McILVANNEY ON BOXING

McILVANNEY ON BOXING

HUGH McILVANNEY

MAINSTREAM
PUBLISHING

EDINBURGH AND LONDON

This edition, 2019

Copyright © Hugh McIlvanney 1996
All rights reserved
The moral right of the author has been asserted

First published in Great Britain in 1996 by
MAINSTREAM PUBLISHING COMPANY
(EDINBURGH) LTD
7 Albany Street
Edinburgh EH1 3UG

ISBN 9781840186055
ISBN 9781845967567 (SDO edition)

No part of this book may be reproduced or transmitted in any
form or by any other means without permission in writing from
the publisher, except by a reviewer who wishes to quote brief
passages in connection with a review written for insertion
in a magazine, newspaper or broadcast

A catalogue record for this book is available
from the British Library

Penguin Random House is committed to a sustainable future for
our business, our readers and our planet. This book is made from
Forest Stewardship Council® certified paper.

MIX
Paper from
responsible sources
FSC® C018179
www.fsc.org

Printed and bound in Great Britain by Clays Ltd, Elcograf S.p.A.

For the Editors, Sports Editors, Subs, Copytakers and fellow scufflers out on the road who have put up with my peculiarities over the years.

CONTENTS

Acknowledgements

The great bulk of this book has, like the rent money over several decades, come from the newspapers that have been my main employers since I moved to London in 1962. I was with *The Observer* for 30 years and it is, of course, heavily represented. But so, too, is *The Sunday Times*, which I joined in 1993 and is therefore the source of much of the material that is being published in book form for the first time. When I offer thanks to both papers it is as much for the original opportunity to go on interesting assignments as for the freedom to make use of the words those jobs produced.

Some other longish pieces were commissioned by *Sports Illustrated* and I am grateful to that distinguished American magazine for their reappearance now.

As always, I am hugely in debt to my agent and friend Geoffrey Irvine, his priceless assistant, Angie Bainbridge, and that other pillar of their office, Wendy Yates.

All at Mainstream have provided their usual mixture of kindness, encouragement and tolerance. Working with them is a pleasure. Socialising is more dangerous, but the rewards justify the risks.

Preface

This book contains a substantial number of pieces written after the appearance, in 1990, of the second of the two previous collections published under the same title. It is natural that much of the new material should be concerned with Mike Tyson, since the heavyweight division holds the greatest fascination for the widest public and Tyson, for the best and worst of reasons, has been easily its most compelling figure over more than a decade now. It is equally natural that in the midst of coverage of Tyson's exploits in the ring there should be two reports, written for *The Observer* news pages, from the rape trial that sent him to jail for three years. Any attempt to cover Tyson's career without dealing with that dark episode would be worthless.

The earlier part of the present book formed the basis of the original edition and retains much of its structure and approach to the grouping of the articles. This means that pieces on Muhammad Ali are used at the beginning and end of the section, so that they enclose and, in a sense, define an era. References to Ali in the latter half of the collection are generally painful, and the pain is deepened by the obligation to acknowledge that his current afflictions are inseparable from the physical trauma he suffered in the ring.

Ali's condition is so sad and so severe that it must have persuaded many that those who want to abolish boxing have a strong case. My own attitude to the issue of whether any decent society should tolerate fist-fighting has been profoundly, perhaps boringly ambivalent for years. The introduction to the first collection is reproduced here because it represents probably my best shot at a consideration of the main arguments. I must admit that as I get older my enthusiasm for the game is increasingly under siege from my misgivings. But the very existence of this book testifies to an enduring compulsion to chronicle fights and fighters. Just when the addiction seems to be waning, along comes an Oscar De La Hoya and the old craving to be at ringside is as strong as ever. I hope the pages that follow make it a little more comprehensible.

Introduction

The Case for the Hardest Game

Now that the British Medical Association has added its influential voice to the fluctuating clamour for the abolition of boxing, some people may feel that a book like this should carry a government health warning. Many millions around the world believe that the fight game is so far from being a legitimate sport that it should be disowned by every civilised society. As someone who not only finds the greatest performers in boxing irresistibly thrilling but has been writing about them professionally for more than 20 years, I am bound to challenge that view. However, I have too much respect for the abolitionists' argument to try to ignore or belittle their central objections. Any supporter of boxing who does not admit to some residual ambivalence about its values, who has not wondered in its crueller moments if it is worth the candle, must be suspect. But many of the attacks made on it are fairly dubious, too. Talking, as a few members of the BMA have done, about 'organised brain damage' and 'legalised grievous bodily harm' is gimmicky sloganising, a case of going into the debating ring with a horseshoe in the glove.

Among doctors themselves there is a conspicuous lack of unanimity about how seriously the brain cells are affected by prolonged involvement in boxing and how the risk compares with that created by less heavily criticised contact sports such as rugby and American football, which might be held responsible for paralysing a higher percentage of those who take part in them. Just as it is natural that fist-fighting should be a profoundly emotive issue, so it is essential that some of the more generalised condemnations of it should be scrutinised. The first point that must be stressed is that deaths in the ring do not make the most powerful argument against professional boxing. If opposition is based on the ratio of fatalities to the numbers participating, boxing is left trailing by motor racing, to name just one other hazardous game. It may be pointed out, too, that fighters don't run amok and kill spectators, as racing cars sometimes do. Motives, not statistics, call pugilism into question.

The most damaging element in the case to be made against it is that it is the one sport in which the fundamental aim of a contestant is to render his immediate opponent unconscious. No matter how you dress it up, that's the tune they're playing in there. Ninety-nine times out of a hundred even the fanciest mover would rather forget about accumulating points and take the early bus home. A sport with such apparently primitive objectives is bound to be seen by many as being morally reprehensible as well as having intolerable physical dangers. Their moral indignation is intensified when they consider the huge sums of money that are often generated by the professional game and the proliferation of non-combatants who insist on grabbing a share of the spoils. Add to that the widespread assumption that most of the spectators at boxing shows are at worst sadists vicariously satisfying a blood lust, or at best benighted souls who somehow feel that they can acquire virility by osmosis in a fight crowd, and it becomes clear that defenders of the sport cannot look for an easy passage. Some civilised men have, when asked to justify their enthusiasm for it, fallen back on facetiousness. One such was the late A.J. Liebling, who wrote about fights and fighters with as much distinction as anyone since Hazlitt (and rather more often than William did). Liebling suggested that if any fighter had gone as batty as Nijinsky there would have been a public outcry. 'Well, who hit Nijinsky?' he asked. And why, he wanted to know, wasn't there a campaign against ballet? It gave girls fat legs.

However, at the end of the day boxing does not have to hide behind jokes or macho bluster. It is an activity so basic that ultimately its best defence is human nature, a flawed argument at any time but one that is not easily trampled underfoot. Aggression is central to all competitive sports and it would be astonishing if there were not many young men left dissatisfied with the sublimation of it involved in ball games, in track and field athletics, in adventure pursuits such as mountaineering or in the racing of horses or machines. Such natures hunger for the rawest form of competition and that means boxing. We may regret that our species has not progressed beyond that appetite but to introduce legislation prohibiting consenting adults from satisfying it would, conceivably, be out of step with recent trends in our liberal society.

Of course, it is a constant, if not always honestly articulated, part of the abolitionists' case that the fighters are hapless victims pressed into reluctant service in the ring by the mercenary and corrupt forces that control professional boxing. It is a view of the business learned mainly from B-movies. (The same mentality holds that every second match is fixed. During one week in the autumn of 1980 the bars of Las Vegas were brimming with characters who 'knew' that arrangements had been made for Muhammad Ali to defeat Larry Holmes, and those of us who argued that Ali had roughly the same chance of winning as Anastasia had of getting a decision over Brezhnev were regarded as bumpkins who should be humoured.)

The point being made here is not that boxing is free of mercenary and corrupt forces. It has a huge variety of doubtful operators, ranging from a minority of outright villains to a much larger group of managers and promoters who blinker themselves against the harsh implications of the deals they make. But what must be said is that in this area, as almost everywhere else, the abolitionists over-simplify to the extent of serious distortion. Certainly some boxers are badly used, but the modern fighter in a country like Britain is usually as much his own man as any professional sportsman is. Anyone who imagines that Johnny Owen was under any kind of duress when he went into the ring for the world bantamweight championship match with Lupe Pintor of Mexico that led to Owen's death in that same autumn of 1980 simply did not know the boy. He was, as it happens, an extreme example of someone who desperately wanted to box. His personality was a small cloud of reticence until he entered the ambience of boxing, in a gym or an arena. Once there, he was transformed from a 24-year-old virgin whose utterances tended to come in muffled monosyllables into a confident, skilled practitioner of a rough but exciting trade. It may be – as I suggested in the hours after seeing him disastrously injured at the Olympic Auditorium in Los Angeles – that Johnny Owen's tragedy was to find himself articulate in such a dangerous language. But the people who say he should have been denied access to that language run the risk of playing God.

Some will declare that only the psychologically inadequate could ever need boxing and there might be some sense in the claim if anyone cares to define psychological inadequacy in the age of the neutron bomb. At a more obvious level of comparison, it seems to many of us that the motorcycle has not only demonstrated an infinitely greater capacity to kill and maim young men than boxing ever did but is rather more readily identified with coarsened spirits. Hell's Angels have caused more public havoc than the members of boxing clubs. To touch on that is not to fall in with those who believe that exchanging blows with padded gloves builds character. The game may have saved thousands of hard-case youngsters from the worst excesses of the street, but few of those salvaged had the instincts of muggers to start with. Most boys who go in for boxing have a deep, combative urge to test themselves and there isn't much of the test about battering an old-age pensioner and legging it with her purse.

Mentioning nobility in connection with boxing is chancy, but exposure to men like Joe Frazier has encouraged such boldness. And Frazier still itched to fight the best heavyweights in the world long after he had retired with a pile of dollars. 'All right,' say the critics, 'tell us what is ennobling about years of having the cranium pummelled, about the absorption of so many blows that the functioning of the brain is almost certain to be impaired.' Reference to all the thousands who have emerged from long hard careers without any evident cerebral damage, such as Gene Tunney (who fought some of the most destructive punchers imaginable and survived stinking rich and intimidatingly sharp into his 80s) or our own Henry Cooper, is no more a conclusive answer than are the greatly improved safety measures and medical supervision. The blatant truth is that there are genuine risks. The relevant question is whether our society considers those risks acceptable in relation to other sports. There is no doubt that fighters consider them so. Naturally, they don't dwell on the possibility of being knocked punchy, any more than a Grand Prix driver thinks of being minced or barbecued in his cockpit. The per capita likelihood of the second is probably much greater than of the first. Jackie Stewart, whose genius was reinforced by marvellous luck, came through a magnificently successful career as a driver unscathed. But Stewart has pertinent things to say about why he put himself in danger so often. He thinks that too much of modern life is wrapped in cotton-wool. 'People who are allowed to live life to the full, to its outer edges, are a blessed group,' he says. The exhilaration of his sport was vastly different from the excitement of a boxer's, but that too is an outer edge.

Fighters are a long way from being wrapped in cotton-wool and further measures could be taken to reduce the threat of major injuries. Perhaps a limited form of headguard should be introduced. But it must be admitted that if the game loses its rawness, it is nothing. If it ever became a kind of fencing with fists, a mere trial of skills, reflexes and agility, and not the test of courage, will and resilience that it is now, then it would lose its appeal for many who are neither sadists nor seekers after the trappings of virility. For some of us boxing, with all its thousand ambiguities, offers in its best moments a thrill as pure and basic as a heartbeat.

Maybe I should not be drawn to it, but I am, and I acknowledge no hypocrisy in deciding in 1980 that I could be at a graveside in Merthyr Tydfil when Johnny Owen was buried and at the ringside in New Orleans a fortnight later when Roberto Duran met Sugar Ray Leonard. Our society will have to become a lot more saintly before the abolition of boxing qualifies as an urgent priority. And until it does I'll feel entitled to write the kind of pieces that follow.

London, August 1982

Part One

The Alpha . . .

It is not inconceivable that the fame of Muhammad Ali has reached more people than have been aware of any other man in history during one lifetime. Mao Tse-tung may have had a slight edge on him, for the old Chairman's home audiences were pretty substantial, but there aren't many other contenders. Through most of the '60s and '70s Ali was certainly better known around the world than any President of the United States or the biggest star in showbusiness. That came about because his huge talent for the most basic of physical contests and his dramatically extrovert nature coincided with an explosion in the communications industry, specifically with the spread of television to the unlikeliest corners of the planet. Television did not merely carry the image of Ali about the globe. It did much to transport the man himself, and the cumbersome circus of the world heavyweight champion, to Kuala Lumpur, Manila, Kinshasa and other places that would have seemed as remote as the moon to Dempsey and Tunney or even to Louis and Marciano. Wherever he went, the cameras followed and so, too, did a planeload of scribblers. Sometimes we needed a Jumbo, sometimes a flying mini-bus would have done, but almost always the travelling group of reporters included enough boxing writers from Fleet Street to surprise and impress the Americans. Perhaps it is remarkable that our country, which has not had even the most tenuous claim to a heavyweight champion since the Cornish-born Bob Fitzsimmons was knocked out by James J. Jeffries in 1899, should continue to think nothing of sending a dozen newspapermen thousands of miles to cover an interesting fight for the title. Not all of Ali's fights were compelling in prospect, or in the event for that matter. But, however dubious the opposition might be, the reporters could usually assume that he or his entourage, the most extraordinary accretion of camp followers ever to live off one fighter, would generate copy.

I calculate that I saw 17 of the major matches in his career and, although one or two correspondents from Britain may have covered a few more, my friend Ken Jones of *The Sunday Mirror* and I were easily the most frequent attenders from the Sunday press. That fact is relevant because journalists from daily or evening papers, and broadcasters from radio and television, are prevented by the shortage of time between deadlines from applying the one technique that offered some likelihood of covering Ali's activities adequately. With him the short sharp interview rarely elicited anything but a stage turn, a revamping of material that might or might not be entertaining but had almost certainly been heard before. By far the best bet was to try to merge in with his life for a day or two or at least for several hours at a stretch, simply to hang around as unobtrusively as possible, eavesdropping on the strange meanderings of his spirit and just occasionally tossing in a few questions when he seemed susceptible to being nudged in directions that suited the eavesdropper. Anyone who took that approach would still have to suffer many of the old vaudeville numbers, maybe a couple of brain-numbing Black Muslim lectures and a little ritual boasting, but unless he was very unlucky there would be something worthwhile among the dross. At some point, perhaps at more than one, during the long exposure to Ali's baroque personality there would surely come a fascinating release of his fancies. Often what came out of the big man at such moments would be hilarious. At other times it would be touched by shadows from darker, more wistful reaches of his mind. On a street called Topaz in New Orleans, in a villa by the Zaire River outside Kinshasa and on the seafront in Nassau, Bahamas, in the hour before dawn, I was fortunate enough to record some of his more private reveries.

Readers may be surprised to find no account in these pages of Ali's first acquisition of the world championship and first defence of it (in the two controversial fights that transformed Sonny Liston from an ogre to a has-been widely suspected of corruption or cowardice) or of the three matches with Ken Norton. The simple explanation is that the Liston episode and Ali's conversion to Elijah Muhammad's version of the Muslim faith occurred before I started travelling on behalf of *The Observer* and, for a variety of reasons, I was also absent when he fought Norton. Since Norton could claim to have had as much success against Ali as anyone who met him in the '70s (Muhammad had his jaw broken on the way to losing their first 12-rounder, very narrowly won their second fight but, on the admittedly unreliable evidence of the television screen, may have been a touch lucky to get the decision at the end of the 15th round of their meeting at Yankee Stadium in September 1976), being elsewhere on those occasions was unfortunate. No doubt, had I been writing sport for *The Observer* in 1973 instead of working on international news and features assignments during a two-year spell with *The Daily Express*, I would have covered the fight in Los Angeles in September of that year in which Muhammad sought to chastise Norton for breaking his jaw less than six months before. However, as I look back, I can say honestly that if I had to miss any of his collisions with men from what could be considered the first rank of his opponents, my preference would always have been to miss those with Norton. The Californian's height and long arms enabled him to box in a style that made problems for Ali. He had a talent for rendering many rounds nondescript, for applying a peculiar form of spoiling tactics at long range, and he favoured an overarm right that caught Ali too often for comfort, especially when Ali was short of maximum fitness. Norton's other substantial asset in the 39 rounds he fought with the greatest heavyweight of our time, and perhaps of any period, was the knowledge that the genius was not a destroyer. Ali could hurt and humiliate opponents and frequently obliged them to make an early exit, but he did not pulverise with a single punch or even with a short, explosive burst of punching. Being spared such a threat meant a lot to Norton, who had more than his share of apprehension when facing knockout punchers. He crumbled spectacularly before Earnie Shavers and, as an elderly practitioner, before Gerry Cooney, and he was thoroughly demoralised in the few minutes he spent inside the ropes with George Foreman. I witnessed that two-round slaughter in Caracas, Venezuela, and the sense of irresistible menace conveyed by Foreman made it impossible for me to believe that Ali would regain the world championship when they came together in Zaire later in that year of 1974.

Foreman's right swings had a habit of battering into the side of challengers' heads with the thunderous effect of the metal ball used by demolition gangs on derelict buildings. And, since Ali had for a long time been an unelusive target for almost anything moderate opponents cared to throw, those of us whose hearts always rode with him were bound to fly into Kinshasa in a gloomy mood. Whatever anybody says now, there was scarcely one good judge in close contact with the pertinent evidence who did not accept that the odds were heavily in favour of Foreman. But the man whose thoughts on the subject mattered most of all refused to be doom-laden. Rather than try in an introduction to identify the elements in Muhammad Ali's nature that equipped him to beat Foreman, to so shatter this frightening world champion's self-belief that at the age of 26 he was effectively finished as a fighter, I shall settle for the hope that the reader will find the clues accumulating as he moves through this book. What the reader will definitely find is the conviction that the opponent who asked Ali the most fundamental questions in the ring, and therefore told him (and us) most about the sources of his strength, was Joe Frazier. Frazier's style made him a helpless victim in his two attempts to cope with George Foreman. As Joe sought to tunnel in on the bigger man, to make his marvellous volume punching tell, he was abruptly wrecked by the bludgeoning assaults on his head. Ali had trouble with Norton and had to survive historic ordeals to establish his narrow superiority over Frazier. Foreman contemptuously annihilated both those men and yet Ali broke Foreman's heart. Boxing is basic but it's not always simple.

Circumstances conspired to make the confrontation in the middle of an African night the most dramatic of Ali's life, if we exclude the time he defied the US Government by refusing to be drafted into the army during the Vietnam War. That refusal caused him to be sentenced to a jail term (one he was never likely to serve but which cast a worrying shadow nevertheless), to be stripped of his world title and prevented from boxing competitively between March 1967 and October 1970. When the Supreme Court finally handed down a ruling in his case on 28 June 1971, there were eight votes in favour of Ali and none against. But the quashing of his conviction could not restore to him the three-and-a-half years that had been taken away or exempt him from the erosions of his leg- and hand-speed, the fractional loss of focus in his timing, that such prolonged idleness was bound to bring to a man who was nearly 29 before he was allowed to resume his career. The Ali of the '70s was an immense performer but he owed much of what he achieved to the outrageous cunning and courage with which he deployed the substantial residue of his powers and to an astonishing capacity to absorb heavy punches. He was a wonder in that second phase of his professional life without ever being quite able to give opponents the feeling (so familiar to such as Cleveland Williams and Zora Folley in the middle '60s) that they were helpless against a blizzard of talents. Unlikely as it may seem, the world never did see the best of Muhammad Ali.

What George Foreman, and those of us who were watching from safe vantage points, saw in Kinshasa was dazzling enough. That match in Zaire was undoubtedly the most enthralling sports event this reporter has ever experienced, but Frazier remains the truest adversary, the purest spirit set against Ali. Muhammad Ali is, overwhelmingly, the central, dominating figure of the stories collected here, but I am anxious that they should represent adequately the other exceptional men involved and, in particular, I hope they do justice to Joe Frazier, who always was a fighter's fighter.

This book begins with Ali and it ends with him. That seems appropriate. It was his aunt, Coretta Clay, who called him the Alpha and the Omega. As far as my experience of boxing is concerned, he justifies the claim. The first series of pieces presented here moves from my early (but not my earliest) encounters with him to the story I filed after the third of his meetings with Frazier, those unforgettable 14 rounds in Manila that might legitimately have provided a climactic and satisfying ending to his career. I was at ringside in London on 18 June 1963, when Ali's attempts to take flashy liberties with Henry Cooper were roughly interrupted by a left hook that went as close to scrambling the prodigy's senses as any punch he ever took in his life. The mysterious tearing of a glove prolonged the rest period between rounds and Ali recovered spectacularly to stop Cooper in the fifth. But that night's action was remarkable enough to make a rematch natural after Muhammad had sensationally won and even more sensationally defended the world championship against Liston. In the three years between the Cooper fights, Ali had only the meetings with Liston, a 12th-round defeat of Floyd Patterson and a points win over the Canadian absorber George Chuvalo. I travelled to Las Vegas for the cruelly comprehensive drubbing of Patterson, but it scarcely resides in the memory as an inspiring episode and I have chosen to start my selection of Ali pieces with a report on some time spent with him in Miami a couple of weeks before he defended his title against Cooper at the Arsenal football ground. The material that takes us from that point in his career to the Frazier fight in Manila makes for a narrative that is easy to follow and requires little additional identification of context other than the dates and locations. The description of George Foreman's meeting with Ken Norton in Caracas may seem to be an interloper in this section, but in 1974 George had the appearance of a destructive missile homing in on Ali's legend. It is now history that he came to earth with a dull thud in Africa later in the year but that report from the tracking station in Venezuela was alarming enough (to me at least) when it was made and is probably worth recalling now, if only to emphasise again what was accomplished in Zaire.

I hope all the passages at arms recounted here are worth the reader's attention. If not, don't blame the combatants. They were rarely boring.

Light and Hard and Ready to Rumble

Whatever the ultimate results of the mounting pressure now being applied in America to the heavyweight champion of the world, one man who is not likely to benefit is Henry Cooper. When Muhammad Ali leaves Miami for London soon after lunch tomorrow he will weigh less in his street clothes than he did stripped for action against the Canadian George Chuvalo in March. He is, in his own words, 'light and hard and ready to rumble' a full fortnight before he is due to defend his title against Cooper at Highbury Stadium.

'I've never seen you looking so skinny this long before a fight,' said one incredulous local reporter as the champion drummed the speed-ball in the Fifth Street Gym. 'If you get any lighter you will be white,' he added and laughed loudly at his own wit. Muhammad Ali did not acknowledge the pun (he rarely sees jokes other than his own). 'Usually I'm 215 lb or more at this stage,' he admitted. 'Today I'm 207. I'm like I was when I fought Liston the first time. When I'm like this I got moves you can't even see, and I punch harder, too. That's how it's going to be from here on. I'm giving nothing away. There's so much pressure. There's draft pressure, alimony pressure, political pressure. They're trying everything to get my title away from me. In Toronto the referee let the man hit me low a hundred times. I'm telling you man, it's a little war. I don't have no return clauses. I got to be well ready.'

For a man seeking that kind of readiness few places have more to offer than the gym that brings a little seedy glamour to the nondescript shops, offices and cheap hotels which make up Fifth Street. One stair up, above a drug store and a shoe repair shop, it is big (30 yards long and almost as wide), bare and busily peopled on most days with successful professionals (Florentino Fernandez, Gomeo Brennan, Luis Rodriguez). A few feet from the ring a machine peddles iced Coca-Cola but the gym's most bizarre feature is a small room with a 'Ladies' sign reinforced by the warning: 'For women only – fighters keep out.' Angelo Dundee, the small energetic Italian who trains and manages the world champion for the group of Louisville businessmen who hold his contract, dismissed the sign as a sexual fantasy. 'We use that place to store equipment. We never have women here.'

They have had one woman this week, however: Oriana Fallaci, the Italian novelist and journalist, a slight, aggressively curious interloper among the snorting, preoccupied fighters. 'Have you seen the de Sade play?' she asked. 'This is it. They're all mad.' When Muhammad Ali shook her hand with his eyes averted she asked one of the sparring partners, Chip Johnson, a big, outrageously good-natured negro who was himself flattened by Cooper in one round, to prove his friendship for her

26

by knocking his employer down. Johnson widened his eyes and showed his gold teeth. 'Better lose a friend than lose my head, ma'am. This man is Superman.'

Unfortunately, Superman has soft hands. Before sparring with Chip Johnson, the less experienced Willie Johnson and, most impressively, with Jimmy Ellis, a boxer of undoubted class who, at 26, is two years older than the champion but only now growing up to heavyweight, he had pads of foam rubber taped across his knuckles. It was about 2 p.m. Outside the temperature was in the high 70s, and soon he looked as if he had just stepped out of the showers. He boxed six sharp rounds, bringing his total sparring so far to about 40 rounds. Ellis's impersonation of Cooper's left hook was close enough to raise a bruise under his left eye. 'I got tagged,' he said later.

To reach the dressing-rooms he had to pass under a large, wrinkled Stars and Stripes, a ponderous cue for questions about his pronouncements on Vietnam that infuriated the majority of Americans. He volunteered no retraction. 'You turn on the radio and you hear: "Twenty-seven Americans was killed in Vietnam today. Two hundred Vietmanese [sic] was killed." Man, it's terrible. I don't like to hear about people being killed. Not anybody.' Then, forced to be more specific about his own attitude: 'America's a white man's country. They got more to fight for than I have.' At that point the conversation gave way to a lecture by Sam Saxon (Cap'n Sam, head of the Black Muslim Mosque in Miami), who has shoeshine concessions at Hialeah and Tropical Park racecourses but makes a more congenial living as bodyguard-companion to the champion. Homilies are Saxon's speciality and he has the kind of physique that encourages people to listen. 'There are 257,255,000 square miles of land in the world,' he announced, throwing in precise figures for the Atlantic and Pacific oceans to show that he knew where the rest of the globe had gone. 'There's room for everybody if they stay where God intended.'

It was agreed that someone who had 'come all the way from London, England', should spend an afternoon with the champion. When he was dressed to go home, in a blue and yellow check shirt and jeans, we walked a hundred yards to a garage where Saxon had parked a white Cadillac. Muhammad Ali was whistling 'A Hard Day's Night' as we drove northwest towards the negro quarter. He stopped, took two metal weights in his hands and began shadow-boxing in the back seat. 'Go round by Sonny's,' he instructed, 'I need a haircut.' The car swung along Second Avenue past open snack counters and cocktail lounges dark as sepulchres to drop us outside 'Nat and Sonny's Downtown Barber Shop and Processing Capitol'. It was closed but a man who unlocked the door said Sonny was expected back momentarily. 'I'll lay around here awhile,' said Muhammad Ali. His idea of laying around seemed to be to move along the pavements at a pace that would have worried an Olympic walker, swooping into soda fountains or disappearing in the gloom of the lounges to kid briefly with the black men who greeted him, and move on as impulsively as he had come. All the time he was enjoying his favourite pastime, talking and playing with children. He cannot let one pass without trying to establish a personal relationship. 'You been good? You gonna give me a hug?' He lifts them high and snuggles them against the smooth, handsome face. Generally they are reserved at first, then recognition shines in their faces as if someone had switched on a light behind their eyes. 'Hey, you're Cassius Clay,' they yell and mob him with questions and demands for autographs. 'Kiss me right here,' one teenage schoolgirl told him, pointing to a discreet spot on her cheek. 'I'm shy,' he said.

After two more checks at Sonny's he signalled a cab, but when we had gone a few yards he told the driver to turn back round the block. We got out and he began to pursue two pretty, brightly dressed young black girls who were crossing the street towards the lounge of the King's Hotel. 'Hey, woman,' he shouted. There was a whispered conversation, then the girls, who had laughed a lot, turned away from the hotel and waved. 'See you,' they called. He turned to me: 'Them girls is prostitutes and I'm trying to convert them.' But he claimed only the most partial success. 'They stopped smokin' but they're still drinking and prostitutin'.'

Finally we took another taxi and drove farther out to the north-west of Miami, to a residential area occupied by lower-middle-class blacks where he has a small, rather boxlike house. Built of cement blocks, it cost around $11,000, appreciably less than the price of most semis in Finchley. In the cramped living-room the only pictures are of Elijah Muhammad and, less conspicuously, the champion. A copy of the Muslim newspaper, *Muhammad Speaks*, is pinned prominently above the sideboard. At one end of the room is a screen for home movies. He likes 'scary horror movies, westerns and science fiction'. Apart from films and TV he contents himself with going for drives or making strange pilgrimages to Miami Airport. Once he was deeply afraid of flying but now he is fascinated by planes. 'It's nice out there, nobody bothers you.'

Three 'sisters' in white smocks (part of the large entourage that helps to keep him comfortable but broke) had cooked a kosher meal in the kitchen that opens off the living-room. After prayers, said with the hands outstretched, palms upwards, Muhammad Ali had salad and cooked vegetables and then disposed of half a dozen lamb chops as if they were digestive biscuits. Later the two of us went for a walk and he played the Pied Piper again. I suggested that even after one failed marriage he must want children of his own. 'I think I will be married before the year is over,' he said seriously. No, he wasn't going steady, but it would not be hard to find the girl. When we were back at the patch of unfenced lawn in front of his home, he flopped down on a sun chair and prepared to hold court among more children. Leaving him, I had the wild thought that if Henry Cooper stayed at home on 21 May and sent along his young son, Henry Marco, Muhammad Ali might give him the title as a present.

Big Match at Highbury

For a man who has unloaded, at a conservative estimate, two or three million words on an ungrateful public since he won an Olympic title six years ago, the heavyweight champion of the world is a deeply mysterious figure. His British opponent in next Saturday's fight at Highbury, Henry Cooper, is describable in one sentence: He is the nicest fellow ever to be about to be defeated for the world heavyweight title.

There was a time when everyone thought that Cassius Clay was equally straightforward: he was a big blabbermouth who talked better than he fought. Since then, he has changed even his name (Cassius Marcellus Clay – 'that my slave name' – to Muhammad Ali) and has come to seem infinitely complex, in turn charming, nasty, arrogant, humble, friendly, aloof, hilarious, humourless, brilliantly alert and weirdly uninformed. It turns out that he isn't even a natural fighting man. In that case, one might conclude, he is in it for the money. But, as it happens, he is broke. Like the weather, Muhammad Ali is something you can experience but cannot define. The other day, in Miami, a white boxing writer, who knows him well enough to accompany him regularly on road runs at dawn, asked me for my interpretation. I had the impression, while I was explaining my bafflement, that he was laughing at my ignorance, but he wasn't. He said the more he saw of Muhammad Ali, the more he too realised he knew nothing about him. The white man closest to him, his manager, Angelo Dundee, can offer no enlightenment. 'People say, "Who is he like, who does he fight like, who does he live like?" All I can say is, like nobody I ever knew.' The champion boasts that he could handle three opponents in one night. If their names were Freud, Adler and Jung they would still take a beating.

When Muhammad Ali arrived here last week, the quiet dignity of his entrance astonished many who still thought of him as the Louisville Lip, the master of egotistical hyperbole. ('Sonny Liston would rather be dropped in the middle of Vietnam with a pea-shooter 'fore he'd fight me again.') Some observers still suspect the new persona, and feel that courtesy and restraint may be merely the latest gimmick. They refuse to accept that at 24 he has at last grown out of his loudmouth period, which he entered even before he won that Olympic gold medal at the age of 18. He insists now that his outbursts were calculated, part of his campaign to get the championship. But this must be an oversimplification. No one with an ordinary view of himself could even simulate such extraordinary behaviour. Many people – including the policeman who introduced him to boxing as a 12-year-old in Louisville, Kentucky – believe that his strident proclamations that he is 'the greatest' have stemmed from lack of assurance, an apprehension bordering on fear. 'It's not a thing in the world but whistling past the graveyard,' patrolman Joe Martin has said.

Muhammad Ali admits that at school he was afraid of bullies, and that he has never been in any way a fighting man outside the ring. 'I've never seen him lose his temper,' says Angelo Dundee. 'He never gets mad at nobody!' However, the suggestions that he was shouting to keep up his courage are obviously much less than the whole truth. Perhaps the true explanation is that his connection with everyday reality has always been tenuous, a characteristic also discernible in his father, Cassius Clay senior, whose life is pervaded by exotic illusions. Dad has had periods when he has claimed to be a sheikh, a Hindu and a Mexican. The champion's own thinking on some subjects has a fantastic quality. The house to which he plans to retire, for instance, is to be a huge, single-storey palace with glass walls, gold furnishings, and rooms whose lighting will change colour according to the gramophone records he is playing – a building with the other-worldly magnificence of a nightmare or a Hollywood film set. Another example of his detachment from reality is his claim that he is immensely popular with the mass of the American people. The animosity towards him, he says, is felt only by politicians in Washington and a few newspapermen.

In fact, most white Americans and some negroes turned against him as soon as he announced his wholehearted and unquestionably sincere commitment to the Black Muslims, the militant black segregationists whose espousal of Islam is based on a refusal to have anything to do with the religions practised by the decadent whites. And when he reacted to the news that he was to be drafted into the army (his appeal against it on the grounds that he supports his parents is still being considered) by saying that he had no quarrel with 'the Viet-man-ese', as he calls them, many of his remaining admirers were soured. Yet, he preserves the illusion of mass popularity. At least, he talks as if he does.

He seems to see his life as a strange, ritualistic play. It may be that the explanation of his rantings is that he has always felt they were required by the script that goes with his destiny. Now there is evidence that his private world is less secure than it was. Such experiences as the hounding he has suffered in the US following his Vietnam pronouncements – which is one reason why Britain is having its first heavyweight title fight since 1908 – and the costly divorce from his wife, Sonji, precipitated by his Muslim convictions have brought on something that looks like maturity. The irony is that this new maturity could make him more vulnerable as a boxer. If he embraces more and more reality, the chances are that he will come to accept the possibility that he can be beaten. He will realise that the incredible reflexes, the superb physique, the mobility and balance that are the essence of his success are ephemeral things. There were intimations of mortality in a conversation he had with Georges Carpentier, the great French boxer of half a century ago, after training in a Territorial Army gymnasium opposite White City Underground station in West London on Thursday. He was amazed to learn that Carpentier – still a trim, handsome figure – is 73 years old. 'How do you stay in that shape living in Paris?' he asked. 'In this jet age it's hard to live so long. Life is such a gamble nowadays. I plan to stay in this business two or three years more and then get on out of it. I'm getting a little tired.' Even here, however, he is not consistent. At other times he says he will go on fighting as long as he can. 'If I didn't box, what else would there be to do?' Undoubtedly, to Muhammad Ali, boxing is much more than a way of earning a lot of money. It is a means of self-expression. 'Put him in a ring, even if it's only in the gym, and you're seeing *him*,' says Dundee. 'That's him at his happiest.'

His boxing method, as his manager suggests, is unique. Letting the arms dangle loosely, so that he can fire from the hip like a gunfighter, is not new. Carpentier recalled that he did much the same. 'You smart,' said the champion. 'This way you can hit from any angle. You can't do that if you are all cramped up in one of them stiff old-fashioned stances.' But what is entirely new is the way he dances around like a flyweight. Even the fast heavyweights of the past, like Joe Louis, carried their speed in their hands, stalking their men with a shuffling motion. 'You're the first man at your weight to fight with your legs,' Carpentier said. Dundee believes that the way Muhammad Ali positions himself in relation to his opponents is a big part of his success. In the plane to London from Miami last week Dundee drew diagrams to illustrate how, when two ordinary boxers face up, each with the left foot advanced and slightly outside the line of the right, a line linking their feet would form a parallelogram. 'That way both boxers are in a position to punch. But if you watch The Kid you will see that he stands so that his feet make just about a straight line with the other guy's, so that they can't hit him without reaching for him. But he can hit them. Because he's got this rare gift, he can float. He doesn't slide or jump in with his punches. He floats in and out in one movement.'

Apart from the soft hands that have been largely responsible for the doubts about his punching power, Muhammad Ali's one serious flaw in the ring is a tendency to flaunt his virtuosity so irresponsibly that he risks disaster. That was what happened when he fought Henry Cooper in 1963 and permitted his smooth demolition job to be interrupted in the fourth round by a humiliating knockdown – the glimpse of fallibility that will draw 45,000 people to the Arsenal football ground next Saturday at prices up to 20 guineas a seat. Cooper has the strongest left hook in boxing, and this type of punch has always been a threat to the champion. He has been knocked down four times, twice in the amateurs and twice as a professional, and left hooks did the damage. When he is caught, however, his recuperation is unbelievably swift. Dundee remembers what happened when he was hit by Sonny Banks. 'Banks came off the ropes and hit him with a perfect left hook and The Kid went down, pole-axed, right on his butt. But what happens? He goes down bleary-eyed and gets up bushy-tailed and goes in and ruins Banks, wastes him. That's when I fell in love with Clay. I said, "You're my baby!"'

There was nothing bushy about his tail after Cooper hit him. Indeed, it was rather close to the floor. He took a short count, was still dazed as he rose and when the bell brought him relief he was doing a fair impersonation of Groucho Marx's walk. His eyes were in separate orbits. A mysterious business over a split glove gave him rather more than the official one-minute rest, but it was still remarkable that he should come out for the fifth round as if it were the first. In a couple of minutes Cooper, bleeding hideously from the cuts around the eyes that have been a blight on his career, was totally beaten.

Those who recall the uncomplicated ballyhoo that marked Cassius Clay's training for the first Cooper fight have been struck by the differences in the way Muhammad Ali has prepared for this one. Mingling with predictable callers from the trade, such as Carpentier and Terry Downes ('How are you today, pretty boy?'), there has been a stream of serious-faced negroes, many of them apparently European adherents of the Muslims. They are invited into the small dressing-room at the White City by Herbert Muhammad, the son of Elijah Muhammad, the embattled leader who directs the Muslims from Chicago. Herbert, a plump, courteous man with a light voice and a passion for photography, was the only one of the champion's party who travelled first-class with him on the transatlantic flight. Dundee, the sparring partner Jimmy Ellis, and the 'conditioner' Luis Sarria, a thin Cuban negro who speaks no English, all came tourist. 'Do you want to know who my number one man is?' the champion asked last week. 'That's him sitting right there. Her-bert Mu-hammad. That is one of the wah-sest men on earth. Son of Eli-jah Mu-hammad, the pah-flest black man in the world. Her-bert Mu-hammad is my adviser, just like the Queen of England, the Pre-sident, Cas-tro and Khrush-chev have advisers. He is the brain. Boy, he IS a brain. I couldn't come here without him. I have to cope with too many brains every day. I couldn't move without him.'

'He is just flattering me,' said Herbert.

'It's a funny thing,' said Dundee pointedly. 'But when you get in that ring you're all alone. All on your own.'

As the one white man in close daily contact with Muhammad Ali, Dundee contrives in the main to ignore the Muslim involvement and get on with a professional job. 'Sometimes I have to con him for his own good. Take his fear of flying. He was scared as hell. Wanted to drive to New York for a fight. I told him it would take 24 hours but he wouldn't listen. Then I said, "You'll be sitting hunched up in a car all the time. Think of all the wear and tear on your body." Well, you know the way he feels about his body, the way he respects it. So he said, "Hey, you're right, man!" and that was it. Now he loves planes.'

Even psychology has not been much help to the Louisville Group, the rich businessmen whose sponsorship launched the champion's career. His relations with them have grown increasingly strained, and when the contract expires in October there may be reluctance to renew it. Though the Group's financial know-how is prodigious (eight of them are millionaires), Muhammad Ali consistently rejects their monetary advice in favour of counsel from his own black advisers. He pays all manner of fees and salaries to helpers he has recruited through the Muslims, and anyone who turns up and makes a convincing claim to affiliation is liable to receive a lavish handout. Such extravagances, plus the cost of his divorce and the $1,250 a month he has to pay in alimony, and the sums (sometimes $200, sometimes $300) which he sends regularly to his parents, have left him with nothing in the bank. That is one reason why, if he stays out of the army, he wants to defend his title four times a year. However, it is doubtful if he will ever earn enough to balance his lack of practicality concerning money. He once demanded that a bank pay him $40,000 in $1,000 bills. 'He has always been pretty hopeless about money,' says Dundee. 'Any bum can sponge on him. At first it was me that made him his allowance for expenses. I used to deuce him to death. He'd say, "Why are you only giving me $2?" Anybody who knows what he is like knows why.'

Compared with the champion's rococo existence, Henry Cooper leads a starkly simple life. He is a good professional who has known disappointments – 11 defeats in 44 contests – but has improved with the years. Now, at 32 and with his fair hair receding, he has probably reached his peak. Cooper turned Roman Catholic to marry his Italian wife, Albina, and he is agreeably sentimental about his family. They will be comfortable when he retires. He is earning another £50,000 for this fight, and nobody begrudges him the purse. Cooper is modest and friendly enough to make even his devotion to clean living acceptable to the wilder spirits in the game.

The money is the only thing he can expect to take out of this fight, for the speed and fluency of the champion's boxing should prevent Cooper from landing his big left hook. The chances are that cuts will end the challenge after perhaps half a dozen rounds. Most people see it as another case of the nice guy coming second. But to me, despite his peculiarities, the man who should come first is rather a nice guy too.

The Fight

Cassius Clay (Muhammad Ali), 24-year-old Black Muslim from Louisville, Kentucky, is still the heavyweight champion of the world. The challenge of the British champion, Henry Cooper, ended bloodily and predictably after one minute 38 seconds of the sixth round at the Arsenal football ground in London last night. More than 40,000 spectators had seen Cooper try bravely, and with some success, for five rounds to force in the big left hooks that offered him his one hope of victory. But, as nearly everyone had feared, the scar tissue around his eyes was too vulnerable to the cutting power of Clay's punches.

The end came with the suddenness of an avalanche. Cooper attempted to rush Clay into a neutral corner, but as he closed he was met with a devastating stream of short left- and right-hand punches to the face. Clay turned him into the corner and as they parted both were sprayed with blood that poured from a widening gash along Cooper's left eyebrow. Cooper said later that it was Clay's head that opened the cut – the same kind as had ended their previous fight in 1963 – but from six feet away those blows looked hard and incisive enough to do the damage.

Now Clay's speed and accuracy and Cooper's courage combined to turn a fight into a slaughter. From his corner, the British champion's brother George and his manager, Jim Wicks, roared him on to a last despairing effort, and he lunged blindly after Clay. But the flow of blood was terrifying. It ran down Cooper's chest, over his shoulder and down to darken the blue of his shorts. Clay skipped away from Cooper's lunges, driving a vast variety of jabs and crosses and hooks into the bruised and swollen flesh around Cooper's left eye. For one awful moment as he backed on to the ropes Clay seemed about to show the least attractive side of his nature. He let his mouth fall open and bared his gumshield in a mocking snarl. But as Cooper responded with desperate anger Clay became serious, and his gloves slashed again and again into Cooper's bloody face. Looking at Cooper, it was incredible that only a minute before he had been intact and still optimistic. Now his situation was quite hopeless and the referee, Mr George Smith, of Edinburgh, needed only the most cursory inspection of the wound to declare the fight over.

Cooper gestured his disgust and frustration and tears mingled with his blood as he was guided back to the stool. He had set his heart on being the only British-born fighter apart from Bob Fitzsimmons – in 1897 – to take the world heavyweight title. At the late age of 32 he had disciplined himself to train even harder than he normally does, and his Italian wife, Albina, had broken her rule to come to the ringside. As he made his way into the ring, preceded by a Union Jack and surrounded protectively by policemen, the great crowd, blocking the gangways and rolling back to a blur of pink faces high under the stands, sensed that this was one of the greatest occasions British boxing has known this century.

In the event Cooper let no one down, least of all himself. He fought to the limit of his powers and for three or four rounds the world champion was perceptibly worried by the determined economy of his opponent's attacks. Cooper did not lose one of the first three rounds and probably took two of them, and it was not until Clay restored the old smoothness to his footwork in the fourth round that wild hopes began to fade. Now instead of a celebration Cooper will have a visit to hospital tomorrow.

Muhammad Ali v. US Government, Houston, Texas, August 1967

'Boxing Is Child's Play Compared with This Fight'

From the beginning, the World Boxing Association's attempt to find a socially acceptable heavyweight champion has left them groping in a twilight of unreality, trapped in the shadow of a man whose right to the title is unlikely to be eroded by a little official ink. The frailty of their arguments was emphasised this week when Muhammad Ali came to Houston for 48 hours and, without even trying, managed to make the current eliminating series seem rather less relevant than a French election without de Gaulle.

Ali's opponent in Houston was the United States attorney Norton Susman and, in spite of being perhaps the first defendant in American legal history to do three miles roadwork in preparation for a court appearance, the champion lost the contest. A motion by his counsel that the order restricting him to the continental US should be lifted to let him box in Japan was curtly denied. Susman, who wears seersucker suits and usually has his handsome features arranged in a slightly patronising smile, succeeded with a counter motion that the restraint on travel should be reinforced by withdrawal of Ali's passport. 'Man, boxing is child's play compared with this fight I've got to face,' Ali had said before the hearing in the Federal Court building. 'This will be rough.' His old gift for prognostication had not deserted him. Of course, it is all going to be rough from now on, as the consequences of his refusal to enter the army close in on him. He believes that he will have to serve a substantial part of the five-year sentence that has been passed on him and occasionally in his presence one senses a deep isolating sadness. At other times his resigned willingness to take what is coming gives way to nervous apprehension about the deprivations of prison life. 'You kinda hate to think about it. I just can't stand lying around in one place at any time. I got to be movin' all the time. My friends tell me that's what's going to be terrible for me. I suppose I'll have to do a lot of studyin'.'

However, the most remarkable element in his reaction to his frightening situation is the frequency with which his natural exuberance breaks through. He is still the most dynamically entertaining personality in sport. Before he left Houston for Chicago he convulsed a tiny audience in the coffee-shop of the Hotel America with a barrage of brilliantly told jokes. Many of them were racial jokes, some were sexy jokes, all were delivered with a range of mimicry and a certainty of timing and memory that few professional comedians would equal. His favourite is an original fantasy. It starts with Muhammad Ali being interviewed at the gates of the prison as he starts his five-year stretch. Booming into the microphone with a deep, theatrically masculine voice that would do well in an aftershave commercial, he says he will serve his time like the man he is. Now it is five years later, Muhammad Ali is leaving jail and the same interviewer asks him if he thinks he will be able to take up boxing again. The answer comes in a high, winsome twitter: 'Well honey, I can't rightly say at this moment . . .'

A gloss on that joke is provided by Angelo Dundee, the little Philadelphia Italian who has trained Muhammad Ali since the days when he was Cassius Clay and whose hustling management put the great man's sparring partner, Jimmy Ellis, into the section of the WBA tournament settled at the Astrodome today. 'The most ridiculous thing I ever heard was that stuff about Muhammad being queer. I know some characters got the idea and it's just crazy. He likes the foxes all right. But he knows how many good fighters got done in by them. He thinks a lot of himself physically. If you say he's narcissistic I'll buy that. He wants to keep his body in shape. That's why he takes it easy with the foxes, just like he does with food. Ever since he went to Africa and got up to 240 lb [17 st 2 lb] he don't want no more of that nonsense.'

Ali admitted to being 16 stone when he came to Houston. 'Hey, will I lose weight or put on weight in prison?' he wanted to know on the first morning. 'They're not too strong on roadwork,' said Dundee. 'I been visiting a few to get accustomed,' Ali told him. 'They say you're all right in them Federal places. You can pay for your own food. You get TV. Only thing you don't get is girlfriends.'

He was wearing a charcoal-grey suit over a white shirt and blue tie with a discreet red pattern. There was a square diamond ring on the little finger of his left hand, a matching watch on the wrist. Between the white, well-spaced incisors he was chewing a toothpick. He had just been formally interviewed and, as always, there was a generous random overspill. 'I see something about that programme "Khrushchev in Exile", and I thought of me, "Muhammad in Exile". We're in the same boat. What was he doing on the show? In his garden an' all that. Don't let it trick you, boy. That old Khrushchev still got power.' As he spoke he was throwing jabs at imaginary targets and when he then went to use the elevator he feinted and hit the button with a short left. He said he was in favour of the tournament because several of the eight fighters involved needed the money. The negro action group who urged that it should be boycotted

36

were wrong. 'Maybe even if there hadn't been all this trouble it would have been a good thing for me to sit out a spell. I was getting so superior, talking to opponents, doing little dances. Nobody believed I could be whupped for real. If I was to get justice and be cleared now and took a week to train, who would believe these people in the tournament could beat me? Maybe I'll announce my retirement in the next few days and that will make the man who wins the tournament the legalised champion. I can always make a comeback if I feel like it when this fuss is over.' He also suggested that he may marry very soon, adding that there is a 17-year-old who would make a suitable bride. 'Then when I came out of jail I'd have a child two or three years old. I'd like to start a family.' Dundee was bluntly sceptical. The possibility does appear remote when Ali muses that it would make good headlines if he retired, got married and went to jail in one week.

Ambiguity was shed along with the frivolity when he spoke of the race riots. 'Pitiful. Whole bunch of people burning up their own homes, own neighbourhood. It's a crazy revolt. An unwise move. Fightin' the maker of the machine-guns. How can you take on the army, all those helmets, all those guns, all those soldiers? It's crazy.

'Rap Brown and those boys can say what they like because they're nobody. Nobody gives a damn. With me it's different. If I went to a negro district they'd come runnin'. I'd have a crowd of 2,500 in no time. It would just take some young fool to throw somethin' and that would be it. He don't care anything about race. He wants publicity. He wants to see a nice fire. I want to keep away from that stuff. Now wherever I go I'm gonna make a point of seeing the police chief himself and telling him where I'm gonna speak. I don't want nobody saying I started the stuff.'

These careful views were carefully reiterated on Wednesday in the courtroom of Judge Joe Ingraham on the ninth floor of the Federal Building, one of the less offensive edifices in a city where much of the architecture seems to be the work of the man who designed Alcatraz and the level of public merrymaking suggests it would make an ideal retreat for monks who have found the temptations of the monastery too much for them.

One of Ali's two white lawyers, Quinnan Hodges, and his coloured attorney, Chauncey Eskridge, entered the court on crutches as the result of two separate accidents and it was a little thoughtless of Mr Susman to accuse them at one point of 'foot-dragging' on procedure. Much of the evidence they offered was in the form of tape-recordings of Ali's statements on TV shows. These were intended to prove that he had avoided any hint of un-American utterances. But Judge Ingraham, a slight, grey-haired Texan who apparently took pride in not laughing at the comedians' cracks on the tape-recordings (which was less of a triumph than he may have imagined) decided that Ali's presence at one peace rally in Los Angeles revealed 'a ready willingness to participate in anti-

Government and anti-war activities'. The judge indicated that the defendant might consider himself lucky not to be confined to one State or one district.

Back in the coffee-shop at his hotel, Ali persuaded Angelo Dundee to buy a steak for 'a poor, washed-up fighter'. Interrupting his noisy enjoyment of the food, he said the hearing, with its evidence of FBI surveillance, had shown him how careful he would have to be. 'A word to the wise is sufficient,' he said and winked solemnly. 'They keep asking me if I'm sincere. Hell, I've had to give up my title and all them millions, I divorced my wife and have to pay all that alimony, and now I'm about to go to jail. And they ask me if I'm sincere. I'm either sincere or I'm crazy.' He paused for a moment, then said wearily: 'Ah, well, I'm flying to Chicago and that old jet don't have to get there.'

Perhaps that is the greatest change the courts and the lawyers and the FBI have wrought in Muhammad Ali. They have made him a fatalist.

Joe Frazier v. Muhammad Ali, New York, 8 March 1971

Superman at Bay

For more than a decade now, whether calling himself Cassius Clay or Muhammad Ali, the man has sought the whole world as an audience. The heavyweight champion has always exerted a fascination that transcends sport, but no previous holder of the title has been able to invade so many lives at so many levels. Compared with him, the most vivid of his predecessors are blurred figures dancing behind frosted glass. When he speaks, he assumes no less than that he is addressing mankind. 'I think,' he told me solemnly the other day, 'I must have the most populous face on earth, exceptin' maybe Nixon's. And maybe even more than his.' The word 'populous' had a kind of surrealist appropriateness, for no one who looks into his face can expect to see one man. He dreams himself anew each morning.

If anything is consistent in him, it can only be the hunger for universal attention, his constantly articulated fantasy that when he puts himself at risk, when he lays his invincibility on the line, the world holds its breath. On Monday night Muhammad Ali will go as close as any athlete ever could to making that fantasy a fact. His fight with Joe Frazier at Madison Square Garden in New York will be filmed, photographed, described in the spoken and written word, analysed and argued over as no sports event ever has been before or is ever likely to be again. Gross takings from the worldwide operation should fall between 20 and 30 million dollars, which is not a painful place to fall. This is – as everyone associated with it freely admits – something else, the greatest, the big apple. Muhammad Ali's craving to be centre-stage in an unprecedented drama is being fulfilled. The fees may be identical ($2.5 million each), and his opponent may be billed as the official owner of a championship that he was forced to yield to the politicians, but there is no doubt that Ali is the greater of two undeniable stars. His magnetism, not the vigorous and beautiful talent of Joe Frazier, will draw the thoughts of the world towards that square of illuminated canvas at the Garden on Monday.

Yet the realisation of Ali's dream may be flawed by a deep irony. His moment of supreme exposure may be his one moment of profound failure: it could be that all these years he has been accumulating an unimaginable audience to witness his final downfall, to be stunned by the stripping away of the Messianic aura, saddened by the revelation that the child of destiny remains a prize-fighter who can be punched apart from his quick wits. 'No one has ever worked so hard on the build-up for his own funeral,' a Frazier supporter said cynically in midweek. That, blatantly, is the sort of sweeping assumption that can never be made about Ali. His achievement so far in his career has not been to stay unbeaten but, in an almost supernatural sense, to seem unbeatable. Frazier, too, has avoided defeat in his 26 professional contests (five fewer than Ali has fought) but while he has done it by dint of fairly conventional prowess, the other man has often appeared to be divinely insulated against calamity. Ali is a magnificently gifted and graceful boxer, the most aesthetically satisfying the heavyweight division has known, but there have been times when his marvellous skills and brimming athleticism might have been insufficient without something that could pass for collusion with the Fates. Adversity, whether created by opponents or the United States draft laws, has been overcome or turned to positive advantage. At the heart of the hypnotic appeal which his personality has for so many of us is an irrational suspicion that here is a man capable of willing his own outrageous image of himself into reality. To attempt such a thing is, however, close to the ultimate hubris, and it is fear of the fall that has sunk admirers like myself in nervous gloom this weekend. There is too much of Sophocles in the scenario of this fight.

If Nemesis there must be, Joe Frazier is classically equipped for the part. He is, as they say around the gyms here, 'all fighter'. Since moving north as a boy from Beaufort, South Carolina, he has lived in Philadelphia, which also happens to be the home town of Angelo Dundee, Ali's trainer. 'Philadelphia,' Dundee has said, 'is not a town. It's a jungle. They don't have gyms there. They have zoos. They don't have sparring sessions. They have wars.' Frazier is true to that background. His work in the ring has a cumulative, percussive urgency, a mounting, destructive rhythm that corresponds to some private music in his head. He is a volume puncher, the most impressive since 'Homicide' Henry Armstrong, who is the only boxer ever to have held three world titles simultaneously. Frazier's appetite for training is frightening. In the days

39

when he worked from 4.30 a.m. until six o'clock at night in a local slaughterhouse, he would face a full schedule afterwards. He first went to a police gym in his teens because he was overweight, and he still burdens himself with special clothing to force the sweat out, especially around his huge thighs. Neither these clothes, nor a leaded belt round his waist, can prevent him from maintaining a pace that would kill many flyweights. Punching the bag, bench exercises, roadwork, sparring, all are done at exaggerated tempo, often to rock music. He is a joyful masochist in the gym, flogging himself without respite in pursuit of the toughness that will make him oblivious of his opponent's aggression, even that of a man who will be four inches taller and – at a predicted 15 st 5 lb – about 10 lb heavier. 'I work so hard in camp, punish myself, and then when I get to the real thing it's that much more easy for me. When the bell rings I'm ready. I'm turned on.'

In fact, he is rarely turned on quite enough at the first bell. It usually takes him two or even three rounds to find his rhythm and, since he is remarkably easy to hit in those tentative minutes, he can anticipate a hard time from Ali's sharp punches to the head. Billy 'Moleman' Williams, who has long been Frazier's principal sparring help, suggests that the first round could be sensational, with Frazier down and in real difficulties. 'But if Joe gets his thing goin', if he cuts off the ring like he does with us in training and gets to Ali's body with both hands, then to the head with that terrific left hook – and forgets his crazy idea of throwin' right leads – then he should take Ali somewhere between the third and the ninth. If Ali gets beyond that point without taking too much, he must be favourite.'

Frazier refuses to believe he is in any serious danger. 'This is just another man, another fight, another pay-day,' he said in his Philadelphia motel this week. He agrees with his manager, a former railway welder named Yancey Durham, that retirement, at the age of 27, is something they should consider after the fight. The success of Cloverlay, the organisation set up by the syndicate of businessmen who handle his money, has made Frazier financially independent, and he does not have to pretend that singing with his Knockouts pop group offers a genuine alternative career. The main function of his music, he claims, is to soothe the savage breast. Cradling his guitar in his lap and strumming amateurishly, he said: 'I play to keep myself calm, to keep from hittin' people or tearing down the wall. I used to have phone bills of $2,000 before I took up music.'

He is a paradox not unfamiliar in boxing, a friendly, church-going family man who leaves his compassion in the dressing-room. 'I like to hit guys and see their knees tremble. I like to feel my strength and go for broke. Clay's a big guy but I've fought big guys before. Movers, too. He says I won't reach him, but that's a broad statement. He will find the ring will get smaller and I will get bigger. I don't see the job taking more than

40

ten rounds. I'll be talking to Clay in there. I always talk in my fights and I've got something special to say to him after all his crap about me being an Uncle Tom. I'll tell you what this fight will be all about – conditioning. And there's no way he's going to be in better shape than me.'

Before his compulsory three-and-a-half-year absence from the ring, no opponent could have been optimistic about being in better condition than Muhammad Ali. But, in the two victories since his return, the nine-minute laceration of Jerry Quarry and the 15th-round knockout of Oscar Bonavena, the exciting elements of his performances have not concealed a definite erosion of his speed. There has been nothing in his training in Miami Beach to encourage hopes that he can rediscover the vast overspill of vitality that swept him to the championship. This time he has talked significantly of being 29, of conserving himself for the night. 'Twenty-nine ain't old but I don't want to go usin' up stuff I need in the ring. That's why I'm quieter than I used to be, not leapin' and foolin' around like I did.'

The truth is that he has done a fair amount of fooling around, haranguing the paying spectators at his workouts, eulogising himself and dismissing Frazier as a second-rate street-fighter, a short-armed hooker who will never get past his jab. But mainly in these moments he gives the impression of remembering a part he played in another show. One striking exception was the day he took Burt Lancaster, who has connections with the promoters, on a Pied Piper's tour of the black ghetto area of central Miami. As Ali leapt from his Cadillac, five years fell away and he was the compelling, hysterically ebullient champion who had led me noisily through the same district three weeks before his title fight with Henry Cooper. 'I bring the greatest movie stars in the world to see y'all,' he shouted, thrusting the nervous actor out of the afternoon glare into the dark interior of a bus. As he strode past Moon's Recreation Hall and the barber shops and drug stores, the crowd around him swelled and Lancaster was not the only member of the tiny white minority who was uneasy. An undercurrent of violence eddied through the blacks who closed in on all sides. Two or three of them challenged Ali to spar, and a tall, wild-looking man in an Apache wig who called himself Nicodemus went at the boxer with dangerous briskness. Ali was their hero, but too many of them wanted to acquire glory by the laying on of hands.

Some of us were given a lift back from the ghetto by Smokey the Bear, a large black wrestler who had attached himself to the camp. He agreed that the situation had been delicate for a few minutes. 'But Reggie would have taken care of it,' he said. Reggie Thomas is a Muslim agent from Chicago who acts as chauffeur and bodyguard to Ali these days. He favours single colours, white or blue, from his flat cap to his pull-on boots. He is small and light-skinned, with the excessively composed features and mobile eyes of the professional bodyguard. Joe Frazier said last week he would never fight in an alley unless he 'was dressed'. He did not have to draw diagrams. Reggie is almost certainly dressed.

Between five and six o'clock in the morning Reggie was to be found easing the black Cadillac around the three-mile perimeter of Bayshore golf course behind Ali's pounding silhouette. Practically every day in the last six weeks or so breakfast was followed by a sleep in the compact penthouse the fighter occupied in a block of apartments (where two Muslim sisters cooked for him and his privacy was forcefully protected) and he was driven to the Fifth Street Gym at 12 o'clock. The big square room was invariably walled in by the bright Florida noon pressing against the dirty windows and the heat was thick as Vaseline on the skin. Ali worked rather perfunctorily amid a motley of engrossed fighters, adding to their noise, to the drum and swish and smack and scuff and grunt, the melancholy cacophony of a boxing gym. Hanging in the air at such times is a muted apprehension, a quiet dread that all this self-denial may mean nothing when the moment comes. One detects among some of the fighters a longing that everything could stay suspended like this, so that a man just sweated and exhausted himself and then showered and drove home through the heat to flop on a coach and mindlessly watch television. Even Ali may have lost his lust for crisis and maybe that was what was wrong with the atmosphere in the Fifth Street Gym.

Or perhaps he is fooling us once again and we are worrying needlessly. Perhaps Rufus Brassell, the sharpest of his sparring partners, is right when he says the great man's talent is virtually intact and the lazy mauling that has often marred his training is an irrelevant joke. Perhaps Angelo Dundee and his doctor friend, Ferdie Pacheco, are justified in saying that Ali, though he is thicker around the middle, is fit to jab and move for 20 rounds if he has to. They insist that Frazier, for all his record of having destroyed so many previously indestructible fighters, will not be able to invade Ali's territory and will disintegrate at the end of the jab. But neither the paid observers like myself nor the locals and holidaymakers who have crushed into the gym in their coloured shirts and dresses, herded in a sweaty cluster like damp confetti, have seen persuasive evidence of all this.

Those of us with an emotional commitment have found more hope in the words of Richard Durham, a black journalist who has been sharing Ali's quarters in Miami to continue the research for a book on him: 'He will win because of his morale. He draws strength from the people. They nourish him and he keeps what they give him. Some men cannot take from the people. If the people give to them it doesn't get through or it just seeps away. He has the power to keep it. It strengthens him the way a parent's love strengthens a child. And, when he has enough of that strength, he can do anything the people want of him. If they want him to win, he wins. They do. He will.'

Just Another Brother ...

In the middle of Tuesday afternoon the lobby of the New Yorker Hotel in Manhattan was so crowded that people who wanted to stay on the ground floor were riding in elevators to take a rest from the jostling. One man tried to reduce the crush by elbowing his way through the bodies and shouting warnings. 'You're creating a fire hazard,' he yelled. 'Get back! You'll have to move back. Somebody could get killed here.' No one moved and he turned away hopelessly. 'All this,' he said, 'for a beaten fighter.'

A few minutes later the door of one of the express elevators opened and the beaten fighter stepped out and attempted to make his way to the street within a straining ring of his black friends and attendants. He was taller than almost anyone else in the lobby, so that his disembodied face rode above the swaying crowd, composed and detached, the lips pursed in a patient expression. He remained undisturbed, signing the pieces of paper that were pushed at him, when his protectors had to give up on their first effort to force him through the main doors. The pressure eased when at last he reached the pavement. Most of the mob fell in behind him, scurrying to compensate for the length of his stride. There were at least 200 people with him when he turned out of Eighth Avenue into the hard wind of Thirty-Fourth Street on his way to the basement garage of the hotel. A tiny black boy, thin as a stick, was held high in his mother's arms for a glimpse. 'Hey, Muhammad, hey, Muhammad,' he called. Then, in desperation: 'Hey, Cassius Clay.' Ali's eyes rolled round slowly in mock rebuke. It took several minutes for the police and his friends to extricate him sufficiently to squeeze him into a black Cadillac. 'Oh, Jennifer,' an attractive black girl said to her white friend as the car door closed. 'I saw him. I saw him.' The white girl laughed. 'I touched him,' she said.

'Muhammad, you're beautiful,' a young white man shouted from the fringe. 'You'll be back. You're coming back.' Ali turned towards him and winked above the hard ball of swelling on his right cheek. As the car edged out and swung tentatively across to the other side of the street, someone muttered that after all Frazier had won the fight. A big man with red hair and a brown outdoor face spun round on the voice. 'He won't win next time. Believe me. Frazier won't win next time.'

It was a moment that no one but Ali could have created, a scene that had very little to do with the usual mobbing of a celebrity. Pop singers and film actors can have young girls scrambling to touch them, but they don't make 16-stone building workers tighten at the throat and offer emotional declarations of faith. Perhaps the most remarkable aspect of that utterly remarkable heavyweight championship fight in Madison Square Garden is that defeat, far from diminishing Ali in the eyes of his admirers, has deepened their feelings far beyond the normal limits of public respect and affection. That suggestion will represent sentimental rubbish to many people, but they are the people who have always been immune to Ali. By no means all of them are racists, blatant or latent. Nor are they necessarily so superficial that they can only see him as a loud-mouthed boor. What is common to most of his detractors is a failure to let themselves become attuned to his spirit, to his dream. To those of us who believe in him, such a failure is astonishing. The beauty of his physical performances, his whole impact as a performer, is inseparable from his bizarre but ultimately heroic vision of himself. Arthur Miller's salesman is not the only man who has to dream. Whoever you are, it comes with the territory. The world would be uninhabitable if all of us dreamt on the epic scale of Ali, but it would be a considerably drabber place if one among us had not done so.

That was why all the sadness of last Monday night was diluted, even transformed, by Ali's refusal to let his dream be diminished. Against an opponent of genuine nobility, one of the most honest wills ever put to work in the prize-ring or anywhere else, he stayed true to himself and everyone who identifies with him. He fought a unique fight, one that was almost baroque in the intricacy of its stratagems. And when all his elaborate attempts to conceal the deterioration of his leg speed, to reduce some of his weaker rounds to a vacuum of restful play-acting, to 'con' Joe Frazier into believing him far stronger and less vulnerable than he was, when all these failed, he took the consequences with magnificent courage.

The white American reporters who screamed, 'Kill the sonofabitch, take his head off, his time's here now,' were blinding themselves to the truth of what was happening in the ring as much as the hotel maid who said: 'So the big mouth got shut up good,' and offered a smile that was an invitation to dance on a grave. They wanted a crucifixion, but if they think that is what they got they are bad judges of the genre. The big man came out bigger than he went in. He lost. There should be no doubt about that. His own claim that he thought he won nine rounds, and therefore the fight, was a confirmation of continuing pride rather than a logical analysis. Exactly the same interpretation must be put on his opinion that, if he had fought Joe Frazier before the politicians put him out of boxing four years ago, Frazier 'would have licked me quicker because I wasn't as strong as I am now'. To say otherwise, as I certainly would, clearly would be seen by Ali as an admission that he is in decline. That, for such a man at the age of 29, is unthinkable. Inevitably, in the midst of all his generous words about Frazier, he finds himself saying that he would have done better with 'a referee from England or Scotland, and judges from Japan and Germany' in place of officials appointed by 'the authorities that took my title away, guys who are a lot more friendly toward the Veterans of Foreign Wars than the Muslims'.

Newspaper stories which gave the impression that he was ranting about having been robbed were ridiculous distortions. During an hour and a half in his hotel suite on the 25th floor of the New Yorker Hotel on

Tuesday, I heard him quietly correct several interviewers who called him 'champ'. 'I ain't the champ,' he said quietly. 'Joe's the champ. I call him champ now. Not before but I do now. I ain't protestin'. He's a good, tough fighter. Not a great boxer but great at his own thing. He puts pressure on you all right, cuts off the ring, and he's the best hitter I ever met. I always thought of him as a nice fella. What I said before, that was to do with the fight. Just the fight. I got to know him pretty good travelling up from Philadelphia before he fought Jimmy Ellis. I was low on money that day and he loaned me $100. He's a nice man with a family, just another brother workin' to make a living.'

Ali was lying back low in an armchair that had been placed to suit the television crews who had just left. He wore a fawn and beige wool shirt and blue slacks. His eyes were heavy and his voice was subdued. He said he was sore rather than tired. The worst pain was at the top of his right thigh, where Frazier's lower left hooks had made regular contact. They had hurt him more there than in the body, he said, contradicting those who had concluded wincingly at ringside that he would be 'pissing blood for a week'. He was suffering less than might have been expected from the bruise on his jaw and kept telling us proudly that it was the only real mark on him. His hands were sore and he extended his right one lightly clenched when anyone wished him luck. He would talk quietly for a while and then fall into silence, glancing absently through a newspaper. Three men who said they were from Blackpool, and gave no reason to question it, had come to deliver an obscenely large stick of rock with 'Muhammad Ali' printed through it. 'What you tryin' to do?' he asked, smiling, 'Give me the sugar diabetes?' 'If you had licked this, you'd have licked Frazier,' one of the three told him. The line sounded no better than it had at rehearsal.

Ali had more practical explanations of what went wrong. 'If I knew then what I know now, I would have done different. If I knew I was gonna lose those rounds when I played about, I wouldn't have fooled so much.' This came across as wishful rationalisation of something that was forced upon him. Such contradictions, the tendency to submerge yesterday's facts in today's feelings, come naturally to him. He is an existential thinker. The truth is that the use he made of his equipment in this fight, though inevitably riddled with all kinds of dangerous exaggerations, was basically the approach that offered him the best hope of winning. No one knew better than he did that his legs had lost the elastic agility and inexhaustible fluency they once had. He knew he could not invalidate Frazier's strength and rhythm by the once favourite technique of 'surrounding' his man, dancing outside the range of his opponent's punches while using his speed, reach and precise timing to pour in his own. At his best, the unequalled mobility had made him as secure as a dive-bomber attacking a wagon train. But a long look at his training in Miami had left me sadly convinced that his foot speed was a memory, that against Frazier he would be obliged to fight flat-footed for much of the time.

It was equally obvious that if he allowed this realisation to commit him to a straightforward slugging war, there would be only one winner and it would not be Ali. He has always sought, and always previously found, a highly specific solution to the problems posed by each opponent and here he appeared to decide that he had more chance of overwhelming Frazier with his personality than with his pared-down talent. In the past he has concentrated on psyching himself into invincibility. Here the emphasis was on psyching Frazier out of belief in himself. From the moment of entry into the ring Ali set out to persuade Frazier that he was taking on impossible odds. The two corners told a story. Yank Durham, Frazier's manager, brought in the minimum help. Ali had half a dozen corner-men, all clad in aggressive scarlet uniforms. A lesser fighter might have been unnerved by the sight of such a red army. But this one was content with the knowledge that Ali would be alone when the bell went. He was only mildly irritated when Ali, gliding sideways past his corner, muttered contemptuous predictions.

When the bell did go, the big man started well, exploiting the anticipated clumsiness of Frazier's early moves with accurate jabs and right crosses. As Frazier pressed in close, Ali smothered his attacks, tangling up the arms and employing the advantage in height to lean heavily on the smaller man's neck and shoulders. If the clubbing hooks got home to the body, Ali exposed his mouth-piece and shook his head in dismissal of their effects, implying that the hitter was punching himself out. In fact Ali was being hurt. He simply takes hurt rather well.

Despite a substantial improvement in Frazier's work by the third, he could not, in my judgement, have won more than two or – at the absolute outside – three rounds up to and including the ninth. Ali had avoided draining himself too severely in this early period, especially in the sixth and eighth, by filling in time with some highly calculated comedy. He held a glove against Frazier's forehead, seeking to ward him off with insulting ease, or stood against the ropes with both hands down, eluding many punches and frowning pityingly over those that landed. Occasionally he rapped his man's face with playful little flurries of his right hand. Spectators who felt that his tactics were insanely hazardous did not appreciate how careful he had to be with his energy. Boxing positively is much more tiring than boxing negatively. Ali knew that if he tried to attack vigorously in every round he would burn out fast. He was more confident of his endurance than his destructive strength, so he gambled on breaking Frazier's spirit rather than his body. It was the boldest bluff imaginable.

This strange mixture of sharp aggression and farcical histrionics went very near to winning the fight. Ali had a superb ninth round, drawing traces of blood around Frazier's nose and mouth and adding to the already distinct swellings around the eyes. When Frazier staggered back, his mouth open in an almost drunken grin, after taking jolting hooks and uppercuts to the head, the fight seemed to have swung decisively. But all this time, in his most frustrating moments, one simple statement could be read into everything Frazier did: 'My time is coming.' Now it had arrived. He rallied in the 10th and in the 11th he took control. At last the left hook reached Ali, who had wearied himself in the ninth, and soon he was staggering around the ring at a crazily reclining angle, like a surf-rider before he loses the board. 'What surprised me most was how often Joe caught me with the hook, with good ones after the 11th,' he said later. His ability to withstand a punch is prodigious, however, and Frazier could not put him down.

For the next two rounds he was catching but not disastrously and in the 14th, managing perhaps the best footwork he had shown all night, he boxed beautifully and won the round comfortably. But he had done his grandstanding too early. In the 15th his legs were leaden. Frazier punished him immediately and before the round had gone a minute a sickeningly violent left hook smashed across the right side of Ali's face, instantly increasing the swelling that had developed there earlier and hurling him flat on his back with his legs kicking high towards the ring lights. Now came one of his worst and greatest moments. Any possible ambiguity about the result was removed by that punch, but so were the unjustified doubts about Ali's heart. Any man (and especially one so close to exhaustion) would have been entitled to stay prostrate after such a blow, but he rolled over without hesitation, was up at the count of two and when he had taken the compulsory eight he went straight at Frazier to hold on through the rest of a brutal round. I found it impossible to give Ali fewer than six rounds, with probably two even, but the 11th and 15th were won so easily by Frazier that he was undeniably in front at the finish.

Joe Frazier, a thoroughly pleasant and admirable man, is also a champion fit to share a ring with any who have held the world heavyweight title. 'I have fought anybody y'all put in front of me and God knows I beat them,' he said afterwards. 'What more can I do? Now I got to live a little, man. I've been working for ten long years.'

Both men say they want to meet again – 'All we need is $6 million split evenly down the middle,' says Yank Durham – and the odds are that all the objections of lawyers and politicians and wives will not prevent a second collision. 'Next time would be different,' Ali said in his hotel room. 'Myself would make it different. When you get as big as I got in this game you get intoxicated with so-called greatness. You think you just have to run three miles a day. That's all I did for this fight. And I didn't rest properly, didn't train hard as I used to. You convince yourself you'll get by on natural talent, that it will all just explode in there on the night. But it don't. Next time I'd run more, get the legs right. That would make it different.' Unfortunately, one remembers the same self-criticism of his preparation for Oscar Bonavena. The signs are that he is no longer capable of driving himself through the endless training that maintained his unrivalled condition, that he no longer has the obsessive, unsuffering enthusiasm for it. He, too, wanted to get home, to his new hacienda-style house in New Jersey, and live an ordinary life for a while, 'washing the dishes, putting out the garbage, landscaping the backyard. We been whupped. Maybe we'll get a little peace now.'

But he was not about to abandon those people who were waiting for him down in the lobby. 'I've never thought of losing, but now that it's happened the only thing is to do it right. That's my obligation to all the people who believe in me. We all have to take defeats in life. We lose loved ones, or a man loses his property or his job. All kinds of things set us back, but life goes on. If so-called great people can take these defeats, whatever they are, without cracking, the others are encouraged. They feel strong.

'If I lost again, I'd say, "That's it. I've had my day." You don't go mad. You don't shoot yourself. Soon this will be old news. People got lives to lead, bills to pay, mouths to feed. Maybe a plane will go down with 90 persons in it. Or a great man will be assassinated. That will be more important than Ali losing. I never wanted to lose, never thought I would, but the thing that matters is how you lose. I'm not crying. My friends should not cry.'

The last time I saw him before he went home he was at the wheel of a caravan-bus that was taking his entourage to New Jersey. As it pulled away through the crowds he gave a slow little smile and waved, like royalty. How else would he wave?

George Foreman v. Ken Norton Caracas, Venezuela, 26 March 1974

The Club Man in Caracas

Of all the cruelties professional boxing can inflict, none is more deeply hurtful than the terrible anticlimax that must always threaten a man like Ken Norton when he goes into the ring against a man like George Foreman. Norton is a beautifully conditioned athlete, a talented fighter and a strong personality whose recent years have been a concentrated preparation for the moment in the Poliedro Arena in Caracas on Tuesday evening when the first bell sounds and the heavyweight championship of the world is at stake. The knowledge of how much of himself is invested in that moment should encourage him to approach it with a dignified optimism, to go to work with pride and conviction as befits a man who is offering his best and is sure that is a great deal.

And yet, all his bright hopes, all his spirit and all his excellence could be laid waste within seconds. One sudden, demolishing intervention by Foreman, one clubbing swing of a right arm so powerful it is almost obscene, may consign Norton's skills, strategies and dreams to oblivion. The long tunnel of discipline and self-denial may lead to the edge of a cliff. When that happens to a fighter of quality in a world title match, the sense of futility is overwhelming. Such an experience is much more than a defeat. It is a little death.

The seeds of this kind of harsh drama are in most fights but here they are assiduously fertilised by a champion who declares in every attitude an absolute faith in raw violence. While Norton talks of the evasive speed of his reflexes, of setting traps, of out-thinking and out-manoeuvring the opposition, Foreman muses on his own capacity for obliteration. In someone who has shortened 36 of his 39 contests in a career unblemished by kindness or defeat, it is an understandable prejudice and one that is enthusiastically endorsed by his trainer-manager, Dick Sadler, a small, round, intensely black man who needs only a little more shyness to be an extrovert. 'Norton gonna stick his head up some time in there and when he do you can write finis,' shouts Sadler.

'Just one time, that'll be enough,' says Foreman. 'When the bell rings I'm goin' out to hurt him. I want to hurt him so bad it's embarrassing to me. I want to hurt him so bad he'll just pass out, just won't be there any more.' He is speaking from the horizontal as he lies under the sheets on a bed at El Poliedro, the latest architectural flourish in this burgeoning capital of a newly reinforced democracy that appears to find South America's first heavyweight championship fight a pleasant distraction after the tensions of the Presidential elections. Foreman is cooling off following an hour of ponderous clowning that passed for a workout. His words come in a bored drawl between yawns but occasionally he seeks to give them emphasis by turning a menacing stare on his questioners. All week he has seemed to be auditioning for the ogre's role that was left vacant when the late Sonny Liston shrivelled to mortal proportions before the iridescent talent of Muhammad Ali. But Foreman's act is confusing. Just when his aggressive surliness is recalling the adolescent terror of the Fifth Ward back in Houston, Texas, the wine-drinking vandal and trainee mugger, he starts to talk like a product of the Job Corps, the community welfare organisation that rescued him from the ghetto, took him to California and steered him towards an Olympic gold medal and his present eminence. Both his speech and his demeanour are riddled with contradictions and the impression conveyed is that at 25 he is still groping after a dramatic identity, a persona formidable enough to fit his status as the hardest man on the planet.

During an hour or two spent with him by the poolside at his Caracas hotel, he lolled truculently under a sunshade, showing more inclination to look at his huge, calloused knuckles or the pattern of his blue denim suit than at any of the faces around him. He objected to the pettiest irritations in a tone that suggested he might decide to make them capital offences and dealt brusquely with points of view that did not echo his own: 'Who are you to tell a big man like me what to think?' But the hostility was often superficial and now and then there was an outbreak of humility that was not unappealing in spite of a tendency towards shop-soiled philosophy. 'People talk about my title but it ain't mine, it belongs to the world. It's the same title that was around before me, before Muhammad Ali or Norton and it will be there when we're all gone. Men don't count, the world is full of men. No matter how hard you step in the sands of life, when a wave comes it washes away all trace of you.' That mood did not last long, however, and soon he was playing the bully boy again, practising the glare that is supposed to melt the backbone, remembering notable feats of intimidation in the past. 'I've missed a guy and seen him cower down and just about say thank you. Even when I look bad I am hurting people, even when I miss they suffer.'

Both he and Sadler insist that he has been in condition for weeks, that his weight gives them no concern, indeed is of no consequence. Yet they have always taken pride in the fact that, all through his professional career, his fighting weight has remained constant between 15 st 7 lb and 15 st 10 lb. If there is a substantial increase this time it can only be to the advantage of Norton, who will not be carrying a superfluous ounce even if he fulfils his intention of coming in a little heavier than usual at about 15 st 2 lb. Despite Sadler's justification of the sparse and erratic training of the past few days, there are people who read omens in it. They suggest that the aftermath of an unsuccessful marriage and the state of his financial affairs, which are in such labyrinthine confusion that he could easily end up as the most highly paid pauper in the history of sport, have gravely diminished Foreman's commitment as an athlete. More succinctly, they say the Las Vegas odds of 3–1 against Norton represent a bargain.

Norton is no more convinced by this glib reasoning than I am. He is sure he has a good chance of winning (I see it as much less good, though it certainly exists) but his confidence has nothing to do with any belief that Foreman has ceased to be an exceedingly dangerous man. 'This is a tremendously strong individual,' says Norton in a voice that is the perfect adjunct to a virile, attractive personality. 'If one of his big punches even half-catches you, you are in trouble. But I have the reflex speed, the agility and know-how to stay clear of those big looping shots, to go inside or outside them. And I'm no more intimidated by Foreman's power than I am psyched by all that imitation of Liston. Waiting around outside my dressing-room, hammering on the door, making with the eye, it's all so childish.

'I fought Muhammad Ali twice, broke his jaw and think I won both fights. How can Foreman psyche me? His power I respect but I'm not awed by it. And if he starts pushing me the way he has other guys, trying to set me up, I'll tell him not to do it again. If he does, I'll hit him in the cup, yes the balls, the testicles, say it how you like. One good turn deserves another.

'I'm no 95-lb weakling. I don't get pushed around. The only guy who ever hurt me in 32 pro fights was José Luis Garcia, the one opponent apart from Ali who got a verdict over me. And the Garcia thing was back in 1970. I'm more mature now, 29 years old, a different fighter altogether.'

That combativeness seems genuine and yet it is impossible to overlook the mental pressure that will be thrust on Norton by being enclosed in such a small space with a destructive giant like Foreman, a man who shrinks the ring the moment he rises from the stool and punches as if he has promised to deliver his victim piece by piece to someone in the tenth row. It is significant that the great Sandy Saddler and Archie Moore, two of the finest craftsmen the ring has ever seen, are happy to work with Foreman, whatever his crudities. These masters recognise that in the end the most telling commodity in boxing is violence and they believe George Foreman has a Niagara of it at his disposal.

Still, it is possible that we exaggerate his ferocity, possible that Joe Frazier was a feeble caricature of himself on the night in Jamaica 15 months ago when he was so brutally separated from his title and his senses. One man who thinks so is Hedgemon Lewis, the leading welterweight contender. 'Even if Ken Norton was not my friend, I would go along with him on technical grounds,' says Lewis. 'George Foreman, for all his strength, does nothing really well. He is just a street-fighter who carries the brawl into the ring.'

True, but those who face him have a habit of being carried out of it. Unless Foreman and his trainer are misleading us about his condition, that may be Norton's fate. I fear a little death.

Dark Thoughts of Africa

The features of poor, devastated Ken Norton are, astonishingly, unaltered. But the face of boxing has been changed utterly. In the past it has been the defeat of a champion rather than a successful defence of his title that has replaced one era with another. Yet there can be no doubt that what happened under the dome of the Poliedro Arena earlier this week made Tuesday, 26 March 1974, the first date on a new calendar in a world where millions of dollars and a kind of immortality can be grabbed with a clenched fist.

George Foreman's five-minute impersonation of the Red Army on the offensive did much more than crush Norton and lay siege to the legend of Muhammad Ali. It lit a fuse that promises to burn across an ocean and detonate the most dramatic event boxing has known. And that is not all.

51

This week also provided confirmation that the power to make the biggest fights is passing from the traditional promoters to a new alliance of international financiers whose muscle comes from Swiss banks and black entrepreneurs whose determination and shrewdness were honed to a resentful edge in the ghettoes of the United States. The decision to match Foreman and Ali in Zaire, a country that has previously had as much connection with the heavyweight championship as Tahiti has with the Winter Olympics, reflects the complementary strengths of this alliance. It was Risnelia Investment, a Panamanian group headquartered in Geneva and one of the principals in a consortium brought together to stage the fight, that first suggested using their existing business links with the Zaire government to sound out the possibilities of an African location. There was immediate enthusiasm for the project and it was in no way diminished when the men from Kinshasa discovered that they could negotiate directly with a remarkable black brother, Don King, a large, theatrically garrulous figure with a hairstyle that suggests, as someone said, that he has just stepped out of a bath on to a bare electric wire.

King's apprenticeship as a deal-maker was served in areas of Cleveland where people are not in the habit of settling disputes through their lawyers. When a man who was involved in a fight with him died some days later, he was sent to jail and it took him four years to convince the authorities that he should not be there. Although King now moves around the highest levels of boxing with a relentless *bonhomie*, his moods are not always as bright as his suits. He was not at his merriest when he found that the handout received by reporters at a press conference held to announce details of the Kinshasa extravaganza stated that the co-promoters were Hemdale Leisure Corporation, a British firm who put up the original $1,450,000 of 'risk money', and Video Techniques Incorporated of New York 'in association with Don King Productions'. Henry Schwartz of Video Techniques apologised instantly for this inadequate billing, telling us that Mr King was not only a director of VT but the one and only man who 'could have brought the Foreman and Ali camps together to sign for this fight'.

The mollifying effect of that eulogy was limited. Don King said grimly that, considering the crucial role he had played in arranging the match, it was an insult that the press statement should 'put me in the back of the bus'.

'This fight will be a tribute to the sports world and more importantly to the black world,' he said. 'Black men will be coming together with mutual respect. It will be symbolic. The prodigal sons will be returning home to Africa, the motherland of black folk. This will be a spectacular such as has never been seen on the earth as yet.'

His language may be Hollywood Outrageous but the hyperbole is forgivable. The show that is due to go on at three o'clock on an African morning this autumn, due to be witnessed by 100,000 in the Stadium of the Twentieth of May and perhaps a billion more in front of cinema and television screens, has the elements to overshadow even Ali's epic confrontations with Joe Frazier. Certainly the prospect is too exciting to be blurred by all the cynicism, financial turmoil and backstage rancour that has been in evidence in Caracas this week. The interminable squabbles over the nationality of officials for the Foreman–Norton fight, the last-minute appointment of an American as non-voting referee, coinciding with the miraculous alleviation of the knee injury that was ostensibly crippling Foreman and threatening to cancel the event only a few hours before, and the government's late refusal to implement assurances that the boxers' earnings would be exempt from tax – all left such a rank taste in the mouth that it is a relief to look back to the harsh simplicity of Tuesday night's action.

Then there was neither argument nor ambiguity. Inside the ring, George Foreman made his own truth and Ken Norton had no power to question it. As one had feared, the challenger suffered a little death and even before the first bell he appeared to be wearing his blue and white gown like a shroud. The impression was that his spirit had been anaesthetised by the implacable presence of Foreman, that he was a victim awaiting his doom. There was never any possibility that he would have long to wait. The 25-year-old world champion has now grown to a full awareness of his fearsome capacity for destruction.

In the brutally decisive second round against Norton, following a first spent stalking and measuring, he moved so inexorably that the sight chilled the blood. Overwhelming strength is one fundamental advantage. His punching method is another. With the exception of the body punches and a jab that can be stunningly orthodox, the pulverising blows tend to come from both hands in long arcs, sweeping diagonally to his opponent's head, and the vast arms often brush contemptuously through efforts at parrying defence. That ability to destroy from a distance will be an immense threat even to Ali, for all the length of Ali's own jab and the speed and ingenuity of his evasions. But Foreman has yet another quality that may prove still more vital in Zaire. It is the effectiveness with which he pursues his man. He quarters the ring with a deadly sense of geometry, employing a perfectly timed side-step that cuts off escape routes as emphatically as a road block. 'I think I am just blessed,' he said from under the cap that was part of the studded denim he wore for his victory party, as he does for nearly every relaxed occasion. 'I hit a guy and it is like magic. You see him crumbling to the floor. God has given me these gifts. I pray a lot and I'm grateful for what I have been given. It is all a matter of blessing and I know it is temporary.' Not so temporary, however, that he expects his talents to fade before September. Muhammad Ali, himself a believer in divine backing, will need another surge of his genius if he is to survive on the continent he craves to impress.

Despite having seen Norton flattened within a few feet of him at El

Poliedro, Ali remains optimistic and so does Angelo Dundee. 'Sure Foreman is a killer if you stand still and let him beat you to death,' says Dundee. 'But who is crazy enough to think Muhammad will do that? Muhammad has the equipment to beat this guy, he knows how to handle that job.'

I, too, know a way to beat George Foreman but it involves shelling him for three days and then sending in the infantry.

George Foreman v. Muhammad Ali, Kinshasa, Zaire, 30 October 1974

Small Cut, Big Problem

George Foreman was cut, but the bleeding may be done by others. That small wound, the kind a child might suffer in the playground and not lose a day at school, may drain from Muhammad Ali the last precious distillation of his great competitive spirit, the reservoir of inspired will that he painfully accumulated as he moved towards the supreme climax of his career. Even those who have observed him since prodigious adolescence, who long ago came to expect the extraordinary of him, were deeply impressed by the sense of imminent crescendo in his preparation for Foreman. But the same admirers fear that at 32, and after a decade of the most extravagant demands on his body and psyche, he had only one such phenomenal effort left in him. He was timing it flawlessly until the awkward elbow of an obscure part-time sparring partner in the Foreman camp made its historic intervention. 'That cut by the right eyebrow would not have incapacitated a man in any other occupation I can think of,' said Pete Hacker, the world champion's doctor. 'I treat a hundred worse than that every month. But for George it was serious.'

For Ali it could be disastrous. The suspicion now is that his psychological clock, set with such precision, can only run down during the delay caused by the injury. Winding it up again may be a task beyond even such a sorcerer. It is as if Canute, having turned back the waves, were to be asked to repeat the trick on the next tide. The intention now is to stage the match at the end of October, and although the new date is six weeks away it seems decidedly optimistic. But whenever (some would say if ever) the fight takes place, we may wince at the sight of Muhammad Ali in over his head. Zaire, as host nation, is already close to being in that position and the men responsible for putting it there are liable to find their embarrassment festering as the eye-cut heals. They sought to bring the circus to town and all they are left with, for the moment at least, is the dust that blows across a vacant site and bitter echoes of the anger and frustration provoked in journalists and broadcasters who came to convey the excitement to the world.

The Zairese people are warm, helpful and charming and they do not deserve to be penalised for the ambition of those salesmen who made promises that local technology and experience could not keep at such short notice. As a global exercise in public relations, a demonstration that Zaire's sophistication had reached the point where it could readily cope with the gaudy juggernaut of the world heavyweight championship (a tribute to sophistication, incidentally, that many countries would happily do without), the promotion is in danger of going hopelessly wrong. This weekend the planes carrying the battalions of media men back to Europe and the United States are in need of extended take-off runs to lift the resentments loaded aboard. The reporters' talk is of telephone calls that would have had more chance of materialising had the wires run into their socks, of telex messages exasperatingly delayed and subsequently, when they began to include complaints about the communications, peremptorily censored. I was told this article was 'wrong' and simply could not be filed from Kinshasa, which is why it is coming from Rome.

The postponement will give the organisers a second chance. Don King, the Cleveland numbers man turned entrepreneur whose vast black presence and tireless persuasion breathed life into the whole unlikely project, says the change of date will create extra expenses amounting to $500,000. That will be a small price to pay for the opportunity to salvage a dream, to prove that the two most celebrated pugilists in the world can indeed meet in their soul-land of Africa and have the rest of the planet as an audience.

President Mobutu is sufficiently identified with the dream to engender assumptions that Risnelia, the company that is the major element in the promoting consortium, represents his money. Mobutu's people are unlikely to feel let down as long as Muhammad Ali is around. They are enraptured by the best-known black man on earth, whether he is promenading among them by the turgid, grassy expanse of the Zaire River or cavorting theatrically through his training sessions at N'Sele, 40 miles from Kinshasa. On several days this week beautiful children, their eyes on guard for a miracle, sat decorously quiet between their mothers and fathers as Ali stepped in out of the bright heat of late afternoon and moved soberly about his exercises and his sparring under a battery of 28 whirring fans. Then as his mood lightened towards the end of the sessions and he began to clown benevolently, shaking hands with one spectator, making a mock lunge at his neighbour, parents and children swayed and bounced in joyous unison and from between gleaming teeth came those high shrieks that are the undiluted expression of pleasure.

George Foreman is the bookies' favourite but to the 22 million citizens of Zaire he could not be more of an outsider if they looked on him, as Ali suggests they will, 'as a Belgium'. Ali's delightful, vibrant young wife Belinda was moved to tears when she first realised the depths of the affection offered to him in Kinshasa. Coming from her, tears meant something. Her usual method of coping with her unique husband is to tease, telling him that she is rooting for Foreman. 'I was on the phone to George and he says he is going to beat you,' she says. The great man rolls his eyes threateningly at her but there is a smile around his mouth. 'That's another reason we gonna whup him,' he yells. 'We fightin' over you.'

At times in Zaire he has given the impression of nearing the point where he would be ready to fight over a lesser woman. 'It's real lonely for me, separated from my family and without the pretty kinda girls around that I'm used to. I'm in jail, I'm sufferin'. But I knew that some day God would test me like this, leave me stranded in the middle of nowhere just to test me. And I've been preparin'.' Anyone who listens in on such a reverie is not entitled to think the man is hypocritical when he declares his affinity with Africans. His ambivalence is natural enough. He does want to be a symbol of the worldwide brotherhood of black men but, to quote his trainer, Angelo Dundee, 'He can't help missing the coffee-shops, the Howard Johnsons and all that bullshit that he enjoys back home. He's stuck with being American.' Sheer homesickness may increase the eroding effect of the long wait ahead of him.

There was something American, too, in his response to the African artist who arrived while Ali was cooling off after training. When the man was pushed through the protective ring of acolytes to hand over a portrait of his hero done on velvet, the subject reacted with suitable enthusiasm but then called for a $100 bill and tried to thrust it on the painter. Even Bundini Brown, who is sufficiently in favour of cash transactions to have bought 7,000 Ali lapel buttons at 14 cents each and brought them to a country where their value has risen as high as six dollars, was constrained to object. 'He don't want your money, man, he loves yo',' wailed Bundini. Walter Youngblood had a solution: 'Give *us* that yard, man, we can use it.' Youngblood, the assistant trainer credited with devising the fish and vegetable diet that laid the foundation of the glowing fitness Ali was showing at around 15 st 6 lb this week, has made a contribution that is worth somewhat more than $100. Everyone in the camp, and not least the central figure himself, insists that he is in the finest condition he has achieved in the last ten years.

Dundee, contradicting Ali's forecast that cuts will be decisive, gives a series of impersonations of both fighters (a sparrow mimicking eagles) as he argues that his man will knock out the vaunted destroyer wherever and whenever they meet. 'Foreman can't live with my guy's movement. Foreman is a walker. No walker can beat my guy. He's made for Ali.' Most of the walking Foreman has done lately has been behind the seven-foot-high fence that encloses the hilltop compound housing his entourage. With its armed guards and its checkpoints, the compound was probably conceived as a fortress to suit the taste of a world champion who is hardly a socialiser. But as he pads broodingly around its confines, studded denim dungarees over his bare skin and his Alsatian Daggo at his heels, he must begin to feel, as Ali obviously does, that the fighters are prisoners of the $5 million each has been promised. 'They give you five million but they work your black ass,' said Ali in another of his unromantic moments. The part of Foreman's anatomy that most people think has been abused this week is, of course, the right eye, and not merely because Bill McMurray's elbow made harsh contact with it. Ferdie Pacheco, a Miami doctor who makes a hobby of tending fighters and has Ali as his star client, says the champion's wound should have been stitched instead of simply closed with the arrangement of plaster strips that is called 'butterflying' because of the double-wedge shape of the pieces of tape. 'Butterflying closes the cut but it does not draw the tissue together properly, so that healing is only superficial and there is a boggy effect beneath the skin. Weeks afterwards a sharp blow will open that cut, and who hits more sharply than Muhammad?'

Pacheco has a point. But will Muhammad be hitting just as sharply when Foreman at last steps towards him in the ring, or will the crescendo that should have thrilled us next week now be denied us for ever? 'Our trouble right now is filling in voids, making sure the wait doesn't get to the kid,' said Dundee. Who will fill the void for us if Muhammad Ali is, as we fear, heading by the slow route to the last exit?

'He's Only a Human. My Guy Ain't.'

The short, humid days are shaped around the midday training sessions and the long cool evenings are filled with talk, with an atmosphere of propaganda as reassuringly familiar as the odours of home cooking. But the hours are peeling away like layers of insulation and soon Muhammad Ali will have to grasp the bare wire of what Wednesday morning could mean to him and the extraordinary cast of helpers and hangers-on who have ridden first-class on his dream for more than a decade.

A great tremor will pass through the whole of sport if he falls to George Foreman, and afterwards the landscape will be slightly dimmer for most of us. For those who have, over the years, been allotted some real or illusory role in his professional activities, trauma will be much more acute. They have made identities for themselves by travelling with the circus and when the big top comes down their egos and their standards of living are likely to collapse with it. Considering what they have at risk, these men – an unlikely collection ranging from the Woolworth's witch-doctor Bundini Brown to a Pennsylvania Irishman called Gene Kilroy who styles himself business manager – are bound to offer some guidance to the balance of optimism and apprehension in Ali's camp. Of course, it would be foolish to equate their spirits with his, but the throb of misgiving that can be detected in their strident predictions of success has a more honourable echo in the realism that steals into his own utterances during his few quiet and thoughtful moments.

The other day he talked of how he would react if Foreman hit him hard enough to knock him down and possibly scramble his senses. He would, he insisted, neither cower like Ken Norton nor stumble into the mouth of the cannon like Joe Frazier. 'I'll be jabbin' and dancin', whuppin' and movin' till my head comes cool again,' he said. 'I'll run if I have to, rassle if I have to. I won't be out at the end of George's arms makin' a target. That's too much to ask if you are in there with me. But shit, the man ain't gonna knock me down.' For emphasis, he rose to demonstrate how to be hurtfully elusive, bouncing around the vast lounge that helps to rank his accommodation with the most luxurious available in the government complex at N'Sele, 40 miles from Kinshasa. As an encore he reached for Angelo Dundee (who is no larger than a trainer has to be) and hugged him roughly off his feet.

'Sonofabitch,' says Dundee every time a tearing pain in the ribs reminds him of the horseplay. 'It kills me if I laugh now and it was laughing that kept me sane through the six weeks we've been here. Since the postponement most of us have been quietly going bananas. Muhammad is the only one who ain't affected. Every day is like a new toy to him. Foreman must have suffered more from the waiting than he has, even if the eye-cut has healed as well as it seems to have done. He's only a human. My guy ain't.

'George is going to find out about his own human limitations here. He wants to pull you on to punches or push you out by the shoulders to a convenient range but he won't be able to do that with my guy. George likes opponents who fight as if they are on rails, advancing in a straight line like Frazier or running in a straight line like Norton. You can kill him with angles. Ali will be either inside or outside the arc of the heavy stuff, and all the time that jab will be jumping into Foreman's face. This could be a repeat of the Liston job. Foreman is vulnerable to mobility and variety. Muhammad will knock him out.'

It is a nice script and in trying to stick to it Muhammad Ali will be able to call on a magnificent will and the substantial residue of the greatest athletic talent boxing has ever seen. He has appeared to shed the years with the surplus weight as he has sweated impressively in the conference hall that has been turned into a gymnasium at N'Sele. Now his torso is a wedge of flexible muscle and his face might belong to a film actor in his middle 20s rather than a boxer of 32 who has been a professional for 14 years. His own declaration that already he weighs less than 15 stone is clearly absurd but he is trim enough to suggest he will enter the ring encouragingly close to the 15 st 2 lb he weighed when he won the world championship from Sonny Liston ten years ago.

After training, Ali sits on the ring apron in his white robe and fantasises aggressively about the wonders he will perform in the 'greatest eeee-vent in the history of the world'. His miracle will, he promises specifically, be the most remarkable since the resurrection of Christ. (It is hard to reconcile the need for such a feat with his dismissal of Foreman as an executioner of nobodies.) Having ranted, Ali gives his associates heart failure by leaping five feet from the ring to the floor, then joins the Californian negro who has been skilfully slapping some bongo drums in a corner of the hall. Ali pounds furiously on the drums, shouting: 'War . . . war . . . war', before striding out into the burning glare of the day.

By comparison, Foreman almost slips into the gym. Each afternoon the world champion leaves his hotel – where he is shut off from the press and public most of the time – and is driven away from Kinshasa's tall buildings to the air-conditioned modernity of N'Sele. He comes to work, not to hold court, and pummels the heavy bags with all the ebullience of a lifer breaking stones. Once every few days he plants himself in front of journalists to answer questions. He does so civilly, but refuses to reciprocate Ali's insults. 'He's a fine man in many ways and I like him a lot. I don't mind all his talk. Talkin' is fun, a lot more fun than what we will be doin' Wednesday. Maybe Ali won't find that too pleasant.' Looking at George Foreman, at the vast, bare cliffs of shoulder that spread out from the straps of his denim dungarees, it is easy to share this last suspicion. The Zairese audiences, who are captivated by Ali, laugh at Foreman's clumsiness in the gym but most men who have faced him in earnest have wished they had an ejector seat instead of a corner stool. He has fallen on them like an avalanche and, despite what Angelo Dundee says, it will not be easy for Ali to stay clear of trouble.

Muhammad Ali is almost certain to fight in flurries, staying away to jab and cross when he can, falling into smothering clinches when the dancing has to stop. Foreman's biggest mistake would be to attempt a calculating fight. If he gives away the initiative he may never regain it. The 25-year-old world champion should set out to be brutal from the first bell, to hunt and destroy, to batter the grace and elasticity and confidence out of a man who would surely be his master if both were in their prime. All this makes for a grim picture and I fear it is the one we are likely to see on Wednesday. As we go to the stadium at that unreal hour we shall be hoping for a miracle but dreading a calamity. Whatever happens those of us who have marched under Ali's banner will not be let down, for he is brave as well as beautiful.

The Greatest, Again

We should have known that Muhammad Ali would not settle for any ordinary old resurrection. His had to have an additional flourish. So, having rolled away the rock, he hit George Foreman on the head with it.

Foreman, roughly disabused of his conviction that all his rivals were entombed in physical inferiority, is by no means the only one left stunned by the blow and that gives Ali a particular satisfaction. He said so more than once in that muted time early on Wednesday afternoon when the turmoil detonated by his achievement had subsided for a few hours. Lying back on the thick cushions of an armchair in his villa, with the windows curtained against an angry sun that was threatening to evaporate the Zaire River as it slid like a grassy ocean past his front door, he talked with the quiet contentment of a man whose thoughts were acting on him as comfortingly as the hands of a good masseur. 'I kicked a lot of asses – not only George's,' he said. 'All those writers who said I was washed up, all those people who thought I had nothin' left to offer but my mouth, all them that been against me from the start and waitin' for me to get the biggest beatin' of all times. They thought big bad George Foreman, the baddest man alive, could do it for them but they know better now.'

As he started the next sentence, Ali remembered the presence of his aunt, Coretta Clay, and the other cook, Lanna Shabazz, who had just been asked to 'fix two steaks and scramble about eight eggs' for him. He checked himself, then shaped rather than spoke the words: 'Ah done fucked up a lot of minds.' That he has, just as he has opened up new horizons for the misled among the faithful, for those of us who have long considered him the most remarkable performer sport has ever produced and yet – with logic, the boxing forecasters' Iago, spitting falsehoods in our ears – found ourselves fearfully predicting that Foreman would be too young and too strong to fall before him. When something as close to a miracle happens, awe befits the onlookers more than analysis but Ali for his part was happy to dissect and explain what he had done.

With myself, one other journalist and his household staff as the only listeners, he rambled for more than two hours through a generally subdued monologue that left out little of what he felt about the fight and its implications. He had been satisfied with the briefest of rests after his pre-dawn exertions and, in the words of his chronicler, Budd Schulberg, had 'talked up a storm' most of the morning. He would do so again later in the afternoon as he ranted happily from one press conference to the next ('Now I can really boast') around his training camp at N'Sele, 40 miles from Kinshasa. But, given his mood in his living quarters at lunchtime, two interlopers were not enough to evoke the usual theatrical reaction, to justify the self-perpetuating stage act. So the scene, despite its occasional hilarity, was an oasis of seriousness, the still eye of his verbal storm.

He was dressed in a short-sleeved black shirt and matching slacks and had kicked off the heavy running boots that are his regular footwear in camp to show white boxing socks with black rings round the top. His wrists and hands were uncluttered by decoration, or even a watch. Apart from a small bruise beneath the right eye and some flecks of blood surrounding the iris (which he attributed to Foreman's thumb), he was unmarked. But he admitted that a left-side rib, which was first cracked nearly ten years ago and has been troublesome since, was again giving him pain. His voice was slightly hoarse, not so much from over-use as from the residual effects of a slight cold that had bothered him before the fight. A fairly severe cough racked him now and again and when it did he grabbed his sore rib and doubled over.

'Muhammad Ali stops George Foreman,' he muttered with his eyes closed. 'Man, that is a hell of a upset. It will be weeks before I realise the impact of this. I don't feel like I'm champion again yet. I can't wait to see all them magazines. They got to say I'm the greatest now, the greatest of all times. I fooled them all. They thought I'd have to try and dance against George, that my legs would go and I'd get tagged. George thought that too. But that was my main thing, not dancin'.

'The trick was to make him think he was the baddest man in the world and everybody had to run from him. Truth is I could have killed myself dancin' against him. He's too big for me to keep moving round him. I was a bit winded after doin' it in the first round, so I said to myself, "Let me go to the ropes while I'm fresh, while I can handle him there without gettin' hurt. Let him burn himself out. Let him blast his ass off and pray he keeps throwin'. Let it be a matter of who can hit who first, and that's me." This was a real scientific fight, a real thinkin' fight. For me it was. Everythin' I did had a purpose.

'There he was swingin' away and all the time I was talkin' to him sayin', "Hit harder, George. That the best you got? They told me you had body punches but that don't hurt even a little bit. Harder, sucker, swing harder. You the champion and you gettin' nowhere. Now I'm gonna jab you." Then pop! I'd stick him with a jab. "I'm gonna jab you again sucker," I'd say and there it'd go. Pop! "Nothin' you can do about it, sucker." He didn't like gettin' hit with those punches. You see his head go on his shoulders, you see it turn every time I connected? And when did I miss?

'I'd jab, then give him a right cross, then finish with a jab. Nobody expects you to finish a combination with a jab. Those punches took the heart away from George. Joe Frazier mighta taken them but they sickened George. When he did all that talkin' about concentratin' on his defence because he was scary about takin' punishment, people thought he was just a big man kiddin' along. But he really don't like punishment and I proved it.

'By the fifth round, you remember when I leaned back on the ropes and gave him all the free shots he wanted and he couldn't do nothin' to bother me, by then I knew George had shot his load. I knew he was through.'

Ali's eyes lifted suddenly and he smiled at Aunt Coretta and Lanna Shabazz, who had winced and drawn in their breath as he talked of that fifth round. 'Were you scared when I let him punch away at me like that? It weren't nothin'. He weren't hittin' no spots, no place vital where he could hurt me. I was leanin' back over the ropes with my head out of the way and my arms was savin' me from real damage on the body. If he'd hurt me I'd have moved. I knew what I was doin'. You know I wouldn't go in there to let no street-fighter mess me around.'

Coretta Clay, a small woman with the firm-boned features of the world champion's father, abandoned herself to a high, ecstatic laugh at the door of the kitchen. 'There'll never be another like him,' she shrilled when she recovered. 'He is the Alpha and the Omega.'

As far as professional boxing is concerned, he pretty well is. When all the outlandish trappings of an extraordinary event have begun to fade and gather dust in the memory, when we have grown vague about the wheeling and dealing involved, about how ethnic pride and financial avarice became ardent bedmates, when we scarcely smile at the remembered sight of Bundini Brown planting a kiss and a 'Float like a butterfly' biro on President Mobutu or the more appealing but equally unlikely spectacle of an attractive young black woman breast-feeding her baby in the third row ringside, where accommodation cost $250 a place without mention of meals – when that distant day comes, what will remain utterly undiminished is the excitement of Muhammad Ali's performance. And for this witness at least the most vivid recollection will not be the inspiration of his tactics or the brilliance of his technique, spellbinding though they were. It will be the glittering, flawless diamond of his nerve.

Many will see what happened in the Twentieth of May Stadium as an exposure of Foreman's deficiencies, of the self-defeating crudity and lack of imagination that had begun to drain him of both energy and resolution as early as the third round. But we are aware of the extent of those weaknesses only because Muhammad Ali refused to be impressed by the punching power of a man who had not been taken beyond the second round in his previous eight fights and who had annihilated the only two fighters ever to defeat Ali. Despite being in the best condition he has known since being forced out of boxing by the US government in 1967, Muhammad at the age of 32 may have had suspicions about the limits of his legs and wind but his decision to invite Foreman to crowd in on him must be seen as an astonishing act of calculated bravery. His ability to function at maximum efficiency, without the slightest impairment of concentration, while the bombs were flying around his head in the early minutes, testifies to a fearlessness that even the prize-ring has rarely produced. And all this after turning back for his dressing-gown and arriving in the stadium less than half an hour before he was due to fight.

The man could pick flowers in a minefield and never miss a bloom. He explains it as simple confidence in his own abilities: 'An experienced pilot flies a plane through a storm without gettin' in a panic. If new things happen he is cool. I have been boxin' 20 years and I'm a pretty good fighter. I can walk into the firin' line with a man like Foreman and I got no fear. Nothin' can happen that I don't understand. I been to school.

'I was a pro nine years before he was. When he got knocked down it was new to him and he was lost. I've been down. I've been humiliated. Had my title taken away. Had my jaw broke. Had so much trouble with my hands for seven years now the doctors been tellin' me to quit. This time they were strong. I was able to hit the heavy bag and I fought without Novocaine injections for the first time in years. But I been through all these things. I know the hard side.

'It was an amateur against a professional, a kid against a man. I tell you somethin', if he had got up I could have humiliated that boy. George has been actin' up with fancy clothes and all that stuff with his dog, and misusin' people, runnin' the press around, talkin' funny when he does talk. He used to be a nice fella but he's changin'. You know how big it makes me to get the title back ten years after I won it from that other big bad bully Liston, to be just the second man to regain the heavyweight championship and the first to win it twice without ever losin' it in the ring. Yet you can walk in on me here and talk to me, no sweat. Tomorrow I'll be back in the ghetto pickin' up black babies and drinkin' soda at a corner store. I talk plenty but I don't act up like George.'

At that moment Foreman was hardly a picture of arrogance. With reddening bumps around both eyes and in the middle of his forehead, and signs that the old cut on his eyelid had wept, he looked and sounded whipped and weary and uncertain as he rested in his Kinshasa hotel. 'I admit he amazed me,' he said. 'Just the distance he could lean back over the ropes was amazin'. And he out-thought me tactically, planned his fight better than I did.' Foreman did not seem to be inventing excuses when he said he had not felt right for four days before the fight. He says he found himself having to take excessive amounts of liquid and this suggests a chemical imbalance in his system that could explain the swiftness of his physical deterioration on the night, though Muhammad would suggest that any man who swings sandbags will tire if he hits nothing but air.

In the villa, having eaten his steak and eggs and drunk a few pints of orange juice, the champion was watching a television cassette of a fight preview with rapt, boyish attention, his mouth slightly open. When he wasn't arguing with the comments of others, he was calling for proper respect to be shown to his own contributions. 'Shhhhh . . . Listen to me here . . . Watch this . . . I was right, wasn't I? . . . I said I'd stop him after seven and he went in eight . . . I even cancelled the rain. It stayed dry for the fight, then an hour after it there was a storm that nearly flooded the place.' This was all bewilderingly true. He bent over the set with a hostile concentration when Foreman's manager, Dick Sadler, came up on the screen. Sadler said his man was a thunderous, murderous puncher. 'No he ain't,' said Ali flatly. Sadler talked of Foreman putting one opponent, Gregorio Peralta, in bed for four days. 'I got outa bed after two hours,' said Ali. 'I put *him* in the bed.' Next we saw Sadler holding the heavy bag while the former champion went close to punching a hole in it. 'Trouble was,' said Ali, as if they could hear him, 'nobody was holdin' me.'

Who can hold him now? Those marvellously timed punches he threw in the eighth round on Wednesday put the promoters as well as Foreman at his feet. John Daly, the English entrepreneur, has already offered him $10 million for a third fight with Joe Frazier, in Beirut, and the expansion of closed-circuit television makes even more enormous sums feasible. Frazier is the likely opponent, though Ali acknowledges the contradiction that he will always have trouble with a man who was pulverised by Foreman. Ali will certainly not retire, partly because he loves the drama of boxing and partly because the money is too good to refuse. He says he has two or three million saved already (for a man who was about to watch *Bonnie and Clyde* on cassette he retains a touching faith in banks, has none at all in investments), but needs more to feel secure.

In a sense, that is a pity, for Wednesday would have made a fine exit. As Coretta Clay says, he is boxing's Alpha and Omega. Now we have seen him, what can it offer us? Maybe both he and boxing should quit while they are ahead.

Muhammad Ali v. Joe Frazier, Quezon City, The Philippines,
1 October 1975

A Kind of Requiem

It takes a rare purity of spirit to irrigate the moral and aesthetic desert that is forever threatening to engulf the world of heavyweight boxing. What we saw in Quezon City, capital of the Philippines, in midweek represented a shining flood of that purity. To say so is not to claim that the third and last meeting of Joe Frazier and Muhammad Ali would leave all who witnessed it ready to embrace the values of the prize-ring. Those 40-odd minutes of unremitting violence must have had the opposite effect on many. They would recoil from the thought that two men who are formidable in so many ways should seek to express themselves through an exchange of suffering, and especially they would wince at the sight of Frazier, his marvellous body reduced to a dilapidated, lurching vehicle for his unyielding will, reeling blindly in the murderous crossfire of the world champion's final assaults.

But whatever misgivings remain about the social validity of professional boxing, there is no room to doubt the worth, the simple nobility of what Frazier and Ali extracted from the harsh context in which they found themselves at the Quezon Coliseum on Wednesday morning. There was nothing morbid or sadistic about the thrill that their performances sent through the blood. What we felt was awe at the spectacle of extraordinary men setting new limits for themselves, pushing back the boundaries of their courage, their physical and pyschological capacity.

With the dramatic images of the fight still filling the memory, there is deep reluctance to listen to all the feverish plans for moving Ali's big top on to another exotic fairground. Naturally, that cosmic promoter, Don King, a hawk in peacock's feathers, is eager to swoop on some more of the millions that are waiting to be snatched around the world. He talks of Munich as having 'the inside track' but admits to a special fancy for Haiti, where even the unsavoury caravan that has attached itself to Ali's heavyweight championship might look wholesome against the local fauna. There are, he assures us, still plenty of governments sufficiently ambiguous about the distinction between prestige and notoriety to want to invest in his kind of promotion. Saudi Arabia, Singapore, Indonesia, Iran . . . the names flow from him like guarantees from a snake-oil salesman. However, Mr King's anxiety to put the show on the road again is not shared by its star. Ali's mumblings on Wednesday about imminent retirement invited as much scepticism as his demands 24 hours later that the purse for his next appearance should be $25 million. But his confession of profound weariness, his pleas for a genuine rest at the end of 12 months that have seen him box 63 championship rounds and amass gross earnings of more than £7 million, were convincing enough.

The morning's work in the Philippines had drained him as none of his previous 50 fights – not even his two defeats, the first epic with Frazier and the night Ken Norton broke his jaw – had drained him. No champion in history has ever had access to a greater storeroom of physical and spiritual reserves, but Frazier seemed to have emptied it, to have forced Ali to lift the floorboards and scrape the very foundations of his nature for the last traces of strength. Ali's subsequent assertion that he wanted to retire as early as the tenth round was familiar hyperbole, but there was an aching honesty about a later admission: 'I felt like quittin' at the end of the 14th, well, not like quittin' but like I didn't want to go no more.' On the way back to the dressing-room his face had the greyness of terminal exhaustion and he moved as if the marrow of his bones had been replaced by mercury.

At first he dismissed any suggestion of talking to reporters, but then he heard that Frazier, with the bruised flesh around his eyes pressing against dark glasses, had undertaken the ordeal. So Ali struggled off his back and pulled on a pair of black slacks. He could not manage his shoes, so he shuffled to the press conference with only his white boxing socks on his feet, leaning heavily on his attendants and bodyguards. Once there, his monologue was muted, solemn and shot through with a direct, poetic eloquence far removed from the doggerel of his more superficial moods, and when he said that going into the 13th and 14th rounds against a man like Frazier was 'the next thing to dyin'' it did not ring false. As always, he bore minimal evidence of the war he had won (only the small lumps and discolorations around his eyes were conspicuous), but he said he hurt everywhere, and each pain was echoed by a tribute to the unique opponent who had inflicted it. 'Don't let me ever again hear anybody put Joe Frazier down,' he had said in his dressing-room. 'That is a man.' Since Ali's own tongue is the one that has lacerated Frazier most vindictively and unjustly, we were anxious to believe in the permanence of his conversion to reality. 'Joe Frazier is a real, real fighter. He is the toughest man in the world. Nobody can put pressure on me like he can, can take what I give and come back to hurt me. If I'd taken the punches he took in there I'd have quit long before he did. He is a man.'

In the evening they demonstrated their recuperative powers in characteristic ways, Ali by calling on President Ferdinand Marcos, Frazier by turning up at a party of his friends in the Hyatt Hotel. A warmth too basic to be called anything but love went out to him as he entered the room with his wife, Florence. He was wearing a dinner suit with the collar of the dress shirt open wide. 'You all havin' a good time?' he called through the microphone. 'You all boogyin' right on in there?' Then he sang a rock song about having a good thing and not wanting to lose it. He had the championship of the world once and lost it, but the best thing he has he can never lose. It is the undecorated grace of his nature.

When he had finished dancing with his wife and one of his younger daughters, he was asked if his feud with Ali had exhausted itself of bitterness, if there would be a mellowing of feeling now. 'I sure hope so,' he said. 'I sure do hope so.' Perhaps Ali at last will help to realise the hope of friendliness, will finally stop allowing obsession with his own ego to distort the huge respect he has always felt for the greatest of his adversaries. In the ring that respect was unmistakable. The fight had an intense dignity, unblemished by any attempt on Ali's part to con or ridicule his opponent. Everything he did was an admission that he was in with an equal. After a smoothly effective start, he was frequently made to suffer in the middle rounds, driven into corners by an aggression as insistent as fire, hammered by left hooks of a ferocity that put his title seriously at hazard. His retaliation was vehement, of course, but it was hard to see how the three Filipino officials (whose scoring of rounds, leaving out those that were even, showed 8–4, 8–4 and 8–3 in Ali's favour) came to have him much better than level entering the 13th. That round virtually concluded the argument, opening with a superb right hand to the jaw that sent Frazier's gumshield flying into the crowd and ending with the challenger's upper face so cruelly swollen that he was unable to see the blows that were smashing into his head. No blind man can fight Ali and at the end of the 14th Joe's corner cut off his gloves.

Frazier is now being pressed to retire, and the most fervent urgings come from those who admire him most, who do not wish to see his greatness rewarded with irreversible damage to body and brain. And if Joe goes, can Ali, who is 33 and feeling it, be far behind? He does not have to be told that their destinies have been inextricably linked. 'I couldn't be what I am without him and he couldn't be what he is without me,' says Ali. 'We been a pretty good team over the last five years.'

There is no one around who could develop a comparable rivalry with him. George Foreman was psychologically dismantled in Zaire. Now he is a tortured and remote figure who refuses to take the fights that might rebuild his confidence. 'I got to talk to George, get him back on his feet,' says Ali, adding that he would welcome the Texan as his next opponent. But for the moment Foreman, who only a short year ago loomed like an ogre of invincibility, stays out of sight, not so much sulking as demoralised, an Achilles whose tent has fallen about his ears. In contrast, Ken Norton, who was devoured by Foreman in five minutes, has been a ubiquitous and muscular presence in the Philippines. He beat Ali once, and took the champion to a photo-finish in the return, but Norton at 31 looks a lot less hungry than he did. He has played a stud in a film and must have found it an untaxing role, for he is surrounded by attractive women of all shades wherever he goes.

With Smokin' Joe gone and Foreman discredited, Ali would find it increasingly hard to invest his doings with a sense of universal drama. The likelihood is that after one or two more fights he will depart the stage and devote himself to such trivia as a $5 billion export business between America and Asia that he promises to supervise. His passing will surely have a cataclysmic effect. The championship he holds can never hope to mean as much without him. What happened in Quezon City may prove to have been a kind of requiem for the heavyweight division.

Part Two

PART TWO

Some of Our Own Who
Could Have a Row

There is a running joke among American boxing writers about the peculiar nervousness that overtakes their counterparts from this side of the Atlantic when a British fighter is in the ring against one of their hard men. They say we give the impression of being scared to drop a pencil because, by ducking our heads beneath the desks to retrieve it, we are liable to miss the fight. In my time at ringside I have been lucky enough to report on the doings of quite a few boxers from this country who have not only shown a marked reluctance to assume the horizontal but have offered enough skill, determination and hurtful aggression to demand the respect and sometimes the capitulation of the best men in their divisions. Some of the outstanding British fighters of the post-war period – such as Randolph Turpin, Dave Charnley, John Conteh, Maurice Hope, Chris Finnegan – do not feature in the dozen or so pieces that make up this section of the book. And yet I have found room for Jack Bodell, who was never in their league as a performer, and for poor Johnny Owen, whose first appearance at the game's highest level of competition brought a tragic, horribly premature end to his life. There is perhaps little need to explain the presence of two pieces on Owen. To leave them out would surely have been some kind of hypocrisy, a sidestepping of the questions committed opponents of the sport that was responsible for the young Welshman's death are entitled to put to someone like myself. I can only hope that what I wrote about John when he was full of life and optimism, enclosed in the warmth of his family and the comforting loyalties of Merthyr Tydfil, and what I wrote on that night when death threw its shadow over him in the clamorous, alien hostility of the Olympic Auditorium in Los Angeles, will relate honestly to the references I make to him in the general introduction to this book.

That the large, ungainly figure of Jack Bodell should surface among so many who were more graceful, more brilliant, or at least far more effective practitioners of the game may surprise some readers. But anyone who cannot feel for the loser in boxing should not be allowed through the door of the arena and for me no one ever represented the poignancy of losing more affectingly than Bodell on the night I have tried to describe. It may be that big Jack did not see himself at all as I did, that his defeat

71

stirred reactions in me which he would not recognise. All I know is that the image of him left alone in Henry Cooper's dressing-room as Henry and a few more of us headed for a celebration party will stay in my mind long after the memory of a hundred more colourful moments has faded.

The other men whose deeds are recalled in this section are so central to the recent history of British boxing that any elaborate justification of their inclusion here would be a ridiculous insult. Terry Downes is still prominent wherever fight people gather (and in several less predictable reaches of society). Sound investment of the money he suffered so willingly to earn leaves him well-heeled and he thoroughly enjoys being flush. He quite likes being flash as well but doesn't shout much about the time and energy he devotes to making life more cheerful for handicapped children. Terry was no stylist in the ring but, as they say around Paddington, where he was raised, he 'could have a row'. He can also talk about fighting better than most and something of his raucous, eccentric articulacy may survive in these pages.

Walter McGowan, from Lanarkshire, had just about the best hands I have ever seen on a boxer from these islands. His extraordinarily fast, varied, damagingly selective punching made him the most precociously brilliant amateur in my experience. As a professional he went to the top but never really overcame his susceptibility to cuts and his propensity to bleed as if he had been hit by an axe. The theme of a huge talent denied by a basic physical frailty is the essence of my account of his second match with Chartchai Chionoi.

Howard Winstone did not bleed with the spectacular profusion of a McGowan or a Henry Cooper but throughout his career he had to live with other fundamental handicaps. An early accident while he was working in a toy factory cost him part of several fingers on his right hand and, being unable to make a satisfactory fist of it, he could never punch properly with it either. He compensated by refining the timing and precision of his left to the point where it had no equal in the featherweight division, was indeed probably the sharpest weapon of its kind in the whole game. His footwork and judgement of distance were equally superb (he could be within his own punching range and still sway away from an opponent's body shots), and all this marvellous equipment was urged on by a heart the size of a town. Winstone in his prime was a true hero, as lovable as we want all champions to be, and going down to visit him when he trained in Merthyr under his manager, Eddie Thomas, was one of the purest pleasures of a sports writer's job. There is much that is exceptional about Thomas, too. Coalminer son of a coalminer, outstanding welterweight champion in his time, he is a giant in the working-class mythology of Merthyr and it was natural that he should have been found using the skills learned underground to extricate, with tender patience, many of the small bodies buried by the avalanche of slurry in the Aberfan school disaster.

Thomas and Winstone made a strong, emotionally integrated partnership and they piled up a lot of success together. I saw much of it in close-up but the material reprinted here deals with one of the three losses to Vicente Saldivar that prevented Winstone from ever establishing that he was the best featherweight of his time. He did hold a version of the world championship for six months of 1968 but the 40-odd rounds he fought against Saldivar, with whom he formed a genuine bond of kinship, told him the truth about his aspirations. Howard's life hasn't been a barrel of laughs since he retired in 1969. Organising his personal affairs was never his strong suit and he may have brought some of the troubles on himself, but that does not reduce the sadness felt by those of us who came to identify intensely with his beautiful spirit in the ring.

Two common factors link Ken Buchanan with Howard Winstone. The first is that Buchanan was managed by Eddie Thomas and the second is that he was an immensely gifted boxer. But the natures of the fighters were very different. Whereas Winstone's personality was generally characterised in his active days by a chirpy, mischievous optimism and only rarely chilled by bitterness towards crudely provocative rivals, there was at the centre of the Edinburgh man a persistent bleakness that frequently took him to the edge of paranoia. His relationship with Thomas was fraught, on his side at least, by tense suspicions but those were no more than an extension of the attitudes he carried out of a childhood riddled with a sense of persecution.

Buchanan did not cower before his persecutors, real or imaginary. He fought them, and the deep reservoir of aggression and stubborn pride that was already forming before he was ten years old eventually made him, to my mind, the most successful fighting man sent out from Britain since the war. Turpin was a more impressive natural phenomenon, Winstone a more inspired mover, Conteh could be more dramatic, but none of our boxers in the last 30 years or so got the job done as consistently as Buchanan. Certainly none of them was within shouting distance of him when it came to winning on the far side of the Atlantic, where the pressures make a night at the Albert Hall or at Wembley seem as relaxed as a sparring session. London is full of experts who will tell you that he would not have lived with Dave Charnley, an earlier head man among the British lightweights. Charnley was a tremendous southpaw fighter but I don't think there is anything in his record to set against the Scot's achievements in foreign rings, a list of successes that was a tribute to an extremely sound, adaptable technique, great physical resilience and fierce morale. Much of Charnley's most telling work was done with short-arm punches and I don't think he would have been close enough often enough to beat Buchanan, whose left jab could be a sickening discouragement, especially when followed by a right cross that was not a knockout punch but did sufficient as the dosage was stepped up to jolt many an opponent towards an early return to the dressing-room. Arguing the comparative merits of fighters whose prime years did not coincide is a pointless exercise but it's fun – and you can shout a lot of bets without having to pay out. However, I'm bound to say that if a promoter with a time machine could match Charnley at his peak with the Buchanan who beat Donato Paduano and Ismael Laguna in Madison Square Garden I'd have to put the arm on the Halifax Building Society and take a heavy swing at anybody who offered evens about Buchanan.

The second of this book's two pieces on that great champion deals with the downbeat occasion of his last but one professional fight, an evening at Wembley when too many years in the business, and some bad breaks outside it, had begun to weary him. An air of melancholy clung to him then, that sense, familiar among outstanding sportsmen in decline, that the rest of life will be an anticlimax, a succession of mundane crises and concerns. Maybe he has had a bit of cheering luck since that night. If not, he won't be too astonished. He has never expected the world to do him any favours, has always tended to assume that most days would call on him to do some battling. That's why he made himself so good at it.

Hostility was never as much of an everyday habit with Alan Minter as it was with Buchanan. But when Minter went to work his eyes held the same hard challenge familiar to anyone who looked the Scot in the face from the opposite stool. Vito Antuofermo was a middleweight champion of the world who expected to get by on toughness and charging, indiscriminate aggression. But his spectacular lack of talent was fully punished when he encountered Minter, who was just as willing to fight and infinitely better equipped to box. In their two meetings for the title Antuofermo was painfully outclassed. Minter was subsequently stopped abruptly by the outstanding Marvin Hagler, on a night when the behaviour of the British crowd was even more distressing than the defeat of the home fighter, but what he accomplished earlier in his career deserves to be set alongside the achievements of our other remarkable post-war middleweights, Randolph Turpin and Terry Downes. Since the early days Minter had struggled to compensate for the fact that he simply did not have a boxer's face. He had the heart, the body and the abilities of a first-class fighter but his face was so subject to cuts, contusions, swellings and sundry other disfigurements that it was a constant liability. It said a lot for him that he usually did conclusive damage to his opponents before they could exploit his weakness. Having had an operation to straighten his nose soon after he retired, he is a handsome man again. On the strength of what he did in the ring, he is also entitled to be a proud one.

Jim Watt is another British world champion who has carried a pleasing appearance and plenty of pride out of the game. The obscurity, disappointments and poor earnings he endured in the first half of his career gave way to thrilling success and fat purses under the management of Terry Lawless. No one could have handled the transformation with more style than Watt. His warmth, quiet, unforced manliness and intelligent, mordantly witty view of life would have made him remarkable in any profession. The Glasgow fight crowd quickly realised that they had found one of their own who was singularly worth admiring, and on his big nights at the Kelvin Hall or Ibrox Park the mutual appreciation was something to experience.

The brief report of Watt's victory over Howard Davis at Ibrox that is offered here was, like the equivalent account of Muhammad Ali's second defeat of Henry Cooper in London 14 years earlier (a piece included in Part One), only part of my coverage of the occasion. Both those fights were Saturday-night events and my reporting took the form of round-by-round description and assessment, telephoned while the punches were being thrown, plus a summing-up delivered as soon as the action was over. In the case of the Watt–Davis and Ali–Cooper matches I have jettisoned the round-by-round 'runners' and reprinted only the sketch pieces dictated at the finish.

Willie Pastrano v. Terry Downes, Manchester, 30 November 1964

The Hungry Bookmaker

The most understandable error in advance assessments of tomorrow night's fight for the world light-heavyweight championship at Belle Vue, Manchester, is that made by Willie Pastrano, the 29-year-old Italian-American from Miami who is defending the title against Terry Downes of Paddington. Pastrano, whose 14 years as a professional have made him a traditionalist, takes the view that the hungrier fighter will win and he assumes that this means him, since he is still rather low on dollars while Downes is credited with holding so much sterling that Mr Callaghan might have been expected to check with him last week between calls to Zurich. It is the fact that Pastrano's mathematics are meaningless which makes Terry Downes such an extraordinary fighter and makes people like myself – who see any rational analysis of the contest as pointing to a clear win for the champion – refuse to dismiss his chances.

Downes, who is six months younger than Pastrano, is not too hard to write off at a distance. His record, even including his brief tenure as world middleweight champion between winning and losing against Paul Pender, of Boston, is very good rather than great; there have always been palpable deficiencies in his technique and he is so far from being a knockout puncher as to have admitted that he 'couldn't punch a hole in a pound of butter'. Of course, to carry such handicaps to one world title and within reach of another requires compensating assets of a remarkable order. You do not have to be close to Downes very long, in a gym or at a ringside, to realise that he has these all right.

What he does have seems to be much more than simple guts or dedicated professionalism. Running through and beyond these qualities there appears to be a seam of the most fundamental optimism, a spirit that somehow impresses as being too positive to be destructible. This is nothing to do with always looking on the bright side. It is, rather, a feeling that no matter how long Downes looked on the black side it would never occur to him to give up. Perhaps the simplest and one of the less inadequate words for what he has is zest. It is what makes the book he has just published – called predictably *My Bleeding Business* – not only tolerable but enjoyable and, in its essence, accurate. Through the corn and the sentimentality and the caricatured language there comes a sense of real individualism and personality.

Maybe it was an accident of family history that gave him experience of living and boxing on both sides of the Atlantic, with a three-year spell as a US Marine thrown in, and maybe it was sheer good fortune that put him in on the betting-shop boom when the returns were astronomical. But things of that kind were always more likely to happen to Downes than to the next man because he goes out and makes things happen to him. He made a world title happen to him when his talents scarcely merited it. Now he has manoeuvred himself into a challenge for another championship after only three convincing but unmomentous victories as a light-heavyweight. He has proved before that character can overcome talent and he may do it again tomorrow night.

Neither he nor his American trainer, Johnny Dunn, entertained any doubts about that as they tapered off training at the weekend in a Territorial Army gymnasium opposite White City tube station. Earlier reports that Downes had looked even less impressive than usual in his sparring were ignored by Dunn, who delivers his opinions with an engagingly pedantic deliberation. 'He is stronger at this weight and he is punching better than he ever did before and his spirit is tremendous. He will be the champion of the world on Monday night. He will win that title. There is no doubt about it.' From the shadow-boxing, the work on the ball, the skipping, it was hard to tell anything about his sharpness but he looked thicker and stronger than before around the chest and shoulders and he confirmed that he has built up there, for he now weighs around 12 st 3 lb trained where he once scaled that much untrained. He does not want to go into the ring any lighter than 12 st 3 lb because he expects to lose 5 or 6 lb if the fight goes the full 15 rounds.

After the workout Downes, zipped into a sleeping-bag, stretched out on the royal blue carpet of the sergeants' mess to relax. He talked easily to a few acquaintances who sat around him on chairs drinking tea. He swears freely but is one of those people in whom it is rarely offensive and often amusing. Occasionally he propped himself up on an elbow to sip from a glass of Guinness. The drink seemed more to the taste of his two-and-a-half-year-old son, Terry, who had been given a sample to put him off and had awkwardly pronounced it 'nice'. The presence of the boy was the ultimate evidence of how far Downes has departed from the monasticism of the old-style fight preparation. He has stayed with his family at his £36,000 home in Mill Hill, done his running around his own grounds and travelled to the gym in his Rolls-Royce.

To Pastrano, sweating away his excess weight and his natural amiability up in Manchester, it all seems strange indeed. He has known nothing like it in all the years since he turned professional at 15. Some of those years were wasted on the mistaken belief that he had to fight at heavyweight. But he discovered the error eventually and made up for lost time by coming in as a substitute against the formidable Harold Johnson and upsetting odds of six to one to take the world title. Past frustrations and the present needs of his wife and five children convince him that he has more reason to be determined than Downes. But Downes is not a man who can live by bread or betting shops alone. A quarter of a million in the bank has not blunted his appetite for boxing titles and all that goes with them.

The chances are that Downes's crowding, swinging attacks will be subdued by the technical superiority of Pastrano, a classic jabber whose balance and incredible durability have kept him from ever finding out what it is like to be on the floor in a professional contest. But if the world light-heavyweight championship is to go to the man with the greater hunger for it, then it is as likely to land in Mill Hill as Miami.

Letting It All Out

When they finally got Terry Downes down from the ring at Belle Vue, Manchester, on Monday night they brought him up the aisle, past the extra press seats that had accommodated *The Rochdale Observer*, a reporter from Chicago and a few more of us, out by the bar and along the short corridor on the right to the cell-like room, ten feet long by six feet wide, where he had stripped for his world championship fight with Willie Pastrano and where he now had to force himself to accept the fact that he had lost.

The end of the fight had come with such suddenness that people all around seemed in various states and stages of shock. It showed as much in the Pastrano supporters as in those who had felt a plunge of disappointment in their stomachs when the best half-hour's work Downes had ever done in a ring was wiped away by one burst of accurate violence in the 11th round. A man and woman, both in their 40s, were standing on some kind of raised platform near an exit screaming and laughing and hugging each other. The woman had her left hand up to her mouth, showing a broad wedding ring. She kept hissing ecstatically: 'Willie, Willie, Willie.' She looked as if she had been left behind from the wrestling that usually occupies the hall.

Behind a door marked 'BBB of C Officials' someone had turned on a radio and Frank Butler, speaking from 30 yards away, was still trying to explain that explosion of class that had saved the tired champion. The door of Downes's dressing-room was being held by a very tall, slim man with a flattened nose whom I had seen a few days before, fitting up a punchball in the TA gymnasium where Downes trained. 'If only he had got over that round,' he was repeating. 'Pastrano didn't know what to do with him. He tried dancing left and tried dancing right but Terry was always there swinging in on him. He was like a door. After the first, he never did a thing wrong. Just as they called him, he was coming home.'

The dressing-room had a washbasin against the bare brick at the far end and unpainted hardboard along one wall, where the street clothes of Downes and his seconds hung on hooks. Two tables had been placed together to form a bench and Downes sat up there with his back to a framed wall mirror marked 'Truman's, Est. 1666'. Reporters and sympathisers squeezed into the room, but at first Downes spoke directly to his manager, Sam Burns. 'I was all right, Sam,' he said, his voice cracking slightly. 'I wasn't half all right. I don't mind losing but I felt all right. I was strong.' His eyes were wet and he kept pursing his lips and shaking his head. 'They shouldn't have done that. The first shot that put me down was a good punch but after that he came with a flurry. It was a desperation flurry.'

'It was a desperation flurry,' said Burns.

'I said to myself, "Don't stand around and get caught by a bad punch. Why get in the way of stray shots? He's wearing himself out. Let's get the hell out of here and take a breather and we'll be all right."'

'You took a voluntary count,' said Burns, as Johnny Dunn, the American trainer, held an ice bag to the bruises on Downes's forehead.

'He was washed out,' said Downes. 'D'you know, I lost it by being professional. Experience cost me the fight. I go down to keep away from stray shots and the referee stops it. He was dead as a kipper. But he suckered the referee. I could go 100 rounds with that guy. It was a terrible liberty to stop that fight. I'm coasting.'

Tears began to come again and Burns and Dunn said together: 'Let it out . . . Let it out.'

'But you wrote in your book that Smythe was the best referee in the country,' one of the reporters said.

Downes managed a joke. 'I'm going to buy back all the books and change them to say he's a bastard.' He added: 'No, I still think he's a good referee but we all make mistakes.'

'Well, this will sell your book, won't it?' somebody said. Downes glared at him. 'Sell the book – that's a lot of fucking good. I could have been champion of the world tonight.'

A tall, middle-aged man, with a dinner jacket and an accent that both suggested Board of Control, pushed his way through. 'If you can't change the decision, don't come in,' Downes said.

'Well, a jolly good try,' said the big man. 'And we're proud of you. It must be a great disappointment but it happens to all of us. What more can we say? Nothing, I suppose.'

A latecomer among the reporters suddenly craned over the crowd. 'Excuse me, Terry, but what do you think of the referee stopping the fight?'

'What do *you* think?' Downes said wearily, then more to himself: 'In Miami I would have expected it but not here. I could have stood on my head. But the guy was desperate. I did the smart thing and went down.'

It was not the objective truth, of course. When he went down the second time, he pitched forward between Pastrano's legs, which is not the way a man takes a voluntary count, and even after the stoppage he was staggering against the ropes. But what he was saying was true enough in an important sense, for it was simply expressing his absolute belief in himself and commitment to his challenge, which was what had made his performance a great one. Any man who gives so much and loses has, in a way, been cheated.

A man with thick-rimmed glasses jostled into the room, saying brusquely: 'Doctor, doctor,' in a Scottish accent. 'Great show, Terry,' he said when he reached Downes. 'How are you? How's the eye?'

'Great. Never felt better. Go and see the referee – he needs his head examined.' He slumped back on the bench again and cried quietly, punching his right fist into his left palm.

A reporter who had written Downes off before the fight asked: 'Was he as good as you thought he would be?'

'Was he as good as *you* thought he would be?' Downes answered roughly. Then, dropping his head on his chest and smiling: 'What does it matter? All the press are bastards anyway. Don't know what day of the week it is, most of them.'

'He's offering you a return – will you take it?' someone shouted from the door.

'Why talk about a return now?' said Downes slowly. 'I had the championship of the world in my pocket and somebody nicked it.'

Chartchai Chionoi v. Walter McGowan, London, 19 September 1967

Blood Has the Last Word Again

Welcome home. Have a glass of vinegar, bite upon a quince. After nine weeks in the United States one might have been permitted to renew contact with British sport through experiences less bitter than the defeats of Walter McGowan and Glasgow Celtic. How do we persuade people that McGowan was a worthy flyweight champion of the world when he held the title for only a few months and has now lost twice to Chartchai Chionoi, a representative of Thailand, where they have but recently learned to box without using their feet? How do we go on boasting about Celtic when their first defence of the European title looks like being brief and inglorious? It's rather hard to be taking things personally again.

McGowan's defeat emphasised the obvious: boxing has always been a primitive trial of the whole man, never a mere contest of skill. In speed, agility, imagination, accuracy, technical know-how, any terms of quality you can name, Chionoi was outclassed. He simply stayed in there and suffered, reassured by the conviction that McGowan would cut, that when he cut he would bleed and when he bled he would lose. It happened that way, as many of us had predicted, but what scarcely anyone had realised was the extent of the injustice that would be inflicted on

McGowan. We assumed the Scot, with his liquid mobility and the insistent regularity of his jabbing, would be ahead when the blood blotted out his scoring. But few had guessed that he would have established such an overwhelming lead. Perhaps only boxing among major sports offers a man the frustration of demonstrating unquestionable superiority at the same time as he is moving irrevocably to defeat.

All men bleed in much the same way, but some do it rather more generously than others, and a man's ability to hold on to his blood is a crucial factor in the ring, one that readily neutralises vast discrepancies in talent. Chionoi remained world champion on Tuesday because McGowan is as close to a haemophiliac as the fight game can accommodate. Wipe the Scot's face with a coarse towel and he's liable to need stitches. The Thai, contrastingly, gives the impression that a woodman's axe would not cut him.

Even medical authorities disagree widely in their explanations of why certain fighters are ruined by cuts while others have hardly any trouble with them. Obviously bone structure and texture of skin are relevant and the blood of some men clots more quickly than that of others. Howard Winstone rarely bleeds freely while Henry Cooper and McGowan have only to be nicked to find the blood spurting spectacularly. It is essential that a bleeder should have an expert cut-man in his corner and the fact that Henry Cooper has overcome his disability sufficiently to hold the British heavyweight championship longer than any other fighter is closely related to the delicate repair jobs done by his trainer, Danny Holland. Many people feel that McGowan's father, Joe Gans, who manages him, should have enlisted the specialist help of someone like Holland. When the suggestion was put to Gans on Tuesday, his reaction was typically aggressive. Joe does not go much on the pleasures of debate. Conversation with him tends to be like attempting to travel in the wrong direction along a one-way street in the rush-hour. 'What does Danny Holland know about cuts that I don't know? I'll take you into a corner and show you that I can stop a cut along with any man in the game. I know I'm being blamed but that's nothing new. It's the least of my worries. My conscience is clear.'

Corner-men in this country find cuts particularly menacing because they are not allowed to treat their boxers with anything more powerful than an adrenalin solution of one in a thousand. In America, where there is less official concern about the long-term effects of ringside operations, seconds employ substances that would dam a river. Willie Ketchum, an old-time manager who now handles the heavyweight contender Thad Spencer, uses a cement-like preparation that has to be laboriously chipped out of the wound after a fight. 'The fighter gets cut, I stop it,' Ketchum says flatly. 'After I've worked on it you could shoot that sonofabitch and he wouldn't bleed.' Needless to say, the ultimate results of such methods are less than decorative.

Tuesday's outcome was especially galling for McGowan because the cut which swung the fight was on the forehead, far enough above the left eye to appear manageable. It seemed that if McGowan had remained cool when the blood began to flow, using his splendid boxing to protect the cut and the big lead he had gained, there was still some chance that the title would be his. Instead, he reacted with desperate, slogging aggression, lunging in with exaggerated left hooks and right swings in vain pursuit of a knockout. Presumably he felt that the disaster had come too early to give him much hope of nursing the injury through 15 rounds. He had begun to bleed in the fourth and the cut was cruelly widened in the next round. McGowan and his father insisted that the harm was done by Chionoi's head but if that is so he had his head inside a boxing glove at the time. In fact, the dramatic damage of the fifth round was caused by one of the Thai's right swings. McGowan had been circling away from these blows cleverly, letting his man stumble clumsily against the ropes. But this time he circled the wrong way and the fight came to its frenetic climax. Ike Powell let McGowan rage through the gore for two rounds, and despite the subsequent protests from the Scottish camp that was as much as could be expected of any referee. With the principal wound worsening and another appearing at the corner of the left eye, Powell's intervention in the seventh round was completely justified.

Naturally the loser's dressing-room was no place for such objectivity. When a few large strips of plaster had been arranged vertically and horizontally above his left eye (there were no stitches but there will be plastic surgery) McGowan and his father sat side by side on a rough wooden table, their legs dangling, their faces sadly composed. Gans's white shirt was spattered with his son's blood. 'I asked Powell for another round but he wouldn't give it to us,' Gans said. 'It wasn't a dangerous cut. If it had been, the boy would have been out of there, world title or no world title. The boy's eyes are my first concern. But it wasn't a bad one. When they see blood they turn yellow.'

'It would have finished in the next round,' said McGowan. 'That's a certainty, boy. He was going in the next round.' He had four brothers and three sisters on hand to agree with him. The rest of us, having seen Chionoi carry his manager around the ring at the end of the bout, were more doubtful. But that display of vigour was a deception. Chionoi collapsed when he was about to leave Wembley Pool and had to be helped back to his dressing-room to recover. Soon afterwards he went along the corridor to console McGowan. Wearing a check cap pulled down over his eyes, a worn raincoat and trousers that finished several inches above his ankles, he was not about to win any prizes as the snappiest dresser in town. The ensemble was not improved when he swapped his cap for Gans's 'bunnet'.

'I no' fight you again,' Chionoi told McGowan. 'Not ever. Tonight after fight my heart stop.' He slapped himself on the back of the neck to show how he had been revived. 'No' fight you again.'

'Just once more,' said Jack Solomons. 'Just once more.' It is difficult to believe that McGowan's one great weakness would not frustrate him again in a third meeting. 'We'll get Chionoi to fight all right,' said Solomons. 'Money talks.' It does, but in boxing blood usually has the last word.

Jack Bodell v. Henry Cooper, London, 24 March 1970

The Sour Taste in Jack Bodell's Pop

The sneering denigration of Jack Bodell has gone beyond a joke. After he had fought unyieldingly through 15 painful rounds against the superior class of Henry Cooper last week, striving to compensate with fitness and heart for his acknowledged deficiencies in skill, Bodell was jeered out of the ring at Wembley Pool. 'Get back among the pig swill,' he was told by a bunch of characters who looked as if they might have more than a passing acquaintance with the stuff. They came jostling out of those seats where all the best fights are fought and yelled at the big man as he squinted sadly past discoloured swellings at the emotional tumult greeting Cooper's restoration to the British heavyweight championship. A cacophony of animal noises made extravagant allusion to the few chickens Bodell keeps at home in Derbyshire. 'You're a clown, Bodell. You wasted your bloody time coming here, you big mug.'

It can be said that the only sensible reaction to such inanities is that of George Walker, who manages his brother Billy's career as a heavyweight. 'When you go into the fight game you go in for the cash. These are the people you despise. They're nothing. All they are good for is buying tickets. If that sort of thing gets under your skin, you shouldn't be in the business.' Of course, George was always a hard man for whom the rustle of bank notes drowned most other annoying sounds. But even in boxing not everyone can develop that kind of skin. Tougher men than Bodell have been hurt by such spiteful assaults on their dignity. The former champion's wife has already said publicly that she has been distressed by the endless baiting. She senses that her man has been subjected to more than the normal callousness of the fight crowd. He has been chosen as the victim of a sustained, sadistic joke. Professional boxers readily learn to live with the antagonism of the mob, to ignore its ill-tempered disapproval. But to fight your heart out and then be met with derisive laughter must be peculiarly sickening. Many fighters have made a good living by playing the clown in the ring but Bodell has always struggled to be taken seriously.

Obviously, when the public, or even a moronic section of it, decides spontaneously to ridicule someone there is not much to be done. In this case, however, the relentless emphasis of London promoters on Bodell's failure to sell tickets, on the unattractiveness of his crude southpaw methods and unglamorous persona, encouraged a contemptuous attitude. The computerised charade between Muhammad Ali and the late Rocky Marciano was enacted behind closed doors, leaving an eerie greyness where the spectators should have been, and when it was shown here one famous matchmaker said: 'Some crowd. Jack Bodell must have been on the bill.' It was a mildly amusing insult, in the same category as the suggestion that Bodell's supporters travel to fights on the back of one motorbike.

Some of the other jibes are made inevitable by Bodell's determination to carry a piece of south Derbyshire around with him wherever he goes. He is a dedicated hick, often dressing in the kind of suits middle-aged men remember encountering at demobilisation centres, and arranging his tie in an elaborate left-handed Windsor that still leaves the knot no bigger than a two-shilling piece. His raw, big-jawed face, and the short hair thinning into single strands where once it made an oily quiff above his forehead accentuate what most Londoners regard as an agricultural appearance, though he started working life as a collier. An accent that seems to broaden as he enters the Home Counties completes the picture of a man who is less than a ready-made hero for metropolitan audiences. All this would be overlooked, indeed its exoticism might be an advantage, if he could fight brilliantly or dramatically. He cannot. His boxing is amateurishly clumsy. His head still jerks into an exposed position as he lunges in with his ponderous right lead, his left is predictable and only modestly damaging and his footwork gives the impression of having been acquired at a school for deep-sea divers.

The statistical healthiness of his record – only ten defeats in 63 contests – can be traced largely to the barging strength of the headlong rush that is his principal tactic, to conscientious industry and to admirable courage. These last qualities are not as commonplace as many imagine, and at two points in the match with Cooper on Tuesday they might have earned a great deal. In the sixth round Cooper, having applied conspicuous pressure in the previous three minutes, began to show evidence of his 36 years, and Bodell took the round easily. But he could never again overcome the difference in technical equipment and punching authority. When Cooper's legs tired noticeably in the 14th the younger man, too, was weary and could not exploit the chance. So Cooper was left, as most of us had suspected he would be, with another great night to remember. Anyone who questions his right to it must have spent the past decade on another planet. To establish how exceptional he is it is not necessary to stress the excitement of his punching, the contrast between the gentle charm of his demeanour outside the ring and the violent courage of his performances inside, or the consistency that has enabled him to hold the British title for more than ten years. It is only necessary to say that on the brink of his 36th birthday he left home to train for six weeks, isolated from the family that is the genuine centre of his life. More than anything else, all those hours of running in cold Kent dawns kept the old man just young enough on Tuesday night.

At home in Wembley some time later, pouring champagne for a small party that included the recruited cut expert Eddie Thomas, Cooper said he was likely to meet the South African Jimmy Richards, and then José Urtain, the Basque heavyweight whose record suggests he has faced a long line of plaster gnomes. These are acceptable names – that of Joe Frazier is patently not – but most of us would take special satisfaction from seeing Cooper retire to enjoy a lifetime of untarnished prestige. Tuesday showed that while he is still too much for any British heavyweight he no longer hooks with the deadliness to worry the best in the world. In short, all that is left for him in the game is money, and he has enough of that to get by.

With Jack Bodell, everything is different. After telephoning home from the ringside on Tuesday, he strode cheerily into his dressing-room, stripped to his boxing boots and shouted for drinks. Someone produced a bottle of lemonade. 'Gimme that bleeder,' said Bodell. 'That's your real south Derbyshire pop. Best in the world.' He drank it down eagerly, telling us between gulps that he hadn't seen the last of the British title and we hadn't seen the best of him. Half an hour afterwards, as Cooper and the rest of us were preparing to leave the other dressing-room along the corridor, Bodell suddenly appeared in his overcoat and plonked himself down in a chair just inside the door of the small ugly room. He had two bottles of beer and was obviously in a mood to be sociable. It was impossible not to feel a warmth for this large, simple-natured, likeable man.

In that strange moment the mindless mocking of him seemed to amount to real cruelty. All of us hesitated, sensing he should have company, but Cooper had a party to host and with a last mumble of inadequate pleasantries we filed out, leaving the loser sitting alone in the winner's dressing-room.

Merthyr versus Mexico

If Howard Winstone beats Vicente Saldivar of Mexico and takes the featherweight championship of the world at Earl's Court on 7 September, the people of Merthyr Tydfil will see it as merely the fulfilment of the natural law. They are already infectiously convinced that Merthyr is in possession of some kind of cosmic championship, that the town and its sons have established firsts or bests in all the significant fields of human endeavour. When Eddie Thomas, Winstone's manager, reminds you that Britain's first coal was dug out from Merthyr hillsides and that the town was once 'the industrial capital of the world' he is simply introducing you to a mounting scale of claimed distinctions which ends in bizarre magnificence: 'First man Albert Pierrepoint hung threw a woman down those coke ovens over there.'

Charles Jones, the Merthyr poet, a man of sharp intelligence and uproarious humour who has elected himself bard and jester to Thomas's court, starts by telling you solemnly in the main street at lunchtime that 'for its size Merthyr has more beautiful girls than any other place in the country, without a doubt'. He finishes at 11 p.m. over a lager and lime in a working men's club by reassuring you with the information that the town 'has the most expert abortionists in the world'. When the club closes there is still a long way to go. Land-locked in a natural bowl 20-odd miles north-west of Cardiff, Merthyr maintains a defiant insularity against most outside influences, including the licensing laws. And Eddie Thomas is one of the few men who can go through a session on two glasses of Advocaat and lemonade and half a dozen pineapple juices and still be offering to sing 'Speak to me Thora' at 4 a.m. The Advocaat is the response to the discovery that he has an ulcer. 'I only hope some of the boys don't start to fancy me when they see me on this stuff.'

The major reason why Howard Winstone is fighting for the world title is that he is the most skilful boxer in Britain, but to understand the real nature of his challenge – his own quiet, unnervous dedication and the support that would have taken three planeloads of his neighbours to Mexico City if the match had been made there – it is necessary to know Merthyr. The simplest way to know Merthyr is to know Eddie Thomas.

Thomas, who held the welterweight championships of Britain, the Empire and Europe, was secure in the town's folklore before he took on Winstone. Now in his 40th year, nearly three stone heavier than he was when he won the titles, he goes around with an open, slightly amused expression, accepting his fame with the affectionate pleasure of a boy who is being praised by the family for passing an exam. In the street he is greeted every few paces and when he drives he is constantly giving toots of recognition on the horn of his red Corsair. It is almost new but already has a dusty veteran look from being driven with rough skill around the tips where ballast is being excavated by the firm he runs with his brother and a friend. Thomas's life is geared to his own impulsive rhythm and he is fantastically unpunctual. His friends can predict where he will turn up but never when. 'He is incredible,' says Charles Jones. 'He is a wild man and yet there is a broad streak of the puritan in him. He is impossible, but he is pure gold.' He is also pure Merthyr, a conscious guardian of the old values that grew mainly out of the mines, where his father lost an arm and where Thomas himself worked even while he was a champion. When we gathered for a training walk on the hills above the town it was beside the row where his father lives and Thomas went in to change into enormous boots, denim trousers and a heavy V-necked sweater worn next to his skin. Winstone wore shoes, slim-fitting trousers and a suede waistcoat over a white shirt. It was sensible enough clothing – he was out to stretch himself, not to sweat – but it emphasised a striking difference between two men who have much in common.

Winstone is absolutely loyal to his environment and says he would never leave it but there is a sense of the modern young man about him that contrasts with the traditionalism of his manager. Winstone likes fashionably cut suits; Thomas wears heavy navy-blue serge. Thomas sings seriously and usually picks songs that have been favourites for 50 years; Winstone is always half-joking when he gives out random lines from contemporary musicals. He leans forward into your face suddenly, affects a deep brown voice and sings: 'We'll find a new way of living. We'll find a way of forgiving.'

Thomas's lurcher followed us on the walk and almost immediately it began to chase sheep. 'Come back, you bugger,' he shouted. 'I'll warm you. I'll warm you.'

'One word from Ed and it does as it likes,' said Colin Lake, one of two Londoners who have been sparring with Winstone. Lake and the other sparring partner, Don Weller, team up with Winstone when he plays his game of baiting Thomas. They call him Jethro, after a television hillbilly, and like to tell about the time they went to a bowling alley in Blackpool and he started to hurl the bowls down two-handed with a fury that threatened to wreck the building. Thomas enjoys it all.

I asked Lake what it was like to spar with Winstone. He jerked his head sideways as if he had developed a twitch and said out of the side of his mouth, 'It's great, just great.' That evening in Thomas's gym it was easy to see what Lake meant. Winstone was sharp even by his own standards. If one left hand missed, he followed with five or six more that didn't, and he threw over his right with an eagerness that forced Thomas to restrain him. 'Box, don't fight,' he was told from the corner. He did eight rounds with Lake and Mick Laud, who must have weighed nearly ten stone. In one of them Lake said something and Winstone suddenly drove him into a corner and punished him with a stream of savagely accurate punches.

'Got him wicked then, didn't you, Col?' said Thomas as the round ended.

87

'That's what I wanted,' said Lake. 'Best way, innit?'

Most of the crowd who had paid half-a-crown to see the workout stayed to watch the long session of callisthenics. Even those who had seen it all before drew in their breath as Winstone moved across the floor by bouncing his stomach up and down on the medicine ball. It was a brutal demonstration of fitness. His new headguard had produced a reddening above the left eye during the sparring and it encouraged Thomas to give him two or three days out of the ring. 'How are the legs, hard?' he asked the masseur in the dressing-room afterwards. 'Lovely, coming along nice.'

'Yes, he's there,' Thomas said quietly. 'He's getting nasty now in the ring. He's ready. So I'll give him a whiff. All we want now is to keep his edge.' Howard Winstone, Eddie Thomas and Merthyr Tydfil would all rather be nice than nasty. But for Vicente Saldivar they are determined to make an exception.

Saldivar the Stalker

Twelve thousand Welshmen will travel to Earl's Court on Tuesday but, unfortunately for British ambitions, only one of them will be allowed into the ring with Vicente Saldivar, who is from Mexico City and at the age of 22 the featherweight champion of the world. Whether the extraordinary skills of that one Celt and the emotional support of the others will be enough to take the title from Saldivar is a question that puzzles even such an authority as Terry Downes, who as a boxer turned bookmaker is better equipped than most to quote odds on the situation. 'Howard Winstone is a helluva boxer but 15 rounds is a long time to keep out of trouble when you haven't got a punch yourself. Still, I fancy Winstone. Maybe it's more hope than judgement. But there can't be anything in it in the betting. About 4–5 the Mexican and 5–4 Winstone. The Mexican must be favourite.'

Downes's opinion – delivered in that unmistakable voice which has something to do with being a cockney and a fighter and with having a nose that has been forcibly remoulded – was formulated after he had watched Saldivar's final sparring session on Friday afternoon in the new Board of Control gymnasium at Chalk Farm in north London. The champion had boxed only two rounds with Love Allotey, the world-rated Ghanaian featherweight, when his manager, Adolpho Perez, called him out of the ring and made it known that Saldivar would not put gloves on again until he went in with Winstone. 'He is ready,' Perez said in Spanish. 'He will continue to do light exercises and shadow-boxing until Monday. But no more boxing. He does not need it.' Those who had seen the harsh treatment of Love Allotey had to agree. Saldivar was sharper and more determined than in any previous workout. He had reached the stage where it is a strain to hold back and twice in the two rounds he opened up in earnest. Love Allotey had not been in serious training and, in any case, a little over six minutes (the rounds were slightly extended) is hardly long enough to get the measure of an unfamiliar southpaw, but Saldivar's performance was undoubtedly impressive. Perhaps most striking is the economy with which he stalks a retreating opponent. He does not chase but slides laterally across the ring to cut off escape routes with the minimum of exertion. It is a technique that could save him a lot of pain against Winstone, who likes his men to charge headlong after him and run the risk of being impaled on the most accurate left hand in boxing.

At training the chain of Saldivar's Catholic pendant emphasised the strong development of his neck. He is deep-chested and altogether powerfully built for a featherweight but, though he was still wearing red woollen tights on Friday, his personal physician insists that there is absolutely no difficulty in making 9 st. Looking at Saldivar it is not hard to accept that he has remarkable stamina. One man who accepts it is Raul Rojas, who challenged for the title in May. Rojas was stopped ten seconds from the end of the 15th round. But the effect of Saldivar's blows tends to be cumulative rather than immediate. Love Allotey said he was a fast and frequent puncher but not a particularly heavy one. This may seem to reassure those who have always believed that Winstone would do well unless he was against what the trade calls a 'banger', someone who throws the kind of stunning punches with which Leroy Jeffery beat the Welshman in two rounds late in 1962. In fact, however, a fighter like Saldivar who can produce an unbroken flow of useful punches may assume the destructiveness of a banger in the late rounds when his opponent is weakening.

Of course, it would be rash to suggest that all the weakening will be on one side. Winstone's left jab is not at all the mere flick that his detractors make it out to be. It jumps into an opponent's face with a vigorous regularity that has sickened many strong men, a fact which is underlined by the way he has shortened his meetings with British challengers in winning two Lonsdale Belts outright. At 26, he still gives an impression of fragility in the ring but there is nothing fragile about his attitude. He has tremendous heart and indeed one of his few flaws is an occasional anxiety to fight when it is politic to box.

There has been much speculation about the eye injury he received in training. The latest suggestion is that reports that he had been thrown by a pony in the Merthyr hills were spread as a smokescreen to obscure the real reason for a break in sparring. This can hardly be true, for the stories about the pony had already appeared in print before Winstone suffered a small, superficial cut on the left eyebrow while boxing on the evening of Friday, 20 August. I was in Eddie Thomas's gym when it happened and the manager was more embarrassed than worried by the injury. In the circumstances, I felt I could not refuse his request to deal lightly with the incident in the article I wrote for last Sunday's *Observer*. The cut healed quickly and Winstone was soon wholeheartedly in action again. His late sparring showed him at his finest, although gauging the incredible precision of his timing against ordinary sparring partners is a bit like setting an astronaut's instruments by an hourglass.

The statistics of both careers are formidable. Winstone has been beaten in only two of his 54 fights and one loss was a highly questionable decision to Don Johnson, who was later brilliantly defeated in Carmarthen. Saldivar has lost only one of 26 contests and 20 of his victories have been taken inside the distance. If Winstone is to win, he must box with iron control for the full three-quarters of an hour. It is a lot to ask but as perhaps the most skilful boxer in the world Winstone will not be intimidated by the job.

If hope and affection and admiration are negotiable currency, I am backing Winstone. If it is a matter of money, then it has to be Saldivar, probably between the 10th and 15th rounds. As Mr Downes says, the Mexican must be favourite.

Decided Long Ago

The world championship contest between Vicente Saldivar and Howard Winstone was one of those fights that are settled in the womb. Saldivar was born with much more natural strength and all Winstone's years of physical discipline, all the dazzling skills and utter fearlessness, could not compensate for that one fundamental discrepancy between the challenger and the champion.

The essence was as simple as that but the event was more complex, which is why it seems worthwhile to recollect Tuesday night's emotion in tranquillity. Even Saldivar's superior power would not have kept his featherweight title if he had not been a southpaw. Because he leads with his right he reduced the effectiveness of Winstone's superb left hand by at least 30 or 40 per cent. The target area was reduced and many of the best jabs were smothered or shut out by the Mexican's right arm and shoulder. As Winstone's manager, Eddie Thomas, pointed out afterwards, the Welshman had to throw a much higher proportion of left hooks and right crosses than he normally would. That was why it was fatuous for people to complain that Winstone was rashly deserting his usual jab-and-move routine. Since the opportunities for jabbing were curtailed he had to stay around and attempt other punches.

The important fact, of course, was not that Winstone met a southpaw but that he met an exceptional southpaw, the only one who holds a world championship at the present time. Saldivar is a good champion: strong, determined, brave, intelligent. Even under pressure he sets himself carefully for the punch, getting in close before he starts work. His basic policy is to do more than his opponent, and if he cannot throw good punches he is prepared to throw indifferent ones. That is why he hits rather often with the inside of the glove, which in turn is why some people thought Winstone might have won. My own view is that Saldivar delivered enough legitimate blows and mounted enough legitimate aggression to win clearly. I thought he took seven rounds to Winstone's five, with three level.

Winstone's wife scored it differently. In the dressing-room, as she kissed her husband's bruised right cheek, she said, 'You won it, lad.'

'No, he just got there,' said Winstone. 'But never mind.' Aside to the rest of us in the crowded, sweaty room, he added, 'You know what women are.' He was lying back on a rubbing-table wearing nothing but a jockstrap. He had just signalled one of his helpers to wave a towel over him but Eddie Thomas said no. As Thomas turned away, Winstone nodded mischievously to urge that the cooling should continue, but Thomas's brother, who is one of the corner-men, said, 'No you don't, you sod.' Winstone gave him an old-fashioned look and a quick kick on the arm with a bare foot. Another friend came forward to the table and Winstone said, 'Here he is, only man in Wales who can eat one spud more'n a pig.'

'Look at 'im,' said somebody beside me, slightly awed. 'He's still wicked.' In Merthyr Tydfil the highest tribute you can pay anybody is to say he is 'wicked'.

Next day, at a lunch given by Winstone for the press, the promoters and some other friends, the tributes were less ironic. He was described as one of the most talented, most sportsmanlike and most popular boxers who ever stepped into a ring. The astonishing thing was not that it was all sincere, but that it was all justified. Winstone and Thomas are such appealing people that it is scarcely possible to do them justice without embarrassing everybody, them most of all.

Scottish Fighting Man

Sports Illustrated, 8 February 1971

Anyone who suggests that the Scots are infatuated with their own image as fighting men has failed to distinguish between infatuation and the real thing. On the corner of any one of a thousand grey streets from Wick to Berwick-upon-Tweed you are in danger of finding people who will earnestly ponder the question of whether it would take one or two Scottish regiments to cope with the Red Army and who will argue persuasively that Benny Lynch, if caught on a sober night, would have floored Muhammad Ali in mid-shuffle.

The fact that Lynch did his deeds as a flyweight is scarcely relevant. An advantage in weight did not help the late Sonny Liston when Peter Keenan, an archetypal Glaswegian who once held the bantamweight championships of Britain, the British Empire and Europe, brought him to order at a party given to offer a Clydeside welcome to the then heavy-weight champion of the world. Liston, in one of his less congenial moods, had knocked a cigar from a fellow guest's mouth and demanded rather loudly that Keenan, too, should refrain from smoking in his presence. 'Listen,' said Keenan, glaring up from the level of Sonny's chest, 'you may be the heavyweight champion, but I have never lost a fight in the street in my life. If anything is going out it's not the cigar. It's you.'

'Aye,' said a voice from the bristling group at Keenan's elbow. 'And not by the door – by the windie.'

Sonny, who was aware that the party was being held several storeys up, cooled abruptly. Keenan then sat down on Liston's knee like a ventriloquist's doll. He called for action from the band, and a fairly conventional Glasgow party was under way again.

Most explanations of the Scottish capacity for personalised aggression embrace ethnic, religious, environmental and economic factors. The population of the country is an amalgam of wild races – Picts, Irish Celts, Norsemen, Vikings, Anglo-Saxons and a few other interlopers – set down in wild terrain, plagued but never overcome by invaders, scarred by the trauma of the Reformation and subjected to the extremes first of agrarian poverty and – more recently – of the industrial version. Whatever emphasis should be put on these influences individually, there is no doubt that their combined effect is to produce an identifiable paranoia. To most Scots, especially to those who inhabit the urban areas of the Central Lowlands, turning the other cheek is the ultimate heresy. They are a small race (there has never been a Scottish heavyweight boxer who could be guaranteed to hit a door if he held it by the handle), but their violence is not a petulant expression of frustration. Their problem is less a suspicion of inferiority than a conviction that the world is conspiring to conceal how remarkable they are.

This convoluted mentality does different things to different people. To Ken Buchanan, a 25-year-old carpenter from Edinburgh, it has brought the lightweight championship of the world and an overnight reputation among American boxing followers as one of the most impressive European fighters ever to cross the Atlantic.

In Madison Square Garden last December, Buchanan and Donato Paduano were put in the ring together as an expensive diversion for a crowd waiting restlessly to see if Ali and Oscar Bonavena would fight as bitterly as they had talked. Paduano, an undefeated Canadian welter-weight previously applauded by Garden audiences as a practitioner of unusual refinement, came off his stool confidently with his shoulders hunched, feinting in close, short-arm patterns. The left hand that jumped into his face was as sudden and unnerving as a water cannon. Paduano tried to regroup his thoughts and sneak a way past or under the hazard. But wherever he went he was met by that sickening jab. It came at him in singles, doubles and trebles, jolting his head so violently that his skull seemed likely to bruise his backbone. All too often for his comfort, the straight lefts were reinforced by sharp hooks with the same hand or swift right crosses. Buchanan, bouncing round the ring with an upright, slightly stiff-kneed action, was invariably where Paduano did not want him to be. The Canadian was 10 lb heavier, but it was clear that this would only compound his embarrassment. By the end of three minutes Paduano's face had reddened painfully, his mouth sagged open and his expression was that of a man who has sucked casually on an exploding cigar. He did no better in the five or six rounds that followed and, though Buchanan tired quite badly towards the finish of the ten-round fight ('I had a cold and breathing got harder'), all three scorecards made him a runaway winner.

Long before midpoint, American boxing writers, most of whom had remained unconvinced when this Limey had taken one version of the lightweight title from Ismael Laguna in San Juan a few months earlier, were turning in the direction of a Scottish writer at ringside with raised eyebrows and pursed lips. 'You told us the kid was good,' they said. 'But he's better than that.' The visitor's accent broadened perceptibly as he proffered suitably modest responses. In the elevator that took them all down to the street after the Ali–Bonavena fight, a hard New York voice kept asking, 'How about that lightweight? How about that? For boxing like that you gotta go back to Robinson.'

When news of the extraordinary success reached Edinburgh, a lot of people began to dredge their memories of Kenny Buchanan. What many could not realise was that Buchanan, brooding in the shadowed interior of his own personality high above the Atlantic, was sorting out his memories of them. From his early boyhood he had harboured a deep sense of persecution, a resentful belief that the other children in his working-class district – and their parents, too – were determined to leave him in despised isolation. Now he saw his triumphs less as a key to popularity than as a bludgeon to put down those who had denied it to him in the past.

There is always tension when he is approached by neighbours from the old days, when the Buchanans lived in a prefabricated house built mainly of asbestos sheeting in a housing project out on the east side of Edinburgh. A man who lived across the road in Mountcastle Crescent at that time made a great show of ribbing Buchanan recently while he was making a personal appearance. 'You've done quite well for yourself,' the man said. 'All those kicks on the arse I used to give you must have done some good after all.' Buchanan spun to face the voice. His eyes are dominated by large black pupils that leave only a minimal rim of blue-grey irises under fair, smudgy brows, and those round and widely spaced eyes stare over the irregular curve of his nose with an intensity that can be intimidating. 'What did you say?' he asked. 'You never kicked me. My Dad would never have let you. And now I wouldn't even let you talk about it.'

When the incident came back to his mind recently, in the lounge of the neat middle-class house he owns on a breezy suburban hill within sight of the huge, girdered silhouette of the Forth Bridge, Buchanan's voice choked and his eyes dampened with anger. He lay back on a leather chair opposite an aquarium which he has built into a wooden unit in the middle of the carefully furnished room, one of the last jobs he did with his carpenter's tools. He wore a sweater and slacks over a slim, straight body conditioned to permanent hardness and his stockinged feet were resting on a round glass coffee table. His wife, Carol, an attractive brunette with the rosy complexion and firm figure to promote health foods, was preparing to entertain the stream of relatives who would pass through on the way to his evening training session. Outwardly they were as relaxed as the domestic group in a television commercial. But Buchanan was looking inward, to a childhood when he walked eerily alone through the Northfield housing project, a nine- or ten- or twelve-year-old boy, exposed and dwarfed by the spaces the planner had laid out for his benefit, divining hostility in every footfall behind him, every face he saw ahead.

He speaks of that time jerkily, in the lilting tongue of the east of Scotland, which shares a glottal stop with the working-class speech of Glasgow but is less harsh and, even among city dwellers, faintly rustic. Words like 'laddie' and 'didnae' proliferate.

'I could write a book about the years between six and fifteen. Maybe I would call it *The Chip on My Shoulder*. Carol is no' the only one who says I've got a chip. Maybe they're right, but I've got reason. The things that happened then, the things that were done tae me, they've left something inside me that will always be there. I didnae have a hard time in the same way as somebody like Rocky Graziano. But I came through it in another way. Nearly all the laddies of my age aboot oor place had older brithers, but there was only me and Alan, and he's three years younger. I had to fight my own battles. The boys roon aboot didnae like me, and neither did their faithers. They were always on at me. I felt some kind of misfit. I think they didnae like me because I could staund up for masel'. My Auntie Joan had given me a pair of boxing gloves when I was eight and a half, and from the time I went tae the Sparta Club I was always being pushed intae fights. Boys would challenge me, but they were always a foot bigger and two stones heavier. I wouldnae back doon, so I had to fight every ither day. When I think how many people looked doon on me, degraded me, I cannae believe in forgive and forget. Once I was gaun home with a bag o' fireworks and the big boys set aboot seven or eight of the boys my own size on to me, and they knocked me off my bike and gave me a kicking. I would be aboot nine at the time, but I can remember the names of every one of those boys. Another time, a woman came and told my mother I had been wetting on her front doorstep, and when my mother asked when I had done it, the woman said midday. I had been miles away in Broxburn with my mother all that day.

'Now all these people are breaking their legs to get to talk to me, but I've no time for them. I remember how they made my life hell. I think of this in the ring. Sometimes I think I want to look doon on them, but really all I want is that they shouldnae be able to come along and knock me out of the road. I've never had a real friend outside the family, certainly nane of my own age, nobody I could rely on. In a fight I was always on my own.'

In his professional fighting, too, there has lately been a tendency to consider himself alone, for he has grown steadily more remote from his manager, Eddie Thomas, a tough and gregarious Welsh miner who was never off his feet in a welterweight career that brought him the championships of Britain, the Empire and Europe and a victory over Billy Graham. Thomas had already made a name as a manager by taking a world featherweight title with Howard Winstone, a left-handed virtuoso from his home town of Merthyr Tydfil. Thomas took charge of Buchanan the moment the Scot stopped accumulating amateur honours and guided him to 33 straight victories as a pro, the longest winning sequence British boxing had seen in modern times. Buchanan, however, was considerably put out when the money he had counted on earning after his marriage did not materialise. He complained that Thomas, who has a running feud with the interests that control the big London promotions, was confining his activities to the private clubs – such as the venerable National Sporting Club at the Café Royal, where there is any amount of gilt but precious little bread.

In July 1969 Buchanan handed his Lonsdale Belt back to the British Boxing Board of Control and said he would rather be a carpenter again than a British champion at the rate he was earning. This move was pleadingly opposed by his father, a short, small-boned man whose grey, combed-back hair and sharp features give a vulpine impression that is immediately cancelled by the sentimental friendliness of his nature. When Tom Buchanan's wife died in October 1969 the event appeared to trivialise the troubles of his elder son. Ken returned to the ring only to lose for the first time, to Miguel Velazquez in Spain. The fight was held in Madrid, where a foreign boxer needs an opponent's death certificate to win a decision, but though most neutrals thought Buchanan had won there is no doubt that he fought below form. 'He had got used to the subdued atmosphere of the clubs and suddenly there were 14,000 Spaniards screaming at him,' says his father. An even more telling disadvantage may have been the fact that Buchanan, no longer training in South Wales under Thomas's supervision, lost track of his weight and fought for the European lightweight title at 130 lb.

Rather surprisingly after that setback, the world championship fight against Laguna was secured. Buchanan was given a fair shake, and he made full use of it. Yet even in this sweet moment there was something to nourish his assumption that the world takes pleasure in misusing him. The British Board, whose policy is to side with the World Boxing Council rather than the World Boxing Association, refused to recognise him as champion. If the Board had been more reasonable, he would not have flown over the pole to Los Angeles in his kilt this week to seek final clarification of his title against Mando Ramos. Ramos is a banger, and Buchanan is taking a big risk for the $100,000 he expects to collect.

He completed his preliminary work last month in the ballroom of a roadhouse a mile or two from his home, and he trained with obsessive, insular purpose. Watching from a row of wheelchairs – placed in front of tables crowded with customers drinking pints of brown beer – was a group of severely handicapped children from a nearby school in which Buchanan has taken a keen interest. He also works readily on behalf of old-age pensioners. But his charitable inclinations stop short of Eddie Thomas. 'I think a hell of a lot of Eddie in many ways,' he said, then qualified the declaration with a string of criticisms that covered everything from Thomas's performance in the corner and his financial transactions to his addiction to falsetto singing. The amity between the two was unmistakably strained, like the comradeship in no-man's-land during a Christmas Day truce.

Mr Tom Buchanan, newly arrived from his quiet job as an office assistant with the local dental service, hovered in that uneasy territory with the air of a man whose function was to catch grenades in mid-flight. 'Of course, I go with Ken,' he said. 'He was definitely persecuted as a laddie, more than I realised at the time. Maybe he is a bit suspicious of people now. But the real point is that he and Eddie are two strong-headed characters, two of a kind. Whatever has happened, I think Ken will stay with Eddie and I think the title will stay with Ken.'

'Kenny will win all right,' said a young man at the ringside, 'because he's such a bloody terrible loser.'

Mando Ramos withdrew because of injury, so Buchanan defended his title successfully against Ruben Navarro instead.

Buchanan and Partner

It will be a healthy irony if the damage done to Ken Buchanan's eyes at Madison Square Garden in the week helps him to see the way ahead more clearly. In the past Buchanan's view of himself and of the relationships crucial to his boxing career has been distorted by factors even more basic than bumps on the cheekbone and lacerations on the eyebrow. The fierce independence of his nature – a solitary strength nourished early in his life by what he saw as the implacable hostility of the world outside his family – has sometimes encouraged an excessive emphasis on self-sufficiency. He has seemed to feel that, with his powerful talent and the loyal support of his father and a few close friends, he could go on dominating the lightweights of the world without the need of professional advice or assistance. Specifically, his utterances and his actions have occasionally suggested that the presence of Eddie Thomas, the Welshman who has managed him since he began fighting for money, is now expensively incidental to his success. Monday night at the Garden may have changed all that.

The outcome of the championship war with Ismael Laguna was, above all else, a tribute to Buchanan's heart and the depth of his reserves as a fighting man. With his jab almost invalidated by the swelling that rose swiftly under his left eye in the third round, severely restricting his vision and multiplying the difficulties of measuring an opponent whose head movement had been a big problem from the start, he had to compromise by coming round into a square, slugger's stance and winning his points with sustained, two-handed pressure. Most boxers, faced with the demand for such an adjustment, would make a respectable lunge at it for a few minutes, then sag into resignation. The Scottish world champion, whose blindingly sudden and confusingly flexible left jab is not only his most telling weapon but the triggering mechanism for all his best combinations, might have been forgiven if he had gone out that way. Yet, far from wilting, he gained in assurance and authority as they moved into the decisive final third of the contest. Time and again he turned back the spidery aggression of Laguna and drove his own flurries of hooks and crosses through the flailing black arms, reducing the Panamanian to an impotence which made it hard to remember that he had twice been a distinguished holder of this lightweight title. Any remaining doubts about the verdict dissolved in the one-sided turmoil of the 14th round, when Laguna was all but overwhelmed. If his head had not fortuitously slipped under the top rope, he would have been a lolling helpless target for the furious assault aimed at him. As it was, the rope protected him during the 15 or 20 seconds in which Buchanan, whose magnificant physical condition was at last giving way to tiredness, could maintain maximum ferocity.

97

'That was a hard one,' Buchanan said as he stepped wearily out of the shower in his dressing-room. 'Man, it was hard. Still, we beat them at their own game.' As he bent over the wash-hand basin to bathe the abused left eye, no one was inclined to question his assertion. The classical boxer had been forced to desert the principles that have taken him where he is, to charge where he would rather have ambushed, to bludgeon when he would rather have pierced. Nevertheless, he had found the strength and the persistent courage and the adaptability to do whatever was necessary to keep the championship. Those who had come to the Garden to see a kind of artist had stayed to cheer a reluctant rough-houser. And Laguna, who precipitated the battle, lived to regret it. An equally significant fact about the fight, however, was that someone else did a job to match Buchanan's. For years the men who work in the corners with American fighters have been presented to us as possessors of almost mystical powers. They are seen, and certainly see themselves, as guardians of potent secrets passed down through generations of the craft in bleak gyms. Of all the legends that surround these men, arguing their superiority over their counterparts anywhere else in the world, the most vivid concerns their ability to cope with injuries and especially to stop the bleeding from cuts about the eyes. The best of them are credited with being able to make the blood clot around a gunshot wound before the smoke is cleared from the barrel.

It was a shock to some of these gentlemen when Eddie Thomas announced in Los Angeles not long ago that, as a corner-man, he would not take his hat off to any of them. It was perhaps a greater shock to any who were within earshot when Harold Conrad, a far from naïve New Yorker who has seen thousands of important fights and always known what he was watching, declared categorically on Monday night that Thomas is the best corner-man operating in the world today. 'That was a helluva job Thomas did in Buchanan's corner,' said Conrad. 'I watch corners and I've never seen one work better. Thomas was like an icicle. No matter what was happening in the ring, how much damage was being done to his guy, he never got flustered. He watched every move in there and he seemed to hand out the right advice, for he turned his guy over to fighting just when he had to. But during the rounds he went on getting ready for what he would have to do in the rest period. That minute really flies by when you've got problems. But Thomas always had all his stuff ready to use and never once looked panicky. Buchanan's a terrific fighter, one of the real ones, but I wouldn't bet that he would have won the fight without Eddie Thomas. That man gives the impression of knowing more about all aspects of working a corner than anyone around right now. Even Angelo Dundee has to bring someone in to do the intricate stuff on the cuts. Thomas and Buchanan make quite a partnership.'

That eulogy, and the extent to which it was merited, encourage the thought that Monday's experience may have persuaded Ken Buchanan that while he would still be a tremendous champion without Thomas, he will always be a better one with him. Tom Buchanan is a vital influence on his son's life, a solid base of affection and trust, but it would be unrealistic to expect the father or any of his friends to cope with the sort of situation that developed in the Garden. That was a crisis only a pair of professionals could have survived. One would not have been enough. Controlling the bleeding from the gash along the left eyebrow, which later required eight stitches on the outside and two on the inside, was a substantial achievement. But the treatment of the large lump that swelled on the left cheekbone in the third was at least as important. When Buchanan came out for the fifth round it was just about noticeable that he had a slight nick under the lump. The small cut 'wept' gently, relieving the pressure of the swelling and improving the sight of the eye. 'That's lucky,' said someone sitting near me. 'Such a neat little cut. You'd almost think it had been done with a razor blade.' I glanced at him curiously. I knew he had been watching the corner but I had not imagined his eyes were that good.

Making delicate facial repairs in the bedlam of the Garden, where the predictable tension was increased by the ear-splitting competition between a full-scale pipe band and a Panamanian group that featured silver, brass and pulsing drums, was the equivalent of threading needles in an air raid. To do it, Thomas had to be nerveless. Ken Buchanan should not lightly dispense with the services of such a man. Their contract is up for renewal soon, almost certainly before the champion has another match, and there should be no snag big enough to stand in the way of a mutual agreement.

Admittedly, Thomas has weaknesses. 'Those bloody bagpipes drove me crackers,' he said as we ate an Italian meal in the early hours of Tuesday morning. 'You know the Welsh invented the bagpipes and gave them to the Scots and the poor buggers haven't seen the joke yet.' Anyone who says things like that needs to be a good cut-man. He never knows when he will have to work on himself.

99

Jim Watt v. Howard Davis, Glasgow, 7 June 1980

Planning to Break a Heart

The toughest judgements on really good fighters are delivered by their own pride. For Jim Watt, the status of champion could never be bestowed by the insertion of a few lines of print in the record books or the clasping of a fancy belt around his waist. It comes down to knowing he's the best and making sure everybody else knows it.

Watt won the World Boxing Council lightweight title in April 1979 and has defended it twice. But he says with quiet seriousness that when he goes in against the black American Howard Davis before close on 30,000 of his own people at Ibrox Park, Glasgow, next Saturday night he will feel more like a challenger than a champion. 'At least, I'll be as hungry as a challenger, as anxious to prove myself,' he said last week after showering off the sweat of perhaps the hardest training of his life. 'I've got the title and I know I'm the man but a lot of people have been saying, "Yes, but there's Howard Davis over in the States." This fight will just clear everyone's mind about it. This is the one that will establish me as the best in the world. I understand one Glasgow bookmaker has made Davis a shade of odds-on to beat me. That guy must be bloody crazy.'

The home-town defector is presumably impressed not so much by Davis's specific achievements in 13 professional fights as by the tradition of excellence he represents and probably by memories of what was seen of him on television at the Montreal Olympic Games. He was one of five US gold medallists in boxing there and some reasonable judges at the ringside thought that of the five he, and not Sugar Ray Leonard, might have the greatest impact as a professional. His hand-speed is still reckoned by many to be at least the equal of Leonard's but much of his punching is done while moving away and therefore rarely has the explosive effectiveness that has destroyed so many opponents of the WBC welterweight champion. Davis has been brought along at a far less spectacular rate (indeed too slowly, according to Sugar Ray's chief counsellor, Angelo Dundee) but he has still managed to earn more than $2 million along the way. Without that dramatic earning power, he might not have stayed in a game for which he had a less than passionate enthusiasm. He was a spellbinder as an amateur but his record since turning professional early in 1977 is not at all terrifying. His 13 straight wins include only five stoppages and he has been on the floor four times. As a fighter who often seeks to burn out the opposition with pace, Davis sometimes has problems with his choreography and, caught with his feet together, is easily unbalanced. But at least three of those knockdowns were real enough.

In July 1978, in Indianapolis, Norman Goins, who is no Jim Driscoll but can bang more than somewhat, sent him sprawling on his back with

100

an overhand right in the first round of a nationally televised match. Then Goins put him down again with a left hook in the fifth. Davis skilfully boxed his way out of trouble and won a unanimous verdict at the end of ten rounds. He won well on points, too, in his most recent fight with Vilomar Fernandez after again being on the floor, but Jim Watt for one was not impressed. 'Fernandez,' says Watt, 'couldn't break an egg. And he's 100 per cent a counter-puncher. Yet he was able to back Davis up. If Fernandez could do that, I should be able to bully him a wee bit. There's no doubt the boy punches at a hell of a speed, in those flurries where his hands are just a blur. I'll obviously have to take quite a few shots but a lot of his stuff is out of range, thrown to finish just two or three inches from your face. I'm glad I'm not fighting him in the States or he might have beaten me on misses.

'When a fella punches out of range like that it convinces me that he's not the bravest. I'll want to be on top of him all the way, making him work every second, not giving him time to draw a deep breath. I don't think he'll fancy that.'

The treatment to be given to Davis has been assiduously rehearsed over the past few weeks in the airy gymnasium above the Royal Oak public house in Canning Town, an area of London that strives to hang on to the flavour of the old East End. Watt's main sparring has been with Kirkland Laing, a stringy, dark-skinned welterweight who has a rich but eccentric talent in the ring. 'He does a better Howard Davis than Howard Davis does,' says Terry Lawless, who is Watt's manager and a pleasant, intelligent man who is never happy unless he has a world champion or several about the place. 'Jim knows that against Davis he's got to be prepared to walk in through the shots and put pressure on the fella like he's never known before. Jim will be encountering hand-speed that he has never met before. But Kirk can give him some taste of it. He does to Kirk what he will look to do with Davis – bring him to his knees with pressure.'

In the ring, Watt was tunnelling grimly into Laing's body, trying to block or smother the other man's long, elastic arms, cutting him off, refusing him the rest that goes with space. They have averaged eight rounds a day, five days a week, like that and Watt has usually had four more with other partners. 'When Kirk has finished at night,' said Lawless, 'he just can't believe he's a stone heavier than Jim. Jim's a tough man. Couldn't you make a mistake by falling out with him at a dance, with his blond hair and blue eyes and not a bad mark on him?

'But it wouldn't be too much of a mistake, because he'd finish up talking you out of it and buying you a drink into the bargain. At work he's something different. It suits him to have the pressure of this fight, the biggest crowd, the biggest atmosphere. He deliberately takes every excuse away from himself beforehand. No talk of injuries or troubles in training. He's not only a proud Scot, he's a proud human being. He's more comfortably off than any of my fighters but he flays himself in training more than any of them. Whatever happens in Glasgow, he won't let himself down.

'Davis will make a hard job but it can be done all right. He has a few strange habits, like turning his head away when he's on the ropes. That could be fatal against Jim because he's got a funny hook with the right that comes from away outside. It comes in on the blind side, hits you out of nowhere, and it could be deadly next Saturday.'

Watt feels he may have quite a number of ways of being deadly at Ibrox Park. 'Davis is a very good boxer but he makes a lot of amateur mistakes,' he said in his rough dressing-room at Canning Town. 'I think I can punish them. I'm not going out expecting to lose the first four rounds because he's fast. They told me I wouldn't be getting to Charlie Nash in those rounds but I stopped him in the fourth. Although physically I may be inclined to move slowly early on, I'm working quick mentally. I'm not going out and getting blitzed. But I'm not going crazy either. I'm just working away there, gradually getting to the other guy.'

One of the substantial advantages for Watt is that Davis will, in two senses, be operating in a foreign country for the first time. Firstly, he hasn't fought outside America as a pro and now he will be in the midst of a roaring mass of Glaswegians. How alienated can you get? Secondly, he will be facing 15 rounds for the first time. 'It just dawned on me driving down to London to train,' says Watt, 'that he's had 13 fights all told and I've had 13 15-rounders. If he feels himself getting tired, the thought that he has never been over the trip could unnerve him. And I think I'll make him tired. I hope to be right on top of him by 10, 11 and 12 and just punch him out.'

Naturally enough, Howard Davis and his two managers, the splendidly named partnership of Rappaport and Jones, have been presenting an alternative script to the Glasgow public in the past couple of days. They are sure that in addition to $325,000 (the Scot is officially supposed to lift three times that amount but finances are never so simple in boxing) they can take home the title. 'Watt can't beat me,' Davis has declared. 'I was ordained to be champion. I have known that since I was 16. I'm quicker than Watt and Watt can't hit hard enough to beat me. He would have to cut off my legs.'

Watt, in spite of understandable worries about having three judges from the far side of the Atlantic, thinks he has a simpler solution than amputation. 'To my mind when I took the championship against Alfredo Pitalua I was fighting a better man than Davis. I think I can break his heart.'

The challenger is 24 and the champion will be 32 in July, so age could be a factor, but in what looks like a genuine even-money fight there is something we can bet on with total confidence. Howard Davis will not break Jim Watt's heart.

Glasgow Saturday Night

Now the world in general and Howard Davis in particular will have to believe Jim Watt when he says that he is the best lightweight fighter of the day. On a sodden Saturday night in his home town of Glasgow, Watt, who will be 32 next month, gave nearly eight years and a convincing beating to the skilled and brave American, a challenger who came to Scotland with an Olympic gold medal and an unbeaten run of 13 fights as a professional.

Davis and most of his countrymen felt that his virtuosity would outclass a man whose early career had been so haphazard that his record shows seven losses in 44 paid contests, but Watt has been a different man since he joined Terry Lawless to claim and twice previously defend the World Boxing Council championship. He has a heart that would not yield to the Red Army and his body, as luminously white as porcelain and inclined to look almost unhealthy against the dark gleam of Davis's negro physique, is trained to a level of fitness that few boxers in the world could match. Those huge assets are served by a southpaw technique disciplined by long years of experience to the point where it punishes the opposition, especially to the body, without obliging the champion to take foolish risks.

Such equipment was too much last night for even a fighter as remarkable as Davis. He sought to break Watt's rhythm with bursts of varied, slashing punches with both hands but Watt utterly refused to be shaken, working relentlessly to the pattern of dogged but never remotely dull attacks that he had planned. Even without a knockdown, the fight had ample excitement and most of it flowed in favour of Watt, who has emerged beyond all question as one of the few genuine heroes of Scotland's sporting mythology. At the end the three officials voted unanimously that he was the winner (145–144, 149–142, 147–144), and all it took then to make for a perfect occasion was a demonstration of sportsmanship from two men who had fought honourably and well. They hugged for nearly a minute when the last bell sounded and their mutual admiration found echoes all around Ibrox.

When the action began it was Watt who stalked after the American, seeking to fulfil his promise of cutting off the faster man and reducing the effect of superior mobility. Davis looked slightly the more tense and he was entitled to do so after listening to the astonishing, prolonged roar, a sound that seemed to come from the bowels of the crowd and swelled to drown the martial din of the pipes and drums that played 'Scotland the Brave'. That roar has washed over Watt in all of his recent successful performances in Glasgow and his opponent could never have heard anything like it before. The sound that greeted Davis was contrastingly hostile but he has been around too long as amateur and professional to be unnerved by decibels and he remained cool as he backed away from the world lightweight champion's initial southpaw probing. He was intent on swaying out of range but did not lean far enough away from one right hand to the head. Nevertheless the round was sufficiently tentative on both sides to be scored even. Davis immediately made a declaration of confidence he meant to maintain all evening by standing in his corner during the interval between rounds and he began the second with a flurry of body punches. He managed a right cross to Watt's face, too, but the Scot, although retreating, was not under serious pressure and when he lost the round it was narrowly and not alarmingly.

The third lifted the Glasgow crowd to their feet in a tumult of expectation. Davis, early on, tried a flamboyant shuffle but soon he was slowed by stiff right hooks to the body. He tried to reply with long lefts and rights but Watt bored in again with more telling shots. Davis breathed heavily and sought to retaliate in bursts but he did not look a happy fighter. Watt took the round. The sixth was another good one for the champion. He produced more quiet, assured excellence and, although the American exacted some reprisal, the round ended with a hard, straight left crossed on to Davis's chin and he reeled back on the ropes, clearly discomfited. Watt was still pursuing him at the bell.

The seventh and eighth were closely and punishingly contested but it was significant that Davis was having to gather himself for swinging surges to keep a balance in the exchanges. Watt, if only by a sliver, probably deserved to take those rounds also. It was the quality of his work, its solidity, as opposed to the more spectacular volume of Davis's assaults, that justified this impression. However, Davis had plenty left, mentally and physically and, in the ninth, with his mouth open in a grimace of determination, he took the fight to Watt and may well have come away with an even round. Nevertheless, there was no denying the simple, true worth of Watt's work and for a time in round ten he added splendid insult to accumulated injury by out-jabbing Davis in the middle of the ring. Ironically it was at this point that his most serious problems to date manifested themselves. Blood appeared on his left cheek, oozing from a swelling beneath the eye, and there was a suggestion of a slight thickening above the right.

Davis spent the 11th trying to exploit the chink of advantage he had opened in the 10th but Watt persisted with spirit and good, sensible boxing and the round was even enough. In the 12th it was Davis's turn to bleed, from a cut near his left eye, and Watt pressed in to use the injury to undermine the American's confidence. Davis had shown plenty of stamina and appetite for the fray but now as the right jabs clipped at the damaged eye he hesitated like someone whose stomach was beginning to accommodate misgivings. Watt was unlikely by this stage to believe that he could, as he had hoped, break the challenger's heart but he looked very much like a winner as he appeared to take that 12th.

Davis sprang from his corner with a slashing attack in the 14th but he found Watt refusing to be moved and before the end of the round thudding right hooks were battering the strength out of the American's body. He was a wild gambler rather than the confident challenger who had come to Glasgow. And at the finish he was undoubtedly a losing gambler.

Onward Virgin Soldier

The Observer, 25 February 1979

Johnny Owen's mother worries when he fights, and so does every other mother who has ever seen him stripped. The British and Commonwealth bantamweight champion has the kind of physique that makes him elusive when he is standing still. His 8 st and 6 lb are elongated over 5 ft 8 in, so that his biceps are scarcely more prominent than his Adam's apple or the veins on his forearm. Indeed, most of Owen's muscles come disguised as skin and bone. His ears protrude endearingly from a face that is small, shy and much younger than could be expected of a 23-year-old who has been boxing competitively since he was ten. When that appearance is juxtaposed with the thought of what he is asked to do in the ring, hearts that are not at all maternal find themselves melting.

On a recent night in Bedlinog, a South Wales village a couple of valleys away from his home town of Merthyr Tydfil, a friendly man in the crowd turned to the boxer's father. 'Dick, you have a lovely son,' he said. 'And I hope you won't be insulted if I tell you how he makes me feel. When I look at him I want to pick him up, put him in a shawl, carry him home and give him a good basin of broth.'

Dick Owen wasn't insulted. He and his wife were accustomed to far more indignant misconceptions about a boy so obsessively dedicated to a fighting career that he has never once allowed himself to be distracted by a girl, has never as much as kissed one in earnest. When her virgin soldier goes off to war, Johnny's mother, stubbornly refusing to watch him take punches, sits at home until she can bear the waiting no longer and then goes to pace around a telephone box higher up the hilly council estate of Gelli-deg in Merthyr, painfully delaying her call until she knows *The Western Mail* sports desk in Cardiff will be able to tell her the result. 'The main reason we've never had the phone put in,' says Dick, 'is that we know we'd be pestered to death by people telling us we should be locked up for letting Johnny fight. Dai Gardiner, his manager, has had to take some terrible stick over that, especially from women. They've called Dai something rotten. He's more like one of the family than a manager, but these characters seem to think he is starving Johnny, then sending him out to get knocked about by sturdier lads. They don't bother to notice that

Johnny won more than a hundred amateur fights and lost only 18, or that he's unbeaten after 17 as a professional and has stopped eight of those professional opponents inside the distance.'

Around midnight next Saturday, in Almeria, southern Spain, Owen will attempt to effect a dramatic improvement in that already exceptional record by taking the European bantamweight title away from Juan Francisco Rodriguez. A glance might suggest that Rodriguez, with only 13 paid fights, is even less experienced than the Welshman but that statistic is deceptive, because the Spanish authorities were so proud of their man's achievements at the amateur level – where he held a European championship and earned an Olympic bronze medal – that for a long time they severely discouraged ambitions of defecting to professionalism. Since joining the harder school, he has kept respectable company, not only making himself head boy on the Continent but putting himself in the way of the world champion, the intimidating Mexican Carlos Zarate. Admittedly, that argument was comprehensively lost after five rounds, but the defeat may be considered less than disgraceful when set against Zarate's record of having stopped 52 out of 53 opponents and having been beaten only once – and that just recently at the so-called super-bantamweight mark of 8 st 10 lb by Wilfredo Gomez. Yet, if the form book invites caution in the approach to Rodriguez, it does nothing to make Owen pessimistic. If there is a line of comparison, perhaps it emerges from Owen's latest success, the points victory last November over the seasoned and impressively capable Sicilian-Australian Paul Ferreri, who had previously given Zarate plenty of aggravation over 12 rounds before succumbing to cuts. The Welshman's apparent fragility has never looked more like Nature's con trick than it was at Ebbw Vale as he came from behind to subdue Ferreri in the last third of the 15-round match.

Rodriguez is known as a boxer of skill and style but one who is inclined to seek rests during rounds and continues to exhibit too many of his amateur habits. He is unlikely to be more slippery than Ferreri and he can forget about taking breathers against Owen, who seems to harbour a deep resentment of the rule that gives him a minute's break between rounds. So the biggest threat to the British champion's challenge may be the eccentricities of scoring in Spain: 'We accept that we'll have to stop the fella to get the title and I expect Johnny to do that, maybe after about 12 rounds,' says Dai Gardiner. After watching Owen in training last week, it was easy to accept that forecast as merely realistic.

Whether running on the scarred hills around Merthyr or working at the gym above the local Labour Club, where the harsh poverty of the facilities makes the fight emporia of New York or Philadelphia look like suites at the Savoy, his application to work is frightening. When the recent snow and ice made the sheep-paths of his roadwork hazardous, he wrapped rags and old socks around his heavy running boots and did his best to maintain his daily schedule of nine-mile slogs. On the one day a week when he is excused gym sessions, he likes to extend the run to 12 miles. His sparring has the intensity of warfare and a night's business can include as many as 15 rounds of it. He has used a handful of experienced and active pros in this his second full preparation for a championship match that has been postponed three times. None has been less than nine pounds heavier than he is but all have had trouble coping with his pressure. On Thursday evening it was the turn of Les Pickett, the local featherweight who is due to fight an eliminator for the British championship in the midweek following the Almeria date. Pickett is not naturally accommodating but he was forced rather than forcing through the eight hard rounds and at the end of each he was gulping down extra air while Owen wandered his corner impatiently with hardly a hint of rise and fall about his narrow chest.

His floor exercises gave further evidence of freakish stamina and, through it all, from the moment he began slowly to accoutre himself for work with the ritualised care of a bullfighter dressing for the ring, there was something even more remarkable: the sense of a man being stimulated and enlarged by submergence in his true *métier*. Earlier, in the council-house living-room bright with a spreading clutter of trophies and decorated on one wall with a lurid green painting of a skeleton presented by a fan, his personality had come across as diffident almost to the point of being fugitive. But in that incomparably shabby gym, with its make-shift ring, patched punch-bag and medicine ball, wrinkling fight posters and an old bath puddled with spit and littered with dog-ends, he grew and brightened visibly with the knowledge that he was a hero at the game in hand, the certainty that he would go out from there to cause a stir in the world. Win or lose in Almeria, he will be doing what he is happiest doing. 'I don't expect to lose,' he says, both the accent and the quietness of voice demanding a straining alertness from the listener. 'I know they say Spain is a hard place to win but it's just him and me at the finish. I really love boxing and I really love training too, for itself as well as for the confidence it gives me. I've got a job as a machine setter in a components factory but I'm happy when I take a fortnight off for a big fight. After all the running and the other stuff in the gym, I know I'm not going to fade. I can go all out from the first bell. It's a great feeling.'

It's not usually so good for the opponent, who finds Owen coming at him with an incessant variety of sharp, hurtful punches, crowding and hustling, undeterred by any but the most forceful counters. Owen's nose has been thickened and polished by all the years of aggressive attention but he has never been stopped and as a pro he has only once been briefly bemused, by George Sutton, who was eventually beaten out of sight. 'The only mark I can remember him getting since turning professional was a tiny one under the left eye in his 13th fight,' says his father. 'His mother played hell when he came home. That was to be the end of it: no more boxing. He wouldn't even let me put something on the bruise. He was so proud about the thought of having a black eye to show.'

Dick Owen did some amateur boxing (the family connection goes back at least as far as Dick's own grandfather, who inflicted a bit of damage in the booths) and all five of his sons were so keen that he had to set up an alfresco gym on the drying green of 22 Heol Bryn Padell, Gelli-deg. 'The boy older than Johnny was really good but gave it up too early and the one immediately beneath him, Kevin, was a Welsh international until he took to the courting lark and packed in the boxing,' he says. 'Johnny's different. He lives for the game and has never looked at a girl. There are enough of them coming for him now but there's plenty of time for that.' John agrees. 'I'd like to be still unbeaten this time next year and we could think about going for the world title. Ferreri's manager said he thought I was near the top class now but we're not rushing. Whatever happens, I think I want to be out of the game by the time I'm around 27. It seems young but, do you see, I'd have been boxing nearly 20 years by then.'

Dai Gardiner, the manager, bearded and still, at 38, carrying the briskness that took him through 13 professional fights with only one loss before a detached retina ended his career, acknowledges that the punching strength of someone like Zarate will represent the decisive question for Owen. 'Can he take one on the chin from a man like that and keep going? That's the only question he's got to answer for me, and we'll just have to find out about that when it comes along. What is sure is that he won't fail because of lack of fitness or temperament, lack of skill or heart.'

In short, Johnny Owen is a legitimate heir to the fighting traditions of South Wales and Merthyr Tydfil in particular. 'This was a hard town in the days when the pits and the ironworks were booming,' says Dick, himself a former miner. 'It had 100,000 people, with Irish, Geordies, Spanish, Italians and all sorts mixed in. Even the women were hard. They had to be. My grandfather had a job underground in the pit and my own mother handled a wheelbarrow in the Dowlais Ironworks.'

The charm of Johnny is that he has inherited that toughness and kept his gentle side. His father again: 'He's mine and maybe I shouldn't say this, but he *is* a lovely boy. He still washes the dishes and clears out the ashes to light the fire in the morning. Nothing changes with Johnny.' Even the Spaniards may find it difficult to complain if he changes things just a little by taking that title next Saturday.

Johnny Owen's Last Fight

It can be no consolation to those in South Wales and in Los Angeles who are red-eyed with anxiety about Johnny Owen to know that the extreme depth of his own courage did as much as anything else to take him to the edge of death. This calamitous experience could only have happened to an exceptionally brave fighter because Lupe Pintor, the powerful Mexican who was defending his World Boxing Council bantamweight championship against Owen, had landed enough brutal punches before the 12th and devastatingly conclusive round to break the nerve and resistance of an ordinary challenger. The young Welshman was, sadly, too extraordinary for his own good in the Olympic Auditorium.

In the street, in a hotel lounge or even in his family's home on a Merthyr Tydfil housing estate, he is so reticent as to be almost unreachable, so desperately shy that he has turned 24 without ever having had a genuine date with a girl. But in the ring he has always been transformed, possessed by a furious aggression that has driven his alarmingly thin and unmuscular body through the heaviest fire and into the swarming, crowding attacks that gave him a record before Friday night of 24 victories, one defeat (avenged) and one draw in 26 professional matches. That record was built up in Europe and its reward was the European bantamweight championship and acceptance as a contender for the world title. Given the basic harshness of boxing as a way of earning a living, no one could blame Owen or his father or his manager, Dai Gardiner, for going after the biggest prize available to them, but some of us always felt that the right to challenge Pintor in Los Angeles was a questionable privilege. Making some notes about the background to the fight on Friday morning, I found myself writing: 'Feel physical sickness at the thought of what might happen, the fear that this story might take us to a hospital room.' This scribble was not meant to imply any severe criticism of a match which, on the basis of the relevant statistics, could not be condemned as outrageous. Indeed, the apprehension might have been illogically excessive to anyone who set Pintor's career figures of 41 wins, seven losses and a draw against the fact that Owen's one defeat had been a blatant case of larceny in Spain and the further, impressive fact that he had never been knocked off his feet as a professional boxer.

Yet it is the simple truth that for weeks a quiet terror had been gathering in me about this fight. Perhaps its principal basis was no more than a dread that the frailty that the boy's performances had hitherto dismissed as illusory would, some bad time in some bad place, prove to be terribly real. There is something about his pale face, with its large nose, jutting ears and uneven teeth, all set above that long, skeletal frame, that takes hold of the heart and makes unbearable the thought of him being badly hurt. And, to my mind, there was an ominous possibility that he would be badly hurt against Pintor, a Mexican who had already stopped 33 opponents and would be going to work in front of a screaming mob of his countrymen, whose lust for blood gives the grubby Olympic Auditorium the atmosphere of a Guadalajara cockfight, multiplied a hundred times.

No fighters in the world are more dedicated to the raw violence of the business than Mexicans. Pintor comes out of a gym in Mexico City where more than a hundred boxers work out regularly and others queue for a chance to show that what they can do in the alleys they can do in the ring. A man who rises to the top of such a seething concentration of hostility is likely to have little interest in points-scoring as a means of winning verdicts. So it was hard to share the noisy optimism of the hundred-odd Welsh supporters who made themselves conspicuous in the sweaty clamour of the hall and brought a few beer cups filled with urine down on their heads. But they seemed to be entitled to their high spirits in the early rounds as Owen carried the fight to Pintor, boring in on the shorter, dark-skinned champion and using his spidery arms to flail home light but aggravatingly persistent flurries of punches.

The first round was probably about even. Owen might have edged the second on a British scorecard and he certainly took the third, but already Pintor's right hooks and uppercuts were making occasional dramatic interventions, sending a nervous chill through the challenger's friends around the ring.

It was in the fourth round that Pintor's right hand first struck with a hint of the force that was to be so overwhelming subsequently, but this time it was thrown overarm and long and Owen weathered it readily enough. He was seen to be bleeding from the inside of his lower lip in the fifth (the injury may have been inflicted earlier) but, since both Pintor's eyebrows were receiving attention from his seconds by then, the bloodshed seemed to be reasonably shared. In fact the laceration in the mouth was serious and soon the challenger was swallowing blood. He was being caught with more shots to the head, too, but refused to be discouraged and an American voice behind the press seats said incredulously: 'I don't believe this guy.'

Pintor was heaving for breath at the end of the fifth but in the sixth he mounted a surge, punished Owen and began to take control of the contest. The official doctor, Bernhard Schwartz, checked the lip for the second time before the start of the eighth, which made the abrupt disaster of the ninth all the more painful.

Pintor smashed in damaging hooks early in the ninth but their threat appeared to have passed as the round moved to its close. Then, without a trace of warning, Pintor dropped a shattering right hook over Owen's bony left shoulder. The blow hurled him to the floor and it was here that his courage began to be a double-edged virtue. He rose after a couple of seconds, although clearly in a bad condition. There was a mandatory eight count but even at the end of it he was hopelessly vulnerable to more hooks to the head and it took the bell to save him.

By the tenth there was unmistakable evidence that the strength had drained out of every part of Owen's body except his heart. He was too tired and weak now to stay really close to Pintor, skin against skin, denying the puncher leverage. As that weariness gradually created a space between them, Pintor filled it with cruel, stiff-armed hooks. Every time Owen was hit solidly in the 11th the thin body shuddered. We knew the end had to be near but could not foresee how awful it would be.

There were just 40 seconds of the 12th round left when the horror story started to take shape. Owen was trying to press in on Pintor near the ropes, failed to prevent that deadly space from developing again and was dropped on his knees by a short right. After rising at three and taking another mandatory count, he was moved by the action to the other side of the ring and it was there that a ferocious right hook threw him on to his back. He was unconscious before he hit the canvas and his relaxed neck muscles allowed his head to thud against the boards. Dai Gardiner and the boxer's father were in the ring long before the count could be completed and they were quickly joined by Dr Schwartz, who called for oxygen. Perhaps the oxygen might have come rather more swiftly than it did but only if it had been on hand at the ringside. Obviously that would be a sensible precaution, just as it might be sensible to have a stretcher immediately available. It is no easy job to bring such equipment through the jostling mass of spectators at an arena like the Auditorium, where Pintor's supporters were mainly concerned about cheering its arrival as a symbol of how comprehensive their man's victory had been. The outward journey to the dressing-room, with poor Johnny Owen deep in a sinister unconsciousness, was no simpler and the indifference of many among the crowd was emphasised when one of the stretcher-bearers had his pocket picked.

There have been complaints in some quarters about the delay in providing an ambulance but, in the circumstances, these may be difficult to justify. Dr Ferdie Pacheco, who was for years Muhammad Ali's doctor and is now a boxing consultant with NBC in the United States, insists that the company lay on an ambulance wherever they cover fights but no such arrangements exist at the Auditorium and the experienced paramedics of the Los Angeles Fire Department made good time once they received the emergency call. Certainly it was grief and not blame that was occupying the sick boy's father as he stood weeping in the corridor of the California Hospital, a mile from the scene of the knockout. A few hours before, I had sat by the swimming-pool at their motel in downtown Los Angeles and listened to them joke about the calls Johnny's mother had been making from Merthyr Tydfil on the telephone they had recently installed. The call that was made to Mrs Owen from the waiting-room of the

California Hospital shortly before 7 a.m. Saturday, Merthyr time (11 p.m. Friday in Los Angeles) had a painfully different tone. It was made by Byron Board, a publican and close friend of the family, and he found her already in tears because she had heard that Johnny had been knocked out. The nightmare that had been threatening her for years had become reality.

She can scarcely avoid being bitter against boxing now and many who have not suffered such personal agony because of the hardest of sports will be asking once again if the game is worth the candle. Quite a few of us who have been involved with it most of our lives share the doubts. But our reactions are bound to be complicated by the knowledge that it was boxing that gave Johnny Owen his one positive means of self-expression. Outside the ring he was an inaudible and almost invisible personality. Inside, he became astonishingly positive and self-assured. He seemed to be more at home there than anywhere else. It is his tragedy that he found himself articulate in such a dangerous language.

The doctors' struggle to rescue Johnny Owen from deep coma proved to be hopeless and he died in the first week of November 1980. His body was brought home to be buried in Merthyr Tydfil.

112

Part Three

Prodigies and Prisoners

One of the advantages of writing about boxing for newspapers in this country is that Fleet Street executives can be persuaded from time to time that a fight on the other side of the world is worth covering even if no Briton is involved. That tendency was strengthened by the eagerness of readers to follow the activities of Muhammad Ali. If Muhammad had signed up to box on the moon, NASA would have been pestered by sports editors seeking quotations for the round trip, with ten days' accommodation in the fight headquarters hotel thrown in.

It is my particular good fortune that *The Observer* have always been ready to consider sending me several thousand miles to report on outstanding foreign fighters other than Ali. The pieces that follow are, in the main, the results of such journeys. A notable exception is the feature on Carlos Monzon in Paris, which was written for the American magazine *Sports Illustrated*. The article on the convict boxers at Rahway State Prison in New Jersey was, plainly, not a conventional sports-page assignment. But perhaps readers won't mind entering that bleak netherworld where formalised violence qualifies as a politeness. At least they will be able to leave it again after a few pages, which gives them an edge over James Scott and the lads.

This part of the book is substantially a celebration of some of the greatest fighters I have ever seen. I hope each of the few pieces does enough to establish its dominant figures in the reader's mind and to pay tribute to their brilliance. The exploits of men like Carlos Ortiz, who was the finest lightweight in the world for half a dozen years, and Carlos Monzon, who was invincible among the middleweights for somewhat longer, could fill a small library. The same is true of Sugar Ray Leonard, Roberto Duran and Larry Holmes, who are also prominent in the pages ahead. All I am doing here is asking anyone who has opened this collection to join me as a thrilled witness of brief, vivid passages from phenomenal careers.

Carlos Ortiz v. Ismael Laguna, New York, 16 August 1967

Ortiz's Peaceful Punch-up

In Morahan's Bar on Eighth Avenue, where they serve Guinness and few
of the regulars are noticeably Puerto Rican, they are still talking with
awed respect of how Carlos Ortiz kept his hold on the lightweight
championship of the world three nights ago.

When the New York Irish praise a fighter of another race something
remarkable must have happened. What happened on the baseball
diamond out at Shea Stadium on Wednesday was remarkable indeed. It
was not that it was a great fight, because no fight as one-sided can be
considered great. It was rather the rare experience of seeing a true
champion impose his talent and his will to a degree that transformed the
fundamental nature of an occasion. Ortiz did much more than make his
ninth successful defence of the title by outclassing and intimidating Ismael
Laguna, the wildly flashy Panamanian who had impertinently borrowed
the championship in 1965. He demonstrated again that he possesses
virtually every attribute required in a professional boxer. He also earned
$90,000 and averted a riot. It was a good night's work.

Since Wednesday the New York papers have carried acid little pieces
mocking the blood-chilling predictions of mob violence that preceded the
fight. But no one was inclined to mock beforehand, least of all those
pressmen who were in the target area during the three recent riots at
Madison Square Garden. Several of them arrived at the ringside with
motorcyclists' crash helmets. 'Those clowns will come down in a minute
if they get stirred,' said one reporter, glancing round the tiered, almost
vertical cliff of the stands, where the flags had begun to wave, the chants
to rumble. 'All it takes is a questionable decision and they'll level this
place.' The press were not alone in fearing that the worst of the previous
disorders might look like a love-in after this collision between thousands
of Puerto Ricans from Spanish Harlem (which had supplied most of the
unpaid combatants on the earlier programmes) and a local Panamanian
element reinforced by at least 2,000 supporters flown in from the
homeland. A request from Eddie Dooley, the chairman of the New York
State Boxing Commission, for extra police to curb the crowds brought a
sharp rebuke from the city's police commissioner, Howard Leary, who
said he found it difficult to understand why the fight had been authorised
in such a racially tense summer.

Racial tensions were not eased at the weigh-in when a dark-skinned
young man in glasses chose to take issue with Bill Daly, who manages
Ortiz. Daly was spieling amiably to some boxing writers in the dingy
front lobby of the Garden, the administrative home of the promotion,
when the Panamanian loomed suddenly in front of him. 'Meester Daly, in
my opinion . . .'

116

'Nobody asked you for your opinion,' said Daly, but the eyes in the pouchy, well-used face were still smiling.

'Nevertheless, in my opinion your boy don't go nine.'

Daly's eyes were smiling no longer. 'How much money you wanna bet?'

'Twenty thousand dollars,' said the young man.

'That my guy won't go nine? Right, we'll all have a piece of that. You're outa your mind.'

'No, no, that's not what I want to bet . . . I want to bet on the fight . . . I . . .'

But Daly's patience had gone. 'Get outa here before I hit you on the chin. Mind your own business. Who is the sonofabitch anyway?'

The intruder retreated. Perhaps he realised that the threats could be regarded as mild from a man who recently snatched a gun out of a policeman's holster in Mexico City in self-defence against a menacing crowd.

Daly might have been less tolerant if he had not just been reassured by the sight of his man weighing in at the limit of 9 st 9 lb, a precision that was equalled by Laguna. Seeing them together, it was unbelievable that the Puerto Rican could get his magnificent torso, his long, muscular, thick-wristed arms into the same poundage as the slim negro. Yet Ortiz, though he has had agonies with weight in the past, did not look at all drawn. Watching him admiringly was a hook-nosed man later vaguely identified as the champion's business adviser. 'What a body,' he said. 'It's a miracle. He's 31 and when you think of the way he's lived . . .' Ortiz's recreational pursuits have never been monkish. He owns one night club and is credited with paying for quite a few others. 'But he's really right this time, mentally and physically. He's so happy about patching it up and being back with Norma and the kids. He's got a wonderful woman there and three kids you could put between slices of bread and eat, they're so cute.'

Across Eighth Avenue, in Loew's Midtown Hotel, Teddy Bentham was thinking a trainer's thoughts. Staring wistfully out of a window, he said quietly, 'Just let Carlos stay young for one more night.' Bentham's anxieties were as superfluous as those of the New York Police. Commissioner Leary had relented in a big way and they were out in strength at Shea, many in plain clothes, hundreds more in wary, dark-blue clusters, accoutred for war. They came braced for a riot and found a recital. Ortiz's virtuosity, his supremacy in every department, made the thought of a complaint, let alone a disturbance, as ridiculous as the betting odds that had installed Laguna as favourite. Laguna was thrashed for six straight rounds, then allowed to win the seventh and ninth and share the eighth while Ortiz accepted Daly's advice to 'take a rest, leave him have a couple'. In the last six it required generosity to give Laguna one and make another even. The Panamanian was demoralised so rapidly that he revealed practically nothing of the frenzied speed, the mounting surges of activity, that had caused so many to overrate him. Too apprehensive to lead, he was constantly jabbed and hooked by Ortiz's left, and throughout the 15 rounds he remained pathetically vulnerable to his opponent's smashing right crosses.

In the dressing-room afterwards, dabbing a damp towel against the minor cuts beside his eyes, wiping sweat from his thinning hair, Ortiz told why he had smiled openly during the fight. 'It was so easy and it was funny to think of all those people who said I would lose, that I was all through. I have been a professional for 13 years and I have been a world champion a long time. A kid like this is not supposed to beat me.'

The last word was with the adviser who had spoken in praise of edible children. 'If only this guy were not such a liver,' he said. 'He could stay around for another ten years and they wouldn't hit him on the ass with a handful of buckshot if he was blindfold.'

Carlos Monzon v. Jean-Claude Bouttier, Paris, 17 June 1972

In This Corner: The Sheep

Sports Illustrated, June 1972

The first mistake the Parisians made was to let one of their airports lose the luggage of Harold Conrad, the New York publicist and boxing entrepreneur, who likes to think that if he stood next to Beau Brummell people would start straightening Mr Brummell's tie. When his bags dropped out of sight in the jabbering acres of the Orly arrival building, Conrad was stuck with the same grey wool shirt for two days. He wore it like a leper's bell, and by the end of the second evening his habitual tributes to the city were having trouble getting past his grinding teeth. 'Yeah,' said a sympathising friend, 'if these guys were going to lose something, maybe it should have been Monzon.'

The man was anticipating the locals' second mistake, which was to persuade themselves, by self-hypnosis at its most convincing, that Jean-Claude Bouttier was France's greatest martial hero since Charles de Gaulle and fit to be in the same ring as Carlos Monzon, the middleweight champion of the world. It was indeed unfortunate for French pride that no one at the airport thought of mislaying the Argentine visitor, because as a fighter Bouttier scarcely belongs in the same country as Monzon, let alone inside the same ring. This is not to say Bouttier was disgraced. He fought as he had trained – with resolution and a sense of responsibility towards those who had let affection and loyalty overwhelm judgement to the point where they shared his quixotic dream. But there was never any serious likelihood that this former butcher boy from northern France could vindicate the most aggressive of the banners flourished at ringside in the Stade Colombes on Saturday night: BOUTTIER – LE BOUCHER, MONZON – LE MOUTON, it said.

Monzon is the kind of sheep to make wolves seek other employment. He is tall for a middleweight, only an inch short of six feet, with a torso that is compact rather than dramatically muscled. His reach is exceptional, but the slim arms do not give that impression of dangling limpness seen in lesser fighters. There is frightening strength in the elasticity of those long muscles, and the whole body has the kind of fundamental power that is deeply embedded in his inherited physiology. He has learned much in his nine years as a professional (not the least of it being the value of using a refined left jab to open the way for the thunderous crossfire of his hooking), but the qualities that set Carlos Monzon apart were given to him in the womb. Technically he is not difficult to fault. He stands up straight, so that his rather long neck puts the handsome head well above the line of his shoulders. 'Like a lantern in a storm,' said a veteran American critic at Colombes. The answer is that pedantry is for those who need it. Monzon's method is related to profound confidence, the conviction that he has the animal authority to dominate almost any man they put in front of him. He has never been knocked down and, as someone once said of Marciano, he finds it hard to forget how strong he is. It shows in his eyes. They look out over the high, moulded cheekbones with relaxed steadiness, following the opponent with a gaze that is thorough but dispassionate. The insistence on hunting by sight like a greyhound, the refusal to fight by Braille, gave Monzon a huge advantage over Bouttier. It was a major irony that the Frenchman should be retired on his stool between the 12th and 13th rounds because the vision of his left eye had been badly flawed by Monzon's thumb. A couple of instances of thumbing were discernible, and by the end of the tenth round Bouttier was already blinking confusedly out of his left eye. The irony lay in the fact that while he had full vision, he made poor use of it.

Bouttier's European title had been won by controlled attacking. The emphasis then was on the systematic application of an economical and impressively vigorous right cross and reinforcing skills – particularly a maturing left hook – that he had acquired on regular tours of gyms in the US. But on Saturday all that gave way to blind lunges, attempts to launch himself, head down, through the violent ambush of Monzon's long arms. His regular reward was to find himself looking at the floor and seeing stars on it. The explanation of this haphazard impetuosity was cruelly simple: Jean-Claude Bouttier, fighting for the big prize in front of 35,000 of his own people, feeling their will welling up in the soft Paris night, was cripplingly overawed. At first the effect was to stun him into a condition close to paralysis. He listened to the introductions with his eyes closed

119

and boxed the first two rounds like a somnambulist, his lips moving nervously as if making a running commentary on a black dream.

Monzon did not trouble to probe for targets. He walked in with the same unhurried stride he uses on the streets, and as he swung he had the air of a man who felt the only risk he ran was of being bored. When Bouttier's spirit reoccupied his body in the third round, the Argentine was obliged to show more concern. Even so, he took enough sharpish rights and firm left hooks to persuade many at ringside that it was Bouttier's round. There was probably only one other, the ninth, that could be seen that way. But it is the sixth that will be remembered. Through the fourth and fifth Monzon stood above Bouttier's groping crouch and slashed him with hooks, and when the bell sent them out again, the same pattern developed, with Bouttier staggering along the top rope as if it were the rail of a pitching ship. Then suddenly Monzon was caught by a left hook that carried the weight of the Frenchman's thick shoulders, the leverage of his steadying legs. Monzon was hurt, perhaps in some slight danger, but his intimidating power of recovery was again immediately evident, and he came back to punish Bouttier painfully. Yet it was when trying a retaliatory punch that the weaker man reeled backward on his heels and, helped by a light blow from Monzon, took a mandatory eight count. Astonishingly, Bouttier managed a further rally, shook Monzon before wrestling him to the floor, took another battering when the Argentine rose, and was still there throwing punches several seconds after the bell. That round should be preserved in a war museum.

Everything that followed had to be anticlimactic. It was, brutally so for the suffering Frenchman. But the fight went on until finally came the cryptic announcement of retirement on the very brink of the 13th, a happening as startling as a splash of cold water. Bouttier, the 27-year-old country boy who had been asked to bring back the championship France last held with Marcel Cerdan in the 1940s, had quit on his stool. But, as they learned that there was to be a hospital examination on Monday to check the possibility of damage to the retina, few of his countrymen were inclined to condemn him. The physical harm that may have been done to Bouttier could be the lesser result of the defeat. He is a warm, instantly engaging young man with the virile looks, intelligence and individualism to make him at once an idol of the masses. However, he readily admits that he is deeply emotional, and no one can be sure about the effect on such a sensitive person of being thrust beyond his limitations. There were hints of a mounting awareness of his situation as he prepared to meet Monzon, and at the weigh-in one could almost see him contract under the clamping pressure. That ritual was conducted in a tiny, cheaply ornate cinema in the foothills of Montmartre. The place, smelling of worn carpets and disinfectant, was crowded on the one side by fans and temporary fugitives from the streetside cafés, on the other by promoters and agents from all over the world who had come with their stockyard gaze to scrutinise Bouttier. The tension that showed then was multiplied as he walked toward the bright square of the ring later that day. On that second occasion his eyes were moist.

He was moved too much by the thought of what he was about to do. Equally, in the future Jean-Claude Bouttier may be moved too much, too hurtfully by the knowledge of what he cannot do.

Sugar Ray Leonard v. Thomas Hearns, Las Vegas, 16 September 1981

Sugar Ray and the Hit-Man

Professional boxing suffers from a permanent glut of expert opinion and over nearly every big fight there looms a garbage mountain of ill-conceived and arrogantly delivered prediction. But this one is different. For once, more minds than mouths are open as Sugar Ray Leonard and Thomas Hearns work through the last increasingly tense days before a meeting that will make one of them the undisputed welterweight champion of the world and earn for both of them sums of money that wouldn't look out of place in a national budget.

In Las Vegas circumspection is almost as much of an eccentricity as sleep, but lifelong lungers are rediscovering caution and so far the betting emporia offering odds on the fight have remained conspicuously unstormed. The leading bookmakers here see the two men as evenly matched down to the last decimal point (at Caesars Palace, the casino hotel where the most profitable altercation in boxing history is being staged, you can bet either one at 6–5 on) and few among the thousands who are willingly crossing the desert to pay up to $500 a seat for a view of next Wednesday's action, can detect a punishable flaw in the layers' assessment. Only deep reserves of intuition or prejudice could permit someone to be dogmatic about what will happen when Leonard, whose speed, spontaneous ingenuity and technical range make the word virtuosity unavoidable, collides with the outlandish physical attributes of Hearns, who has a reach that is a threat to chins in the next county and develops enough leverage when he punches to knock down a small building. Having no particular resentment of buildings, he has contented himself with battering men and all but two of the 32 victims he has claimed in an unbroken run of success as a professional have made an early and often hazy return to the dressing-room.

Meanwhile, since emerging as perhaps the most brilliant Olympic champion of 1976 in Montreal, Leonard has been paid upwards of $25 million for the 31 fights that have seen him move steadily towards the World Boxing Council welterweight title, relinquish it briefly and then regain it from Roberto Duran on a night when the amazing Panamanian, who had previously been less readily subdued than a forest fire, went out with ignominious tameness.

With such credentials on both sides, and Leonard's WBC championship as well as Hearns's World Boxing Association title on the line, it is not surprising that the unlikely group of promoters drawn together by the event – lawyers, a rock concert impresario and a college basketball coach – have a hard time keeping the euphoria out of their voices when they report on how the tickets are going. The unsentimental people who run Caesars Palace foresee no problems about taking the $6 million needed to give them the profit they demand of the 25,000-seat temporary arena built alongside the hotel. And that gate money is only a fraction of the return expected by Caesars, where anyone seeking a room over the next few days had better be able to prove that he has the kind of credit back home to allow him to bleed away $20,000 at the gaming tables. The guaranteed presence of high rollers is the factor that has made this Las Vegas hotel the new headquarters of world boxing, leaving traditional strongholds like Madison Square Garden to squirm impotently as plans are worked out to construct the cliffs of scaffolding that will support the 30,000-odd live spectators who are likely to watch Larry Holmes defend his heavyweight championship against Gerry Cooney around March of next year. Those stands will probably be erected above the track being laid for the Grand Prix motor race to be hosted next month by Caesars, an organisation sufficiently brash to think about operating its own space shuttle if satisfied there are big enough bucks to be hustled.

Keeping distant company with those of us at ringside will be a television audience of 300 million. They will be scattered about the globe but, naturally, the huge majority will be concentrated in closed-circuit locations around the United States and the sales figures for these are already extraordinary. Radio City Music Hall in New York disposed of its 6,000 seats before an advertisement had appeared in a paper. The entire promotion is nearly certain to gross close to $40 million, which will leave the huge earners of the past, notably Leonard–Duran I and Ali–Holmes, trailing. Once the technology associated with the swiftly growing pay-TV market is properly into its stride in a year or so, even these figures – and the $10 million or more that Leonard should put in the bank (Hearns, much less dramatically rewarded throughout his career, will collect maybe half as much) – are sure to be dwarfed. All sense of perspective is liable to disintegrate when we remember that just after the Second World War Sugar Ray Robinson, generally acknowledged to be as great as any fighter in living memory, took his welterweight championship into the ring against another master of the trade, Kid Gavilan, in a New York fight that was given second billing on the card and cost only $40,000 in purse money. Today Robinson would have to hire a train to take his wages home.

As this reporter's mind, more accustomed to wrestling disconsolately with the implications of the electricity bill, reels away from the financial miasma of Leonard versus Hearns it is at once a relief and a thrill to encounter convincing evidence that the two principals are driven essentially by a desire to gain the kind of credit that has nothing to do with banks. They know that the history of their unforgiving business will see each as the yardstick of the other and each wants desperately to be champion with a validity that extends beyond his own era. They approach the test with all the seriousness it warrants but without bitterness. Hearns, whose 22-year-old face ages towards bleakness when he sets its small features behind the moustache and sparse tuft of goatee beard in preparation for going to work, lets the expression relax to fit the soft, attractive voice when he speaks of his liking for Leonard as a man and respect for him as a boxer. The reciprocation seems equally sincere. When asked if he was experiencing any of the harsh animosity he had felt towards Roberto Duran, Leonard's almost beautiful face opened into the smile that always tempts photographers to check their light meters. 'There's no possible comparison,' he said. 'Thomas Hearns is a nice young man. I like the guy. But that Duran ... wheeee ... man ...'

Still, neither of them will have any qualms about inflicting hurt on Wednesday evening. Gauging their relative abilities to do so is scarcely simplified by the word of how they spend some of their time away from the training sessions. Thomas (the Hit-Man) Hearns apparently has an enthusiasm for teddy bears, is uncomfortable if he has to sleep without one and prefers to do his box-watching with such a cuddly item at his side (if he has taken in some of the American programmes I have come across lately, the teddy bear must feel insulted). Leonard, when not relaxing with the attractive wife and young son who have adjoining rooms in his suite, likes to watch horror movies. 'He enjoys seeing that crazy stuff where people are getting their heads cut off or monsters are coming out of closets,' says Mike Trainer, the attorney mainly responsible for filling most of the Leonard closets with money. Decapitation, or a fairly gruesome modification of it, is the treatment the Hearns camp have been promising Leonard. 'Ray, it's only gonna take one punch,' declare the yellow T-shirts worn by the droves of bucket-carriers and purveyors of obscure assistance who flurry around Hearns at training in the bare, airless Sports Pavilion of Caesars Palace.

The WBA champion has been steered up out of the Kronk gymnasium in the hostile wasteland of Detroit's West Side by his manager-mentor Emanuel Steward, a 37-year-old black man with high intelligence sharpened by survival courses in the street, a forcefully persuasive nature and personal ambition so intense that it comes out of him in waves. It was outrageously optimistic of the manager to write to the World Boxing Association last week 'respectfully demanding' that Leonard be made to put up his WBA light-middleweight (154 lb) championship along with the welterweight titles at stake here. But a respectful demand is about the least aggressive approach anyone can expect from Emanuel Steward. Many, including Leonard, insist that Steward has stifled Hearns's independence, made him a mechanical, programmed fighter, first cousin to a robot. 'Steward walks around like a big shot,' says Leonard. 'He has taken advantage of Tommy Hearns's career to make himself better known than Tommy. I have no affection for the guy.'

Leonard will have much less, says Steward, after Wednesday. He is impatient with those who argue that his man has been hiding a clutch of severe technical limitations behind the advantages derived from being 6 ft 1 in tall, having a reach of 78 inches and being able to punch with freakish power against men too incompetent, and sometimes too petrified, to get out of the way. That reach is four inches longer than Leonard's but the critics say that Hearns's considerable residue of amateurishness will make it easy for Sugar Ray, who knows a bit about the geometry of the ring and has a dazzling flow of countering combination punches, to neutralise the unusual height and length of arm. 'That's what they'd like to believe,' says Steward. 'But Tommy has proved, amateur and pro, that he can box. He won't go in blasting like a madman. He has the left jab and the overall flexibility to set Leonard up and the hand-speed to take the chance when it comes.' Hearns, who can talk engagingly on his own behalf, elaborates convincingly on that theme but the emphasis has been on strength as he has sparred ferociously for up to a dozen rounds a day with about 15 different helpers. Several have been world-ranked middleweights, and lighter men were understandably scarce after one young prospect, Marlon Starling, had his jaw broken by a blow with an 18-oz glove.

Leonard does not mean to be available for the jaw-breakers. He and his impressive corner partnership of Janks Morton and Angelo Dundee see his fluency of foot movement, especially the lateral slides that will take him away from Hearns's right and then back in to unload with explosive speed and deadly variety to the head and body, as the key superiority. Eddie Futch, a tutor at least as widely admired and rather more venerable than Morton and Dundee, is sceptical. 'I don't care how much lateral movement a guy has, in order to punch he must come to you and when he comes he's got to bring that head,' says Futch. He tips Hearns but Eddie is a Detroit man.

Leonard's riposte is unforced. 'I know how to fight Tommy Hearns, how to deny him leverage for his power, which definitely is awesome if you let him use it. I won't run because that would give him his distance and momentum. I'll be there all the time but not directly in front of him, where he wants me. I'll move, keep him off balance when I'm outside and punish him when I'm inside, where he can't work effectively. He won't cope with my tempo, my range of movement and my variety of punching.'

Unsurprisingly, Dundee agrees. 'Ray will have a dozen answers for anything Tommy can do. This kid could feint you out of your jockstrap and I'll tell you something else – he'll be the puncher in this fight. He's juiced up. He's hot for it.'

No one will count on staying cool in the ring on Wednesday. Specially reinforced television lighting will raise the temperature by 20 degrees and at the relevant time of 7.30 p.m. that could mean a reading close to 100. Psychological sweats may be more decisive, however, and the younger, rawer Tommy Hearns could be the victim. His confidence has been nourished by the repetitive spectacle of opponents keeling over and, if Leonard refuses to go early, Hearns's self-belief may wilt. Sugar Ray Leonard survived a frightening ordeal against Duran in their first fight. He went to the bad place and came back a mature hero of his game. I have taken a little of the 6–5 on, and I think he has enough talent to carry even that ominous burden.

Lou, Duane and Good Old Chuck

After a championship fight whose best rounds were fierce enough to justify heat shields and asbestos balaclavas at the ringside, all the arguments about points-scoring are bound to seem insultingly academic. But they are far less offensive than the lack of perception and common sense afflicting the three Nevada judges who, in Las Vegas on Wednesday night, came within four and a quarter minutes of contriving a result that would have been scandalous even by the fairly elastic standards of professional boxing.

If Sugar Ray Leonard's battering assault had not forced the referee to take the outrageously brave Thomas Hearns into protective custody after one minute 45 seconds of the 14th round, the distortions already perpetrated on the scorecards of those judges would have made a draw or a defeat for Leonard a real possibility. At the start of the 14th one of them, Chuck Minker, had the World Boxing Council welterweight champion trailing by 125 points to 121, while Duane Ford showed Hearns leading 124–122 and Lou Tabat favoured him by 125–122. These figures had been produced by incompetent and irrational application of a system that gives ten points to the winner of a round and is meant to reflect his superiority in the lower total allocated to the loser. Logically, three minutes of pretty closely contested action might be scored 10–9. Where there was a huge difference in the quality and effectiveness of the work done, the marking might be 10–8 and if one man all but overwhelmed the other 10–7 would be legitimate.

There was no hint of such an acceptable coherence in the judgements of the men appointed to monitor the dramatic fluctuations witnessed in sweaty temperatures under a darkening sky by the film stars, politicians, gamblers, sportsmen and hard-case fight fans who contributed to an audience of 23,600 in the temporary arena set up over the tennis courts of

Caesars Palace Hotel. You didn't have to be John McEnroe, who was in a front-row seat, to object to the way the shots were called. Had Hearns survived that 14th round, he would presumably have lost it by a two-point margin on all three cards, as was the case in the violently one-sided 13th. However, had Leonard's exertion diminished his own aggressive capacity by the start of the 15th (and an earlier passage of the fight indicated that to be quite likely), Hearns might have been able to struggle through that last round without suffering really spectacular damage. It would then have been impossible for him to lose.

By keeping the discrepancy to one point in the last he would have left Tabat's scoring all square and the advantage given to Leonard by Duane Ford would have been neutralised by good old Chuck, who should not be allowed out without a guide dog. And, of course, if the World Boxing Association champion had managed as much as final-round equality on one card he would have won, and Thomas Hearns, not Sugar Ray Leonard, would now be the undisputed master of the world's welterweights. Apparently some of the world's millions who watched the fight on television saw nothing wrong with the judges' scoring or its implications. They must be granted the indulgence due to anyone who is at the mercy of the camera's inability to maintain a true perspective, its failure to differentiate consistently between blows that make genuinely telling contact and others that mean little. But surely even such remote observers saw enough to make them disagree with the official view that it was reasonable to put Hearns 10–9 ahead in the fifth round, during which relevant hostility was scarce and the edge attained had to be small, and then divide the fighters by exactly the same degree in both the sixth and the seventh, when Hearns was the reeling victim of a sustained and profoundly damaging bombardment.

The brilliantly timed and executed left hook over his own lowered right hand that precipitated the troubles in the sixth was acknowledged by his manager, Emanuel Steward, to have had a numbing effect that was never fully cleared in the remaining rounds. Certainly he had only his unbelievable gameness and the vast reserves of natural strength contained in his elongated frame to prevent him from crumbling conclusively in the seventh. After those three minutes of controlled punishment from Leonard, whose venomous exploitation of virtuoso technique made it seem that the wrong party had been dubbed Hit-Man and Cobra, Hearns returned to his corner a hunched, almost shambling figure, unrecognisable as the supremely confident 22-year-old who began the night so assertively. To equate what Hearns achieved in round five with what Leonard inflicted in the two subsequent sessions is to compare a shower of rain with an air raid. That Tabat, Ford and Minker did so is testimony to their obsession with the convention that 10–8 is not warranted unless there is at least one count. They chose to ignore the fact that Hearns took the kind of beating that might have put an ordinary man in bed for a month. Their interpretations were as eccentric as that of the referee, Dave Pearl, when he decided against registering a knockdown in the 13th after a murderous, unhindered attack by Leonard ended with Hearns sprawling backwards through the ropes. He had been pushed, said Pearl. All of us had better hope we never encounter such pushing in a bus queue.

When a resumption of the mayhem left Hearns squatting miserably by the same part of the ropes before rising shakily to take a standing count that was interrupted by the bell, the judges could not avoid recording a two-point inferiority on their cards. Three points would not have been out of order and that sort of marking, along with the proper response to the sixth and seventh, would have rationalised their scores appreciably, if not quite enough to satisfy the majority of ringside watchers. 'Hell, a punch that your opponent hardly notices shouldn't mean as much as one that rings the guy's chimes,' said one of the most respected American boxing writers on Wednesday night. He agreed with a colleague who holds that the present scoring system should be replaced by one that gives zero to the loser of a round and awards the winner anything from a minimum of a single point to a maximum of five, a gulf so remarkable that it should bring about the automatic termination of the contest. Both insist convincingly that it is ludicrous to have the ten-point system when it requires something like a slaughter to create a two-point margin. They argue that the scoring should incorporate the old principle that 'the guy who gets beaten up is the loser'. This may appear to be a crude maxim but anyone who thinks that professional boxing can be reduced to a formalised metaphor of violence rather than the real thing, to a sport as bloodless as modern fencing, is deluding himself. You either take it for what it is or reject it. And if you accept its harsh realities you recognise that Ray Leonard practised them to far greater purpose than Thomas Hearns did on Wednesday. You accept that the calculations of Ford, Tabat and Minker were nonsensical.

Ford, when pressed about the peculiarity of giving the fifth round the same weight as the sixth, said it was 'a borderline 10–8'. Tabat would make no concessions. 'I don't have to justify anything,' he said. 'Has the spoiled kid been crying?' Leonard, in spite of a pervasive weariness and the painful swelling that had spread up from his cheekbone and nearly closed his left eye as Hearns's punches found and exacerbated a training injury, had no tears on Thursday morning. But there was a bitterness tinged with more paranoia than might be expected from a man of 25 whose midweek earnings should lift his gross profit from boxing close to $40 million. He was making a generalised accusation, certainly not homing in on Wednesday's judges, when he said: 'They don't want me to win. I can't win a close fight. If I don't stop a man, I'm going to lose. I accept that.' He feels that his success, his wealth, his golden-boy image are widely resented. 'They see this kid smiling and the smile rubs them wrong. They hear that I made a few millions and that bothers them.' In particular he senses animosity among many of the friends who grew up with him in Maryland. 'They all bet against me. These are guys who have gone to college and now they are working in a seven-eleven store [a reference to the supermarkets that stay open from 7 a.m. till 11 p.m.]. After they pay their bills maybe they can afford a six-pack of beer. They see a paper: "Leonard Makes Millions". They want to puke. They say, "That little guy, he's nothing much. I knew him all his life. What's he doing with that kind of money? I hope you get your butt whipped, Leonard."'

For Hearns, who tried so manfully to whip his butt, Leonard had nothing but warmth and expressions of respect once the war was over. It was a surprise that suggested miscalculations by Emanuel Steward when the 6 ft 1 in hero of Detroit's embattled ghettoes weighed in at 10 st 5 lb, 2 lb inside the welterweight limit, but he was, as ever, freakishly strong. The tall man's assurance, the long and jarring left jab and the constant threat of bombing right crosses made Leonard an apprehensively alert fugitive in the first two rounds and enabled Hearns to build a clear if less than towering lead by the end of the fifth. The next two were disastrous for Hearns and he lost the eighth too, but in the ninth he was encouraged by evidence that Leonard was temporarily punched-out and worried about the left eye. From then until the 12th Hearns, reversing roles to become the smooth, circling, jabbing boxer, did reasonably well in a quiet way. But Leonard had not forgotten that his earlier, frighteningly destructive spell had been engineered by going flat-footed and sliding into the danger area, boldly drawing and slipping Hearns's heavy stuff to make openings for his own selective fire. In the 13th he rediscovered his stalking energy and the results were devastating. The 14th was unrelieved calamity for Hearns and referee Pearl said later that he noted between 24 and 28 hurtful and unanswered punches before he stopped the fight.

Those of us who were seated a few feet in front of Leonard's wife and seven-year-old son at that time shuddered at the thought of how they would have reacted had the flood of pain been submerging Sugar Ray. As it was, one reporter believed he had heard them pleading with Leonard to quit but when their group shouted, 'Let's go home, Sugar,' they meant him to exit over a prostrate Hearns.

Mrs Leonard proved there was no bad blood by laying a kiss on Tommy's cheek afterwards. He in turn praised the winner as 'a hell of a person' and a great fighter but said the stoppage was premature and there must be a rematch. 'Detroit, I shall return,' he declared resonantly.

First Leonard, who wants to remain at welterweight for the time being, would like to silence Aaron Pryor, an unbeaten contender whose tongue can be as unruly as his behaviour often is between matches. Hearns might consider moving up to meet the wayward but immensely talented Wilfredo Benitez at light-middleweight, the division in which Leonard may soon be obliged to relinquish his World Boxing Association title.

Ahead for either of them there could be a high-earning confrontation with Marvin Hagler, ruler of all the middleweights. Before long, however, there must be thoughts of putting Leonard and Hearns together again. If that happens, no one who has any sense will be writing off the younger man but Leonard's equipment becomes more impressive by the day. 'Ray is not just an accomplished boxer – he's an accomplished human being,' says Mike Trainer, the lawyer who manages the champion's extensive financial interests. 'He's not a wise-ass. There are boxing people who mistake intelligence for wise-assery.'

What boxing people don't usually misunderstand is a talent for fighting. Even the astonishing firm of Tabat, Ford and Minker might see the point about Sugar Ray the next time their business mixes with his.

Fighting for Freedom

Filed from New York after spending a day in Rahway State Prison, New Jersey, September 1981

American fighters train in establishments you are not likely to confuse with a Knightsbridge health club. Just the smell on the stairway leading up to Muhammad Ali's old sweatshop at the Fifth Street Gym in Miami is a reminder that the game has its roots in pretty crude places and anyone who tried to walk across the desperate streets of West Detroit to Thomas Hearns's alma mater, The Kronk, could expect to arrive in a plastic bag – or several.

When it comes to training quarters with a hard-nosed reputation, however, the title-holder is to be found 20-odd miles along the Jersey Turnpike from New York City. James Scott, who is one of the leading light-heavyweights in the world, conditions himself there and so do seven more professionals and about 40 amateurs. Whatever their other deficiencies, those boxers don't lack discipline. They are inmates of Rahway State Prison, one of New Jersey's maximum security penitentiaries, a house of correction whose 1,170 residents include men mean enough to make Bad, Bad Leroy Brown yell for his mammy. Some of the more theatrically frightening prisoners take regular sessions with batches of juvenile delinquents from the surrounding area, little seminars that are meant to show the adolescents what is up ahead if they graduate to serious crime. A few of the niceties of prison life, such as male rape, are vividly evoked. The theme is rehabilitation, or at least deterrence, by terror. British television audiences recently saw how the scheme operates in a documentary called 'Scared Straight'.

The Scared Straight project and the boxing programme at Rahway are both in the charge of the same man, a stocky (5 ft 7 in but strong enough

129

to tackle heavyweights before his amateur boxing career ended) lieutenant in the prison service named Alan August. His involvement in such attempts at regeneration draws approval from liberal onlookers but August is no bleeding heart. Even at work, in his open-necked shirt and beige suit with a metal badge the size of a door-knocker hanging over the handkerchief pocket, he does not bring do-goodery of the Lord Longford school immediately to mind. His rigidly coiffured hair, the wide, dark moustache and a voice shaped in Elizabeth, New Jersey, are all more appropriate to the line of employment he plans for himself: 'If there is a big sale for the book I'm writing about my experiences, I'm gettin' outa here, gonna buy a nightclub. Air traffic controllers tell you they have a stressful job but they should try this.' As a man who has had, at different times, one inmate sitting on his chest with a knife at his throat and another rudely interrupting a committee meeting to batter him unconscious with a piece of wood torn from a corridor bench, August is entitled to talk about stress but he is anxious to emphasise that the relationship between the staff of 400 at Rahway and the prisoners is probably better than that at any comparable institution in the United States. He says there have been only three suicides and two murders within the walls in the 13 years he has been there. That, considering the calibre of client, is amazing.

August feels that the boxing programme has helped to keep the peace and Peter J. Fenton, the Superintendent of Rahway, agrees with him. Fenton is black and that is not remarkable, since two-thirds of this prison's population are black and the remaining third is split between whites and Hispanics. For photographer Michael Brennan and myself, the Superintendent's office acted as a kind of decompression chamber in reverse, a place to ease the adjustment between the normal world and the depths of Rahway. The penitentiary had begun to have an oppressive effect even as we approached its surprisingly low, straw-coloured mass across the industrial flatlands of New Jersey. Initial entry was through the glass doors of a foyer as innocent as a hospital's and, with identity established and Augie as escort, we were soon drinking coffee with Mr Fenton. It was only later, as we passed into the working area and the cell blocks, that we had our hands branded with a stamp that would show up under special light beams and forced ourselves to lose count of how many walls of steel bars we stepped through and how many doors were slammed and locked behind us.

'I came from an inner-city background myself and I learned to box before I learned to speak,' said the Superintendent. 'It's in you. Some people when they reach the age of 40 will still think they can resolve every problem with their fists. It's all they know. That type of man won't sit still to learn carpentry or become a mason. He won't go through the educational programme.

'We have quite a number of people here whose natures tend to be on the violent side. Since they were kids on a ghetto street corner they have been that way. We give them an opportunity of exhibiting their wares, show-casing their talents in a legitimate way. Not only can they use their fists but they can earn money doing it.'

James Scott, who at 35 has been in prison most of his adult years and is now serving life for a first-degree murder alleged to have been committed to cover up an armed robbery, is the programme's star and his professional fights inside the fortified perimeter of Rahway – several of them covered by nervous cameramen of national television – have earned him $110,000. Most of that purse money has gone in fees to lawyers who are having an uphill struggle to persuade society to take a more benevolent view of him. When Scott was found guilty of the armed robbery, perpetrated in Newark in 1975, he was sentenced to a term of 30 to 40 years but the jury then was unable to decide if he was guilty of murder. Lieutenant August is convinced that the revival of the murder charge, and the holding of a belated and conclusive second trial, had something to do with the provocative publicity created by Scott's successes as a convict-boxer.

Not all Scott's earnings are spent on his case. He is allowed to pay out $104 a month for the steak and eggs he consumes relentlessly every day. The other prison boxers are given an enriched diet at the State's expense for a short period before their matches. 'These guys aren't sitting around eating lobster tails,' Superintendent Fenton points out. 'It's mainly a matter of getting a piece of high-protein meat to give strength. There are 200 other people in the prison who are on special diets because that is what they need. So nobody looks on this as any kind of rip-off.

'Apart from the benefits for those guys who are active as boxers or trainers, timekeepers or referees on the programme – we have one person who made it back out on the street, took his referee's licence and is refereeing fights out there – the boxing has many good side-effects for the whole population. The institution is safer because we are channelling the violence of inmates who might otherwise be acting out on those around them, bumping people, showing macho-energy. The disciplinary record is much better. And I think the population feel far better because of what our boxers have done. They appreciate the distinction of being the only institution that has major televised boxing shows, of having their own guys perform and being able to watch along with the world.'

There is always a clamour of outsiders who want to be in the small live audience at the Rahway fights. 'You get Assemblymen, police chiefs, all kinds wanting to be in on a little bit of history,' says Fenton. 'They go around talking about it for three months afterwards.' Such tourists are always well segregated from the main body of prisoners, who usually watch on closed-circuit television in their cells. If those lonely spectators envy the boxers and their attendants, that active group are in turn demanding more freedom than they are likely to get. They are asking to be permitted to go through the gates and into the outside world for fights.

That would, as Lieutenant August says, produce nightmare problems of security, perhaps the need to frisk everyone who entered a public hall. But when we met half a dozen of the convict professionals and their trainers in a bare-walled office deep within the prison the talk of going on fighting expeditions outside filled the room with forlorn imaginings. The sheets of paper pinned on the noticeboard gave the schedule for urinary examinations and other depressing punctuations of the prison routine, but the chat was all of Atlantic City, the Vegas of the Jersey shore. Dressed in casual civilian clothes or tracksuits, exchanging relaxed banter with the officer they call Augie, the men exuded a sense of privilege, none more so than Scott. All the others deferred to 'Scottie', some with a reverence blatantly infected with fear. He took their diffidence as natural. Modesty is not one of his handicaps. Dwight Braxton, who recently obliged Scott to accept only his second defeat in 22 fights, had also done time in Rahway and said before the meeting that he remembered the other man 'walking around like he had a Superman cape on his back'.

Scott fought a strangely reticent, largely retreating fight against Braxton. He was still bothered by a healing cut when he went into the ring but there seems a chance that the defeat was associated with his age, from which he subtracts two years, and the fact that neither he nor the Rahway ambience could intimidate the alumnus in the opposite corner. His talk of the occasion now does not have the ghetto enforcer's ring of earlier utterances. 'They don't give me credit for the way I fought and beat Braxton,' he says unconvincingly. 'Most fighters go out of the game with scar tissue, and stuttering. You want to go out so that you can enjoy the money you make. You don't want to be throwing a punch every time a bell rings.'

Scott's skin is noticeably lighter than that of the other men who were in the room. His face often affects a look of street knowingness and his physique, prodigiously developed in the endless hours available for training, is sufficient to discourage anybody who thinks he might not know as much as he makes out; he does. He had come down from his personal office to be with us and he soon made it clear that he felt interviewers should be as readily influenced as the other inmates: 'You writers can be helpful by pushing us guys towards true championship contention. The boxing programme should never have been started if they don't intend to give us title shots. I was ranked number two by the World Boxing Association and then they dumped me in 1979 because I couldn't get release to fight outside the prison. We should be allowed out, even if we have to go handcuffed. Tell them that. Don't write the conventional article. You got to put some exciting adverbs in there. Tell them about that English guy John Gully.'

Gully was a Bristol man who emerged from debtors' prison at the beginning of the nineteenth century to become heavyweight champion of England and a Member of Parliament. Scott's knowledge of him probably comes from *The Ring Record Book*, although there is much less narrow literature – collections of essays, books on psychology, history, public speaking – piled beside the TV set and in front of the loaded rack of clothes in his cell. His mention of John Gully had obvious significance. We are told that Gully's boxing ability encouraged admirers to pay his way out of jail. 'We are fighting for recognition and freedom,' said one of Rahway's boxers, expressing the dream of an early parole that is behind all their sweating in the gym and suffering in the ring. They want to fight for titles first, if not a world title then a US title or at least a national prisons title. But they hope for more than that. There is, inevitably, much talk of having been framed or unjustly sentenced. 'I'm only in here for a $230 robbery,' says Scott – and, at another point, 'Locking you up, it has a diminishing effect.' So too, thought the visitor, has blowing someone away with a handgun.

As he showed us out of Rahway, Lieutenant August paused by a filing cabinet to produce three weapons that had been made by prisoners in unofficial handicraft sessions. One was an almost perfect sheath knife, another a mallet whose head detached from the handle to reveal a six-inch spike and the third a heavy laundry pin twisted into a deadly sticking tool. The boxing programme creates an atmosphere in which such items are less likely to be used, although August admits that one member of the team missed a fight after being found quietly manufacturing a bomb. 'He is a good fighter but he can be a pain in the ass,' said the lieutenant.

August looked thoughtful as we left, like a man wondering where to put the dance floor in a nightclub.

Part Four

Part Four

... and the Omega

As I have suggested earlier in this book, Muhammad Ali could have done himself and his legend a favour by retiring after his third fight with Joe Frazier in Manila. Instead he fought on for six more years, making a bad exit inevitable. But first there were a few good times, such as the reclaiming of the world heavyweight title from Leon Spinks in New Orleans (a win that gave Ali the unequalled distinction of holding the championship for a third time). The conversation I had with him before that fight was one of the most bizarre and entertaining even he ever contributed to my experience as a reporter.

He talked up a storm again before he fought Larry Holmes in Las Vegas but in the ring there he was a pathetic nonentity, an insult to what he had been. In the Bahamas, against Trevor Berbick, he compounded the insult. That was an abysmal episode, just about as depressing as a sports event can be. Of course, a far deeper sadness surrounded Ali once it became clear that his long career in boxing had caused him to be progressively ravaged by Parkinsonism.

Dreaming of Another World

Nowhere, not in Kuala Lumpur or Manila, beside the log-cabin mosque at his camp on a Pennsylvania mountain or by the turgid sweep of the Zaire River, has Muhammad Ali ever contrived a less likely or forgettable setting for the utterance of his dreams. He was lying naked under the stars, stretched on a quilt that was laid out behind the low hedge that screens the brick-floored patio from a patch of neat lawn at No. 463 on a street called Topaz in a middle-class suburb of New Orleans. It was shortly after five o'clock on Thursday morning and he had just run for 30 minutes through the heavy Louisiana night, pounding out three or four miles along the shores of a nearby lake as part of the unwontedly rigorous training schedule he has imposed on himself in preparation for what the T-shirts of the faithful are hailing as the Third Coming: his attempt next Friday night to win his return match with Leon Spinks and so become the first man ever to reign three times as heavyweight champion of the world.

Now, as the insects whirred in the trees along Topaz, anticipating the muted sound of the water sprinklers that would go to work when the hot dawn came up, he was a sprawling shadow outside the front door of the house he had rented to take him away from his besieged suite and the thronged lobbies of the Hilton Hotel downtown. As always, he had remained modest enough to leave a small towel draped across his thighs, although he had no company here other than a couple of bodyguards from the New Orleans police department (who seemed about as sensitive as the guardians of the law usually are in the Deep South), his Cuban masseur, Luis Sarria, two of the bucket-carriers from his entourage who had come hustling out from the Hilton after being left sleeping when the boss started his run even earlier than usual, and two reporters from London who had ridden the helpers' coat-tails in the knowledge that Ali is at his least strident and most captivating if caught in those still and private hours when most of the world is abed.

Sarria rubbed the soles of Ali's feet and, as he relaxed, that compartment of his head that is constantly engaged in the production of his own Superman cartoons began to work overtime. His voice was a soft, confidential drone as the images of dramatic happenings, past and to come, crowded his imagination. He started quietly by insisting that he really meant it this time when he said that the defeat of Spinks would be his last fight. It was true that several earlier threats of retirement had rapidly dissolved but now, with his 37th birthday only four months away, the cruelty of training was becoming unbearable and the need to translate himself into a new and wider context was too urgent to be denied, he told us. To achieve that translation ideally, however, it was necessary to assert yet again his uniqueness as a boxer, necessary to put the 25-year-old

138

upstart Spinks in his place, reduce him to the role of a bit-player in the cosmic events enacted around The Greatest.

Ali's voice became animated, vivid with prediction. 'So I'm out there with him in the Superdome, and the world is amazed. This ain't the fat man that took him casual in Las Vegas last February, that didn't train or eat good, that listened to all the talk about how easy he would be, saw him as just a kid out of the amateurs with seven nothin' pro fights to his name, a novice who didn't belong in the ring with the best heavyweight of all times. No, this is the real Ali, lookin' beautiful and movin' fast, goin' for him from the first bell, attackin', attackin', no rest, crowdin', hurtin', pop, pop, with the jab, then the right hand, the hooks, the combinations, pressure he can't take. It's a mismatch, by seven or eight it can't go on, the referee is jumpin' in to stop it. It's all over. Muhammad ALLEE is champion of the world for the third time. This is a miracle . . . and then I go and pick up my briefcase, get in my Lear jet and fly off to see some President of a country somewhere.'

'Can I go?' asked Lloyd Wells, who is one of the 22 people here on Ali's payroll for this fight and was getting ready at that moment to list in a notebook the sequence and number of punishing abdominal exercises his employer would soon perform on the rubbing-table.

'Yeah,' said Muhammad absently, while Sarria's hands fluttered, black as crows, over the oil he had spread in a glistening film on a body already looking harder and more athletic than it has done in three years. At one point Sarria hovered like a diviner above the stomach, then tapped gently to elicit a hollow sound.

'Water,' he said, using one of his few words of English.

'I know,' said Ali, 'from now till the fight we'll cut it right down, dry out and lose five or six pounds more and go in there about 218. No more of Dick Gregory's juice and vitamin mixtures. They're keepin' weight on me.'

'I could kiss you for that,' said Lloyd Wells, leaving the outsider to wonder if the reaction was unconnected with resentment of Gregory, the comedian turned humanitarian activist and nutritional expert who has been advising Ali on diet and advocating in particular the virtues of lemon and lime juice and of kelp. Jealousies are intense and bitter among the motley group that draw sustenance from the great fighter's generosity and, although Gregory can be financially independent of the intrigues and hypocrisy, he cannot escape being a target for the backbiting.

Stretched on the table, placed like an incongruous fugitive from a gymnasium in the middle of the well-furnished suburban living-room, Ali was letting his thoughts drift up and away from such squalid trivia as pay cheques. 'Think of what it will mean to be the first man ever to win the heavyweight title three times. That's somethin' worth taking a lot of hurt for. It's somethin' I'll have for the rest of my days. Each morning when I wake up, whether the sun is shining or there's rain or snow, that will be there. You can lose an arm or your health, your wife or your life, but they can't take that away from you. Nobody could deny I was the greatest, greater than Marciano or Louis, greater than Jack Johnson. Wherever I went, people would say, "There he goes, there ain't never been nobody like him." Think of how it would help me in my work with my new project, my real life's work, the WORLD organisation.'

WORLD (the initials stand for World Organisation for Rights, Liberty and Dignity) is a little something he dreamed up while hob-nobbing with Brezhnev on his recent visit to Russia. The concept envisages persuading tens of millions of his admirers around the globe to pay a membership fee of $25 a head to provide the basic financing for a headlong assault on every major problem on earth, from famine to leprosy to racism. Earlier, on the patio, soliloquising about a scheme he claims is so far advanced that the US Government should be approving tax exemption 'in about a week's time', he indicated that, naturally, he would be putting all his accumulated resources at WORLD's disposal and that he had been promised specific assistance by friends as diverse as folk-singer Johnny Cash and President Muammar Gaddafi of Libya. 'Most of the hatred on the earth is because people don't understand each other. Americans hate Russians but maybe they wouldn't if they'd been there like I was. Ain't it somethin' that Brezhnev knew about me, that the hell I'd raised had reached him and he wanted to meet me? He made me a kind of ambassador to let folks in America know more about his country. I found there was a lot of peacefulness over there. I never saw so much peace in my life. In a grocery store you can put your money down on the counter and nobody will grab it. You can walk in a park at night and nobody will bother you. I'm not sayin' I'd like to live there. There's a lot that's dull about it. The clothes is dingy but it's for sure that everythin' ain't bad.'

The wonderful naïveté of his interpretation of life in the Soviet Union, like the simplistic optimism that sees WORLD as something between his own United Nations and the Red Cross ('It would take a thing as big as that to give me fulfilment after what I've already done'), seems at first to make stark contrast with the intensity of his professional effectiveness as a boxer. But both are fed by the deep reservoir of dreams in his nature. The difference is that as a boxer he has the will and the equipment to transmute fantasy into fact. Whether the alchemy will work once more at the age of 36, when he is faced with an opponent who is the living embodiment of fierce and hungry youth, is a question only the foolish answer glibly. Ali's respect for the question is declared in the extreme dedication he has brought to his training over the past two months. His attitude was exemplified at the house on Topaz on Thursday morning when the presence of myself and a colleague encouraged him to shatter his record for the total of abdominal exercises completed in a session, driving himself through more than 500 without a hint of cheating.

From the early summer days of running and chopping trees in

Pennsylvania to roadwork, callisthenics and serious sparring here in New Orleans, he has sweated in a way that has been alien to him since his third meeting with Joe Frazier in Manila in October 1975. When he disrobes at the Superdome next Friday the world will see his body just about as fit as he can make it at his age. But it is the erosion that remains invisible that will threaten him. Can all the systematic honing of his physique restore the swiftness of reflex, the judgement of distance and sharpness of timing that once made other heavyweights look as if they had sludge in their veins?

It is unlikely. For a long time now he has been reachable even with crude and ponderous punches and there has been no notable reversing of the trend in the latest sparring with a series of moderate partners. 'Guys who could only have waved to him in the old days now land solid,' says Harold Conrad, a New York aficionado who has been watching him throughout his professional career. 'Spinks is a natural fighting animal who just keeps coming with punches. Some are good and some are nothing, but there are so many of them that as long as he is in there he will lay plenty of hurt on Muhammad. He could even do the damage we have all been dreading if he stays there long enough. People say Muhammad threw away the first fight in Vegas with bad tactics, by playing about in the early rounds. But I'm not so sure it was a matter of tactics. With the doubtful condition Ali had then, if he had warred with Spinks early on he would have been knocked on his ass in the later rounds. As it was, he was able to hang on through 15 but Spinks kicked the shit out of him and won from here to Calcutta.

'This time Ali is in shape. He's worked like a sonofabitch. But that old bum with the white beard will be on the stool along with him and he could take the scythe to Ali's legs long before the 15th. So I think it would be crazy for Ali to go for a points win. I think he's got to street-fight this kid. He's gonna be at least 20 lb heavier, he's learned a lot of meanness in 58 pro matches and nobody has more fighting heart than he has. He should go out blasting at the first bell and try to ruin Spinks by halfway. It will be hard, for Leon don't discourage easily. But I believe Ali has one big night left in him and I'd bet on him to do the job.'

The diagnosis, the prescription and the prognosis are echoes of my own thinking about a conflict that could be one of the most melodramatic even Muhammad has provided. Leon Spinks, offering a gap-toothed stare of preoccupation under the flaring Afro as he moves through his training to the constant, amplified din of funky disco music (it tows him from the open doors of a van when he runs, shudders in waves about him in his gym at the Municipal Auditorium), is not seeking to con anybody when he presents a different script. His programme has been haphazard and not without its enervating diversions but he is likely to be much the same unremittingly aggressive force as he was last February. At 25, he has not learned the habit of apprehensiveness and perhaps he never will. Ali has had 50 professional fights more than he has but the 11-year discrepancy in age may be equally important.

'I am a natural fighter and a natural winner,' says Leon Spinks. Those are excellent credentials but next Friday night they may be invalidated by a man with more than a trace of the supernatural.

No Nemesis, Just a Novice

There was just too much history bearing down on Leon Spinks in the New Orleans Superdome on Friday night, and he was left feeling as mesmerised and helpless as a boy trying to shovel against an avalanche. Muhammad Ali's Third Coming to the heavyweight championship of the world was an exercise not so much in brilliance as in contrived inevitability. He and half the people on the planet wanted this victory so badly that Ali, having tortured his 36-year-old body in training to the point where it was once again an outrageous instrument of his ambitions, was able to spit on the calendar and turn the fierce youthfulness of Spinks into something humiliatingly self-destructive. Seven months ago, the 25-year-old from the St Louis ghetto looked like an inescapable Nemesis, a force strong and irreverent enough to close an era as he swarmed through the disintegrating remnants of his boyhood hero's resistance to take the title in Las Vegas. On Friday night he looked what his record said he should be: a brave and powerful novice, burdened with inexperience and the extreme limitations of a recently converted amateur.

These 15 rounds were less of a championship match than a procession, a New Orleans parade without a jazz band. There was scarcely a hint of serious discomfort as Ali established himself as the first heavyweight to take the title three times, and did so, unbelievably, more than 14 years after he first made monkeys of the forecasters by draining the ogre out of Sonny Liston. Here, after a first round in which his punches were extravagantly mistimed, he swiftly found distance and rhythm and set a pattern that frustrated and all but demoralised his opponent. Even when the three Louisiana officials had taken the fifth round away from Ali because they felt his holding during those three minutes amounted to fouling, none of them could leave him with a total of fewer than ten rounds. The referee, Lucien Joubert, gave ten to Ali, and four to Spinks, with one even, and so did one of the judges, Ernest Cojoe, while the second judge, Herman Duitreix, had it 11–4 with no even rounds. Few of the unofficial cards at ringside could credit the loser with any more, and many gave him less. It was a tribute to the persistence of his spirit that he took the 14th, and perhaps the 15th, too, as Ali's legs and arms began to tire after 40 minutes of astonishing fluency. But, leaving out the question of rule violations in the fifth, it was hard to accept that the defending champion had done more than share any of the other rounds.

Spinks had come to the ring with more handicaps than any young boxer could be expected to carry in only the ninth fight of his professional career. There were about 70,000 people in the soaring vastness of the Superdome (easily the largest indoor crowd boxing has known), and most of them – from the celebrities like Jackie Onassis and President Carter's mother, John Travolta and Kris Kristofferson, to beer-slugging red-necks on upper tiers so remote that they might have been in the next county – were vociferously prejudiced. Spinks was booed as he ducked through the ropes as champion, and, as if Ali's friends weren't enough of a problem, his own corner was such an overcrowded Babel of confusing advice that the one man most likely to provide a constructive theme between rounds walked away from the chaos after the sixth. George Benton, an outstanding middleweight when he fought out of Philadelphia, and now a skilled tutor who did much to channel Spinks's natural violence into profitable aggression in Las Vegas, had said during the champion's haphazard training that he was being prevented from offering maximum assistance. 'They're cutting my throat, stopping me from helping the kid,' he had said then. Now, as he moved disconsolately through the hysteria of the ringside audience, he muttered: 'What can I do? There are ten people up there in that corner. What can I do? There are too many amateurs up there.'

That was true, and the sad fact was that the boy wearing the gloves looked like one of them. Spinks had affected an unworried grin, showing the gumshield like a surrogate denture, as Ali danced away from his charges or repelled him with flicking jabs and single and double hooks in the early rounds. But his depression became blatant as Ali's strength refused to wane, as the older man blended glimpses of his former foot-and hand-speed with punishing improvisations learned over 18 hard years against the toughest men in the world, tricks that enabled him to war as well as box with such as Liston, Frazier and Foreman. Spinks felt the heel of the glove and the bare hardness of the forearms more than once. Above all, he found his most hopeful rushes smothered at birth by the holding that Ali has developed to a level where it has less in common with a boxer's survival technique than a wrestler's belligerence. Lucien Joubert, perhaps responding to the collective desire that came down in waves from the rim of the arena and with silent force from the countless committed millions beyond, permitted far more of that clutching, hauling and spinning than had been seen last February, and the challenger benefited from the referee's leniency.

But such questionable passages would have been rendered insignificant if Ali had not linked them with surges of selective, effective attacking, circling fleetly and watchfully, jabbing with increasing confidence and accuracy, sometimes hooking off the jab, releasing the occasional brisk combination of hooks and uppercuts, looking to land overhand rights, always adding to his overall control, causing his victim's eyes to cloud with the realisation that the discrepancy in class was irreversible. 'Get him, Lee,' a female member of the Spinks party at the ringside shouted repeatedly in a voice that grew more shrill as her man slid hopelessly behind. 'Beat him on his head. Give him what he give you.' 'I think he'll need something from that black bottle Ali reckons he used last time,' a sarcastic reporter suggested. By that stage, Leon looked in need of a soda siphon, and a chance to break it over Ali's skull.

Spinks had indicated during the preliminaries a heavy awareness of what an ordeal the evening would be. Ali was solemnly, almost morosely, undemonstrative, and any Muslim praying he did was unaccompanied by conspicuous gesture (he may, of course, have been relying on the celestial canvassing of his manager, Herbert Muhammad, son of the founder of the Black Muslims, who spent the entire contest with his eyes cast down and his lips moving silently while Angelo Dundee gave brisk advice and Bundini Brown and the others in the corner jabbered and whooped). After dropping on to his knees and closing his eyes for a long Catholic prayer, Spinks spent nearly a full minute before the bell embracing his brother, Michael, a fellow Olympic champion in Montreal. He appeared uncharacteristically conscious of the weight of the occasion, and that impression was reinforced later when he admitted to interviewing journalists that he had been unable to concentrate with the intensity that a title defence demands. 'My body was ready, but my mind wasn't on the fight,' he said, and quickly became bellicose when pressed on the strangeness of that omission. 'Maybe it was because I had a lot of other things on my mind, a lot of problems that come with the heavyweight championship,' he offered, eventually. 'Who knows? I don't. That just wasn't me in there, period. But I won't cry because I have lost once, it won't keep me from sleeping or from going back to the gym.'

Nor did it keep him from congratulating Ali or declaring that the master is still his idol. Ali in turn described Spinks as a gentleman and made the familiar prediction that the man he had just outclassed would end up as champion after he had gone. He made it clear, however, that he was in no hurry to step aside. 'The title is too hard to get,' he said. 'I'm not goin' to give it up without thinking. I'm going to sit down for six or eight months and think about it. Then I'll decide whether to fight again. I would never want to go out a loser. I've always wanted to be the first black man to retire undefeated, and to do it now after being champion three times would be somethin' no one could ever equal. I have made suckers out of all of you. I was training three months before you knew it.

'That couldn't have been Ali in that ring tonight. It couldn't have been the old man, the washed-up 36-year-old fighter dancin' through 15 rounds against a 25-year-old boy. M-a-a-a-a-a-n, that was a miracle, and can you imagine what it means? I was great in defeat, what will I be to the peoples of the world after this? I'm going to get on with settin' up my WORLD organisation to help the poor folks of the world, to help the hungry and those with diseases and famines and all kinds of problems.

'If you think I have done something now, wait till you see what I do as president of WORLD. We now have tax exemption, we now have a charter. We're going to have offices all round the world, an office in the Kremlin, an office in Bangladesh. I'm going to Moscow in about another month to see President Brezhnev. I told him I'd go back to see him after I regained my title. About 16 presidents have now given their approval to WORLD. It's going to be helping people all over the globe.'

When he listed the sources from which he had drawn help in beating Spinks, he began with Allah and moved by way of Dick Gregory and his vitamin-charged juices to the doctor who had prescribed 'half a pint of ice-cream and a big hunk of honey, 30 minutes before the fight'. There were plenty of smiles around the room, but few sneers. If he put on wellingtons to cross the Okinawa Deep we'd have to rate his chances at only slightly odds against.

Larry Holmes v. Muhammad Ali, Las Vegas, 2 October 1980

Shooting for Immortality

For nearly 20 years Muhammad Ali has been imposing an extravagant fantasy upon his life but somewhere, surely, reality is crouching in ambush, waiting to take revenge. It would seem that Larry Holmes is about to give reality some vigorous assistance. Ali has come back, less than four months short of his 39th birthday and after two years of debilitating retirement, insisting that next Thursday the most remarkable fist-fight ever to break out in a car park will make him the heavyweight champion of the world for the fourth time.

When he beat Leon Spinks in September of 1978 to become champion for the third time, the feat was unprecedented. But that match was for the World Boxing Association version of the title and Spinks was a raw upstart, lately out of the amateurs. This week it is the World Boxing Council championship that is at stake and Holmes, at the age of 30, is a mature and brilliantly equipped heavyweight who has won all 35 of his professional fights and stopped 26 opponents, including the seven who have challenged him since he took over his title slightly more than two years ago. If Ali can give eight years and a beating to such a man, we shall have to stop insulting him with words like miraculous.

He is, of course, joyously aware of the dramatic outrageousness of what he is attempting. As he leaves his training sessions at Caesars Palace Hotel in Las Vegas he is apt to part his white robe theatrically and declare:

'This is the first miracle.' The condition of his body is indeed astonishing. He has shed 30 lb, ridding his torso of the fat that enveloped it like a greasy, shapeless quilt a few months back. The pendant breasts have gone and as the skin has tautened across his chest and midriff the planes of his face have regained their previous handsome definition. To complete the impression of rejuvenation, he has used a black-blue dye on his hair and the overall effect is enough to make an ordinary 38-year-old man hide in a geriatric ward. Angelo Dundee, who has worked with Ali since the teenage days in Louisville, Kentucky, is not exaggerating when he says that the most vital appurtenance of his preparation for this challenge has been the mirror. Simple narcissism has always been a major tributary to the deep mainstream of his pride and there is no doubt that through the bleak slog of running and bench callisthenics and punishment in the gym he was sustained by the mirror's daily testimony that he was beginning to look pretty once again.

But the event scheduled for Thursday evening in a temporary outdoor arena specially constructed in the parking area of Caesars Palace (at a cost of $800,000 and with an attendance of 24,000 and gate receipts of $6 million in mind) is not a beauty contest. The question that only violence can answer is whether Ali's physique, which looks just about as trim and imposing as it did when he stunned the boxing world by making a physical and psychological wreck of the awe-inspiring George Foreman six years ago, still possesses the power, flexibility and capacity to endure that it did in Zaire and again in 1975 against Joe Frazier in Manila. That fierce collision in the Philippines with the noblest of all his rivals offered the most recent convincing glimpse of the greatness of Ali. He fought eight more times between that night and his retirement as a reigning champion in 1978 but none of the performances, not even the reversing of a humiliating defeat by Spinks, represented him at anything like his best. When he bowed out of the game it was with the acknowledgement that Holmes, already the holder of the WBC title, was the best heavyweight in the world and that fighting him would not be a good idea. How can anyone logically conclude that the intervening couple of years have improved Ali's chances? Yet in the betting shops along The Strip in Las Vegas Holmes can be backed at odds of 9–5 on, which is not a cripplingly short price for an ostensible good thing. Anybody who wants to bet on Ali can have no better than 7–5 against.

Some have sought to explain these odds by reference to the inevitable rumour that the fight has been made the subject of an arrangement, carefully choreographed to give Ali victory, set up a return and so on and on and on. Holmes dismissed these sinister fairy tales with bitter simplicity. When asked his price for throwing the fight, he said: 'My life.' It is unthinkable, he adds, that there should ever be a day when his three daughters would go to school and have other kids baiting them because their father couldn't beat Muhammad Ali when he was 38 years old. 'I'll tell you – if there was some dirty business, Don and I would find the mother that did it and git him.' The Don in question, who flows about as quietly as Niagara, is Don King, the promoter of Thursday's little *divertissement* and a man who has steadily been making himself more central to Holmes's career than the champion's official manager, the far-from-gruntled Richie Giachetti. King talks of Holmes as 'my son' but the hard facts of drawing power have obliged him to pay Ali $8 million while asking Larry to be content with $3.5 million plus a percentage of the revenue from the closed-circuit televising of the match across North America and in 40 or 50 countries around the world, including Britain.

On the basis of fatherly affection and economic self-interest, King would have no reason to look kindly on an 'arrangement' and his determination to be regarded as Mr Clean can only be intensified by the awareness that his name has already been linked with the FBI investigation into alleged wrong-doing in boxing. The promoter, who used a four-year prison sentence to extend his education and change the direction of his life after a manslaughter conviction interrupted his activities in the Cleveland numbers rackets, speaks freely about the investigation, as he does about anything else that is mentioned to him. Apparently believing that oratory begins and ends with vocabulary, he loads his sentences with dubiously pronounced polysyllables and then sprays them over his audience like buckshot. But he can be amusing on the FBI. 'I say I'm a bad nigger but I don't think I'm bad enough to take on the FBI. So don't put me in that position, that's a very untenable position for me. I don't want to play J. Edgar Hoover. I don't wanna mess with his spirit. I wanna leave him alone, let him lie quiet.'

The tone was less lighthearted when King turned to stories carried in a British Sunday newspaper that quoted a Harley Street neurologist as saying that films of Muhammad over the years betrayed symptoms of brain damage. King argued heatedly that such a long-range diagnosis should be challenged by the medical profession and by Muhammad himself, perhaps through a $2 million court action. Earlier, Dr Donald Romeo, who was appointed by the Nevada State Athletic Commission to examine Ali before this fight, referred scathingly to claims that the great boxer's kidneys and brain had been permanently damaged in the ring. 'So he takes some blows to the region of the kidneys and there's blood in his urine – big deal,' said the good doctor, who seems to have learned his bedside manner from James Cagney. 'It clears up in a day or two, end of story. They talk of brain damage? That's also a bunch of bunk.' Anyone who had just come from the Los Angeles hospital where young Johnny Owen lies desperately ill after suffering severe brain injury in his bantamweight title fight with Lupe Pintor was bound to wince at such words. Boxing can ill afford to be smug about this issue.

Somewhat more reassuring is the fact that three days of comprehensive tests at the famous Mayo Clinic in Rochester, Minnesota, gave Ali clearance to fight. When he went there on 22 July he weighed 237½ lb. The bound diary that records that information traces his daily progress in detail, work done and weight lost since he started serious training at the beginning of April. He was 251 lb on the fourth of that month (1 lb under 18 stone) and he was down to 221 lb last week. But is the streamlining merely cosmetic, or is he genuinely strong and fit? The best case for an affirmative answer is made by a bare, functional rubbing-table that is a jarring interloper in the main bedroom of Suite 301-2 at Caesars Palace, where the orange furnishings cosset everything but the eyes. It was on that kind of table that Ali toiled through an endless series of abdominal and back exercises to build the condition that made him too much for Spinks in New Orleans. Even more relentless torture has followed the runs he has been taking before dawn on a Las Vegas golf course. Two days ago the diary showed that an aggregate of 13,947 exercises had been completed. The statistic may have limited significance but it is an important symbol to Muhammad Ali, proof that he has paid his dues yet again and is ready to rumble. 'Look at me,' he said, dancing around the bedroom carpet in slacks and fitting shirt, throwing left jabs and crossing rights to within an inch or two of a nervous interviewer's face. 'Isn't that somethin'? I was a fat man, up to 253 lb. I wanted to get money in the bank. So I tricked Holmes into fighting me. If I had looked like this, he would never have agreed to fight me. My mother, my wife, everybody closest to me, they're all shocked by the change in me. I'm about as thin as I was when I fought Henry Cooper. No sugar, no soda, no soft drinks, no milk – just water, that and six months of steady work, that's what's done it.

'Now they're saying I only look good. Well, we'll see. That's their latest excuse. First I was too old and too fat. Now they're saying, "He's skinny and he looks pretty but he's not strong." That's as crazy as saying I've got brain damage. They'll find out on the night. Holmes is supposed to have a great jab but on a scale of 100 I'd say mine is 90 and his is 75. His combinations don't mean nothin'. I'll just cover up and wait till he gets tired.

'He runs out of gas by about the eighth or ninth round and I'll pressure him, wear him down. He'll look for me to dance, run, rope-a-dope. But I'll go straight for him from the first bell. If I can get that jab out and keep my distance, it's my fight. Holmes can jab but sometimes it don't come all the way. When that happens, pow! I'll get him with my straight right over the top.

'I'm shooting for immortality and I'm on the doorstep. Holmes can't beat me.'

While in Ali's suite, it is hard to remain insulated against his optimism. The place is charged with life, filled with his scurrying, chattering children and his womenfolk and sometimes with the less attractive presence of vying members of a bloated entourage, characters whose only visible quality is adhesion. The man supports enough people to populate a small country and he gives the impression that the well will never run dry.

But Larry Holmes can kill that illusion. All he has to do is fight to the true limit of his ability. He is magnificently fit and he knows that the threat to his mind is the most crucial. The heat exerted by Ali's personality can reduce an opponent's brain to a puddle of confusion. If Muhammad undermines him psychologically, then Holmes's one discernible physical deficiency, that tendency to run out of energy prematurely, may be disastrously exacerbated. The champion's attempts to compete verbally with Ali have been clumsy failures but he insists convincingly that it will be different in the ring. 'He was a great fighter but he has stepped out of his time into my time,' said Holmes. 'I was his sparring partner for four years and I know all there is to know about how he fights. Whatever he tries, I'll do what is needed to beat him, to knock him out. At a distance, I'll be too fast for him. I'll out-jab him. If he covers up, I'll break his ribs or murder his kidneys. If he wants to rassle, I'll show him a few holds. I'm going to stop him, retire him for good.'

Picking against Ali, the greatest hero figure modern sport has known, is extremely painful. But here it would be cowardice and hypocrisy to do otherwise. I believe the mirror is telling him lies. He may be the most celebrated victim of a looking-glass since the Lady of Shalott.

A Legend at Hazard

The ring activities of Muhammad Ali now have all the grace and sporting appeal of Russian roulette played with a pump-action shotgun. If he seriously considers inflicting on himself and his admirers across the world another experience like Thursday night's disaster in Las Vegas, there may be a case for taking him into protective custody. To go on trying to sustain the illusion that his middle-aged body can fight as effectively as it did ten years ago is, clearly, to risk grave physical harm, and that is not the only danger. His pride and his legend would also be at hazard, for there can be no doubt that if Ali, the most electrifying athlete of his and perhaps of any generation, ever again earned millions as negatively as he did last week he might begin to be mistaken for a fraud and a bore.

The talk about mounting another ill-advised and unjustifiable challenge for 'that other half' of the heavyweight championship currently held by Mike Weaver should be smothered immediately and for ever. Official prohibition of any such mad adventure is not easily achieved in a sport where supervision is ludicrously fragmented and altruism is giving away too much weight to the dollar. However, there should surely be particular efforts made by any who have a claim to leverage – from journalists and broadcasters to members of governing authorities – to preserve

Muhammad Ali from the penalties of his own fantasies and the avarice of some who might mislead him. It is impossible to exaggerate the pathetic discrepancy between the bankrupt Ali who succumbed so helplessly to Larry Holmes, failing to last the distance for the first time in his life, and the thrilling master who was too much in his time for such forbidding heavyweights as Sonny Liston, George Foreman and Joe Frazier. The unquestionable lesson is that it is no longer his time.

In the open-air arena at the Caesars Palace Hotel, all the emotional support from a naïvely optimistic majority in the crowd of 25,000 could not lift him out of his chronic torpor. As Holmes jumped the left jab into his mouth and patiently identified openings for crossing rights to the head and hooking attacks to the body, the man who had three times been champion of the world was reduced to making faces. And even those defiant expressions gave way to a betrayal of pain and confusion as each successive round brought nothing but more systematic punishment. Holmes has learned a great deal on his journey from the role of Ali's sparring partner to that of holder of the World Boxing Council heavyweight championship, with a professional record that showed 35 straight victories before this fight, and his cool, sharp, unhurried aggression piled discomfort on a challenger who was soon looking every day of his 38 years. But, before the evening was over, all of us who have a special attachment to Ali had reason to be grateful that the old man was being taken apart unvenomously by a pro (one who feels respect and even love for him) and not by a young slugger out to make a name through dramatic mayhem. 'There are a couple of kids around who might have killed Ali if they had been in with him as he was tonight,' one of the most knowledgeable American boxing writers said late on Thursday.

Ali's own ability to remain standing when hit by punches that would fell other strong heavyweights only increases the long-term threat to his well-being. 'Me being so proud, I wouldn't fall and I probably would have got hurt,' he acknowledged in a hoarse, weary voice on Friday morning. 'I didn't like the idea of stopping the fight at the moment they did. I didn't know who stopped it. Now I realise what happened and what *would* have happened to me, I'm glad they did stop it. I was gettin' tireder each round, I was gettin' weak. I've never been so drained in my life.' The fact that the steady slaughter was ended in the interval between the 10th and 11th rounds was, in large measure, Ali's reward for retaining the calm expertise and objectivity of Angelo Dundee in his corner throughout his career. There was some controversy and no little distortion afterwards when reporters sought explanations of the blatant rowing that took place at the time of the stoppage between Dundee and Drew 'Bundini' Brown, the erratic black man who has been corner-hand and amateur sorcerer to Ali over the years.

Brown's version was that he had wanted to pull Ali out two rounds before Dundee, as chief second, was ready to do so and that eventually he, Brown, had terminated the fight. But from a position a few yards away and on that side of the ring this observer gained the firm impression that Bundini's interventions had precisely the opposite motive. Dundee endorsed that view convincingly and with good humour. 'Did I stop the fight? Is the Pope a Polack? Sure I stopped it. It was my right. I was in charge of the corner. Bundini was grabbing at my sweater, hollering "One more round, one more round" but the well had run dry, there was nothing there to give. I'd told Ali as early as the fifth that if he didn't start throwing punches I was going to stop the thing. Then, when he took a really bad beating in the ninth, I knew that one more round was the absolute limit he could have, however much he wanted to go on. When the tenth just brought him more hurt, that was it. I didn't care what Bundini or anybody else said. They're saying that Herbert Muhammad as manager stopped the fight from the ringside but I didn't have to wait for word from Herbert. He gives me *carte blanche* when I'm in there.'

While the arguments swirled around his head after the relentless suffering of the tenth round, the loser sat silent and apparently remote on his stool, staring blankly ahead of him. He admitted next morning that he had not realised what was going on until he looked across the ring and saw Holmes's seconds lift their man off his seat and hoist his arms in a winner's salute. Ali made a miserable picture as he was assisted away from the ring. The flesh around both eyes was badly bruised and swollen and his face was a confession of exhaustion. Once back in Suite 301–2 of Caesars Palace he was given the drug ananase to help disperse the bruising and went to bed desperately worn out.

But he had enough spirit to joke quietly with Holmes when the champion came in to sit on the edge of his bed for a quarter of an hour. There was an unforced warmth in their banter.

'Man, you're bad,' said Ali.

'Look at the teacher I had,' Holmes answered. 'Hey, you ain't gonna fight again, are you?'

'Oh yeah, I'm comin' back for Holmes ... Holmes ... I want Holmes.'

'You wanna go a few more rounds now?'

'No, I'm tired.'

He was that all right but it did not keep him from being up again and on the apron of the ring at 4.40 a.m. Las Vegas time to perform for breakfasting New Yorkers (at 7.40 a.m. in their city) on the 'Good Morning America' show. A few breakfasts may have been spoilt when he borrowed from General Douglas MacArthur and declared: 'I shall return.' Many of us would be glad of someone to play the part of Harry Truman, who put MacArthur out to grass. Ali's lawyer, Michael Phenner, advised him to cut back on his speculation about meeting Weaver or the South African Gerrie Coetzee, who challenges the WBA champion in Bophuthatswana later this month, in any statements he made to the press on Friday. He agreed. 'I know they could chew up my ass,' he said. But his overall tone was chirpy enough. 'I feel pretty good,' he told Phenner, and added archly: 'We got the money all right, did we?'

He was still cheerful later in the morning when he came out wearing a black shirt, grey slacks and dark glasses to talk to those of us who had been permitted to pass through his private security force into the suite. 'I felt a lot worse after losing to Frazier and Norton and after beating Foreman,' he insisted. 'Frazier in Manila was terrible. I couldn't get up for the press conference. Psychologically, I am all right. You have to be a champion in losing as well as winning. If your attitude is controlled by your condition then the condition will conquer you. My attitude is in control. I make you think I'll die if I lose, that I'll jump off a building. But it don't bother me.'

That claim was as hard to accept as his rationalisations of why he had lost. The weight reduction that he had been hailing as a miracle a couple of days before was condemned as disastrous. 'I'd have fought better weighing 250 lb. Going from 260 to 217 was too much. I was slim, looking like I was when I started out, but I was weak. I was dehydrated. In ten rounds in that heat I didn't perspire. There was no sweat in me. I wasn't right at all. If I told you all the problems I had it would sound phoney and I don't like making excuses. One trouble was with my left arm, a pulled muscle. I couldn't throw my jab. In the gym I felt weak and the last two days I couldn't jog a mile. I didn't win a round. His sparring partners could do better than I did. I knew I was in trouble after round one. I sat on the stool and said to myself: "I'm in big trouble."' The memory produced the slow, warm smile that was to light up his abused face frequently during the day. 'I was dead tired after that one round and there were 14 more to come.'

He refused to commit himself about a comeback. 'I'll wait about a month, get my weight back, stay in shape, then go into the gym with Matthew Saad Muhammad, the light-heavyweight champion, and Mustafa Muhammad, the contender who is going to fight him. I'll do about seven fast rounds with each of them and I'll know if I should carry on.

'If I do, I'll train with heavyweights and have wars in the gym. I won't just be playing. This time I didn't throw punches in training, got into the habit and didn't throw them in the fight. In the condition I was in, Holmes was great. He fought a good fight.'

There was nothing but mutual generosity at the crowded final press conference attended by the two fighters. Ali had pleasant greetings for Holmes and his wife Diane and kisses for their baby daughter Kandy. When someone shouted that he was 'still the champion in my heart', Ali said quietly, 'I want to take your heart and turn it over to Larry. He *is* the world champion.'

Said Holmes, 'Ali does not owe boxing anything. Boxing owes Ali everything it is possible to owe. Without him there would be no million-dollar pay-days and no Larry Holmes as he is today. I love the man and I truly respect him.'

'Then why did you whup me back there?' Muhammad called from the other side of the platform. It would have been nice if we could have believed that he was riding out of the hardest game on the swell of laughter.

Muhammad Ali v. Trevor Berbick, Nassau, The Bahamas, 11 December 1981

Falling Idol in Paradise

He continues to recite the commentary for an epic but what we are seeing is not so much a B-movie as a cruel cartoon. Muhammad Ali can still preach and philosophise, boast and charm and predict. What he can't do is fight, at least not within a light-year of how he once did. The genie is gone from the bottle forever and Ali is ready to be dumped along with the rest of boxing's empties.

To do a little dumping at the Queen Elizabeth Sports Centre in Nassau next Friday night, Trevor Berbick won't have to prove himself an exceptional heavyweight. He will just have to show that he is fairly good at being young. When he leaves his stool to begin the 61st fight of a professional career that has spanned 21 years and made him the only man in history to hold the heavyweight championship of the world three times, Ali will be five weeks and two days short of his 40th birthday. Much more than half of his life has been punctuated by physical ordeals, and the wearing effects are both blatant and considerable. Berbick, a Jamaican based in Canada, only recently turned 28 and has strength and willingness to compensate for the crudity of his technique. If he does not make easy work of the old champion, any laughing Berbick allows himself on the way to the bank should be done behind a false beard and dark glasses. He says the promoters of Friday's ill-conceived event, a consortium headed by an Atlantan called Jim Cornelius but operating closely if not always effectively with the Bahamian Government, wanted him to act anonymous from the start. 'They pushed me over to Freeport on Grand Bahama, 150 miles from Nassau, gave me inferior training facilities and tried to make me feel like I was a second-class citizen,' he complains, with as much bitterness as the friendly island voice can manage. 'Cornelius is an Ali man. But it didn't work out the way they wanted. I'm living better than Ali is. I got a villa at the Bahama Princess Hotel and the manager lets me train there in comfort. That's why I said it's like a vacation, man.'

153

As Berbick expressed his contentment between prolonged yawns, lying back on his bed in Villa No. 2 at the Princess, he was offering a reminder of the one lifeline that may be available to Ali now that he has been set helplessly adrift by his own fantasies and the greed of others. It is not the least of the ironies associated with what is happening here that the central figure's best hope of avoiding serious harm is his utter loss of credibility. Berbick is 16 st 3 lb – compared with 15 st 5 lb when he laid the basis of a reputation by brawling confidently through 15 rounds with Larry Holmes, the World Boxing Council heavyweight champion, last April – and he insists that he will be unconcerned if his weight stays as high as it is. His preparation seems to have been as desultory as Ali's own. Both give the impression that they wouldn't run if they had diarrhoea and there is more sparring on the average Saturday night in a Glasgow pub than has been seen around either camp.

Of course, the two men have very different reasons for keeping the traditional masochism out of their schedules. Berbick cannot help feeling that he can afford to be lenient on himself. Ali does so little because that is all he is able to do. The fat rolls and creases around his middle and the muscles whose strength and elasticity and endurance were once the wonders of the sporting world are clogged with a fatigue that will never leave them. He shed most of the fat abruptly and unnaturally before he challenged Larry Holmes in Las Vegas 14 months ago and found that his appearance of reasonable fitness was a terrible illusion. He was stopped after ten rounds by a champion who took him apart without enthusiasm or a hint of cruelty.

Ali says that he went into the ring with Holmes at around 15 st 2 lb and the effort of making himself as light as he was in his fighting youth and the effect of pills he had been taking for a suspected thyroid condition combined to make him sick on the night, leaving him short of breath and with a racing pulse. Four days after that painful débâcle, he had the first of three intensive examinations by medical specialists at the University of California, Los Angeles. Their declaration that he has suffered no appreciable damage to his body or his brain during two decades of professional boxing – that, in fact, his 'current health status is excellent and there is no evidence from a health standpoint that he should be limited whatsoever in his activities' – has been used in a leaflet raid on newspaper editors and television executives by the promoters of the so-called Drama in Bahama. The doctors' testimony is indeed reassuring, and that of the neurosurgeon and the neurologist is especially so to those of us who have been alarmed over recent years by the diminished physical presence of the man and a mumbling diffuseness of speech that seemed to be something quite apart from the whispered monologues that were always an element of his routine in better years. 'The patient tended to talk softly and to almost mumble his speech,' the doctors reported. 'But when questioned about this, he was able to speak appropriately without any evidence of a speech disorder. He was evaluated by both a neuro-surgeon and neurologist who felt that his speech pattern was not pathologic.'

That is great news but all the report means at the end of the day is that Muhammad Ali is in good shape to mow the lawn or to help his wife carry the groceries. When it comes to judging how well he is equipped as a 40-year-old for fighting ten rounds against somebody a dozen years younger, Angelo Dundee might be a better witness than the lads at UCLA. 'He's scared,' Ali says quietly of Dundee, whose hustler's coolness and mastery of emergency procedures in the corner have been Ali's perennial safeguards against the destructive hysteria of his parasitic entourage. 'Angelo thinks I shouldn't be fightin'. He's coming in to work the corner but he thinks I'm shot, my legs have gone. But Angelo's not me. He don't know what I've got.'

At that point what he had most conspicuously was comfort and temporary insulation from the dangers ahead. He was reclining on the blue and white floral cover of his bed in Suite 642 of the Britannia Beach Hotel on Paradise Island, a resort enclave linked by a bridge to the spread of mainly nondescript buildings that sustain Nassau's identity against constant counter-attacks by the sand and greenery that were there before them. The curtains were drawn to close out the morning glare as well as the noise of seaplanes roaring under the supports of the bridge on their way to take-off and the more sociable din made by the clinking of bottles as they were carried to the fancy yachts moored at the marina. It was a difficult place for warlike thoughts to flourish and Ali, wearing only a pair of brown slacks and looking handsomely overfed, did not present the image of a man about to storm another impossible peak of athletic achieve-ment. But that, he told us, was what he was about to do. He was going to clear Berbick out of his path inside the ten rounds allotted for the purpose and then he would take care of Mike Weaver, the World Boxing Association heavyweight champion, and, probably, he'd go on to prove to Larry Holmes and the rest of us that he had been an invalid in Las Vegas last autumn. By taking the world title for a fourth time, he would make us think hard about the saying that records are made to be broken. 'They'd have to change that and say, "Records are made to be broken, all but Muhammad Ali's."'

He repeated that amended version several times, intoning it with an actor's clarity. No one has been able to explain to him that fooling around with dreams of immortality can shorten your life, and lying back on the bed he was dreaming of nothing less. 'When a man does some-thing like I'm doing it's always unpopular until he does it. Then they make statues of him. He's got a name that never dies.' When he sought to put next Friday into a manageable perspective, as much for himself as the two or three others in the room, he went to the sources he always calls upon at such times: to his love of attention and his need (an addict's craving) for drama and specifically for the drama of being an aggressively non-conforming black man in a white man's world.

'The hard part was working for the fight before people knew there was a fight, working when the press weren't writing about it. I trained better today knowing you were here, knowing I'm 40, that I'm not supposed to be doing this. Y'see I'm a rebel. Vietnam ... I didn't go, joined the Black Muslims at a time when negroes were scared to walk to Muslim mosques, on the stands with Elijah Muhammad, preaching the doom of America, standing next to the boldest black man ever to hit America ... didn't fly the flag in those days, called the white man the blond-haired, blue-eyed devil. Standing right there with BAD Muslims. I'm right there. That's the man. That badder than ... man, this fight is easy.

'Look at the kind of man you're dealing with. Weigh up my life, you won't be surprised what I do. I'm right there with white people in Georgia and Mississippi, preachin' that America's lynched, slaved, burned, robbed us. Raped our women. White men ain't no good, never be no good. We were preachin' that stuff. That takes more of a man than to fight Berbick. I like controversy, I like drama. I just don't know how to be scared about these things.

'I guess I should be scared, maybe it's gonna hurt me, kill me one day. I've been shot at in Georgia and I've been shot at driving my car down the road in Fayetteville, Arkansas. Bullet went through the windshield, came out the back window. Rentacar.'

With that nod to verisimilitude he turned back to the present: 'This doesn't look rough to me. Berbick puts his head down and swings like an old woman. I'll eat him up. You must realise I been fighting since I was 12. This is just another boxing match.'

A moment later he yielded to an alternative point of view. 'You're right, I'm gamblin'. Yeah, you're right. I'm the world's highest roller. Those guys shootin' for a thousand dollars a roll in Vegas are small-fries. I'm bigger than them. But I don't believe I'm gonna be a shadow of what I was. I believe I'm gonna be right on that night. It's true, I take punches. Look what it's gotten me. I'm rich. I'll probably take some more punches. I have to.'

His imperatives and his finances remain equally mysterious to outsiders and what he says about them gives little clarification. He suggests that he will receive $3.8 million for this fight but $1 million is a more convincing figure. (The adversary he has respected most in his fighting life, Joe Frazier, took $85,000 plus expenses to box a draw with Jumbo Cummings in Chicago on Thursday, and left the ring knowing the scorecards had done him a favour.) In any case, according to Ali, the purse is incidental. He has come back to inspire the black peoples of the earth.

He didn't look too inspired himself as he moved at a sauntering pace through the warm, still darkness before Thursday's dawn. His breathing was noticeable on the curves of the Paradise Island bridge and as we took to the cracked streets of Nassau's shopping quarter he slowed enough to give his three Fleet Street escorts delusions of well-being. He had a heavy rubber corset around his middle and he fingered it occasionally for signs of sweat as he talked of the demands made on his time by such as Jimmy Carter and Leonid Brezhnev. Now and then a passer-by was invited to spar but recognition was sluggish and there were no jokers ready to co-operate. It was a strangely melancholy trudge past the shops bravely calling themselves department stores, the cheap restaurants, the dry cleaners, and there was quiet relief when the sun came up. By that time we were passing Peanuts Taylor's Drumbeat Club and heading along a straight road beside the sea. Ali stopped at a T-junction where the side road led to a lumber yard and shadow-boxed perfunctorily. Under his tracksuit parts of his body that used to be taut were bouncing around. Then we piled into the limousine that had been trailing us and rode back to the hotel. A man who has missed the last bus after the bars close takes more out of himself on the walk home than Ali had done with what we were supposed to regard as roadwork.

He had been happier the day before when he ordered a video-machine to be switched on in his room so that he could call some shots against Berbick while the Jamaican rough-housed with Holmes on the screen. 'Look at him, he's in hittin' range now and I'm jabbin' – pow, quicker than Holmes, pow, I'm eatin' him up. I can't miss him. He comes at you, puts his head down and swings like an old woman. He's easy.'

His standard training session is depressing: some half-hearted slamming of the heavy bag and a couple of rounds of poignantly ordinary shadow-boxing. Easily the best part is his patter to the tourists who turn up to watch. His humour has worn better than his boxing and it is made irresistible by the warmth that comes from his sense of being a continuous presence in millions of lives for nearly 20 years. 'Y'know, all people 25 years old have been hearin' about me since they were seven,' he said to a few of us the other day. 'My wife is 25. She heard about me changin' my name when she was eight. The whole generation that's now in power – governors, mayors, policemen, cab drivers, all the people at the prime of life – all of them been following me since they were babies.'

It's true and it's enough to make you hope that next Friday Trevor Berbick won't be a competent heavyweight, that he won't even be good at being young.

The King Who Went Out on a Dustcart

Graceful exits are rare in professional boxing but few great champions have gone out more miserably than Muhammad Ali in the Bahamas on Friday night when he lost on points to Trevor Berbick in a thoroughly inept fight that was the melancholy centrepiece of a memorably shabby promotion. The most remarkable career the game has ever known was, we must earnestly hope, brought to its final close by a tinny rattle from the Bahamian cow-bell that was dredged up from somewhere to impersonate the timekeeper's instrument the bungling organisers of the event had neglected to provide. When the incongruous noise signalled the end of the tenth round Ali, who had been forced to acknowledge the full, sad cost of serving more than half of his 40 years in the prize-ring as he laboured unsuccessfully to hide the decay of his reflexes, timing and athleticism, was well behind on the scorecards of all three judges.

Berbick is the kind of lumbering, slow-armed swinger he would have first embarrassed and then demolished in his dazzling prime but even the additional sluggishness imposed on the Jamaican's work by conspicuous idleness in training could not save this pathetically diminished Ali. Against an opponent who, as a 28-year-old, at least had youth to compensate for dubious fitness and extreme crudities of technique, the man who set a record by winning the world heavyweight title three times, scuffled quietly and with decreasing conviction towards a defeat that only the prejudiced in his own camp could seriously question.

To see him lose to such a moderate fighter in such a grubby context was like watching a king ride into permanent exile on the back of a garbage truck. The one blessing was that he was steadily exhausted rather than violently hurt by the experience. But even that consolation was worryingly diluted when most of his inner circle, from his wife Veronica to his manager Herbert Muhammad to his recently acquired friend, John Travolta, thrust distorted and dangerously reassuring interpretations of the fight into his head. 'I don't want him to fight but you people are brainwashing him into thinking he did badly tonight,' Veronica told reporters in Ali's dressing-room afterwards. 'You had made up your mind about the fight you were going to see before you came here.' She insisted that her man had done more worthwhile punching than Berbick, who had been barely hitting him. The theme was parroted by a chorus of voices of which Herbert Muhammad's was the most significant. 'You done good,' said Herbert. 'I don't agree with that decision.' 'Everybody knew you won,' said Veronica, talking again into Ali's left ear. For someone who didn't want to invite further exposure to physical hazard, she was making free with the illusions.

Her words had an effect on Ali that some of us found alarming. He was sitting on a wooden bench against a whitewashed wall and when she sat down beside him he was a slumped, infinitely weary figure, answering

158

questions in a drained whisper as beads of sweat formed on his chin and dropped on to the folds of flesh around his middle. Even his wife's arrival did not animate him noticeably as he admitted that out in the ring he felt old for the first time in his life (a statement to remind us that he believes genuine illness contributed substantially to his helpless passivity when he was stopped after ten rounds by Larry Holmes in Las Vegas 14 months ago).

'Father Time caught up with me,' he said so faintly that only the two or three of us at the front of the crowding group of interviewers could make out the words. 'I feel tired. Berbick was too strong, more aggressive. I just had the feeling I could do this thing. My mind said do it. But I know I didn't have it out there. I did good for a 39-year-old, did all right considering I'll be 40 in five weeks.

'I thought Berbick was shorter than he is. I didn't know he was so strong. He tagged me with a couple of hard ones and they tired me a bit. There's nothing to worry about, this is not going to bother me. But I think it's too late to come back. I always say that after fights these days but who knows how I'll feel next week.'

That last sentence was liable to stir misgivings in many around him but the resigned, exhausted tone kept our concern in check until John Travolta, crouching at his feet, and Veronica at his side fed him their views about how well he had done. Ali quoted his wife and the actor immediately as if they had touched an optimistic nerve in himself. 'Veronica and John Travolta, they tell me it was so close, that I won. Was it close?' A smile spread across his aching face, obscuring for a moment the slight bruising beneath his left eye and the tiny area of discoloration by the right one. The fatigue seemed to be lifted briefly from his body. There was in those few seconds the definite threat of another nightmare up ahead, the bleak possibility that the words he was hearing would nourish his own capacity to dream away reality.

But yesterday he indicated firmly that he will be steered towards unambiguous retirement by the memory of how feebly he coped with the modest problem set by Berbick, the realisation of how far he has declined from the towering standards of the past, how totally he has lost the blurring hand-speed, the dancing mobility, the entire thrilling range of virtuosity that made him unique among heavyweights. His brilliance was always idiosyncratic, shot through with outrageous improvisations that blithely violated tenets of the game most fighters regard as sacrosanct. Imagination, balance, elasticity and blinding quickness enabled him to use techniques – such as constantly pulling his head away from punches instead of moving inside them, punching while his feet and body were eccentrically positioned – that would have brought disaster to less inspired performers. But his days of being a magnificent heretic belong to another time.

Once his speed and co-ordination deserted him, he was bound to look worse than ordinary because he did not have the remnants of an orthodox method to hide behind. At the Queen Elizabeth Sports Centre in Nassau he was just an ageing, overweight ex-champion who was no longer troubling to keep the grey out of his hair, no longer able to keep Trevor Berbick's clumsily directed blows out of his face. Much of the action in the early rounds was so riddled with ponderous incompetence that scoring it was largely a negative exercise, but Berbick was marginally less ineffective than Ali and edged ahead. The great man could neither measure nor synchronise his punches convincingly and generally he was reduced to pawing flurries. Just occasionally, as in the fifth, which he won, he managed a fleeting semblance of the old sharpness and caught Berbick with left jabs and passable imitations of right crosses. In between these limited rallies, however, he allowed himself to be bulled to the ropes and when the referee, Zack Clayton, refused to let him hold and wrestle, too many of the younger boxer's haphazard hooks and swings thudded against his head.

Assaults of that kind gave Berbick clear, if unimpressive, superiority in the fourth and seventh and what happened in the eighth was a tribute to the courage Ali will never lose. In that round he went up on his toes and bravely attempted to jab and dance, stick and move. The crowd, swollen to a sizeable, noisy audience in the dusty baseball stadium by the promoters' willingess to sell tickets at a fifth of their face value, chanted his name in their eagerness to be persuaded that they might see a small miracle. It did not come. Ali took the eighth but was soon settling heavily on his heels again and when he was on the wrong end of the undistinguished doings in the ninth and tenth there could be only one result. The two judges who gave the verdict to Berbick 99–94 may have been a touch generous to him but the official who had it 97–94 was scarcely exaggerating.

When Ali mumbled afterwards that Berbick would need to make only reasonable improvement to have a favourite's chance of winning the world championship, he was unlikely to find widespread support for the opinion. The Canadian-based West Indian had looked far more fit and vigorous in his brawling 15 rounds with Larry Holmes last April but it is hard to imagine that he will ever be more than a strong rough-houser.

On Friday, Berbick was glad enough to get a night's work done and collect his wages for it. He had held out until nearly six o'clock, the hour when the first match was due to start at the stadium, to secure what he considered to be ironclad guarantees that James Cornelius, the tall, belligerent black man from the United States who heads the promotional consortium, would pay the outstanding balance of his purse money. Cornelius – who has been publicly accused by Don King, currently the biggest operator in the fight business, of having led a group of five men who beat him up and threatened his life over a contract wrangle in Freeport last week – is not too brisk at coming up with the ironclads.

While reporters from around the world milled about endlessly at the fight press centre on Paradise Island awaiting developments, somebody joked that Cornelius's arrival had been delayed because there was some difficulty over raising the $2 toll needed to get across the bridge on to the island. What was obvious was that the malodorous enterprise billed as the Drama in Bahama had not been quite the source of prestige the Bahamians had anticipated. In the end they must have felt that they needed it the way Bermuda needs the Triangle. Or Muhammad Ali needs another comeback.

Apart from being discouraged by his own decay, Ali may have found the seediness of Mr Cornelius's arrangements inclined to sour him against the sport that has dominated his life. The programme began nearly two and a half hours late with gloves in such short supply that some pairs had to be unlaced rather than cut off the fighter's hands, so that they could be used again. Down-the-bill boxers had to strip in cramped proximity to one another in ludicrously overcrowded dressing-rooms before going out to answer the cow-bell. It was all a disgraceful mess and the flavour of it was not improved by the violence with which Ali's strong-arm battalion repelled pressmen and broadcasters who tried to follow the loser into his dressing-room.

Inside, there was a contrasting tranquillity, especially when Ali's attractive 11-year-old daughter from his previous marriage squirmed on to his knee to hug and kiss his battered head. His mother, too, squeezed through the jostling cluster of interrogators to embrace the most famous son in the world. 'Good try, honey,' she said and then to us: 'I didn't cry. I'm glad he didn't get hurt. I'm glad that's it. I'm not worried about his losing. I'm just glad he didn't get hurt.' Angelo Dundee, who has run Ali's corner for 20 years, was another who was happy about that but one or two on the fringes of the entourage looked as if they suspected they were about to be hurt – by being deprived of regular swellings around the cash pocket.

Everyone in that room was having thoughts about how it would be when Ali had left this scene behind for ever. A wire-service reporter was being more pragmatic. He was asking the fighter if, when he had quit, he would find time to talk President Gaddafi out of sending Libyan hit-squads after President Reagan. With Muhammad Ali that is supposed to be a practical inquiry. As was said after that Roman heavyweight was done in, when comes such another?

Part Five

Further Dispatches

What follows is a selection from my writing on boxing over the last dozen years or so. All the newspaper and magazine articles used have been transferred directly to the book, warts and all. The positive and negative effects of this approach are equally obvious but I feel the advantages outweigh the disadvantages. Even when an early profile of Barry McGuigan ('Fighter With All Ireland in His Corner') tells of a deep warmth between McGuigan and his manager, Barney Eastwood, and later coverage of the Clones man's exploits reveals a bitter split in the partnership, the contradictions bring no embarrassment. On the contrary, they show how an almost filial bond between McGuigan and Eastwood gave way to mutual and litigious hostility. The story of Ireland's most exciting fighter is an enthralling one but it has had more than its share of shadows.

Of course, sad stories are never hard to find in boxing. All too often the game's cruelties seem too much to be balanced by its exhilarations. But at this point I shall spare myself and everyone else another confession about a lifelong enthusiasm increasingly assailed by misgivings.

Fighter With All Ireland in His Corner

The Observer, 21 October 1984

Nothing any sportsman anywhere does over the next year or so is likely to mean as much to as many people as the performances in the boxing ring of Barry McGuigan. In Ireland, where one man's hero can be the next man's villain, the emotional identification with this remarkable 23-year-old is so deep and so close to being unanimous that it sends an awed shudder through a witness from outside the island.

The regular fights at the King's Hall in Belfast that have been the principal means of moving McGuigan to the brink of a challenge for the featherweight championship of the world are occasions of such melodramatic intensity that they make a lot of other boxing shows seem like altercations in a library.

It is not simply that the old bare arena out in the Balmoral district near the southern edge of the city is strainingly filled with partisan humanity (even a formidable commando of doormen and stewards cannot hope to restrict the crowd to the official limit of under 8,000), or that the heaving crescendos of cheering threaten to separate the walls from the roof. The feeling in the place is better understood when you look at the faces of those who are roaring the name of the pale, muscular figure whose crowding momentum is shrinking the ring.

Whether they are in the couple of front rows where a seat costs fifty pounds or standing up in the long galleries packed with ten-pound customers who have queued for seven or eight hours to improve their chances of a decent pitch, McGuigan's devotees are exultant when he goes to work.

Their shining eyes and glowing cheeks can't be attributed to the drink or two they may have taken on their way to the fight. They have, quite simply, been transported, lifted clear of the chilling divisiveness that eddies through the streets beyond the doors and given a solidarity that is no less real for being temporary.

'While they are in the hall they are Barry McGuigan United,' says Barney Eastwood, the contender's manager. 'The old prejudices will come to the fore again soon enough in plenty of cases but I'll tell you this – the wee fella could walk up the Falls Road or the Shankill Road any day and not a man or woman would lift a hand to hurt him.' The claim is strengthened by the knowledge that McGuigan's supporters' clubs are to be found in both the Republican Falls and the Loyalist Shankill.

It would be foolishly glib to trace the width of his appeal to a refusal to let sectarian barriers dominate his own life. He is a practising Catholic who married a Protestant girl raised across the street from him in Clones, a little County Monaghan town only a few miles inside the Republic of Ireland; who added British citizenship to his Irish nationality in order to

166

fight for a wider range of titles; who carefully avoids emblematic colours in his kit and is accompanied into the ring by a peace flag; and who recently moved with his wife and young son to a whitewashed house overlooking a small lake just ten minutes' drive from Clones but, as it happens, 50 yards on the Fermanagh (Northern Ireland) side of the border.

That flexibility of attitude towards boundaries, geographical or mental, finds favour with many but obviously not with all of the people around him. McGuigan's status as a true all-Ireland hero has more basic origins. It relates on the one hand to the powerful and persistent hunger for such a phenomenon and on the other to the considerable charm of his personality and the exciting dimensions of his talent.

A few have sought to be snide about his Mr Nice Guy image, but his mixture of boyish modesty and natural courtesy has proved equally irresistible to the elderly ladies who wait in line on fight nights to wish him well as he leaves the Bangor guest house he has shared with them during the final weeks of training and some of the hardest residents of that old tough town along the road.

To the latter group his solicitousness, his choirboy's manners are made all the more attractive by the certainty that once he is through the ropes they will give way to the kind of inspired destructiveness that has always been beyond the huge majority of European boxers. Then his dark blue eyes will have an ominous directness and the man who has to face him will wonder how so much sustained ferocity can be generated by someone who stands a fraction over 5 ft 6 in tall and weighs 9 st.

A major part of the explanation is, of course, the quality of his movement as he closes on an opponent. Some fighters think they are being shifty, that they are bobbing and weaving the other fellow into bewilderment, when their manoeuvres are in fact trundlingly predictable. But there is a constantly disconcerting variety about the fluent mobility of McGuigan. The swaying of his torso, the dipping of his shoulders, the smooth adjustments of his feet and, above all, the percussive, cumulative rhythm of his punching are all invested with a ruthless sense of purpose that can be read in the steady gaze he offers from beneath the black hair he has recently coated with oil, to make himself even more slippery.

The general excellence of his technique – and vital specifics such as the jolting authority of his left jab and the savage economy of his left hooks, particularly the terrible body shots that make opponents wish their rib cages had been constructed by Harland and Wolff – would be enough to declare him exceptional in any generation of British champions. However, a great deal more than skill and courage is needed if the fierce Latin Americans who now hold two separate versions of the world title are to be challenged with confidence.

Fortunately, McGuigan does have a great deal more. Those victims who suspect him of being unnaturally strong are not hallucinating through their sufferings. Physically he is fairly extraordinary. Apart from the deep reserves of power he has built up by an addiction to fitness that stretches back far into his childhood and makes him a confirmed tee-totaller and non-smoker today, as well as an outrageous glutton for the gym, he has one or two priceless assets which heredity rather than discipline has provided.

Most notably, he has unusually long arms (his 70 in reach is reckoned to be at least three inches above the average for boxers around his division) and at the ends of them are remarkably large, hard hands, the sort of ideal hammers that mean far more to a pugilist than the public tend to realise. In the days when Clones was an important rail junction in Ireland, a small-scale Crewe, McGuigan's paternal grandfather was legendary among his fellow railway workers for the size and strength of his hands and at school the young Barry was invincible when the boys played a primitive game of conkers in which their clenched fists took the place of chestnuts.

A dispute about the wrappings of his hands during his long and success-ful amateur career (only three defeats in 90 senior matches and the climax of a Commonwealth Games gold medal in 1978) so aggravated him that he ripped off the bandages, went out with the gloves over unprotected knuckles and did nasty damage to his right hand. That injury might have struck those who followed him then as freakish, because he was inclined at that stage – and indeed for some time after turning professional – to rely almost exclusively on the deadly brilliance of his left. It goes without saying that since he teamed up with Barney Eastwood both fists have been properly cushioned against unnecessary abuse but the right has been obliged to start paying its way in the ring.

Eastwood is head of a family firm whose turnover from 32 betting shops and a number of amusement arcades, along with substantial interests in property, guarantees that he does not have to look to the fight game for his next million. Even in his schooldays, when he was an outstanding Gaelic footballer until a flirtation with the alien sport of soccer caused him to be banned, his greatest enthusiasm was for boxing. Having grown up with a gift for making money, he had enough of the stuff to do some promoting in Belfast during the 1960s. But he was discouraged by the lack of backing from the boxing authorities and dropped out for a decade and a half, until a glimpse of Barry McGuigan on television revived his dream of taking an Irishman by way of noisy nights at the King's Hall to a championship of the world.

Nowadays it is Stephen Eastwood, third youngest of Barney's family of six sons and a daughter, who is the promoter and the 52-year-old father concentrates on the management job he has handled not only with judgement but with a consistently warm concern for his protégé's welfare. Nobody ever built the sort of business Eastwood controls in a town like Belfast without being wise to the ways of the streets and anyone who has tried to outwit him on a bet, at a dog track or the ringside, won't expect him to be out of his depth among the high rollers of international boxing.

Already they must have noted the achievement of raising McGuigan to number four in the rankings of both the World Boxing Council and the World Boxing Association while avoiding really punishing fights. The third of his pro career brought a questionable points loss against Peter Eubanks but four months later, in December 1981, Eubanks was convincingly stopped in the return and his mild impertinence remains the only blemish in a sequence of increasingly impressive performances that reached a total of 24 with the two-round win over Felipe Orozco, of Colombia, at the King's Hall last Saturday night.

Infinitely more serious than the experience with Eubanks was the depression that overwhelmed him after Young Ali, a Nigerian he had knocked out in London in the middle of 1982, died after lying for months in a coma. McGuigan went into prolonged retreat in the countryside around Clones, with only his handful of dogs as companions, and there was a definite danger that he would give up boxing. Eventually, he says, it was his sense of obligation to all the people who had contributed to his progress that persuaded him to carry on.

Coming from him, the statement has no phoney ring. He has forged a link with millions of strangers, so it's not surprising that the bond with his own large family and the many home-town friends who are almost as close as relatives should be as basic as an umbilical cord. The McGuigans tend to have something to lift them out of the ordinary, whether it is the singing that took the lively, immensely likeable father, Pat, to third place in the Eurovision Song Contest of 1967 or the golfing ability that gives Barry's nearest brother Dermot a handicap of three or four. To a degree, Barry is prosecuting his talent on behalf of all of them.

His development as a fighter has been calculated and systematic. One of its key passages was a trip to the US on which McGuigan violently disillusioned a few local slickers who thought to take liberties with the country boy from across the water, and, to his more lasting benefit, acquired the coaching assistance of Bobby McQuillar. McQuillar, a black man in his 60s, is a gymnasium sage who in another time took decisions over such masters of the game as Sandy Saddler and Joe Brown.

Until his health failed recently, McQuillar was in the habit of coming from America, with perhaps three sparring partners, to supervise the last phase of training at the custom-built gym above the Eastwood bookmaking headquarters in central Belfast. 'Like Kenny Buchanan, who also taught Barry a hell of a lot on visits over here, Bobby McQuillar and his boys weren't easily paid,' says the manager, with a smile. 'But really you couldn't put a value on what those sessions did for us.'

McGuigan himself vividly endorsed that view when he rose from the breakfast table at his father-in-law's hotel in Clones last week to demonstrate a few McQuillar moves. He is a spirited talker, whether he is discussing the tragedies of contemporary Ireland, the happiness of his marriage to his attractive, dark-haired wife Sandra, or the shrewdness and generosity of Barney Eastwood's guidance. But he is never more assured than when he talks about the technicalities of his trade.

Suddenly by the table, to satisfy his manager, he was stripping to the waist to let us hear the thudding, rhythmic noise that comes from his shoulders when he punches, a slightly eerie signal of his power. Then he simulated a left hook to the body. 'Bobby McQuillar says that no matter how good the condition a man is in he can't get his liver in shape to take these hooks.'

The body he would like to be assaulting soon is that of Eusebio Pedroza, the Panamanian who holds the WBA version of the feather-weight title. Pedroza is an outstanding champion who has made a long string of defences in an amazing variety of locations and he reinforces his legitimate effectiveness with a consummate mastery of more dirty tricks than any ten other fighters would be liable to know. Yet the odds are that Barney Eastwood will try to tempt him to Belfast rather than pursue the Puerto Rican Wilfredo Gomez, the WBC champion, who is easier to hit but strikes back with more devastating effect.

'I think Barry would be the outsider with either of them, maybe 5–4 or 6–4 against, but he'd have a tremendous chance. He's like a Classic horse who has never been off the bit. I believe when he has got to go the Derby trip you'll see something very special. I hope I am right because, apart from admiring him so much, I really love the boy.'

That puts B.J. Eastwood in a rather large company.

Donald Curry v. Colin Jones, Birmingham, 19 January 1985

Scales Tip towards Curry

There was a moment early last Wednesday evening when some of us who harbour a natural limey desire to see Colin Jones of Gorseinon, South Wales, take the welterweight championship of the world from Don Curry of Fort Worth, Texas, found our already meagre optimism abruptly and significantly diminished.

It happened in one of the two big, bare rooms that constitute the Birmingham gym in which both fighters are completing training for their lucrative collision a few miles down the motorway at the National Exhibition Centre next Saturday night. But the scene did not rely for its effect on the esoteric paraphernalia of a boxing sweatshop.

It might just as easily have occurred in Boots (provided the shoppers were able to cope with the sight of a handsome black man stepping naked on to the scales) because the most relevant point about Curry's work on Wednesday was not the economically brilliant technique he displayed in sparring but the wave of relief and pleasure that spread out from his own tired body to put wide smiles on the faces of his manager and trainer, Dave Gorman and Paul Reyes, after they read his weight at the end of the session.

We all know that fight people are not above concealing their anxieties with a little Thespianism and the light but almost exuberant slap on the back Reyes gave Curry as they walked away from the weighing machine may have been for the benefit of those who were watching for confirmation of persistent reports that the World Boxing Association champion is no longer comfortable and strong at the welterweight limit of 10 st 7 lb. But the camp's satisfied mood seemed believable and so, too – always allowing for a marginal, morale-boosting leniency towards himself – did Curry's quiet declaration that he had just made 10 st 10 lb.

He looked drained and weary but nobody was entitled to make much of that. Since the residue of the jetlag produced by a protracted transatlantic journey that brought him into Britain on Monday morning had been compounded by sustained if easy-paced exercise in sweat clothes – which included skin-tight, rubberised trunks of the kind waterskiers wear and a plastic tunic – any evidence of bright-eyed liveliness might have had racing men among his audience calling for a saliva test.

As it happened, he would have found difficulty in obliging. His mouth had been sucked dry by the skipping and ball and bag punching that gathered his perspiration on the floor in puddles so substantial that Reyes was constantly mopping it up with towels. When Curry asked for moisture during his labours the trainer dispensed it so parsimoniously he might as well have used an eye-dropper.

This, clearly, was a boxer suffering to put himself within reach of the stipulated poundage sufficiently early to avoid a crisis in the days or hours leading up to the weigh-in. That impression was strengthened when Dave Gorman said that after Wednesday they would want several days of privacy (without being scrutinised or interviewed) in which to make the last concentrated surge of their preparation. Obviously they don't need closed sessions to rehearse tactics. In common with most outstanding fighters, Curry will ensure that he is not lumbered with preconceptions when he comes off the stool at the first bell. He will bet on his ability to assess Jones swiftly and accurately once the war is on, confident in the knowledge that his equipment is more comprehensive, more varied and more reliably destructive than the challenger's. So the wish to train in private is, presumably, associated with the traditional reluctance to let outsiders see your man hurting himself to shed weight. The question for Jones's supporters is whether they can take any real encouragement from this muted drama of the scales.

Curry is tall for a welter at 5 ft 10½ in and, although his torso is slim and his noticeably long arms have the elastic muscles of a fluent puncher rather than the cumbersome bulges of a weightlifter, he is not at all stringy and there is no surprise in hearing him talk of moving up in stages to

171

challenge for the junior middleweight (11 st) and eventually the full middleweight (11 st 6 lb) title.

He says he will leave the welterweight division after Saturday's assignment because the only two men who could provide credible and financially rewarding opposition around that weight – Milton McCrory, against whom Jones drew and then lost in two 12-round World Boxing Council championship matches, and Aaron Pryor, of the devastating attack and dishevelled mind – are not about to put themselves in front of him for business. But there can be no doubt that the long hours imprisoned in the sort of gear that turns his own body heat in on him like a furnace are becoming less tolerable even for someone who has just turned 23 and brims with dignified ambition.

Yet it is almost certainly inadvisable for us founder members of the Admirers of Colin Jones Society to draw reassurance from Curry's weight worries, just as it would be a mistake to imagine that the damage he did to the metacarpal bones of his right hand in winning the world championship over 15 punishing rounds against the tough Korean Jun Sok Hwang five fights ago will recur as a serious handicap. It is worth noting that Curry has no truck with the old-style heavy bag that hangs, intimidatingly solid as a load of cement, in most British gyms. He prefers a much lighter, far more yielding inflatable version from America and his insistence that concern about jarring wear and tear on his elbows is the main consideration isn't totally persuasive.

However, it is a fact that the hand injury didn't prevent him from demolishing Roger Stafford in one round six months after becoming champion, taking a second and thoroughly convincing victory over the estimable Marlon Starling and stopping Elio Diaz and Nino LaRocca. Those four engagements were title defences and Curry's performances in winning all 20 of his professional fights, combined with the achievements of a remarkable amateur career that embraced 400 matches and would surely have brought an Olympic gold medal but for the US boycott of Moscow in 1980, are enough to make some of the best judges in the States regard him as a talent worthy of being hailed as a legitimate heir to Sugar Ray Leonard.

His midweek sparring in Birmingham was too academic to invite detailed assessments but throughout his rounds with Daryl Robinson, infinitely the more informative of his partners, his quality was unmistakable. In the ring he is a relentless watcher of his opponent, following every move with a concentrated alertness that enables him to spear precise, hurtful punches through openings that lesser practitioners wouldn't even see. He has the perceptiveness, technical flexibility and innately sharp timing of the developing virtuoso and those who know him best say he can also employ his shoulders and elbows to fairly brutal purpose when battling inside, at which he excels.

Curry himself identifies defensive skill as his prime asset and, despite all the sanguine speculation about Jones finding him less elusive than McCrory, he is likely to present the Welshman with a frustratingly difficult target. Although he has been boxing since early in his schooldays, Curry is virtually unmarked. The line of his nose may have been fractionally adjusted but that is scarcely perceptible and an almost total freedom from cuts has left his face smooth and appealing beneath hair that is swept away from the forehead to resemble a floppy cap worn back to front.

Normally Colin Jones, with his craggy, coalfields features, bony prow of a nose and spiky crewcut would make a warlike contrast with the champion. But Colin has let his hair grow a bit for this fight and, with the glasses he wears when off duty, he looks like the personable young businessman he could easily be if he didn't apply such healthy scepticism to the flood of propositions attracted by the three-quarters of a million or so he has grossed while becoming the best-paid British boxer in history.

The glasses have the additional value these days of obscuring the ominous scar in the flesh between the right eye and eyebrow that commemorates a savage cut inflicted by Billy Parks before Jones stopped the American in the tenth round in the latter of the two inside-the-distance wins he has had since losing to McCrory. Anyone who fancies betting on our man at 7–4 against (Curry is 5–2 on) should be informed that the wide range of punches exhibited by the champion in training included not only a selection of body shots calculated to exploit Jones's probable vulnerability to that kind of assault but a chopping left which often slashes in as a double hook and appears perfectly designed to reopen that ugly cut.

Of course, Colin Jones at his most aggressive might tunnel through to deliver his own hooks and, whether slammed in with the left or the right hand, these have the explosive power to flatten any welterweight in the world. He says he will seek to land a couple of the big blows in the first round 'to let Curry know what it's all about' and feels that an average of half-a-dozen decent hits per round afterwards will progressively tighten his grip on the WBA title (he remembers that Curry was knocked down by Jun Sok Hwang). But as he talks there is about Jones an aura of relaxation, almost a tranquillity that can only disturb his backers. He is trained to hard fitness and has followed all the classic rituals, even removing himself from his wife's bed for more than a month before going to Birmingham, yet it is impossible to trace the belligerent edginess of previous campaigns.

He comes across as a man who won't spare himself in earning about £100,000 next weekend (notwithstanding the fact that Curry will collect three and a half times as much) but for whom success would be a pleasant bonus. It is conceivable, too, that his thoughts occasionally drift to the strenuously denied charge of grievous bodily harm that will take his brother Kenneth and himself into Gowerton Magistrates' Court four days after the fight. None of this makes for optimism.

My respect and affection for Colin Jones are considerable but the bookies' odds look just. Don Curry seems so skilful, so quick, so hard, so hungry and so likely to keep enough of his strength at 10 st 7 lb that if our hero carries his banner through more than half the 15 rounds we'll have no complaints.

Bloody End for Jones

Colin Jones's attempt to take the World Boxing Association welterweight championship from the brilliant Texan Don Curry was always more of a hopeful dream than a realistic challenge and it ended in bloody, tearful disappointment and an ugly threat of riot after only 36 seconds of the fourth round at the National Exhibition Centre in Birmingham last night.

Plastic bottles were showered towards the ring as the fight was stopped at the instigation of an official ringside doctor, David Targett, and more were aimed at Curry as he moved through the ropes and headed for the dressing-room.

Prolonged and bitter scuffles broke out in parts of the arena and the whole place rumbled with a belligerent discontent that might have damaged the reputation of British crowds as much as the disgraceful turmoil which erupted at Wembley Arena when Marvin Hagler took the world middleweight championship from Alan Minter. In fact, nothing comparable with that nightmare developed but one of the bottles thrown at Curry was reported to have struck an American television man, so we are guaranteed a fair dose of critical publicity on the other side of the Atlantic.

The frustration of the thousands who had come to support Jones was understandable but their reaction was as illogical and unjustified as it was reprehensible. Jones was clearly and painfully a defeated fighter when the referee, Ismael Fernandez, of Puerto Rico, interrupted the assault on him and called for Dr Targett's opinion.

The Welshman had fought with all the courage that is basic to his nature but never had a remotely convincing answer to the speed, volume and variety of the punishment poured at his head by a 23-year-old who may be the finest technician in the game today. The stream of viciously accurate left jabs, right crosses, two-handed hooks and occasional jolting uppercuts had already rocked Jones ominously by the end of the second round (having brought blood from inside the loser's nose in the first). And when, in the third, Curry first drew a further trace of blood from near the right eye and then, far more calamitously, opened a deep and terrible gash across the bridge of Jones's nose, a beating for our man was not only certain but imminent. All the smoothly hurried work of Eddie Thomas in the British corner before the start of the fourth could achieve

174

little against the huge problems created by that gory slash – which looked as if it might spread like a grotesque extra mouth – and Jones responded to the bell with the grim awareness that Curry's sharp and powerful blows would home in on the wound.

Of course, they did and the fourth was barely half a minute old when blood, not for the first time, had the decisive say about the future of a fighter from these islands. As Dr Targett tenderly fingered the cut he winced slightly and began to shake his head. Soon he was muttering the words Jones had not wanted to hear and immediately the Welshman's shoulders began to heave, his forehead fell miserably against the blue top rope and tears mingled freely with the blood.

The words that came from him were predictable because he has no more affection for being taken out of a fight than most of the men who come to the ring from the valleys of South Wales. 'I am so ashamed and disappointed,' he said. 'I feel so stupid that it has been stopped like this. I had so much fight left in me. I suppose now I ought to retire.'

Eddie Thomas, though his spirit always goes into the ring with his men, managed sufficient objectivity to say: 'I'd have liked Colin to complete that fourth round but I think probably I'd have pulled him out myself pretty soon. Really, I can't disagree with the decision.'

Nor could anyone who saw the fight through eyes unblurred by beer or prejudice. Even when Jones was landing solid hooks on Curry he never once suggested that he could do more than fleetingly halt the American's scientific dismantling of his ambitions. Jones took chances, leaving his body open as he leaned out wide to arc in the left hook, but such gambling did not bring the power to drive Curry backwards. Instead the black champion merely licked his lips, maintained that calculating stare of his untroubled eyes and went about his work with cumulative destructiveness.

Every punch he throws is premeditated, a subtly contrived act of violence. He never guesses. He watches intensely, assesses, deliberates and delivers with a speed and precision that few if any fighters at any weight in the world could match. Without doubt Colin Jones will recognise this morning that he cannot be numbered among that minority.

All suspicions of weight troubles, all talk of Curry's weak hands had to be put away as meaningless history while Curry offered his own judgement of his performance: 'Sugar Ray Leonard could not have done a better job than I did tonight. Jones wasn't nearly as strong as I thought he would be and I had an easy victory. I am the best fighter in the world.'

Marvin Hagler v. Thomas Hearns, Las Vegas, 15 April 1985

Hearns Cornered by a Man Possessed

Around the terrible simplicity of what Marvin Hagler did to Thomas Hearns there has gathered over the past week a small cloud of convenient rationalisation.

Its principal expression is a series of slightly exasperated questions. How on earth could Hearns elect to fight Hagler relentlessly through that terrifyingly intense and savage first round? Why didn't he jab and move? Why weren't those seven-league legs employed to carry him out of range of his opponent's most destructive ordnance?

Perhaps such thoughts are natural enough but suggesting them to Hearns at the height of his crisis would have been about as realistic as telling a man caught in a forest fire to look for messages carved into the trees. He was concerned in those long minutes of searing violence not with tactics or strategy but with battling for his life.

The fighter who had come off the stool at him when the first bell sounded was not a Marvin Hagler anyone had ever seen before. He was a man possessed, the very incarnation of furious hostility, an enemy who shrank the ring with the heat of his malevolent intent.

All of this may persuade some people that organised retreat offered the best hope of survival and ultimate victory. Retreat to where? And, in any case, can they honestly imagine that Thomas Hearns, The Hit-Man – a pugilist whose self-belief has always been inseparable from the conviction that if his right hand landed with full effect the victim of the assault, however strong, must come apart in front of him – would admit that his firepower was inferior without even trying to match it with Hagler's?

One round was surely the least he could give himself for gambling his blasting equipment against that of a world middleweight champion who had always been a heavy hitter but never noted for instant demolitions. Given his temperament, his record and the genuine provocation exchanged between these two men, Hearns was bound to attempt all-out war before he settled for a guerrilla campaign. How was he or anybody else to know that when his ambition met the hot gale of Hagler's obsessive commitment the result would be a first round that was probably the fiercest, most devouringly competitive ever seen in a major professional fight?

It is now history that what was devoured in those three minutes was Hearns's chance of adding the full middleweight championship to the light-middleweight title he currently holds, his dream of proving that all the muscles he had piled on to his tall, attenuated frame had made him suitable company for bigger, harder men.

To those at ringside that surge of mayhem seemed to go on forever ('I was praying for it to end – I thought I was going to have a heart attack,'

176

said Harry Mullan, the editor of *Boxing News*, afterwards) and when the bell intervened at last it was almost an impertinence to separate the two fighters on a scorecard.

Two of the judges, including our own Harry Gibbs, gave Hagler a 10–9 advantage and the third put Hearns ahead by the same margin. But maybe the right evaluation was made by an American friend who said he had scored it 11–11. Those figures are impossible, of course, but that merely made them appropriate to what he had just seen.

Hagler had prepared for the start by standing in his corner pummelling his own body and shaven head with his gloves, as if the aggression that was welling in him was too overwhelming to be contained through the few seconds he still had to endure before he could let it flood over Hearns.

Hagler's appearance at the end of that first round was equally significant. He was already cut and showing other signs of damage but his features remained in vivid focus, glowing with the concentrated belligerence he meant to bring back out for the second.

Hearns, in ominous contrast, wore the faintly blurred look of a man whose brain was beginning to have difficulty in transmitting signals to the distant frontiers of his long body. It is here that another fundamental objection can be made to all those neat theories about how Hearns should have deployed his resources in Las Vegas. If we acknowledge that he wasn't about to consider boxing on the retreat until he'd had a go at asserting himself in the first round, we are obliged to examine his capacity to apply that defensive policy by the time he was coming out for the second.

The truth is that he was not in particularly good shape for that or any other ploy. Hagler's awful pursuit had, in the last half-minute of the first, wrought profound havoc on both Hearns's confidence and his co-ordination.

There is evidence that at his fittest Hearns is barely able to maintain fluency, balance and counter-punching effectiveness when going backwards. His legs are too much like those of a wading bird to be ideal for a boxer. They serve well enough when he is bombarding his opponent, because then he can plant his feet firmly and unload from a solid base. But Hagler never once gave him a glimpse of such luxury, hounding him all over the ring with a mixture of primitive bloodlust and brilliantly improvised techniques.

There is an unprofitable tendency to forget that Hagler is, and has been since his youth (he was a middleweight at the age of 16), a master of the essentials of his trade, so much so that he was voted the outstanding participant in an amateur tournament whose entrants included Sugar Ray Leonard.

The use he made last Monday of the huge arsenal of skills he has accumulated during his many years in the game was not at all refined. But it was as inspired as it was dramatic. When he violated basic tenets of the sweet science his timing, especially with that extraordinarily versatile right hand, was so devastatingly excellent that Hearns was constantly at hazard.

Usually if a fighter jumps off his feet to aim punches the results are either negligible or ludicrous. Hagler contrived to make extravagant leaps and still land perfectly executed rights to the head.

Whether he was leading with that hand, or switching to the orthodox stance, he rarely dealt in anything as straightforward as a jab. Hooks, swings and anything else that might rock or demoralise Hearns were hurled across with what might have been mistaken for wild abandon. In fact only Hagler's spirit was really wild, for there was always a pronounced element of calculation in what he did with those powerful arms.

His spontaneous measurement of distance was invariably impressive and even when he was swinging roundhouse punches they had a habit of connecting. It was a blow almost meriting that description (a right, naturally) that began the third-round slaughter of Hearns. Two more rights clubbed into the taller man's head before he went down to sprawl helplessly on his back near his destroyer's corner.

A warrior's reflex brought Hearns unsteadily to his feet as the referee's count passed eight but his faculties were still scattered around Caesars Palace arena and there would have been no justification for letting him continue. He had, in a sense, been falling for most of the eight minutes the war lasted. Throughout the second there were clear hints that those freakishly thin legs were giving way under him. He was tripping over his own feet because he wasn't sure where his own feet were. Limbs that had never been likely to dance him out of danger were now having trouble keeping him upright and their chances of winning that battle were reduced to nil when cuts on Hagler's forehead and underneath his right eye spread blood across his face and made him still more frighteningly determined to kill off the opposition in a hurry. The more Hagler bled the more certain it was that Hearns would be sacrificed.

Now boxing has to recognise this long-reigning middleweight champion as one of the outstanding performers that most distinguished of divisions has known. (This reporter had begun his tiny share of the process as early as Monday morning by laying off some of the bets on Hearns mentioned in this space last week.)

Thinking of him along with other contemporary middleweights is enough to make a matchmaker feel like an undertaker. Perhaps Marvin will have to overcome his prejudice against meeting men above his weight and tackle Michael Spinks, the world light-heavyweight champion.

There is only limited enthusiasm for the idea of one awestruck observer of the deeds on Monday night. 'Who should Hagler fight after that?' he was asked and answered with a shiver: 'How about Russia?'

Magnificent McGuigan Is King

Barry McGuigan became surely the most rapturously acclaimed winner in the history of European boxing when the intensity of his aggression wore down the magnificent resistance of Eusebio Pedroza and battered the great Panamanian's World Boxing Association featherweight championship away from him over 15 rounds at the Queen's Park Rangers football ground in West London last night.

The predictable announcement that the referee and two ringside judges had made the 24-year-old from Clones, Co. Monaghan, a unanimous points winner produced the most euphoric scenes witnessed at a sports event in this country in decades. Those of us who had considered it a privilege to have a close-up view of McGuigan's unforgettable perform-ance began to have second thoughts as thousands of his Irish supporters crowded around the ring in a feverish, smothering swarm.

McGuigan's father, Pat, had sung 'Danny Boy' before the start, but now there was no possibility of a singing celebration. What came from the dancing, back-slapping throng was a blurred tumult that foretold a party which would last for a week at least and spread from the Irish pubs of Shepherd's Bush to every corner of that island across the water.

McGuigan had lived up to all the promise of an astonishing career which had seen only one insignificant stumble in the 26 fights that led to last night's challenge. He had refused to be frustrated or diminished by the wonderful talents and unbreakable spirit of one of the finest champions the featherweight division has ever seen.

Pedroza showed bewildering class in the first few rounds and even when McGuigan penetrated the stockade of inventive skills he erected around himself the Panamanian was revealed as an even greater hero than his admirers had declared him. He was battered down to the canvas in the seventh round, hammered close to helplessness near the end of the ninth and often during the last three that belonged so unequivocally to McGuigan he was reeling about the ring, looking out grimly above an evil swelling on his left cheek. But he refused to be broken.

That Barry McGuigan at last made him bow out of his championship is a triumph which can hardly be exaggerated and no one now is entitled to oppose very strenuously the claims some of us have made that this young man is the most dramatic fighter to emerge from these islands in many years.

The first three rounds had to be scored for Pedroza as the Panamanian boxed with cool brilliance on the retreat while McGuigan sought to find his range. 'Here we go' the Irish majority in the 25,000 crowd had chanted, from throats well lubricated in the Shepherd's Bush pubs, when the *Rocky* theme played their man into the ring. But not surprisingly

McGuigan needed a little time to develop the devastating rhythm that had swept aside all opposition on the way to the challenge.

In the first Pedroza backed away with a swiftness that betrayed respect for McGuigan's power, but was never flustered as he thrust out his long jab and occasionally crossed the right. It was not a punishing round but the Panamanian did most of the scoring and the same applied to the second round. His was the sharper, more accurate work but there was evidence that the advantage he had at the end of that round might be academic because McGuigan was continuing to press forward with a confidence that encouraged his supporters to be optimistic.

It was impossible even for a prejudiced observer to fail to admire the excellence of Pedroza's boxing in the third. But although he took that round, one thudding left hook by McGuigan as they broke after a clinch suggested exciting happenings were imminent.

The Panamanian's extraordinary height for a featherweight (5 ft 10 in) made him hard to reach and the length of his arms created extreme awkwardness when the two men closed. However, McGuigan was not in the least discouraged and was out in the middle of the ring waiting to go to war at the start of the fourth as Pedroza came slowly from his corner. That round was much more even in terms of scoring than its predecessors and no less rugged. The world champion had already been warned by the South African referee, Stanley Christodoulou, for holding and for letting his punches drift low.

McGuigan, for his part, was not inclined to be gentle and his head had a tendency to wander towards his opponent's thick moustache. The fifth provided three more minutes of often unscrupulous violence, with Pedroza earning a further reprimand for swinging low. McGuigan was getting stronger rather than weaker at this point and Pedroza, for all his impassive expression, must have felt concerned.

There was even more pronounced roughness in the sixth round of what was shaping to become a memorably unrelenting struggle. McGuigan had three warnings for minor misconduct, notably his old habit of forgetting where the waistline is, but self-belief was growing in him with every minute and his expression as he went back towards his manager, Barney Eastwood, in the corner was one to cheer every Irish heart in the stadium. What occurred in the seventh was sufficient to make his vast following ecstatic. He kept boring in through the champion's skills and near the end of the round the dark sky above the football ground was almost split by a massive roar as McGuigan caught his opponent with a brutal right hand to the head near Pedroza's own corner.

Those marvellous legs that have carried the older man through 19 defences of his title suddenly wilted and when a left hand crashed against his head he keeled over on to his side. He climbed bravely to his feet to take a mandatory eight count but at the end of the round the signs were that his championship might be heading across the Irish Sea.

Of course, this dark, serious-faced man is the truest of champions and he came back in the eighth to box superbly and fight ferociously, so much so that he probably took the round.

But that hardly seemed to matter in the ninth as McGuigan's fury enveloped him again. The climax of the challenger's aggression once more came near Pedroza's corner and this time, too, it was not the famous left hook but another thunderous right that started the bad troubles for his victim. That blow was followed by a calculated flurry of hooks and the champion's long legs looked like going completely. There were several heavy punches landed by McGuigan after the bell and as Pedroza teetered back to his stool he showed particularly the effects of three numbing right hands.

The 10th round was quieter, but in the 11th McGuigan, whose face shone with an eagerness for the fray, was crowding in cruelly again on a struggling veteran. Now his body punches were clearly telling and twice Pedroza dropped on one knee to claim the rest he sorely needed. In the 12th McGuigan maintained the pressure and despite Pedroza's persistent capacity for skilful rallies, the Irishman was the controlling influence.

All of the assessments of what had gone before now appeared scarcely relevant. They meant no more than the wonderful techniques Pedroza had exhibited to take his early, deceptive and by this time almost forgotten lead.

McGuigan was utterly, punishingly in command and his progression to the title one of exhilarating inevitability.

Lloyd Honeyghan v. Donald Curry, Atlantic City, 7 September 1986

A Shocker over Cocktails

The brief, harsh dramas that change the lives of fighters are often enacted in memorably peculiar places, but few have been as jarringly inappropriate as the setting provided by the Atlantic City Boardwalk last weekend. There, in 18 minutes of astonishing action, Donald Curry was transformed from an undisputed champion of the world into a battered former welterweight, with lacerations and violated bones where his aura of invincibility had been.

Both the deposed champion and his successor, Lloyd Honeyghan, the London-based Jamaican whose swiftly destructive hands painfully convinced Curry that he can no longer defy nature by forcing his tall frame into 147 lb, were clearly too preoccupied to worry about where they were doing business. But spectators did not have to be burdened with an exaggerated sense of history to feel that a boxing upset of such magnitude should have been witnessed somewhere other than the gaudy showroom at the Caesars Atlantic City Hotel Casino. Any genuine fight fan in the invited audience of around a thousand was in danger of having his cheek distractingly brushed by the leading edge of one of the cocktail waitresses going about her chores as if Buddy Hackett held the stage.

Admittedly, many Americans had imagined in advance that there might be an element of comedy, perhaps even of farce, in the proceedings. If they cared at all, they shared Curry's scepticism about Honeyghan's list of 27 straight victories as a professional. They also reflected reassuringly that in the course of this century only two challengers from Britain – Ted (Kid) Lewis in 1915 and 1917 and Alan Minter in 1980 – had left the US with world titles.

Curry appeared to have the perfect credentials for maintaining that inhospitable tradition. After enduring only three defeats in more than 400 bouts as an amateur, he had matured into a beautifully controlled, consistently lethal professional. Hunting his victim by sight, never resorting to the crude Braille readings of opponents that are favoured by too many boxers, Curry picked and executed his shots with a devastating economy. It took him only 16 professional fights (11 of them won by knockout) to earn the World Boxing Association welterweight title in 1983. After he made himself the undisputed master of the division last December, with a two-round demolition of the World Boxing Council champion, Milton McCrory, there was a widespread willingness to accept that in any pound-for-pound assessment of contemporary fighters, only Marvelous Marvin Hagler was in Curry's league.

While the Curry legend was growing, however, so was the man. From his home base in Fort Worth came persistent hints that Curry, who looks every bit of the 5 ft 10½ in given as his official height, found sweating down to 147 lb an increasingly arduous process, and so last year he began to take matches at the junior middleweight limit of 154 lb. But, having dropped back to welterweight and having proved strong enough to destroy McCrory, he overrode the opinion of his manager Dave Gorman that it was time to move up permanently. The omens implicit in the long hours he had spent in plastic sweat suits were forgotten amid the acclamation of the violent triumph over McCrory. Although Honeyghan could not possibly have known it, his time was coming.

As it happens, the 26-year-old West Indian has never been one to lack faith in his destiny. At the age of 12, three years after moving to England, he saw a telecast of one of Muhammad Ali's wars with Joe Frazier and announced to his father, Sylvester, that he had decided to be a world champion fighter. From that moment nothing – not even the considerable talent he had shown for cricket – interfered with his declared ambition. But a personality that is sometimes more interesting than endearing, one in which extrovert loudness coexists with obsessive privacy, has troubled his pro career. It was teaming up lately with Mickey Duff, the most successful entrepreneur in European boxing, and Bobby Neill, a

Scotsman who was British featherweight champion from 1959 to 1960 and is now the country's best trainer, that gave Honeyghan's career its decisive impetus.

When he arrived in Atlantic City most observers reckoned that all he had to commend him was an eighth-round knockout of Horace Shufford in Las Vegas in May, and that did not count much for someone planning to get in the ring with the likes of Curry. But the challenger bellowed his confidence all over town and backed up his vaunting by betting $5,000 on himself at 5–1, this despite more commonly quoted odds that put his chances at 6–1 or more. 'I want people to know how much I believe in myself,' he said. 'I can't wait to start punching Curry on the head. I'm going to smash his face in.'

Honeyghan came fairly close to fulfilling that coarse prophecy on Saturday night. He and Neill had agreed that the essence of their strategy must be to force Curry to back up, and their plan took immediate effect as the challenger attacked with surging verve and a variety of accurate punches to take the first round easily. Then, early in the second, Honeyghan caught Curry with a tremendous driving right that hurled the champion across the ring. Curry managed to close and hold long enough for his head to clear, but he was already bleeding from the mouth. Honeyghan compounded the champion's miseries with a sharp combination to the head before the end of the round.

Curry reached far into a substantial spirit to try to turn the fight in the third and fourth rounds but, although he won both, he was never for a moment in total command, never recognisable as a man who came to this job with seven straight knockouts behind him. By the end of the fourth round, an awareness of imminent calamity was seeping into Curry's head. 'I had been too relaxed all day,' he recalled later. 'I usually want to get a little nervous, but I didn't feel that way. I couldn't get into the rhythm, and during the fight I was weak and sluggish. I had no strength in my legs, and my timing just wasn't there. I wasn't myself.'

That wasn't surprising since he had burned down from 168 lb to meet Honeyghan. Curry was not himself because part of him had been left in puddles on the floor of a gym. What remained might easily have been deposited on the floor of the ring in the fifth round, which saw Honeyghan punishingly regain control. Curry looked a beaten fighter before an accidental butt from his opponent's cropped head in the sixth opened an alarming gash under his left eyebrow. Honeyghan worsened the cut with ripping head punches, and ringside doctors were merely endorsing the view of Gorman, and of the loser himself, when they ruled that Curry should not come off his stool for the seventh round. Instead, he went to a nearby hospital to have some 20 stitches applied around the damaged eye and one to his lower lip. Despite all that, as well as the pain of a broken nose, the 25-year-old ex-champion called a press conference at 1.30 a.m. on Sunday and talked with such dignity that no one was inclined to dismiss his vow that he will be back to spread havoc among the junior middleweights.

Honeyghan, holder of all three versions of the world welterweight championship, faces an early defence of his crown against Johnny Bumphus, the International Boxing Federation's No. 1 contender, but the real money fight on his horizon should involve 1984 Olympic gold medallist Mark Breland. That could be a year away.

The new champion says he has no fear of any fighter – only of fame. He had better work on that problem. Hammering Donald Curry was no way to stay out of the limelight.

Marvin Hagler v. Sugar Ray Leonard, Las Vegas, 6 April 1987

The Illusion of Victory

It is not only in Las Vegas that professional boxing's system of scoring shows all the intellectual consistency of rolling a pair of dice.

Don't blame the desert air for the rush of blood to the brain that caused Jose Juan (Jo Jo) Guerra, a WBC judge, to make Sugar Ray Leonard a winner by ten rounds to two over Marvin Hagler while another official, Lou Filippo, was giving the 6 April fight at Caesars Palace to Hagler by seven rounds to five. If the record of judges sanctioned by its State Athletic Commission is anything to go by, Nevada is a congenial environment for officials with the glorious eccentricity of mind brought to his work by Guerra. But bad decisions know no boundaries.

The simple truth is that at this stage of its long and erratic history, prize-fighting is still nowhere near establishing any consistently accurate means of measuring performance. If the comparative effectiveness of two fighters is so difficult to calibrate (or so open to extravagantly subjective interpretations) that Guerra and Filippo can contradict each other as outrageously as they did, then even when everybody stays honest, boxing clearly carries a far higher risk of recurring injustice than any other sport.

When judges talk about focusing on paramount criteria – on identifying effective aggressiveness, clean punching, ring generalship and quality defence – they are merely emphasising the complexity, perhaps the impossibility, of the exercise. Much of the time all they can do is review a fighter's performance, much as a theatre critic would an actor's, making the pseudo-scientific adjustment of putting their impressions into figures.

No one has ever understood the boxing judge as reviewer of theatre better than Sugar Ray Leonard. Even Muhammad Ali, who substituted histrionics for real fighting often enough in the latter part of his career, was usually more concerned with disconcerting his opponent and getting the crowd on his side. Leonard sought those dividends too against Hagler.

But the overriding priority for him appeared to be the manipulation of official minds.

Naturally, to achieve that end, Ray had to bring a lot to the party. Physically and mentally, he was astonishingly strong, sharp and resilient after what had been, essentially, a five-year layoff.

Thus, looking and moving so much better than anyone had a right to expect, Leonard was in a position to exploit the Schulberg Factor. This phenomenon – a compound optical illusion – may not have been discovered by Budd Schulberg, the novelist and fight aficionado, but he receives credit here for pointing it out to a few of us who were asking ourselves how Hagler came to be so cruelly misjudged. Budd's reasoning was that people were so amazed to find Sugar Ray capable of much more than they imagined that they persuaded themselves he was doing far more than he actually was. Similarly, having expected extreme destructiveness from Marvin, they saw anything less as failure and refused to give him credit for the quiet beating he administered.

What Ray Leonard pulled off in his split decision over Hagler was an epic illusion. He had said beforehand that the way to beat Hagler was to give him a distorted picture. But this shrewdest of fighters knew it was even more important to distort the picture for the judges. His plan was to 'steal' rounds with a few flashy and carefully timed flurries and to make the rest of each three-minute session as unproductive as possible for Hagler by circling briskly away from the latter's persistent pursuit. When he made his sporadic attacking flourishes, he was happy to exaggerate hand-speed at the expense of power, and neither he nor two of the scorers seemed bothered by the fact that many of the punches landed on the champion's gloves and arms. This was showboating raised to an art form, and the brilliance with which it was sustained was a tribute to Leonard's wonderful nerve, which is cut from the same flawless diamond as Ali's.

But, however much the slick ploys blurred the perceptions of those on the fevered sidelines, they never broke Hagler. He has a different kind of spirit, but it is no less resolute than Leonard's. The hounding intensity that kept him unbeaten through 11 years from 1976 will soon be a memory, but he had enough left to press on through his early frustrations and throw the superior volume of hurtful punches. I'm convinced Hagler won the fight; a draw, and the retention of the title, was the very least he deserved.

'It's unfair, man, it's unfair,' Hagler said helplessly to the master illusionist at the end. That's an old cry and – given the haphazard way boxing judges its heroes – all too often a true one.

Ring of Caution

The Observer, 6 March 1988

There will be a comeback before the come-back for Barry McGuigan.

The first serious fight in the renewed professional career of the former featherweight champion of the world will not, he insists, take place in a public ring, with crowds and clamour and a big purse at the end of it. It will be a small and private war conducted behind the locked doors of a boxing gym.

For that engagement, McGuigan and a highly paid volunteer from among his sparring partners will put aside the heavily padded gloves favoured in training and pull on the eight-ounce kind used in official fights. The Irishman will dispense with all the other mitigating accoutrements of the gym, stripping down to the essential equipment of his trade, but the opponent will be allowed the type of headguard that is now standard in amateur competition.

McGuigan is determined that what ensues will be much more than a dramatised sparring session. Talking about it last Thursday, he could not quite keep the throb of anticipation out of his voice. 'We'll go at it for five, six rounds, really have a contest behind closed doors. I'll wear no head-guard and, for starters, I'll find out again what it is like to get hit with those eight-ounce gloves instead of the 12-ounce sort the lads have been wearing in our work.

'But I think the other fella will be glad of his headguard because I will be using the light gloves, too, and that will be some change after those blubbery 14-ounce things I am wearing in training. I have been feeling so good for so long in the gym, satisfying myself more in sparring than I ever did even when I was world champion, and I can't wait to get a taste of the real thing. So I want to give myself at least one private contest, maybe two, before I start throwing punches in public.'

He knows, of course, that even such conscientiously staged dress rehearsals cannot possibly tell him whether he is right or wrong to return to the ring. The comeback is not so much a tradition as an affliction in boxing, a recurring proof that fighters are hopeless judges of their own limitations, ready in far too many cases to go on trying to con the calendar until a sense of mortality is harshly imparted by another man's fists.

But two significant facts separate McGuigan from the generality. The first is his youth (he turned 27 last Sunday) and the other is the peculiar combination of pressures that caused his estrangement from the fight game after the literally agonising loss of his World Boxing Association title to the Mexican-American Stevie Cruz in Las Vegas 20 months ago.

That defeat, or rather the bitter circumstances surrounding it, made an open wound of the acrimony and mistrust that had been quietly festering between McGuigan and Barney Eastwood, the manager who had seemed more like a blood relative on the exciting, skilfully planned climb up through British and European championships to recognition (along with Azumah Nelson of Ghana) as one of the two best featherweights in the world. The bad feeling has since put Eastwood and his protégé in opposite corners in court several times. One hearing left the older man obliged to pay his ex-fighter £650,000 as money due from previous earnings but still holding a legal claim on McGuigan's services if he resumed his career. After further exchanges between heavyweight counsel in Belfast last week the soured partnership was finally dissolved when Frank Warren, the London promoter who has taken charge of McGuigan's ring activities, paid Eastwood £200,000 to relinquish his stake.

The volatile Belfast bookmaker took his leave with a volley of hard words (like 'big-headed' and 'unworkable' and 'ungrateful') but the target of the criticism declines to respond in kind. 'We had great times together,' he says. 'Things went wrong but an endless slagging match won't do anybody any good.'

He has the look these days of someone who has endured as much bleakness over the last couple of years as he is likely to need for a while. The face, with its frame of black hair and thin moustache, is still capable of the slightly Gallic jauntiness of old. But occasionally its pale features appear drawn and overshadowed by recent wearing experiences, by far the most devastating of which was the death of his father last June. He finds his immediate family life – with his wife and three young children in the second home he has established near Hemel Hempstead, Hertford-shire, because his true heartland in Clones, County Monaghan, was less than an ideal base for his burgeoning commercial interests – richly fulfilling but there is always a tightening of his throat when Pat McGuigan is mentioned.

Obviously, he would not be disregarding a formidable bank balance and heading once more towards the hazards of the ring if he did not believe that his father would have approved. His own conviction is that the real Barry McGuigan did not lose the world title, that he never even turned up on that smotheringly hot afternoon in the Nevada desert in the summer of 1986. He says the heat of the south-western US had already drained him during his preparation and the disparate complications of ear and ankle trouble had left him so low that he pleaded with his manager to be granted a postponement of his defence.

As he waited for the first bell, he was depressed and alarmed by a feeling of extreme heaviness in his arms and his forebodings were miserably justified once the fight was under way. He had often started slowly in the past but before the ordeal in Las Vegas he always found it easy to move quickly up through the gears until he had achieved the searing, relentless momentum that has, on memorable nights in Belfast and London, burned away the resistance of such considerable adversaries as Juan LaPorte and Eusebio Pedroza.

Against Cruz he could not believe his own impotence. 'He hit me a couple of fairly ordinary punches in the third and fourth rounds and my legs started to go. When LaPorte hit me he almost took my head off. But, though I felt a huge fuzz in my head for a second or two, I was all right again straightaway and strong as ever. When Cruz hit me I was clear as a bell but my legs were going. My biggest asset always was that I could fight all night long but here I was tired, wiped out after three rounds. It was like pushing through water to throw punches. It was crazy and horrible and it could never have happened to me if I had been anything like myself.'

Those of us who watched queasily at ringside as McGuigan – previously the embodiment of surging, aggressive verve – struggled with extraordinary courage against the deadly torpor that had invaded his body like a disease will never forget the pitiful blankness which spread across his eyes before he sank to the points defeat that was the first he had suffered since surrendering a decision to the eccentricity of a referee at the start of his life as a pro. Certainly there was an unmistakable core of injustice in that nightmare but can the man who went through it really want to risk more of the same?

There are many strands to McGuigan's declaration that he does. He points out that he will be going to scale at the super-featherweight limit of 9 st 4 lb and thus avoiding the torture involved in forcing himself through the last barrier between his natural ultimate of 9 st 2 lb and the classic featherweight level of 9 st. At nine-four, he argues, all the fierce strength that was his pride will be restored and he is adamant that his technique, far from eroding, is showing marked improvement as the result of lessons learned in increasingly studious sparring and from watching some of America's outstanding fighters at practice. He is understandably committed to the belief that a blend of the European and American styles gives him maximum effectiveness and he will employ sparmates and a training adviser from across the Atlantic as he approaches the match he is scheduled to have around late April.

When he meets Frank Warren today to discuss details of that assignment (of course, it is almost sure to feature opposition from the States) thoughts of having a shot at a world title soon afterwards will be brightened by his opinion that the domain of the super-featherweights is not desperately intimidating at present. Neither he nor Warren will want the political entanglements inseparable from the WBA championship, which is held by the South African Brian Mitchell. Warren has firm contractual arrangements with the International Boxing Federation's champion, Rocky Lockridge, but he defends in April against the dangerous Harold 'The Shadow' Knight.

The WBC ruler of the division, Azumah Nelson, whose favourite hobby used to be bad-mouthing McGuigan, would be the man to bring in heavy money. Since Nelson is nearly 30 and may have shown his age lately by being knocked down before winning a split decision over Mario Martinez of Mexico, perhaps he need not be seen as an ogre if McGuigan is indeed the exhilarating warrior he was.

This is a big question, for this is not the realm of Eddie the Eagle, where a man can make himself a chat-show hero by dint of effrontery and incompetence. All we on the sidelines can do is worry and wish Barry McGuigan well.

King of the Ring and Lord of Chaos

The Observer, 20 November 1988

The extreme disorder in the life of Mike Tyson was almost enough in itself to ensure the emergence of Don King as the most potent single influence on the heavyweight champion's affairs, an eloquent black Iago at his ear.

Confusion is King's element. He is boxing's Lord of Chaos, a masterly exploiter of the fight game's permanent state of anarchy, its chronic lack of any widely accepted system of business or code of behaviour.

'There was no criminality,' said Joseph Spinelli after playing a prominent part in a prolonged FBI investigation of King and other boxing promoters a few years back, 'because there are no rules that govern this industry . . . It's just a mess, and Don King is smart enough to know how to exploit that mess.' Spinelli, who has made further investigations in his current role of New York State Inspector General, calls King's contracts 'horrible' and then adds: 'But in the world of boxing they're legal. In my mind they're nothing more than legalised extortion.'

Harsher words have been applied to King in the course of his extraordinarily swift rise from Cleveland's Eastside ghetto (where his precocious predominance in the gambling rackets was interrupted by imprisonment for killing a fellow hustler in a street fight) to commercial sovereignty over world boxing and especially its most lucrative component, the heavyweight division. Apart from the attentions of the FBI, which were focused on him for several years in the early '80s, he has blithely weathered the intensive probings of Grand Juries and the hostility of the IRS, the US tax authorities whose persistence proved too much even for Al Capone.

When he and his long-serving secretary, Constance Harper, vice-president of Don King Productions, were indicted by a Federal Grand Jury in Manhattan late in 1984 on 23 counts of income tax evasion, filing fraudulent tax returns and conspiracy, he was exposed to the risk of up to 46 years in jail. But – forsaking the diamond rings and gold pendants, the velvet trim, ruffles, spangles and sequins that frequently enable his appearance to echo the garish hyperbole of his marathon monologues –

he came on as a soberly dressed and respectful witness and was acquitted by a mainly female jury, a number of whom clustered round him afterwards for autographs.

When he talked some time later of his series of troubles with the Justice Department, he had obviously washed the courtroom meekness right out of his famous hair and was back in verbal overdrive. 'They went down the list of every conceivable charge known to man,' he said. 'Racketeering, skimming, kickbacks, ticket scalping, fixing fights, preordaining fights, vitiating officials, corrupting judges, all the way down to laundering money. Everything but the Lindbergh baby. Instead of using me as the true attestation of the American Dream, they threw the book at me.'

And of the fact that Connie Harper drew a short jail sentence, he said simply: 'Spite. They couldn't lay a glove on me, so they took it out on her.'

King's prodigious capacity for survival (there are some who explain the outrageous vertical sweep of his coiffure by saying he was given the electric chair and walked away when the straps were undone) cannot fail to impress even his many detractors in boxing. It is a quality he has been developing since childhood, mainly because his background gave him no option. He was second-youngest in the large family fathered by a Cleveland steelworker who died on 7 December 1941, but not from the bombs the Japanese dropped on Pearl Harbor that day. Clarence King was killed ('consumed' is the word used by his celebrated son) by a ladleful of molten metal. His widow used the $10,000 'tragedy money' to move the family from the hard-core ghetto to a mixed neighbourhood named Mount Pleasant but their circumstances dictated that none of them could be excused bread-winning duties. At the age of ten Donald manifested the enthusiastic talent for hustling that remains the supreme force of his nature, starting by selling his mother's roasted peanuts around the 'policy houses', usually condemned properties where blacks crowded in to play an illegal numbers game that is a kind of bingo of the streets.

Though he finished his studies at John Adams High School and was attracted to the idea of continuing his education, the numbers racket pulled him in. By his 20s, Cleveland police files described him as a policy czar and that meant real money for a mathematical wizard now known as 'The Kid' or 'The Talker'. It could be dangerous, of course. The porch of his house was blown up, his saloon was torched and 30 No. 5 birdshot pellets were sprayed into the back of his head from a 12-gauge shotgun.

There were deadlier consequences when a dispute over $600 owed to him by a minor numbers man, Samuel Lee Garrett, got out of hand outside a tavern on the corner of East 100 St and Cedar Avenue on 20 April 1966. He testified later that Garrett had followed him from the bar to his car parked by the kerb and attacked him, that his own punching and kicking response was self-defence. To the arresting officers, the accused (who gave his occupation as self-employed grocer) explained the presence of the loaded but unfired .357 Colt Magnum in his hand by saying he was alarmed by Garrett's efforts to pull something out of his pocket. Garrett, a tall, thin consumptive with a drug habit, was found to have massive brain injuries and died on 25 April. He was 34, the same age as King.

Various versions of the Garrett death form a familiar element in Don King's biographical notes but what is less well known is that it was the second time he had faced a murder charge. In December 1954, he shot and killed a man named Hillary Brown who was firing at him while robbing a numbers house King operated. That shooting was deemed justifiable homicide and he was released.

The Garrett case brought a conviction for second-degree murder that was reduced by a judge to manslaughter and sent King to the Marion Correctional Institution for four years. His time as No. 125734 in Room 10, Cellblock 6, was his Road to Damascus, a transmutation given mystical significance, certainly in his own accounts, by the discovery of the liberating and uplifting power of books. Since his release in 1971 he has been cumulatively credited with a reading list that might have filled in a life sentence for Methuselah.

Pericles, Socrates, Demosthenes, Marx, Engels, Kant, Hegel, Schopenhauer, Nietzsche, the Apostle Paul, Thoreau, Jefferson, Franklin, Jesus, Voltaire, J.K. Galbraith, William Jennings Bryan, Donne, Kahlil Gibran, Rostand are just a sprinkling of authors he is reputed to have absorbed in the intervals of becoming so intimate with Shakespeare that he refers to him as Bill. Many of the favourites in his vast arsenal of half-remembered quotations come out mangled (he was once heard lauding the teachings of St Thomas Aquinine) but it's worth a journey to hear how, in his rapid, piping delivery, he savours a line like 'Sweet are the uses of adversity'.

Only a fool could fail to see that behind King's unconvincing flourishes of erudition an extremely high intelligence and truly fecund imagination are at work. What makes them devastating when brought to bear on the anarchic arena of fight promotion is that they are allied to a deep, almost joyful dedication to the hustle, a love of devious stratagems and blinding extravagances of showmanship. 'If press conferences were outlawed, he'd give up the game,' says an American reporter.

For all his immense wealth, he cannot at 57 sit still to enjoy the pleasures of the 179 rural acres he owns in Ashtabula County, Ohio, where his second wife Henri has decorated their huge, much-windowed house with a catholicity of taste that embraces Chinese screens, antique clocks, a swimming-pool shaped like a gigantic boxing glove and featuring a six-foot fibreglass Statue of Liberty, and an indoor tableau of stuffed animals lorded over by a snarling lion because 'Don's a Leo'.

On the contrary, in spite of recurring rumours about health problems, he is tirelessly seeking to woo Mike Tyson away from Bill Cayton, the champion's legitimate manager. King is a notoriously charming suitor, though those who have fallen out with him know that the sweet talk and literary allusions can give way to the sort of violent vituperation that is particularly menacing when it comes from a man who stands 6 ft 3 in without counting his hair and weighs upwards of 17 st. A remarkable proportion of his business associations end in litigious acrimony, often with him making an out-of-court settlement.

More than a few client fighters claim to have suffered because, they allege, King exerts a monopolistic control over whole areas of their trade, effectively exploiting his son Carl's position as a manager of boxers and his own heavy influence within governing bodies of the sport, and often leaving the men who bleed in the ring cheated or drastically short-changed.

Yet, between bouts of carousing that have encouraged his squat body to balloon, Tyson seems taken with King's entreaties. Perhaps Don can again rely on skilful playing of the black card, the call of brother to brother that won over Muhammad Ali and his Muslim manager Herbert Muhammad a decade and a half ago, sending Ali to Zaire for the Rumble in the Jungle with George Foreman and starting the transformation of a recently discharged convict into a global legend.

Don King has travelled a long way since his days in Room 10, Cellblock 6. He has dined at the White House and won a battery of awards for contributions to ethnic and humanitarian causes. His successful plea for the Ohio Governor's pardon in the Garrett case was backed by Jesse Jackson and the widow of Martin Luther King.

But neither he nor Mike Tyson is ever likely to forget the raw streets both have come from and for the moment that bond probably means more than money to the younger man. Perhaps Tyson will be lucky and never find himself thinking like his outstanding predecessor as champion, Larry Holmes, whose career was run by King and who now says: 'Don King doesn't care about black or white. He just cares about green.'

Lloyd Honeyghan v. Marlon Starling, Las Vegas, 4 February 1989

Shadows Fall on British Dreams

At a time when a friendly omen would not have come amiss, there was naught for Frank Bruno's comfort in Lloyd Honeyghan's first and probably last experience of fighting in Las Vegas.

Logically, Bruno should have no trouble in persuading himself of the irrelevance of Honeyghan's ordeal, since each man certainly is an island when it comes to coping with the hazards of the ring. Yet if, as would be only natural, sinister shadows have begun to flit around the edges of the heavyweight challenger's mind in the dwindling days before his rendezvous with Mike Tyson, he will find no consolation in a comparison of what he and last weekend's loser brought to the desert.

Lloyd Honeyghan came here with the welterweight championship of the world, a big reputation and a high opinion of himself and, in the assessment of bookmakers, an odds-on chance of keeping all three. He left so traumatised, physically and mentally, that there would seem to be a strong case for giving up the game while the balance between sufferings endured and riches earned is still acceptable.

Bruno headed for Vegas yesterday from his training camp near Phoenix, Arizona, carrying far more good wishes than convincing credentials. He has conquered many hearts but is the champion of nowhere and, unfortunately, lovability is no substitute for talent when someone like Tyson is coming off the other stool.

This month of February is shaping to provide the British with a superfluous reminder that boxing is more implacable than any other sport in destroying chauvinistic illusions – and in inflicting nearly unbearable hurt on individuals along the way. To see in close-up what that battering defeat by Marlon Starling had done to Honeyghan was to shudder again at the harshness of the fight game.

Standing by Honeyghan's chair in a bare room off the Sports Pavilion at Caesars Palace Hotel, watching helplessly as he huddled forward almost into the foetal position while excruciating pain spread out behind his closed eyelids from the hideously swollen right side of his face, at least one reporter who has found boxing irresistible all his life wondered not for the first time if he had the right to be so captivated by it. Is it, I was obliged to ask, mainly the fear of being dismissed as an ageing hypocrite (of being bracketed with those bores we could all name who find it easy to turn sourly moralistic about sex as soon as their own juices start to dry up) that keeps the misgivings sufficiently in check to let me go back to the ringside?

Maybe. Or perhaps it really is something in boxing that no other sport can produce, not just the rawness of its excitements but the opportunity it thrusts upon men for the most basic kind of heroism, grace not merely under pressure but under siege. That explanation is made more tenable by the insistence of most fighters that any attempt to stop them from doing the thing they do best would be an intolerable invasion of liberty. But, obviously, their enthusiasm for a dangerous trade doesn't automatically grant the rest of us a licence to encourage them to take the serious risks inseparable from it.

Positive discouragement was appropriate after Honeyghan's 25-minute exposure to the hostile superiority of Starling. There was, of course, much more than physical agony in the sadness that hung around him like an isolating cordon as he awaited the ambulance which would carry him to a local hospital for a precautionary examination. He had taken an eagerly proclaimed optimism and so much else to that ring a few yards away and now he was back with nothing but a few tributes to the gameness with which he had gone down to a nine-round thrashing.

Thoughts of how unendearing his ways can be in better times, how aggressively perverse and crudely egotistical, did nothing to make his forlornness in defeat any less moving. It was hard to relate bombast and self-promoting hyperbole to the crumpled figure who kept muttering that all he wanted was to be home with his children. There was a feeling that everything and everyone surrounding him had become part of a nightmare and that he would not be rescued from it until he was thousands of miles away and back among his family.

Seeing him like that made it almost a source of guilt for some of us that we had begun to imagine such a dismantling of his dreams, if not on this night then on another not too far up the road.

Notwithstanding the excellence of his record, the extravagant admirers who tried vainly to sustain the argument that he was one of the very best fighters Britain had produced were ignoring doubts about the staying power of his body and of his concentration as well as weaknesses in technique, like a tendency to throw punches on a round trajectory and a recurring openness of stance that creates vulnerability to head shots for which the good natural timing of his own hands cannot always compensate.

Once Starling had established at Caesars Palace that the strains of an up-and-down career had not drained too much out of him, we knew that Honeyghan's second tenancy of the World Boxing Council welterweight championship was over. I saw him as the winner of the first three rounds (and he shook Starling in the third with a big, heavy right hand that might have been crucial had the point of impact not been so high on the head) but it was unmistakably ominous that he opted for simply shovelling in blows at an extraordinary, self-exhausting rate instead of seeking the precision and subtlety needed to gain more than occasional penetration of his opponent's skilful defence. When Starling came back strongly in the fourth to dominate and all but outclass the champion with the sharp, chopping effectiveness of his counter-punching, the decisive trail had been set.

It was, as far as Honeyghan could tell later, in that fourth round that a searing pain developed in his upper cheekbone, wide of the right eye. Whether or not his layman's diagnosis of damage to a nerve had medical validity, no one can dispute his account of how horrible the implications were. 'The least flick with a jab was like somebody shoving a knife into my face. It was killing me . . . I got on my toes and started to dance because I didn't want to get hit on the face.'

'Get him, Marlon,' a contorted mouth beside me at ringside screamed at that point. 'He's running like a dog.' Lloyd was running like a wounded man, which makes a much sadder sight. He stood and fought when he could but he was doomed long before the referee's intervention in the ninth. The swelling on his jaw was grotesque and the bruising about his mouth so bad that he could not clench on his gumshield, which was frequently dislodged to fly into the crowd like a symbol of departing hope.

The British could sense in the Las Vegas air more than a hint that this bad night was a rehearsal for another.

Mike Tyson v. Frank Bruno, Las Vegas, 25 February 1989

A Prize Beyond Reach

As if his own muscle and readily summoned malevolence were not enough, Mike Tyson will have the weight of history in his punches when he starts throwing terrible hooks at the head of Frank Bruno on Saturday night.

The experience of a century tells us that Britain does not breed heavyweight champions of the world and as Bruno moves down the aisle towards the ring at the Las Vegas Hilton it won't take too much imagination to see him as jostling through a clammy throng of disconsolate ghosts, a spectral crush of all the many hopefuls we have sent out to be battered in pursuit of a prize we were apparently not meant to win.

It is true that this latest challenger has specific reasons for refusing to be identified with the catalogue of humiliations visited on his predecessors. He is different from all of them, and not just because he is black. The combination of size and punching power makes for a more relevant distinction. Henry Cooper hit more explosively but was almost a light-heavyweight and, while Joe Bugner had bulk comparable with Bruno's 6 ft 3 in and 16½ st, the Hungarian-Englishman's inherent passivity sometimes prompted the thought that he had the physique of a Greek statue but fewer moves.

Bruno has greater aggression than Bugner but fluency is a major problem for him, too. Nor is his tendency to think and execute ponderously in the ring the only significant defect he carries into the most profitable and dangerous engagement of his professional life. Indeed his disadvantages are numerous and substantial and, since they include an inclination to crumble dramatically under heavy bombardment, every argument for recognising him as a new kind of British contender must be swamped by the conviction that he will end his quest as the vast majority of the others did: outgunned and horizontal.

There is real pain in having to make such a prediction, for the big man is no less appealing at close range than the public at home perceive him to be. A current of relaxed, mutual pleasure spreads through his bantering exchanges with reporters, who yield happily to his mixture of modesty, openness and inviolable charm and even come to savour their familiarity with some of his deadpan one-liners.

It is only when he rises to leave, to return to the lonely reality of why he is here, that a few of us suddenly feel presumptuous about taking warm, easy enjoyment from his company in such circumstances. Then we wonder again if there is something too comfortable, perhaps even patronising, about the gushing emotionalism of the nation's attitude to a man approaching the climactic phase of a seemingly doomed mission.

Naturally, Bruno insists that he does not read the script that way. When he finished his final sparring session on Thursday afternoon (having totalled 158 rounds in the two months or so he has been in America, not to mention the 85 he did between the several upsetting postponements that Tyson's marital and managerial disputes imposed on this fight) he was full of upbeat utterances. He was, he said, 'mentally beautiful, physically beautiful'. It would now be just a matter of remaining cool about the job, staying loose with stretching exercises and short runs on a nearby golf course where he expected to be kept alert by the carnivorous intentions of 'some serious dogs'.

No, he didn't think he had stopped sparring prematurely and he knew for sure that Mark Wills and Terry Armstrong, the last survivors of the seven partners he has used up since late December, were glad to take their wages and call it quits. 'Those fellas are in a bad way, they have nothing left,' confirmed George Francis, the challenger's trainer for the past couple of years. 'They deserve medals. They've needed painkillers to stand up to all the bruising Frank's given them.'

We had observed first-hand at a public workout 24 hours before how much suffering Wills and Armstrong, two stocky journeymen, had brought on themselves by their quixotic attempts to impersonate Tyson's rumbustiously aggressive ways. In Johnny Tocco's classically dilapidated gym in downtown, blue-collar Vegas, where the scruffy walls are plastered to the low ceiling with posters proclaiming the violent propensities of an extraordinary diversity of fighters (from Bad News Wallace, a Nevada State champion, to Ali, Hagler and Duran), they excruciated stoically under some of the most effective attacking this witness has ever seen from Bruno in training. Considering his intrinsic limitations, and the 16 months he has been without a fight since demolishing the bloated remnants of Bugner, he looked fine.

Particularly impressive were the unwonted frequency and sharpness with which he threw left hooks. In close, he essayed left and right uppercuts and if they did not work he bore down powerfully on his man, pushing him towards the floor in what was plainly a rehearsal of a scarcely legal manoeuvre designed to neutralise the champion's deadly infiltrations.

'The rules don't count when you fight Tyson,' said Terry Lawless, the manager who is seeking to make Bruno the fifth winner of a world title sent out from his East London stable. 'He tears up the book. We know a lot about him because we've been watching him since he was a kid. Frank sparred two rounds with him when Tyson was 15 or 16 and then when Mike was 17 Frank worked a full week with him, doing about 30 rounds. I was very pleased with what I saw. Tyson has improved tremendously since but Frank has got a lot better, too.

'Whenever Tyson has a fight coming up you see nothing but film clips of him knocking people over, everywhere you go. It's brilliant propaganda. I think Jimmy Jacobs started it and since Jimmy died it's been kept going. The repetition of all those devastating knockouts helps to keep the world in awe of him. Maybe the world should be in awe of him. But it does seem that so far his opponents haven't fought as if they wanted to win.

'We know how to fight Mike Tyson but doing it may be another matter. It's always a hell of a lot easier on this side of the ropes.' That last truism never had more point than it does in relation to the current heavyweight champion of the world, who deliberately exudes unnerving menace from the moment he leaves the dressing-room without even the minimal niceties of gown and socks to muffle the rawness of what he is about.

His most recent opponent, the outstanding light-heavyweight Michael Spinks, had not lost in the 12 years before they collided in Atlantic City last June. But the mere thought of the ferocity he was going to encounter melted Spinks's resolve like a snowflake in a furnace and within 91 seconds he had drowned in his own dread to become the 31st victim to be stopped by Tyson in a brief, prodigious career of 35 uninterrupted victories.

Bruno has been blatantly susceptible to nervousness in previous fights and a number of his most committed admirers acknowledge a danger that he will freeze on Saturday. They do not imagine that the sense of impending nightmare created by Tyson's ritualistic arrival in the ring will be diminished by the fact that the two or three key handlers who accompanied him down the aisle when he was under the guidance of Jimmy Jacobs and Bill Cayton will now give way to an egregious entourage of Don King's red-jerkined flunkeys.

There was no doubting Bruno's sincerity when he told us in Tocco's gym that he would go to meet Tyson entirely unafraid. But that was in Tocco's gym. 'I don't fear him one little bit and I mean that from the heart,' he said. 'I don't give a shit if he comes on with the entourage, with 20 people around him. I'm not fighting them – I'm fighting him.'

If the mean edge implied in that avowal is genuine and can be maintained it will be a good ally. But can big, endearing Frank Bruno possibly match the depth of psychological and physical hostility that comes naturally to the frightening 22-year-old he faces? Their backgrounds alone establish a gulf that favours Bruno everywhere but in the primitive space they will share at the Hilton.

He was brought up with plenty of street experience in South London and was sufficiently unruly to be sent to a boarding school for difficult boys. But he was never a law-breaker, was raised within the warmth of a loving family and has now formed another of his own. His brother Michael (at 39, twelve years older than Frank) is here and will soon be joined by their mother and the mother of Frank's two young daughters.

He tells us much about where he is coming from when he says: 'My mother is an evangelist, a Christian lady and she doesn't want me to do boxing – I don't think any mother would want her son to fight – but my mum would rather me do boxing than be a mugger or a robber.'

By the age of 10 or 11, Mike Tyson was a mugger and a robber in Brownsville, Brooklyn, one of the worst ghettoes in America, the sort of environment of which he says now: 'When I was young, coming up, it was a sign of weakness to admire someone else.' Soon he was in correctional institutions and would have been heading for serious crime and probably an early death had not the late Cus D'Amato rescued him and channelled his capacity to terrorise into boxing.

The assumption that his love-affair with the game has been a model of steadfastness compared with the luridly volatile marriage to Robin Givens that ended with a quickie-divorce in the Dominican Republic on Tuesday was challenged the other day when he said that 'since I began boxing at 13 I must have quit 200 times'. But it is unquestionably the central passion of his young life, whether he is performing in the ring or being animatedly erudite about its history. He lives to expand his role in that history, declaring that he 'would rather win and get nothing than lose and get $20 million'. Ominously for Bruno, he means to break the record set in 1900 by James J. Jeffries for the fastest knockout in a heavyweight title fight, which stands at 55 seconds.

Looking at the great muscular slabs of his body from a distance of three feet, seeing it looking perhaps harder and lighter than it has been since he came to the top, made sharing his faith easy. Then he added further chilling persuasion: 'Sometimes I hit a guy with a punch I thought had missed. I say to myself, "Did I hit him?" – and he's lying there snoring.'

When Tyson was last seen working out in public two and a half weeks ago, his timing was still slightly ragged. But the word from pummelled sparring partners is that he has since conscientiously honed himself to a brutal efficiency. They say the troubles in his life (having taken a day off to make an ex-wife of Robin, he found his ex-trainer, Kevin Rooney, coming at him with a $10 million breach of contract suit) don't weaken him but translate to viciousness in the ring.

If Tyson is at his best, it is inconceivable that the Frank Bruno who was all but scrambled by Jumbo Cummings, knocked out by 'Bonecrusher' Smith and pulverised by a fat and already declining Tim Witherspoon can take home anything more than the $3.6 million he is due to be paid. For all his physical splendour, and advantages in height and weight, he will be like a labrador at the mercy of a wolverine. I think he will be savaged and that on Sunday morning Britain will still be awaiting its first convincing claim to the heavyweight championship of the world.

Tyson has much faster hands, is more venomous and clearly the better boxer, with an under-appreciated range of head and body movements that enables him to bring his blasting punches in from a terrifying variety of angles. If Bruno reaches the fifth round it will be a surprise and an achievement.

If he goes on to win, in spite of his fragile chin and suspect stamina, he can do another commercial – for miracles.

It's a Good Time for Bruno to Go

The rest of the world should not sneer at the eccentric way the British read a fight. Had the ringside analyses at Dunkirk been dominated by logic, there would have been a strong case for throwing in the towel and civilisation might only now be making a comeback after a long spell of premature retirement.

Yet it must be said that in the less momentous context of Frank Bruno's battering defeat by Mike Tyson the motives for refusing to face the facts come across as nowhere near as compelling. On the evidence of the last week, all the principal reactions to a hectic quarter-of-an-hour in Las Vegas seem dubious: the public's, Bruno's own and, most conspicuously, that of the deal-makers who control his career. Obviously no one has any right to question the fighter's interpretation of what happened in those five rounds, no matter how many subjective adjustments to reality it incorporates. Anybody who performs as heroically as he did through such an intensity of experience is entitled to leave objectivity to others.

Leaving it up to the British public to be objective is, of course, a pointless exercise and never more so than when our mysterious relationship with heavyweight boxing is involved. Considering that we cannot lay convincing claim to a single heavyweight champion (Bob Fitzsimmons left Cornwall as a boy and was shaped by the Antipodes and America before he won the title in 1897), the depth of excitement stirred by a long succession of doomed contenders is as strange as the compulsion to construct myths around the failures of certain favourites among them, notably Tommy Farr and Henry Cooper.

Bruno, like the much smaller Cooper, can mix dramatic power with vulnerability and he lacks none of the modest, man-in-the-street charm of the young 'Enery. So, whatever the complex psychological basis of this country's freakish enthusiasm for any native son with the remotest pretensions to being a challenger for the world heavyweight title, the phenomenon was always sure to visit all its blessings and its drawbacks on big Frank.

The disadvantages have been predominant amid the astonishing hysteria that has attended his homecoming from the US. Adulation is fine, and there is no doubt that he earned a good deal of it, but there have been worrying currents running through the excessive celebration of his performance.

Particularly troubling is the sense that, for the past month or more, there has been a widespread tendency to treat him not like a sportsman at all but as some kind of alternative source of the instant sentimentality and conveniently packaged drama provided by the television soaps. Dangerously implicit in such a flood of crudely focused attention is an inclination to distort what occurred last weekend into something resembling a triumph, which it clearly was not.

With so much misleading tumult in his ears, it is not surprising that Bruno should resent anyone who suggests now might be the time to turn away from the pain and risks of the ring towards the life of a high-earning celebrity that is his for the taking. However, it is that message this peripheral voice is obliged to deliver.

He stresses that he is only 27 years old and that boxing is his job. But the fight game is not a place of employment to be compared with any other. Too many of its most distinguished figures have finished their careers feeling like a man in a bank vault who is trying to stuff as much as possible into the bag before the heavy door swings shut on his head.

It was not the lure of huge sums of money but a simple dream of glory, his genuine hunger to be champion of the world, that drove Bruno to make such hurtful sacrifices in the protracted preparation for the collision at the Las Vegas Hilton and to rise so impressively above his previous form once inside the ropes.

'Frank missed a year of his children's growth to concentrate on getting the training right, and you know how much he thinks of those two little girls of his,' said Terry Lawless when we talked 24 hours after the manager had watched helplessly (save for the towel he could and did toss into the ring as a token of submission) while all the effort, all the long-nurtured hopes and carefully rehearsed strategies, came to nothing before the disciplined violence of Tyson's climactic assault. 'It wasn't cash that made him put up with the separation. He's looked after his dough and he didn't need this fight to be comfortable financially, with a good income from outside boxing. How many TV commercials a year do you need to live pretty well?

'As far back as a year ago we had a very serious discussion and I questioned whether he needed to go on. I had to be absolutely sure he wasn't going in with Tyson because of the money, that it really was the title he wanted to fight for. He was adamant that he desperately wanted the championship of the world.'

Lawless is equally adamant that he was one of the tiny minority of professionals in boxing who honestly believed that Bruno's aspirations were realistic. 'I could see him doing it,' he said. 'I felt the troubles in Tyson's life outside the ring would tell on him as the fight went on and that the absence of Kevin Rooney from his corner would be vital. There's no doubt I was right about the corner – the guys in there didn't know what day it was – but the fact that Frank got knocked down just a dozen seconds into the first round pretty well ruined the chances of finding out if, in the later stages, Tyson would become anxious and start wondering how all the nonsense of last year had affected him.

'Of course, the knockdown shouldn't have happened but, no matter how much sparring you do, 16 months between fights can leave you not quite ready for that opening bell and all it means, all the pressure that's lumped on you. Frank wasn't really hurt when he went down, more surprised and embarrassed, but it took away some of the confidence he had carried into the ring.

'I've never known him more calm and together before a big night. In the last couple of days before they go in, fighters can die. But he was perfect. Even at the weigh-in, where he usually sweats up, he was great. I'd say the psychiatrist who worked with him, using hypnosis, definitely had a good effect. The doctor was sensible about what he could achieve. "Remember," he told us, "one big whack on the chin and everything said here might not matter."'

Perhaps the most significant single element in Bruno's memorable showing against Tyson was the way he withstood an appreciable number of major whacks on the chin. Those of us who thought such durability was beyond him must, in decency, acknowledge that we did him an injustice. It would seem we must yield to the theory that when he is fresh he is resilient enough and that he is undermined by fairly ordinary punches only after general tiredness has set in.

That contention had always appeared to be contradicted by the first-round havoc wreaked on his nervous system by Jumbo Cummings back in 1983. But Lawless says that a change in schedule caused Bruno to be hustled into the ring earlier than expected that night, with the result that he was still mentally dishevelled when Cummings came at him.

Tyson's lightning knockdown might have produced similar confusion but Bruno refused to disintegrate. The quality of will he summoned for an assignment he plainly recognised as the fight of his life made watching him one of the most moving experiences offered by a British boxer in recent years. To me, even the illegal tactics he employed had a core of honour, for they represented a declaration of nerve, a refusal to be intimidated by one of the most accomplished dirty fighters now operating.

Holding with the left hand and cuffing with the right may have been rather amateurish villainy and referee Richard Steele's understandable decision to deduct a point for it in the first round would have been more acceptable if he had punished Tyson for throwing a blow while Bruno was on the floor, deliberately punching after the bell and freely using his elbows, forearms and head. What is certain, however, is that roughing up Tyson (which was planned beforehand by Lawless and his trainer George Francis and sensibly persisted with in spite of a 'last warning' by the referee) made the champion lose his temper and become a snarling, out-of-control brawler instead of the skilful, calculating destroyer he is at his best.

Had Bruno boxed more openly, seeking by orthodox means to make room for his punches, the chances are that the champion would have settled to a rhythm behind his jab and remembered to throw body punches to create openings for the bombs. And the end would probably have come earlier than the final seconds of the fifth.

As the world knows, the methods Bruno favoured did bring him one glorious moment of opportunity late in that feverish first round. When Tyson was steadied by a right and then severely jolted by a left hook as he sought to hurl in a big one of his own, his legs juddered sideways and his face blurred. Had Bruno had the natural reflexes to shift position and drop a brutal right hand on him then, had Bruno been the kind of man who inhabits the ring as comfortably as a Roberto Duran or, for that matter, a Tyson, we would have been teetering on the brink of an impossible upset.

But Frank is not remotely such a man and that moment is the best he is ever likely to know as a fighter. He should cherish it and head for quieter ways of making a living.

It will help if Terry Lawless lets the strong compassionate streak in his nature come through. 'When you get up in the corner you have to act the tough guy,' he told me in Las Vegas, 'but sometimes you really want to put a bag over your head, run out and wait for someone to tell you the result when it's over. When you get close with fighters, and I probably get too close, you want them all to retire, particularly the big guys, because where they work it is a rough, tough business.'

Such thinking is not weakness in a boxing manager or anyone else. It is humanity. Let's hope its strength will be deployed against the temptation of an immensely lucrative return with Tyson, should that be on offer.

It could be a dreadful mistake to tangle with such a force of nature twice. The San Andreas Fault precipitated a lot less violence than it might have done in April 1906. But San Francisco isn't asking for a rematch with the earthquake.

Mike Tyson v. James Douglas, Tokyo, 18 February 1990

When an Ogre Looks Forlorn

The assassin's swagger with which Mike Tyson intimidated other men also served to keep his own demons at bay and now he knows it will never come as easily again.

Deep down in a private world that has always been filled with flitting shadows, is Tyson responding to humiliation in Tokyo with snarling defiance or does he realise that, even if the loss of his heavyweight championship to James 'Buster' Douglas is temporary, something more basic has gone forever?

The career of an ogre of the ring tends to be a one-way street with a cliff at the end of it. Sonny Liston and George Foreman were demythologised with startling suddenness, although George is currently doing an effective job of hoisting his ageing and overweight body back up the rock face to riches.

But Liston and Foreman were both undone by Muhammad Ali, who confronted them with the greatest arsenal of gifts the heavyweight division has ever seen. Tyson, at 23, had his dreams of invincibility pulverised by an opponent whose credentials suggested beforehand that he had the same chance as a trout being dropped into a bathtub with a hungry pike. If there is a Richter Scale for sporting earthquakes, what happened in Japan last Sunday would have to be considered two or three points clear of any other shock in twentieth-century boxing.

Don King's scandalous attempts to minimise the devastation could only exacerbate in the end the damage done to the principal victim, Mike Tyson. It was predictable that King would mount blustering protests about the length of time Douglas was on the canvas after he was left in a sprawling daze by a classic right uppercut from Tyson in the last seconds of the eighth round. The promoter tried to harry the notoriously malleable officials of the World Boxing Council and the World Boxing Association into accepting the monstrous contention that by failing to be precise in his counting the referee had permitted a knockout in the eighth which invalidated a total demolition of Tyson in the tenth.

Of course, the referee's voice is all a fallen fighter is obliged to heed and, in any case, the battered Tyson could not escape the raw truth of what he had been through. All the hustler's rhetoric from King did was draw a merciless bombardment of contempt and indignation from across the world and by the time he and Tyson turned up together at a press conference in New York on Tuesday they had no option but to acknowledge James Douglas as the legitimate, undisputed champion.

King's conciliatory tone in Manhattan had nothing to do with an uncharacteristic upsurge of decency. Looking for fair play from him is like asking a wolverine to use a napkin. The former racketeer's survival instincts had told him that he had gone too far, that even amid the incorrigibly sleazy standards which constantly prevail outside the ring in professional boxing his conduct was being exposed as despicable and he had better pull back from the brink – if only to protect his investment.

The investment sat alongside him, wearing dark glasses to conceal the left eye that had been blinded by an ugly ball of swelling for several rounds before Douglas completed his historic destruction in the tenth. There was good reason for Tyson to be subdued, almost plaintive, in the hotel next to Grand Central Station (all he wanted was the rematch, he insisted mildly, and then he would put everything right) but what many of us are anxious to know is why he was nearly as subdued from the moment he entered the ring in Japan.

As someone whose experience of the fight has been restricted to the two-dimensional testimony of a television screen, I have no right to over-vehement interpretations. But after hours with the video machine I am left with the bemusing impression that the Tokyo Dome housed a contest between two ringers. Maybe both men's fingerprints should have been taken before the start to confirm that they were who they purported to be.

James Douglas was certainly unrecognisable as the often dispirited journeyman who scuffled around the heavyweight division throughout the 1980s, incorporating serious blemishes into his record. Being stopped by David Bey, Tony Tucker and the spectacularly unfamous Mike White was bad enough but there was probably even more embarrassment in an eight-round draw with Steffan Tangstadt, a Norseman who could scarcely pillage a hairdressing salon. And in gathering these negative references, Douglas occasionally invited suspicion that his appetite for conflict was less than voracious.

Yet courage and commitment were outstanding among the array of pugilistic virtues he brought to his meeting with Tyson. One theory is that a tornado of tragedies that has swept through Douglas's personal life recently has given him a new perspective about the hardships of his business, convincing him that he had learned to cope with more desperate hurt than Mike Tysc ~ould inflict on him. There is no doubt that he had become increasingly formidable in the run-up to his challenge, winning six fights in a row and five of them inside the distance, but his performance in Tokyo amounted to an almost miraculous raising of his game.

The 29-year-old from Columbus, Ohio, was a remarkable heavyweight last Sunday, big (16½ st and, at 6 ft 4 in, five inches taller than Tyson), fast, determined and skilful. Douglas did not just beat Tyson. He administered a terrible hiding, one that made the scoring of the American judge Larry Rozadilla (88 points to Douglas, 82 to Tyson at the end of the ninth) only the merest touch excessive and made that of his Japanese counterparts look like manifestations of dementia. Masakuzu Uchida had the scores level after nine and Ken Morita had Tyson one point ahead, which indicates that he would have given Pompeii the verdict over Vesuvius.

That Douglas was far ahead before landing the punches that ended the fight should not be disputed. The real question concerns the identity of the man he beat. My anxiety to give full credit to someone who tossed every dismissive prediction back in the forecasters' teeth cannot rid me of the conviction that the real Mike Tyson never showed up in Tokyo.

His face offered strangely soft lines instead of the usual sculpted menace and his body, too, lacked tautness. Where previously he had prowled through preliminaries with contained but vibrant truculence, here he looked simply morose. There was no ominous flexing of the neck and shoulder muscles, no hint of smouldering aggression in the eyes. He looked as if he might be sick and he fought that way, without fire or rhythm, devoid of the skipping liveliness that normally makes his footwork deceptively competent and the spontaneous adjustments of range and timing which make his fierce blows connect. Some of us have long been convinced that his squatness and limited reach would make him vulnerable one day to a tall, crisp-punching opponent of true quality (convinced that the young Ali for one would have outclassed him) but Tokyo was surely a misrepresentation of his own tremendous assets.

A pathetically amateurish corner did not help but mattered less than the debilitating influence of his private life and the rust encouraged by having just 93 seconds of ring action since the Bruno fight in February 1989. Most damaging of all, perhaps, has been his alliance with Don King, who has precipitated decay in practically every fighter with whom he has been associated. King gives no evidence of really believing in boxing, or in fighters come to that. His obsession with his own grotesque persona and with labyrinthine wheeling and dealing seems to make him a ruinous contagion.

If Tyson means to rehabilitate himself for the rematch with Douglas that could be contrived by paying Evander Holyfield to postpone the challenge he was due to present on 18 June in Atlantic City, he should start by distancing himself from King. But he may find that even more difficult than quietening the clamour of doubts that must now be raging in his head.

Hero of the Non-Militant Tendency

The Observer, 30 September 1990

Maybe it is because boxing at its most serious can be such a bleak and painful place, even for the visitor, that so many people react with warm indulgence to George Foreman's outlandish campaign to recapture the heavyweight championship of the world. He brought his caravan to London last week, subjected the populace to a relaxed but relentless bombardment of huckster's patter and aphorisms minted in Humble, Texas, and then appeared briefly in the ring for an engagement that was slightly less competitive than shooting fish in a barrel. As he departed for home, he could have been expected to leave a wake of bitter disgruntlement over the poor value for money he had delivered. Yet such booing as there was at the London Arena was both limited and mild. Clearly, a majority in the crowd had derived from last Tuesday evening pretty much the kind of pleasure they anticipated.

That they were willing to settle for so little was, of course, a tribute to the peculiar appeal of Foreman's personality and his past. For all the trundling antiquity of his current presence, he comes trailing clouds of distant glory, carrying echoes of the great heavyweight era he shared with Ali, Frazier, Norton and a cast of exciting extras, and the drawing power of those associations is considerably heightened by the sheer niceness that has overtaken this one-time ogre in a captivatingly mellow middle age. There is, however, another element discernible in the Foreman saga, one that may have more long-term significance for boxing. It is the extent to which he underlines the readiness of promoters and their audiences to go for 'events' rather than contests, to identify more than ever before with the showbusiness factor that has always been integral to the fight game. Among heavyweights in particular, it has never been necessary to guarantee a decent match to pull in a crowd. A sense of drama, of occasion – however spuriously contrived – has always been the key promotional device. But in an age when television is the principal creator of entertainment standards, when celebrity invariably means more than ability in the rating of a performer, the spread of showbiz criteria in boxing is inevitably accelerating. Given that such thinking has so overwhelmingly invaded the middleweight division, it is natural that heavyweight boxing should go even further over the top. Big George is handily placed to cash in on this non-militant tendency.

Part of his attraction these days may well be the comic-strip air of unreality that surrounds his endeavours. Though some of the 24 opponents who have fallen to him in his latest comeback (including, presumably, the hapless Terry Anderson, whose blubbery shape finished nose-down on the canvas in Docklands) must see things differently, there is no question that many who have witnessed his slow-motion mayhem have responded as if they were watching not a genuine fight but the mock violence of professional wrestling. There are traces of relief about being able to laugh and joke over action that amounts to a euphemism for the cruelty the ring too often accommodates. London Arena in midweek certainly offered a different experience of boxing from that encountered eight days ago at the Albert Hall, where Jim McDonnell went much closer to death than any man should be taken in pursuit of a sport. And there is no doubt which was the truer reflection of the grim essence of the business.

It would, perhaps, be better in many respects for all of us if boxing could be transformed into the undeadly ritual enacted by Foreman and Anderson. But it cannot. For George, too, reality will soon assert itself, dedicated though he is to a quietly fantastic view of his own exploits. There is a wonderful charm about the zany inversion that characterises his comparison of his prowess in his 20s with what he claims to be his attributes at 42. Discussing the days when he was a terrifying force in the ring, he comes on, without a hint of the phoney, as Mr Humble from Humble, not only lavishing compliments on the destroyer of his legend, Muhammad Ali, but dwelling on how he was put in his place during his time as Sonny Liston's sparring partner and insisting that Joe Louis 'probably would have creamed me because he would have hit me with so many combinations'. However, once on the subject of his current form, he puts his imagination into overdrive. Apparently he has not merely absorbed the mastery of defensive technique in gymnasium tutorials with Archie Moore but has so benefited from the old virtuoso's teaching that everything from footwork to economical execution of his punches has improved dramatically.

Reconciling that testimony with the visual evidence provided in Docklands is scarcely necessary, since George's tongue was almost boring a hole in his cheek. In the lumbering, gigantic flesh, he reminded me of a Bill Shankly comment on a striker of yesteryear, Martin Chivers. 'The big boy's deceptive,' said Bill. 'He's slower than he looks.' Mind you, George could hardly be slower than he looks. The blow that flattened Terry Anderson was in transit so long it could have been done in oils before it landed. Even the contact it eventually made did not appear too devastating but other punches he has thrown lately, notably the cruncher that did for Gerry Cooney, have confirmed that the old murderous power can still be visited on anyone foolish enough to wait around for it.

The chances are that none of the three heavyweights who could bring George a fortune by fighting him – Mike Tyson, Tyson's Tokyo conqueror James 'Buster' Douglas, and the man Douglas defends against next month, Evander Holyfield – would be so helpful. Nor would the fellow a number of insiders are beginning to see as the likeliest large lad of all, the black Canadian Razor Ruddock. My own most vivid image concerns what a fit and hungry Mike Tyson (if we ever see such a Tyson again) would do to George. The promoters wouldn't dare risk flimsy floorboards that night. Tyson could expect to be granted a series of free hits before George got under way. And I fear the elderly charmer would come down like a dynamited chimney stack.

A Drowning Man in Fat City

The Observer, 28 October 1990

Pacifism is an honourable creed but a man's public espousal of it looks less than noble when he has just accepted $20 million to go to war. As James 'Buster' Douglas lay at Evander Holyfield's feet – blinking placidly up at the ring lights like someone whose thoughts of throwing back the bedclothes have been discouraged by word that it's raining outside – he was not committing any heinous offence. Being overwhelmed by an instinct for self-preservation, even being at the centre of one of the most ignominious abdications in the long and not always glorious history of the heavyweight championship, does not transform a decent, likeable individual into a despicable villain.

No one should feel inclined to challenge the claims of the loser's uncle, J.D. McCauley, that he is 'still a great human being'. But James Douglas must plead guilty to a colossal deception, one perhaps perpetrated on his own nature as much as the world at large. It consisted of passing himself off for years as a fighter when that was something he was never truly equipped to be. He certainly looked the part briefly in Tokyo last February when he shattered belief in Mike Tyson's invincibility by not merely knocking out that frightening champion in the tenth round but coming off the canvas in the eighth to do it. However, there were unmistakable signs that Tyson presented only the feeblest impersonation of his powers in that fight and now it appears equally probable that, as suggested in these columns a week ago, a unique combination of pressure and opportunity for once allowed Douglas to transcend the natural limitations of his personality and lifted him to a level of performance he may never reach again. Many insisted that a better guide to his softer, truer self was to be found in the blatant inclination to surrender he displayed when being stopped three times earlier in his career. Those capitulations were seen as representing a distaste for the pains of conflict too basic to be eradicated, and the Holyfield débâcle makes the contention almost impossible to refute.

Physical size, family background and a respectable athletic talent conspired to carry James Douglas into places where his fragile spirit was constantly under siege, and last Thursday evening, amid a vulgar showbiz clamour beside a Las Vegas hotel, it crumbled with humiliating finality. In truth, of course, his will had cracked a long time before that moment of collapse in the third round of his first defence of the heavyweight title. Pride had obviously deserted him at an early stage of the hopelessly undisciplined training programme that sent him into the ring as an 18-stone fat man, more than a stone heavier than he had been in Tokyo. The destructive scale of Douglas's self-indulgence conveyed itself to those around Steve Wynn, the owner of the Mirage Hotel and provider of the mammoth purse monies that caused this fight to set financial records, when concern about the defending champion's weight encouraged them to monitor his room service charges. They knew they were dealing with a phenomenon once an order had been called in from Wynn's sauna, which had been opened up specially for the boxer's convenience. The bill for the sauna snack was $98. As he stooped between the ropes on Thursday, all pendulous breasts and Michelin middle, it was apparent that Buster hadn't wasted a cent.

Seeing such a blubbery leviathan coming towards him, Holyfield (who weighed about 15 st) may have wondered whether he should be throwing punches or firing harpoons. In the event, the unbeaten challenger, glistening with fitness and oozing confidence through every well co-ordinated assault on a miserably passive target, soon contrived to give his opponent what proved to be an irresistible glimpse of the exit. One minute into the third, Holyfield let a wild and gigantic uppercut from Douglas miss his face by fully 18 inches while rocking back on his own right foot to deliver a perfect right-hand counter-punch flush on the jaw. As the victim was spun off balance, there was a fairly solid collision of heads, which went largely unnoticed but became crucial in explaining Douglas's subsequent suspicion that he was bleeding. A following left hook from Holyfield swung harmlessly over the sprawling champion's right shoulder but there was no need for further contact. Douglas was ready to be drowned by the melting of his commitment.

There should be no attempt to question the quality of the blow struck by Holyfield or, for that matter, of any aspect of a beautifully orchestrated performance that gives the former cruiserweight the right to be regarded as a worthy holder of the most lucrative championship in sport. Equally, Douglas had absolutely no option but to go down from such a punch. It was what he did once on the floor that will haunt him for the rest of his days. Having landed on his left side, he raised himself on to one elbow and rubbed his right glove across his brow and the region of his right eye before looking at the glove as if seeking traces of blood. Then, as he sank back to flatten his shoulder on the canvas, he twice used his left hand to rub his face and across his nose and did more checking to see if anything had been left on either glove. Study of the videotape of the count seems to show that Douglas's eyes were clearly focused as he examined the gloves and Mills Lane, the referee who was tolling the seconds over him, says: 'He didn't try to get up. I'm not saying he could have gotten up but he didn't try . . . His eyes looked good to me. You're born with a ticker – they can't give you one.'

Lane's was among the mildest of the professional judgements voiced on the fact that Douglas remained stretched on his back long after Holyfield's whooping corner-men had literally leapt over the prostrate form to engulf their astonishingly impassive winner. Some of the comments were offensively heartless, such as the declaration by Mike Trainer, adviser to Sugar Ray Leonard, that 'Douglas is a dog – a piece of junk'. That kind of remark typifies the callousness that often eddies through boxing. But what Eddie Futch said is harder to ignore. Futch is a 79-year-old black trainer and manager whose experience of the fight game's realities goes back to a time six decades ago when he used to spar with Joe Louis. He is just about the most respected figure in American boxing, not least because concern for the welfare and dignity of fighters informs everything he does. Yet Futch, choosing his words carefully, said late on Thursday: 'I thought Buster Douglas was disgraceful tonight. He allowed himself to get in such poor condition that he had nothing. His judgement of distance was gone, his timing, he had no snap. He landed one punch in the whole three rounds and for the heavyweight champion to come in in that kind of condition was just outlandish.' On the manner of Douglas's going, the great veteran was no less direct: 'The things that he did – rubbing his face and looking at his gloves to see if there was blood there – showed that he was aware of what was going on. He was conscious and could, in my opinion, have gotten up at that time. But he chose not to do so. Maybe he has his own reasons.'

When asked for reasons, Douglas (his face a heartbreaking mirror of the confused gloom that had settled on him) could only mumble haphazardly about trying unsuccessfully to pick up the count, about rubbing his face because he thought he had taken a glove in the eye, about regrets over failing to find rhythm or momentum. Meanwhile, his trainers, the previously mentioned uncle, J.D. McCauley, and John Russell, bridled aggressively when questioned about methods which included declining to weigh their charge at any time during his preparation. The consensus was that their approach, whether merely lax or grotesquely eccentric, had been ultimately disastrous. Their argument that Douglas's flabbiness could not possibly have contributed to his downfall in such an early round, that he simply had an off night and was caught by a good punch, is patently nonsensical. The ludicrous, long-range uppercut that invited Holyfield's decisive right counter was the desperate gesture of a man who had been struggling against his own gross lack of fitness from the first bell, testimony to the pathetically blurred sense of distance and timing Eddie Futch so witheringly condemned. No doubt it would be best now if Douglas took his extravagant earnings and retired, leaving the fighting trade to others, like Evander Holyfield, who have more appetite for its rigours. If the $20 million he drew here, and the further $31 million that was promised for a rematch with Mike Tyson, could not dissuade him from indulging the wrong kind of hunger, he should not be surprised to find Steve Wynn regretting that Thursday's set-to was not on a winner-take-all basis.

As it happens, the winner will take plenty. Holyfield is already lined up to pit his impressively honed athleticism against the lumbering remnants of the powerful armoury with which George Foreman intimidated the heavyweight division until that day in Africa 16 years ago when Muhammad Ali abruptly invalidated his ogre's licence. The new champion is due in the spring to be paid $20 million for coping with the 42-year-old Foreman and if, as expected, his vastly superior movement keeps him away from George's ponderously delivered bombs, he should win comfortably and travel on to an even richer engagement with Tyson – probably around September of next year. Provided Tyson is capable of rediscovering the destructive intensity that came naturally to him before he behaved like a ringer in Japan, he will be the real test of whether an extraordinary array of specialist helpers – from computer analysts to body builders to a ballet teacher – have been able to turn a cruiserweight into an outstanding heavyweight. Serious doubts persist in this quarter but it must be admitted that Holyfield did not look a negligible item at the Mirage. Even an impending divorce action that threatens to make a mess of his image as a highly moral Christian did not impinge on his searing concentration.

For the moment, there is a guarantee of lively entertainment from the geriatric ward. George Foreman has already begun his propaganda bombardment. He was shouting at the weekend that, in spite of the encounter with Douglas, Holyfield has yet to find out what it is like to come up against real bulk. George said he was going to continue to eat every ice-cream and burger in sight. 'When you push and shove against me you are going to be taking on all the franchises,' he assured the champion. 'My foot weighs more than you do. You'll go when I hit you with my senior citizen's punch.'

'It's not about the size of the man, George, but the size of the heart,' said Holyfield. 'I eat hearts,' the old man responded. 'I eat chickens' feet. I eat everything.'

He eats up newsprint, that's for sure.

Dubious Dealings in Xanadu

The Observer, 24 March 1991

Impropriety was the unlikely word being tossed around the boxing circles of Las Vegas over the past week. It seemed as out of place as a Henry James character in a Mario Puzo novel. Skulduggery, chicanery, larceny are all terms that occur more readily to critics of the fight business in its modern Xanadu. Yet here they were, not even talking about outright impropriety but merely the risk of the shadow of the thing. Mealy-mouthed circumlocution was almost epidemic.

The reason for all the caution was obvious enough. Most of those who had witnessed the seventh-round ending of the heavyweight fight between Mike Tyson and Donovan 'Razor' Ruddock were convinced that what the referee, Richard Steele, did was wrong. Where they had trouble was in trying to work out why he had done it. Some felt that any explanation of Steele's decision to intervene with barely a glance at Ruddock (who was standing clear-eyed and incredulous against the ropes by the time the official waved his arms to terminate the action) had to start with the fact that he makes his living in a casino owned by Steve Wynn, whose Mirage Hotel had contracts with Don King, Tyson's promoter, extending beyond last Monday's match. But reluctance to impugn the integrity of Steele, a popular man who happens to be an ordained minister, restricted probing journalists to the suggestion that it was at the very least foolish of the Nevada State Athletic Commission to appoint a referee who had such professional ties with parties involved in the fight. In short, they had invited suspicions of, yes, impropriety.

They surely had, and the extent of their wrong-headedness was emphasised by confirmation that Steele had returned to the US on Friday, 15 March, after refereeing in Tokyo, then handled a world title fight in Vegas on Sunday, 17 March, before going into the ring with Tyson and Ruddock the following evening. Given the likelihood of disorientation implicit in such an itinerary, was it any wonder that he was so uncertain about the details of the heavyweight assignment even after it was over that he tartly corrected an interviewer by insisting it was scheduled for ten rounds, when in fact it was a 12-rounder? There have been reports that the Nevada Commission believed Steele's physical stature (he has kept the strapping, handsome figure of the pro light-heavyweight he once was) would help him to maintain discipline between two big men. But that reasoning cannot be reconciled with their appointment of Mills Lane, who is small, bald and relentless as a terrier, to control the James 'Buster' Douglas–Evander Holyfield championship meeting back in October. As it happened, Lane did not need much of his feisty efficiency on that occasion, which found Buster in a mood to tuck himself under the covers with a good book and a direct line to room service. It is, however, difficult to imagine that lack of size would have prevented the hard little district attorney from being far more of a martinet than Steele, who limited himself to a few ineffectual warnings – mainly between rounds – in response to constant flouting of the rules last Monday night.

Ruddock's habit of using his long arms to entangle his shorter opponent and subject him to the leaning tactic so dear to Muhammad Ali in his declining years was hardly legal, but the referee's passivity gave greater benefit to Tyson, who persistently punched low and now and again butted like an old-fashioned Glasgow street-fighter. Of course, it would be outrageous to blame Steele for the way the evening climaxed in uproar, with rival corner-men treating a worldwide audience to one of the most prolonged and squalid brawls ever seen in the ring after a major fight. But, for whatever reason, he was miserably inadequate and all the pious irrelevancies introduced by his apologists cannot obscure that simple reality. Such people have been telling us (with an air of profundity) that it is better for a referee to intervene a minute too soon than a second too late. They appear to think that truism can justify their position. Certainly they show no sign of seeing the hypocrisy in their attitude, of recognising that it is totally unrealistic to endorse professional boxing as it is currently conceived and yet argue that a fight should be stopped the moment a man has been staggered by hurtful punches. Maybe boxing should not be endorsed. Maybe it should yield to the condemnation of those who feel that the violence endemic to the ring is more than a decent, humane spirit can accept. But the characters who claimed that Richard Steele got it right in Vegas were playing a dishonest game. They went to ringside to watch prize-fighting and then sought to cushion themselves against its harsh demands, one of which is that a man who is upright, clear in the head, free of any dangerous or debilitating injury and eager to fight should be allowed to do so.

Donovan Ruddock was in such a condition when Steele reached to take the gumshield from his mouth. Even Dr Ferdie Pacheco, who was Ali's physician in the great years and remains understandably 'soft' on how much suffering should be countenanced in the ring, criticised the stoppage as blatantly premature. Ruddock had been left momentarily dazed and reeling when hit by a flurry of hooks from Tyson late in the seventh round. One brutal left had crunched into his jaw and, although the right and left that followed swung undamagingly over the target's shoulders, a further right and left made sufficient contact to compound the effect of that first bludgeoning punch. So Ruddock was in bad shape as he spun drunkenly sideways to come to rest against the ropes with one arm dangling over the top strand. But he had already demonstrated a capacity for quick recovery when dropped by Tyson late in the third round, though he was undoubtedly glad to hear the bell ring almost as soon as he rose at the count of six (when he landed on the floor in the second it was more of a freak trip than a knockdown).

Now, in the seventh, the Jamaican Canadian was to be given no chance to recover. While Ruddock was lurching away from Tyson's attack, Steele was already thrusting himself into the former world champion's path with arms outspread. The movement meant that the referee was facing away from the fighter he was purporting to rescue. At best, the only sight he could have of the man he was making a loser was out of the corner of an eye. What he should have been doing was looking directly into Ruddock's eyes to assess his ability to continue. Instead Ruddock, unmistakably in command of his faculties, was left staring in disbelief at a back view of the Steele gestures that ended the fight. 'What?' he said with such indignation that the word could be lip-read from the middle of the crowd. Had Tyson been waved in again, he may well have been odds-on to do his own stopping before the end of the seventh round, which had two-thirds of a minute to run. In spite of fighting well below his best standards, he had won five of the six rounds completed and even when halted in his tracks and severely shaken by heavy punches in the sixth he had so convincingly weathered the bombardment that he was able to come off his stool full of aggression at the next bell.

However, the substantial probability of defeat for Ruddock – who had fought bravely but with an amateurish reliance on blasting in left hooks so huge and imprecise that they often made him resemble a hammer thrower who had forgotten to let go – was not the issue. Steele wasn't there to judge his prospects of pulling off an upset, just to gauge whether or not he could defend himself. The answer struck me as unequivocal at the time and repeated viewings of the tape have reinforced an angry conviction that welled up at ringside: had Tyson been in Ruddock's condition, badly discomfited but *compos mentis* and ready to battle on, the referee would never have dreamt of declaring him a beaten fighter. Perhaps a standing eight-count would have had a rationalising influence but the Nevada Commission allow such a refinement only in very special circumstances, for example when a boxer becomes enmeshed in the ropes. On this matter, too, Steele revealed a tendency towards confusion, for he counted while Ruddock was on his feet and shrugging dismissively after that fluke knockdown in the second round.

Naturally, the principal effect of the furore is to feed enthusiasm for a rematch and Don King and Murad Muhammad, Ruddock's promoter, are already talking cosily of the jackpot it will bring. One horror for those of us who are asked to chronicle such activities is the thought of another series of press conferences featuring King and Muhammad. When teamed up, they surely have no challengers for the ranting and raving championship of the galaxy. As far as the fighters are concerned, Tyson would again be favourite second time around but last Monday made many suspect that his finest performances may be behind him. His attacks were ploddingly unimaginative, almost devoid of the foot, body and head movement which conveyed such an electric sense of vitality and destructive variety when he was building the momentum of the rampage that ended up so suddenly at the feet of Buster Douglas in Tokyo 13 months ago. Generally he was content to tunnel in grimly, plant himself, and seek to force big single shots through the protective mesh of Ruddock's arms. Prior to that conclusive flurry, he had hardly thrown a combination worth the name.

He still looks like the deadliest heavyweight of his day but I can think of two or three from the not so distant past who would have encouraged me to bet fearlessly against him. Start with Ali, Sonny Liston and George Foreman in his prime – which was, of course, many years before big George started to regard McDonald's as his favourite opponent.

Fat Chance for King of the Burgers

The Observer, 14 April 1991

The scale of George Foreman these days suggests that he should be located by lines of longitude and latitude. He is not so much a prizefighter as an historical site and some feel that if Evander Holyfield has a problem at the Atlantic City Convention Center on Friday night it may be in summoning up the callousness to be an archaeological vandal.

Any incipient squeamishness will, of course, be overcome when he remembers the undisputed heavyweight championship he is defending, the $20 million he is being paid to do so and the multiples of that figure which could accrue from future fights. Another incentive to destructiveness should be the knowledge that failure to deal summarily with the 42-year-old challenger will encourage many to see Holyfield as a fraud, an unworthy guardian of the world title Foreman lost to Muhammad Ali nearly 17 years ago. That, if we close our ears to the disingenuous babblings of the promoters, is the truth of what is about to happen here. Foreman is not just an old fighter. He is an old fighter whose athletic capacity was irrevocably rusted by a full decade of inactivity between 1977 and 1987, ten years in which he punched nothing more threatening than a Bible. Is it really surprising that some of the punches he now throws at opponents could be timed with a sundial? Perhaps the greatest triumph of this comeback has been ensuring a steady supply of the kind of victims who hang around to be hit by such assaults, like suicides in the path of a lumbering freight train.

They have given Foreman a record of 24 straight wins (23 inside the distance) since he cut down on evangelical preaching to return to the ring four years ago. Only one, Adilson Rodrigues, at No 10, was a ranked contender when called to the chopping block. Yet big George has contrived to trample over their carcasses to this opportunity of making history, and a pay-day which guarantees him £12.5 million and looks like bringing somewhat more. Since he insists on an autonomy almost unheard of in his business – personally handling everything of importance, from the wrapping of his hands before a fight to the selection of opponents – he deserves the wry tribute of the American boxing writer who says he is going to vote for Foreman to be named Manager of the Year. Promoter of the Year might be a possibility, too. No one, not even the nemesis of his previous incarnation, Ali, ever did a more astonishing job of selling a fight. Muhammad, after all, had rather more to work with than the remnants of an immense gift that are currently at his old foe's disposal. By presenting himself as the man from Cheeseburger Mountain, or maybe the man who *is* Cheeseburger Mountain, a jolly champion of all bad-diet freaks who claims to consume junk food and ice-cream with the voracity of a garbage chute, Foreman has captured the imagination of the multitude who dream of seeing a middle-aged fat man make nonsense of the natural laws of physical decline.

It hardly matters that insiders tell us he is happier eating fish and chicken. There is more publicity mileage in his wistful assertion that the only shadow over his fondness for the island of St Lucia, where he has done two separate spells of training for this engagement, is the lack of fast-food joints. When he had his first Atlantic City workout on Friday afternoon he revealed the familiar contours of a small continent. Looking at his belly, which is hard enough but of aldermanic convexity, it was easy to believe him when he said he weighed 19 st and did not expect to be below 18 st when he faced Holyfield (though a shade over 15½ st was standard in his prime nearly 20 years ago). Bulk and strength are his principal assets now, his supporters tell you. No doubt they were satisfied with recent images of their man at work on his 200-acre ranch near his birthplace of Marshall, East Texas. The photographs showed him in harness, hauling a truck in the manner of Geoff Capes in a strongman contest, splintering an oak tree with a lumberjack's axe and casting a hungry eye over the cattle that are the practical members of his varied menagerie. He looked like a throwback to an earlier age of pugilism, especially when contrasted with the sight of a flawlessly sculpted Holyfield in training amid the chrome glitter of hi-tech conditioning equipment in a Houston gym, 200 miles away.

Here on the Jersey shore they train, four hours apart, in the same converted conference room at the Trump Plaza Hotel. But the differences in approach remain stark. While Holyfield grinds through the punishing schedule that has piled two stones of extra muscle on to what was by nature a cruiserweight's (13 st) physique – a programme which sometimes causes his accomplished boxing adviser, George Benton, to look askance at the contributions of a fitness consultant, a weightlifting coach and a charming lady ballet instructor hired to increase flexibility – Foreman's performance has as much to do with vaudeville as violence. On Friday he sparred ten rounds with five partners, keeping the exchanges sufficiently gentle to make his refusal to take rests between rounds less of a strain than it might have been. Sensing that spectator interest was flagging at one point, he collapsed under a blow that wouldn't have dropped his mother and reclined briefly with his head on the bottom rope. Afterwards he leaned on the top rope as if it were a lectern and his large, crumpled face glowed with undiluted happiness under the glistening dome of his shaved skull as he unloaded the one-liners. 'What distance do I run in the morning? It depends how far my bedroom is from the kitchen . . . Certainly there should be a mandatory retirement age for fighters – 65 . . . I weigh 265 lb now but I won't eat breakfast on the day of the fight, so I'll go in at 250.'

He exuded such warmth and fun that somebody, remembering the brooding, intimidating presence he once was, said it was as if he had retired as Sonny Liston in 1977 and come back as Ali. Yet the odds-makers in Las Vegas do not see him as a joke. Though Holyfield is a hot favourite, anyone wagering on Foreman is given only 11–4 against. It is an amazingly short price considering the date on his birth certificate and the still greater disadvantage of that eroding decade of absence from the ring. The calendar has been defied by boxers before now, most remarkably by Archie Moore, the legendary light-heavyweight who is on hand as resident strategist in the Foreman camp. Moore claimed he was a mere 44 when he made a final, and successful, defence of his world title but his mother, who might be regarded as a more reliable witness, reckoned he was 47. Either way, The Mongoose was considerably beyond the age of 38 which made Jersey Joe Walcott the oldest man ever to hold the heavyweight crown. Neither achievement offers a legitimate analogy with what Foreman is attempting. Both Moore and Walcott had a scarcely interrupted commitment to their trade from their teens to retirement. Throughout those years, fighting was for them just another day at the office. If Foreman proves capable of taking ten years off and then reclaiming the title, either he is something miraculous or Holyfield and Mike Tyson have built their reputations in a heavyweight division peopled by pygmies.

Plainly this is no golden age but surely it is not as bad as such a result would make it. Holyfield himself may fall in the end to the hazards that always accompany manufactured bigness in the ring. Tyson, though seemingly diminished nowadays, would be fancied to blast him aside. But on Friday Holyfield will step forward as a superbly prepared athlete of 28, 6 ft 2 in and perhaps 15 st, with the vigour of youth and a warrior's heart even his least charitable detractors dare not question. His unblemished record of 25 victories (21 stoppages) features few notable names but it is rather more impressive than Foreman's shopping list. Big George's most potent weapon is the sense of his brutal, almost super-natural, power that seeps through from the past. Even contemporary

fighters who never saw him at his frightening peak have an eerie awareness of what an awe-inspiring figure he was until Ali pulverised him,
body and soul, in the small hours of an African morning in 1974. They
realise with a shudder that in 71 contests only Ali and Jimmy Young, in
March 1977, have beaten him. However, when his cheerleaders try to tell
us he is a deadlier executioner today than he ever was in the '70s, they are
being ridiculous. A boxer can never fully exploit his strength without
muscle elasticity and sharp timing, which is where age does weary and the
years of idleness condemn.

Much is made of the sequence of accurate punches with which
Foreman finished off Gerry Cooney, and it was certainly a memorable
display of assault and battery from an old gentleman. But by that stage of
his sad career Cooney was a magnet for destruction. The two men coming
together at the Convention Center are devout Christians and at least one
of them believes in miracles. I am stuck with the mundanities of the form
book. It indicates that Holyfield will so discomfit Foreman with youthful
movement and crisp combinations that, after a few rounds, he will be
wearing the flummoxed, ill-used expression to be seen on the faces of
senior citizens who have rashly tried to cross the street in heavy traffic.

Unless the game is even more outlandish than we thought, there will be
no title for yesteryear's man. Just the kind of cheque that comes in handy
for a father of nine.

Foreman Fails with Honour

The Observer, 21 April 1991

The mere remnants of what once made George Foreman a fearsome
heavyweight champion were enough to call in question Evander
Holyfield's right to be considered a worthy holder of the title. Let there
be no doubt about the comprehensiveness of the beating Holyfield
inflicted on his 42-year-old challenger over 12 rounds at the Atlantic City
Convention Center on Friday night. For 36 minutes Foreman, boxing's
most remarkable revenant, padded forward stubbornly into a volume of
punishment that swamped his own sporadic and cumbersome attempts at
retaliation and by the end of the fight the discrepancy in performance was
certainly far greater than the official scorecards suggested. Yet there was
no reason to argue with the loser when, still buoyant behind dark glasses,
he said afterwards: 'He had the points but I made the point.' In fact, big
George had made at least two that must be heeded.

The first was that the second career he launched four years ago after a
full decade of eroding absence from the ring was fuelled by more honest
commitment, had less to do with mercenary hokum, than its

accompanying welter of hype indicated. And the other, perhaps more telling, implication of his ability to go the distance was a substantial hardening of the persistent suspicion that beneath the rippling bulk of Holyfield's zealously enlarged physique there lurk the limitations of the cruiserweight he was born to be. There should be no stinting of praise for the natural strength, durability and resolution that enabled Foreman to propel his 18½-stone mass relentlessly, if ponderously, at his opponent virtually from the first bell to the last without bothering to rest on a stool between rounds. But given that his lumbering, elderly man's aggression was being met by a meticulously trained 28-year-old who is designated the undisputed heavyweight champion of the world, the venerable monument could have expected to be brought tumbling down long before the 12 rounds had run their course.

Holyfield had a glaring opportunity to produce such a finish as early as the last half-minute of the third round, when a burst of accurate hooks to the head abruptly undid Foreman's co-ordination, leaving the large shaven skull bobbing helplessly on his shoulders like a beach ball in surf. The champion was allowed to bombard the defenceless target at will through the final 15 seconds of the round, relishing the freedom to lunge his 15 stones in behind every punch. But – though Foreman was soon reeling blindly towards a neutral corner, his great head now lowered like that of a bull awaiting the kill – Holyfield found then, as he would in several similar episodes later, that he simply lacked the raw power to gain a knockdown, let alone a knockout.

The 17,000 spectators, who had already been nervously stirred by an unscheduled crackle of fireworks up near the roof of the Convention Center and the alarming sight of thick smoke spreading from another corner of the hall (it proved to be from nothing deadlier than a smoke bomb), noisily signalled a gathering belief that what had threatened to be a farce might turn into a drama. But, of course, the action was essentially too one-sided to justify that description. The profoundest danger for Holyfield was not of losing but of failing to swell the respect he feels has always been unfairly withheld from him. Unfortunately, there was little about his victory to alter the majority view that he is an interim tenant whose lease of the heavyweight title will be terminated whenever he confronts Mike Tyson. That former champion has shown signs lately of being much less than he was. But it is impossible to escape the conviction that, had he been permitted to blast at Foreman's jaw as often and wholeheartedly as Holyfield did, the proceedings would have been briefer and more brutal. Tyson, for all his squatness, is a true heavyweight and he hits like one.

Holyfield is a likeable individual and a more than decent fighter, a sound technician who boxed with sufficient control and threw enough sharp combinations to establish a superiority over Foreman that was ridiculously insulted by the scoring of one of the judges, Tom Kaczmarek.

Even when he had deducted the point referee Rudy Battle rather harshly took from Foreman in the eleventh round (the low punches which Battle objected to several times during the fight appeared to owe less to villainy than heavy-armed crudity), Kaczmarek had Holyfield winning by only 115 to 112. That was an offensive distortion. Eugene Grant's 116 points to 111 was also niggardly and Jerry Roth's 117–110 was definitely as close as I could have made it, even giving the giant all the best of it in his three strongest rounds, the second, fifth and tenth. Foreman never sought to take a backward step but almost invariably he was advancing into the cannon's mouth. It was a blessing for him, and may ultimately be a damning curse for Holyfield, that the champion's armament is not as heavy as it should be.

Amid a gusher of mutual admiration at the post-fight press conference, Foreman happily nurtured the wishful thinking of those of his supporters who imagined he had more than once come within a whisker of flattening Holyfield. He did reach the champion with a swinging right in the second round, spinning him theatrically off balance and going on to discomfit him so noticeably that the session could be scored for the senior citizen. Then in the fifth Holyfield's head was snapped back cruelly by a huge left jab and his work rapidly became ragged as Foreman, for once looking deliberately unhurried rather than laborious, found his head with worthwhile punches. And again in the tenth there was unmistakable discomfort for the favourite as he was caught with two chopping rights and weariness obliged him to initiate the first prolonged clinching of the fight. However, such glimpses of encouragement for Foreman were vastly outweighed by the many periods when, as he joked later, he suspected that the rival camp had slipped a mule into the ring and set it to kicking him. If Tyson had been granted the same opportunities, George might have felt he was keeping company with a Clydesdale.

Apart from the third, the ninth was the round in which Holyfield most conspicuously revved up the abuse he administered consistently to his opponent's head. It ended with the challenger wearing a dazed, slightly pathetic expression on a face which had long before become puffed and reddened under punishment. Yet the tenth round, with its contrary trend, emphasised dramatically Holyfield's inability to punch with permanently draining effect. He was content afterwards to move quietly towards the points win that would have struck his admirers as an improbably humble objective at the start.

When Holyfield, who is still unbeaten after 26 pro fights, subsequently faced the multitude purporting to be media at this event he looked healthy and relaxed. But, understandably, he had the subdued demeanour of someone reflecting that there must be cosier ways of spending the hour before midnight. George had, he acknowledged, surprised him with the deceiving speed of his jab and had 'proved at 42 he has a granite chin'. No, he was not in trouble at any time. 'George caught me with good shots but

I never gave him the chance to follow up. He cut off the ring and made me do things I didn't want to do sometimes but I did out-hustle him and land more punches. The toughest thing was the relentless pressure George put on. In every moment of the fight either I had to be punching him or he would be punching me. I felt I was fighting a smart fight. My strategy was to break George's momentum.' He was sure Foreman had not hit him as hard with a single shot as Michael Dokes had done. But whereas he had stopped Dokes, and everyone else encountered since mid-1985, the old man had insisted on staying around. 'George wasn't as easy to hit as I thought he would be. I thought I would rain on him. But I did hit him with all I had and for five years when I hit guys with all I had they went out. George didn't. He proved he had determination and a granite chin.'

Foreman duly delivered an answering salvo of compliments. 'If I had to lose I am glad it was to such a fine gentleman,' said George. Naturally he had a kind word for himself, too. 'I didn't retreat, did I? I kept the fight coming all night. My legs are so strong and I wanted the senior citizens to know I didn't need any advantages. I didn't sit down at all, though that mule kicked me a few times and I wanted to lie down. The door is open for me now. I might go out and get off the cheeseburgers and on to turkey legs – naw, I'm going to stay on cheeseburgers.'

As he headed back to Texas and his nine children with his share of the spoils from the most financially productive fight in history, the possibility of further lucrative gigs could not be ruled out. Many in Atlantic City have been wondering what Muhammad Ali, who appeared as the now familiar ghostly presence in the ring before the fight, made of all that has happened recently to the man he shattered so completely in Zaire 17 years ago. On the evidence of Friday night, it must be said that George Foreman's past is likely to prove greater than Evander Holyfield's future.

The Tortured Morality of Little Wars

The Observer, 29 September 1991

Hypocrisy is never slow to arrive at the bedside of a seriously injured boxer. It comes from both sides of the abolition debate. People who would readily endorse political policies that inflict violence on the grand scale, economic or military, are eager to take the moral high ground on the conveniently narrow issue of whether men should be licensed to punch one another in public. But all their glibness does nothing to excuse the blinkered irrationality and shabby special pleading that run through most of the countering arguments advanced by defenders of boxing, especially those who draw profit from the professional ring without stepping inside it.

Clearly, as someone who for more than 30 years has earned part of my living from writing about fights and fighters, I must accept that I belong among the justifiers, and frequent declarations of ambivalence do not relieve me of the responsibility. How much mileage is left in ambivalence, you may ask, as Michael Watson clings precariously to life in a London hospital and a bantamweight called Fernie Morales lies similarly imperilled 5,000 miles away in California? The answer, rendered no more adequate by being honest, is that I don't know. What I do know is that anyone who continues to feel inclined to make a case for boxing should renounce once and for all the embarrassingly simplistic comparisons evoked last week by such interested parties as Mr Barry Hearn, the promoter of the super-middleweight championship fight with Chris Eubank that took Watson to a neurosurgeon's operating table.

When Hearn invited us to judge the physical dangers of prize-fighting alongside those presented by other sports, he was reaching for the hoariest and most easily discredited defence of the business in which he has recently become a major influence. Some of us are tired of repeating the blindingly obvious truth that numbers of injuries and fatalities have never constituted the most potent condemnation of boxing. Surely everybody should accept by now that motive, not statistics, calls pugilism into question. There is no other activity designated a sport in which participants are officially encouraged to knock their competitors unconscious. Abolitionists may be dredging for emotive language when they say that the central objective of boxing is the systematic traumatising of an opponent, but their claim is near enough to reality to deepen the uneasiness of many of us who go regularly to the ringside. That fundamental matter of motive, the awareness that every time the bell rings we are acquiescing in the basic commitment of one fighter to incapacitating another, has more power to accuse than even the occasional heartbreaking calamities such as the blighting of the prime of Michael Watson. Other sports have produced far more dramatic death tolls. Motor racing may be considerably safer than it was in the era two decades back when Jackie Stewart found himself standing over the graves of a handful of rivals and friends in as many months, but the ratio of deaths to the tiny number of drivers involved will probably remain more depressing than any comparable statistic from boxing. However, even the fierce mutual antipathy of Ayrton Senna and Alain Prost could never send them off the grid with the hurtful intentions a fighter brings off his stool. Their aggression is formalised, given speed as its metaphor, whereas the boxer's is as raw as the survival instinct. And, for all its hazards, motor racing allowed Stewart to leave it with three world championships and without a scar, physical or mental.

Compare his present circumstances with the predicament of Muhammad Ali, not only one of the most inspired of boxers but perhaps the most universally acclaimed and captivating figure in the entire history

222

of sport. Whatever anyone says about the complexity of Ali's medical condition, about the onset of Parkinson's or any other affliction unrelated to the ring, it is impossible for me to believe that the premature twilight that has descended on his life has nothing to do with the frightening volume of blows rained on his beautiful head once the spring had left his legs. Of course, it is easy to trot out the names of outstanding fighters who have lived to be old and happy, and with all their marbles. But the current plight of Muhammad and the memory of an afternoon spent with Sugar Ray Robinson in his Los Angeles home several years before he died, of finding the man who was arguably the greatest master of the hardest game a sad, confused remnant of himself, are not easily outweighed in the mind.

One question to be faced at this point is whether, had they known about the wretched lows that lay ahead, Ali or Robinson would have been prepared to forgo the incredible highs of their extraordinary careers. It is an issue just as likely to be raised by the fate of a lesser fighter. Nine years ago, in an introduction to a collection of pieces I had written on boxing*, I referred to such a case, that of an outrageously thin, poignantly appealing bantamweight from Merthyr Tydfil:

* That introduction is, of course, reproduced in this book, which may make the lengthy quotation from it seem less natural here than it did in the newspaper piece.

Anyone who imagines that Johnny Owen was under any kind of duress when he went into the ring for the world bantamweight championship match with Lupe Pintor of Mexico that led to Owen's death in the autumn of 1980 simply did not know the boy. He was, as it happens, an extreme example of someone who desperately wanted to box. His personality was a small cloud of reticence until he entered the ambience of boxing, in a gym or an arena. Once there, he was transformed from a 24-year-old virgin whose utterances tended to come in muffled monosyllables into a confident, skilled practitioner of a rough but exciting trade. It may be – as I suggested in the hours after seeing him disastrously injured at the Olympic Auditorium in Los Angeles – that Johnny Owen's tragedy was to find himself articulate in such a dangerous language. But the people who say he should have been denied access to that language run the risk of playing God.

Though I can still identify with most of that, the idea that it would be a violation of individual rights to declare boxing illegal impresses me a lot less than it did. Such a concern might be overwhelmed by the worry that many of us, by making our small contributions to the huge worldwide edifice of organised boxing, are encouraging generation after generation of boys to choose its primitive thrills and dangers when they might otherwise opt for alternatives that involve playing at war rather than engaging in a miniature version of it. The assertion that abolition would merely drive fist-fighting underground – leading to a sleazy proliferation of clandestine promotions in which the blood lust of the lowest class of spectators (quite a few of whom showed up at White Hart Lane last weekend) would be satisfied with brutal disregard for the welfare of the contestants – is a long way short of being an answer to the abolitionists. Such squalid bootleg brawls occur now and there would certainly be more of them if boxing were outlawed. But, apart from the fact that dread of practical difficulties is no justification for running away from an ethical problem, it is madness to deny that the number taking part would be reduced to the merest fraction of the present total by a ban on amateur and professional boxing.

Talk about the steady improvement in safety procedures represents another unconvincing argument. Headguards, shorter fights, shorter rounds, quicker stoppages, better medical supervision – none of these affects the core element that sets boxing apart from every other sporting endeavour: its primeval essence of destructive motive. That is why the lingering belief that Michael Watson should not have been permitted to start the 12th round against Eubank, that the evidence of pathetic disorientation and gross vulnerability discernible from my seat 25 feet away might have persuaded his corner or the referee to end the fight after the terrible violence of the 11th, has only limited relevance. Watson was not a victim of negligence or bad judgement but of the basic nature of his profession.

So where does that leave a marginal witness like myself in relation to the big debate? I have been soliloquising on the subject for years now and this morning I have not moved much beyond the point I had reached after watching Lloyd Honeyghan battered by Marlon Starling in Las Vegas in February 1989. I know that, in spite of all the foregoing arguments, I want to be there when Mike Tyson fights Evander Holyfield for the true heavyweight championship in November, I want another look at the best pound-for-pound fighter in the world today, the great Mexican Julio Cesar Chavez. The enthusiasm comes tinged with guilt but it is real. How much mileage is left in ambivalence?

Sad Tale of Beauty and the 'Beast'

The Observer, 2 February 1992

Whatever judgements it may eventually deliver on its central issues of suffering, guilt and innocence, the Mike Tyson rape trial has already illuminated the frightening extent to which America is in thrall to an almost mystical concept of celebrity.

The British, who gave the world Beatlemania and who continue to drool over a peculiar range of icons from soap opera actors to the royal family, are anything but slow to be in awe of the famous. But much of what has happened during the past week in a small, characterless room in the City-County building on Market Street, Indianapolis, has emphasised the unique eagerness of Americans to be dazzled by any triumph over anonymity, regardless of how it is achieved. A minor manifestation of the power of celebrity to distort normal values – but one, nevertheless, that made several onlookers shudder – occurred immediately after Desiree Lynn Washington, the 18-year-old college student whose accusations have exposed Tyson to the possibility of 63 years in jail, had given the Marion County Superior Court vivid details of her allegations of sexual brutality against the former heavyweight champion of the world. The remarkable composure that marked Washington's performance on the witness stand seemed suddenly to drain out of her slight (7 st 10 lb) body as her testimony was interrupted by the ending of Thursday's sitting. She looked shaken, like someone being led away from a bad accident, as she was helped out by a female member of the prosecution team. And as the two women disappeared from view, half a dozen of the 17 members of the public allowed into the trial crowded round the rail separating their seats from the well of the court and waited happily for Tyson to sign autographs.

Its muted nature did not prevent that scene from forming a common thread with the circumstances in which Desiree Washington first met Mike Tyson on 18 July last year, the moment when the most highly paid and publicised figure in sport arrived abruptly, along with a rhythm and blues singer called Johnny Gill, among 23 girls rehearsing for the Miss Black America beauty pageant that is an important element of the Black Expo staged annually in Indianapolis. The effect, as described by the State of Indiana's leading prosecutor, Greg Garrison, was instant pandemonium. 'Well, the girls go nuts,' Garrison said in his opening statement to the jury of eight men and four women. 'Everybody is so excited that these celebrities are coming in. Some of them went for cameras, and some of them bolted for the celebrities.' It was, he suggested later, the same compelling attraction of fame that governed Washington's response when, at 1.36 the next morning, Tyson telephoned from his limousine to the hotel room she was sharing with two fellow contestants in the pageant.

The prosecution's evidence is that, having first argued against the boxer's pleas that she should join him in the limousine, she was persuaded to change her mind by his insistence that he 'just wanted to talk' and by her room-mates' speculation that he was likely to show her around some of the late-night parties where other celebrities might still be encountered. Having got out of bed, she dressed so hurriedly that she kept on the polka-dot underwear that was part of her sleeping attire, but even in her haste she remembered to pick up the camera she had used earlier to have photographs taken with her improbable date. 'You can say, "I went out with so and so", but if you have a picture, then that's neat,' she told the court brightly on Friday morning. Such priorities, which seem characteristic of the High School girl she so recently was, especially when expressed in the light, perkily innocent voice that could belong to a 13-year-old, do nothing to assist Vincent Fuller, senior partner in Williams and Connolly, the Washington DC law firm widely hailed as the most effective forensic machine in the US, and the man spearheading a defence effort costing at least $2 million. Fuller, a greying 60-year-old with glasses, a slightly professorial manner and a voice that is strong but has a tendency to be blurred by the courtroom microphones, is heir to a tradition established by the founder of the firm, Edward Bennett Williams, who until his death in 1988 was considered the finest American trial lawyer since Clarence Darrow. However, so far in this case he has exhibited surprisingly little of the brilliant capacity for absorbing and deploying detail that has brought him his greatest victories – such as the 1982 verdict that declared John Hinckley, charged with the attempted assassination of President Ronald Reagan, not guilty on the grounds of insanity, and the acquittal in 1985 of Don King, the electric-haired promoter who is currently Tyson's mentor (some would say Iago), on 23 counts of income tax evasion, filing fraudulent tax returns and conspiracy. In this archetypal Midwest city, whose principal claim on global attention is a car race, Fuller's Eastern Establishment sophistication has counted for less than the folksy guile and occasional bare-knuckle aggression of Garrison.

At 43, Garrison has such an impressive record in the Indiana courts that he is frequently wooed away from his private practice to handle particularly vital State prosecutions on a contract basis. He has been soberly suited in front of Judge Patricia J. Gifford, a proud member of the notoriously conservative Daughters of the American Revolution, who might not be amused by the cowboy boots and leather braces he sometimes wears. But with his long, lean frame and head of thick, carefully cut and swept back hair, he is made for dramatic interventions and he has revealed plenty of the sense of theatre left over from the time he was training to be a concert pianist. Far from being intimidated by the heavy artillery drawn up against him, he has been relentlessly combative. He is unfailingly sharp in identifying reasons for an objection, and not above slamming the table in registering it, and more than once during his opening address his appeal to the jurors was so intimate that he almost climbed into the box with them. Garrison's force of personality ideally complements the assets of his star witness. Desiree Washington is petite and attractive, with shoulder-length black hair. She has turned out on one day in a grey suit and white blouse, on another in a tasteful turquoise dress, but always she has presented a powerful combination of girlish charm, alert intelligence and lively spirit.

Inevitably, there has been muttering that the image she offers from the stand, like all the distinctions she has accumulated at school and beyond her impeccable involvement in the affairs of her Rhode Island community, will strike the predominantly young, working-class jury as too good to be true, as proof of a precocious ability to put herself across convincingly in the interests of well-honed ambition. Williams and Connolly have the reputation of taking few prisoners in their legal battles, and of shooting those they do, and it is no shock that Fuller has strenuously sought to foster any suspicions about the accuser's genuineness. His initial statement made clear his intention to brand her as an unusually mature young woman, one 'who bears false witness against Mr Tyson' out of mercenary motives. 'It is our contention that Miss Washington has not been victimised but compromised,' said Fuller. 'She wanted to be with him (Tyson), but she found herself treated as a one-night stand. Desiree Washington has a compelling desire for money. Throughout the pageant, money is a frequent subject of her conversation. Indeed, on the day she meets Mr Tyson and believes she is going to have an engagement with him that evening, she's heard to say such things as, "He's got money. I'm going out with Mike Tyson. He's rich. Did you see what Robin Givens got out of him? Besides, he's dumb."'

The defence must intend to call witnesses to testify to such utterances, which Desiree Washington has resolutely denied she ever made. But whatever other voices speak against her, the impact of the alleged victim's own version of her ordeal in room 606 at the Canterbury Hotel, a few downtown blocks from the court and only one from the room at the Omni Severin Hotel that she was sharing last July, may remain so convincing that Fuller will have to risk summoning his client to the stand in an attempt to undermine it. It is her evidence that within minutes of being lured to 606, by Tyson's pretext of having some brief business there, she was totally helpless under a savage sexual assault by a man more than twice her weight, one of the strongest athletes alive. Her description of the attack that has resulted in one charge of confinement (for restraining her on a bed), two of deviant sexual conduct (digital penetration and cunnilingus) and one of rape was as horrifying as Garrison indicated it would be when he began by saying her 16-stone captor had hurled her around like a rag doll.

Questions about why she did not report the alleged rape until nearly 24 hours after leaving Tyson's room surely cannot carry much weight, since it was the arrival of her parents in Indianapolis and their subsequent urgings that precipitated the report. Equally, the view that her credibility suffers drastically from her controlled demeanour in court is peculiar, almost a demand that she deny the natural resilience of a bright, spirited teenage nature. Pressed on why she rose only two or three hours after such an ordeal to go ahead on that Friday and the following days with the full exhausting schedule of beauty pageant events, in spite of being 'in a cloud' and feeling a lot of pain between her legs, she said firmly: 'I played softball for about 12 years. I've had fractured ribs and fingers and stuff like that, and I always make the play and finish the game before I quit. I mean, I just don't quit. I was in pain, and I just beared it. If I was a quitter, I wouldn't be here now. At 18 years old, I didn't need this media stuff, but I believed in my heart I was doing the right thing, and I prayed about it, and I finished what I started.'

A few yards across the court from her, seated in his usual place at the defence table, wearing one of the variety of expensively unspectacular suits he favoured throughout the week, the deadliest pugilist of his time may have been wondering if he will be allowed to see one of the most astonishing careers in the history of the ring through to a conventional finish. But the thoughts going through the large, cropped head tilted forward from the muscular slabs of his shoulders were unlikely to be concerned with the vast sums of money, perhaps upwards of $100 million, riding on the judgement that awaits him. He can be assured that Don King and several others will grant such matters all the pondering they require.

The current heavyweight champion, Evander Holyfield, is no more than an inflated cruiserweight and the merest of pretenders to the domination of boxing's most lucrative division Tyson exerted between 1986 and his shatteringly unexpected loss to James 'Buster' Douglas in Tokyo in February 1990. Tyson was the youngest man ever to win a world heavyweight title and, though he has been without it for nearly two years and is already betraying traces of serious decline at the early age of 25, he has continued to look so superior to any prospective challengers that it was hard to put a ceiling on his projected earnings until the present charges cancelled an imminent match with Holyfield. But everything in his past experiences should have warned him of the danger of such a crisis involving the law (and his Indianapolis predicament is scarcely eased by the fact that elsewhere the reigning Miss Black America, Rosie Jones, has filed a $100 million suit against him for sexual harassment). From the earliest days of a childhood split between two of the most desperate ghettos in America, the Brooklyn districts of Bedford-Stuyvesant and Brownsville – where he was a gun-handling mugger at primary school age and is credited with more than 40 arrests before he was 12 – to his brief, stormy marriage with the actress Robin Givens, he has never been far

from trouble. Only the wildly optimistic believed that he had been permanently rescued from his origins by Cus D'Amato when that eccentric but
inspiring theoretician of boxing and life took him out of a reformatory for
hard cases in upstate New York and became his guardian. All his prodigious progress as a fighter, his climb towards titles and riches, never lifted
him far above the violent waywardness he had developed in the ghetto
and when D'Amato's death was followed by that of the old guru's managerial protégé, Jim Jacobs, Tyson's career was soon awash in bitterness
and litigation. Such conditions provide a natural habitat for King and
before long Tyson was committed to an alliance with that self-promoting
promoter, which was not guaranteed to increase his chances of either
long-term prosperity or immediate tranquillity.

A tiny echo of happier times in the D'Amato household near Catskill,
New York, has been offered in recent days by the presence in court of
Camille Ewald, a homely woman in her 80s who was Cus's companion
for many years and is one of the few people for whom Tyson feels a deep,
trusting affection. The conspicuous absence of another member of the
Catskill group is, however, more significant. He is Jose Torres, former
light-heavyweight champion of the world and author of a book that
chronicles a number of the memorably turbulent episodes in Tyson's life.
The defence was delighted to be able to prevent Torres from appearing as
a witness, which is understandable considering that one passage in his
book quoted Tyson as telling him in 1986 how he liked to hurt women
when he made love to them.

It was another Mike Tyson the public saw at a religious rally in
Indianapolis on Friday night. Emerging for the first time from the
seclusion he has maintained since the start of the trial, he joined about 350
banner-waving supporters at Christ Missionary Baptist Church, where
the Rev Melvin B. Girton led the chanting of 'We love Mike', and the
crowd sang hymns and tirelessly shouted hallelujahs. State Senator Billie
J. Breaux said they had come to see justice done to everybody. 'We have
come tonight because a brother is in a fight for his life, and a sister is in a
fight for her future, and we are trying to retain our dignity.' Another
female speaker earned a standing ovation when she declared: 'Black
women, we must remember that our bodies are temples and we control
them. If we don't respect ourselves, who will?' The man accused of
defiling one temple applauded and smiled.

Tyson, who had prayed publicly with Jesse Jackson just hours before
he took Desiree Washington to his room last July, brought Friday's
emotional evening to a climax by moving his bulk up to the microphone
and reading from a prepared statement: 'I fight with God and with God I
can't lose,' he said. Having just one juror on his side might be enough.

As he signed his autographs in the courtroom, the beleaguered
heavyweight may have been tempted to make a link with an even more
incongruous scene involving his friend King after the tax case acquittal in

1985. On that day the clamour for autographs came not from spectators but from the jury that cleared him. One woman asked if she could keep his pen.

Forget that a New York State Inspector General once described the contracts King writes as 'horrible'. That pen had been in the hand of a celebrity.

The Raging Bull in the Bedroom

The Observer, 9 February 1992

After waiting nearly two weeks to have his say in a trial that threatens him with 60 years in jail, Mike Tyson took the witness stand to pour out lurid endorsement of a defensive strategy apparently aimed at proving he is an aggressive, foul-mouthed sexual predator but not a rapist. In the high, slightly lisping voice that is forever at odds with the menacing hulk of a former heavyweight champion of the world, Tyson spent 75 minutes late on Friday afternoon enlightening a jury of eight men and four women in the Marion County Superior Court about the blitzkrieg of ghetto directness that is his favoured way of wooing. He told how he was firmly laying down the conditions of a date within minutes of meeting Desiree Washington, the 18-year-old college student he is accused of raping during her participation in the Miss Black America beauty pageant here last July. The girl had been swiftly disabused of any notion that he might fancy going to the cinema or having dinner. 'I said, "That's not what I want to do . . . I don't have that in mind. I just want to be with you, I want you."'

'Did you say anything else?' asked Vincent Fuller, the renowned Washington lawyer who is leading the boxer's defence against one charge of rape and two of deviant sexual conduct (another, of confinement, has been dropped as redundant).

'Well, it's kind of crass,' replied Tyson. But, given a little prompting, he repeated the words: 'I explained to her that I wanted to fuck her.' Her response, he claimed, was equally forthright: 'Sure, just give me a call.'

When Washington had mentioned that he was 'kind of bold', he had put her straight on that issue, too. 'I said, "That's the way I am", I just want to know what I'm getting before I'm getting into it.'

For day after day before their client came to the stand, through witness after witness, Fuller and his hugely expensive team sought to establish that that indeed is how Mike Tyson is. They seemed positively to encourage a series of Washington's fellow contestants to characterise him as someone who moved among the 23 Miss Black America entrants like a stud in heat, groping bottoms, spraying propositions in all directions, freely employing obscenities both to declare his intentions and to dismiss girls who objected to them. Plainly, the defence has set out to persuade the jury that Washington – who alleges that Tyson brutally assaulted her in his suite at the downtown Canterbury Hotel in the early hours of 19 July last year – knew exactly what she was heading towards when she accepted a telephoned invitation to rise from her bed in the Omni Severin Hotel and join him in his limousine. They have doggedly, if not always effectively, attempted to create the impression that she was consumed by a mercenary desire to become involved with a man who is both famous and wealthy at the age of 25. Every move they made was meant to present her as just the kind of girl on the make who would behave as Tyson in his testimony insisted she did. He said, in absolute contradiction of his accuser's sworn description of how their brief time together developed, that she was kissing him enthusiastically from the moment she joined him in the limousine. By the time they were let into his room by his bodyguard, Dale Edwards (who is alleged by the prosecution to have been downstairs when the couple entered suite 606), she was, according to Tyson, ready to sit on the bed and react agreeably to more touching and kissing.

Soon, he told the court, they plunged into frantic sexual activity. 'As I'm kissing her, she was moving fast. She was dropping her jacket, you know, getting her jacket off quick. And I'm just kissing on the neck and around the ears, back of the neck and chest and nipples, the stomach. I believe she had a white shirt on as well. She was trying to get that off, so I came back while she was taking that off. She had taken off those shorts, she had – I'm sure she took off the shorts . . . and the underwear dropped to her knees, and I pulled them all the way off.' Tyson said he had then taken his own pants off and when asked what happened next he looked embarrassed; 'Man, my mom is right here,' he said, referring to 86-year-old Camille Ewald, who was for many years companion of his late guardian and boxing mentor, Cus D'Amato. Hesitantly, he went on: 'I had – I was having oral sex with her.'

Then Washington had told him urgently to come up, indicating that she wanted him to insert his penis, and he had done so and engaged in intercourse for 15 to 20 minutes before respecting her wishes by having his climax outside her body. Afterwards, he continued, while she was rearranging her hair in front of a mirror, she had gone through a little dance. 'She was in the mirror doing her hair, a little dance, like shoo, shoo, shoo, doing her hair.' It was, he declared, only after she had turned down his offer to let her stay the night and he had made it clear he was too tired to walk her downstairs, that Washington became irritated. She had left the room and he had gone to sleep for a while before being roused to catch an early-morning plane to Cleveland, in keeping with a schedule he says he had planned well in advance.

It was a remarkable catalogue of behaviour to associate with the image of Washington put before the jury by the prosecution, a tiny (7 st 10 lb), girlish personality with the voice of a 13-year-old, one whose many accomplishments at High School and in her Rhode Island community had not prevented her from remaining unworldly to the point of naïveté. Certainly the voracious commitment to consensual sex seemed hard to reconcile with the evidence of Mary Belle Washington, earlier in the week, about the long-term effects the experience with Tyson has had on her daughter.

The jury in this case will carry away many vividly disturbing memories, not least that of the fire that swept last Tuesday night through the Indianapolis Athletic Club in which they were staying. The blaze killed two firemen and an elderly resident and so affected the state of mind of one of three original black jurors that he was replaced by a reserve, who happened to be a white man of 44. However, it is doubtful if anything will remain with these members of the public brought into the miserable courtroom drama longer than the voice of Mrs Washington as she lamented the remoteness that had come over Desiree in the weeks after her return from Indiana to Rhode Island: 'And one day she said to me, "Mom, I'm not Desiree any more." I said, "Yes, you are." She says, "No, I'm not Desiree any more. Desiree is gone, and she's not going to come back."'

Naturally, the defence has painted a different picture. In particular, it has offered remarks said to have been made by the student in a ladies' room at the Omni Hotel (which is less than a block from the Canterbury and provided three-to-a-room lodgings as well as practice facilities for the pageant girls) as among the most significant ever uttered in a lavatory. A fellow contestant, Madeline Whittington, said she was washing her hands in the rest-room at the Omni when Washington, in the midst of 'primping, putting on make-up, lipstick, taking things out of her purse', confirmed to her that she was going out with Tyson. 'Yes, of course I'm going,' Whittington reported Desiree as saying. 'This is Mike Tyson. He's got a lot of money. He's dumb. You see what Robin Givens got out of him.' Corroboration came from Cecillia Alexander, one of the very few witnesses who have conveyed to a court what they heard while in a lavatory stall. Alexander also testified that, while in less confined circumstances, she heard Washington answer some teasing about her 'husband' Tyson and his inability to speak well by saying, 'Mike doesn't have to know how to speak well – he'll make all the money, and I'll do all the talking.'

The girl with the most spectacular name in the case, Parquita Marionette Nassau, who was born in Liberia and raised in Atlanta, Georgia, swore that she, too, overheard that line about the division of earning and talking responsibilities but she had more impact as a witness to Tyson's conversational style. She said that when she made a comment to the effect that Southern girls like to cook, he had replied: 'That's good, because I like to eat; and I'm not talking about food.' Then she told how he looked at a handful of pageant contestants around him. 'He said, "I want to F you, and you, and you. And bring your room-mate, too, because I'm a celebrity, and you know we do that kind of thing."' Nassau herself had complained when 'he felt on my behind' and he had apologised profusely. But he told her: 'If you don't want to go out with me, I could move on, because I could have any one of these bitches out here.'

Greg Garrison, the engagingly theatrical 43-year-old who is leading prosecutor for the State of Indiana here, has consistently demonstrated enough spirit and intellectual nimbleness to outscore the 60-year-old Fuller. But he has sometimes found himself following unlikely lines of questioning as he has tried to convince jurors that the accuser was not only excessively susceptible to Tyson's celebrity but simply did not encounter enough of the crudities experienced by other contestants to recognise that a date with him could be dangerous. Garrison has been obliged to seek answers indicating that much of the time the fighter was polite, warm and thoroughly congenial, the kind of individual from whom Desiree Washington might readily accept one of the friendly hugs he was lavishly distributing, someone she was liable to believe when he suggested they should have a talk and do some sightseeing around 2 a.m. The prosecutor elicited some welcome co-operation in that area from Tonya Traylor, a defence witness who asserted that four-letter words were so much part of Tyson's normal vocabulary that they were not offensive. 'And so if he's going to say, "I'm going out the door", he may say, "I'm going out the F door". But I don't take that personal, because he's talking about a door.'

Lawyers on both sides have been taking their opponents' tactics very personally indeed and the naked hostility that has swirled through many of the exchanges almost went out of control at the beginning of the week when the defence tried to introduce three new female witnesses. The women were said to have come forward with a story about having seen Tyson and Washington 'all over one another' in the boxer's limousine as it pulled up in front of the Canterbury Hotel early on the morning of 19 July 1991. Garrison, who did not hear of their existence until Sunday, opposed their introduction with such vehement hints of 'bad faith' on the part of the Washington heavy brigade that both Fuller and James H. Voyles, a hero of the Indiana bar who has been recruited to the Fuller team but treated pretty much like a message boy, made passionately indignant protests about the impugning of their integrity.

Judge Patricia J. Gifford put it on record that everybody's integrity was utterly unstained. But, showing a face suffused with anger under her short blonde hair, she added: 'I presume I would be remiss if I did not also indicate that the court does not appreciate being put in this position in the middle of a trial that's taken a great deal of effort if there is any possibility that it was done with the idea of causing some kind of reversible error.' That acknowledgement of a suspicion that the defence may already be wondering if they will be in need of an appeal can only increase the tension of the two or three decisive days of this trial that lie ahead. Most observers think the pressure of reasonable doubt will come to Tyson's rescue. But at least this is one fight in which he cannot pre-empt the voting process with a knockout.

Mike Tyson was found guilty and served three years in jail.

Big Man from Tyson Town

The Observer, 8 November 1992

Riddick Bowe has an interesting way of describing how he means to spend next Friday evening. 'I'm going to knock out that little man you all call the heavyweight champion of the world,' he says with a slow and friendly smile.

The words are less easily ignored than the usual pre-fight mouthings, because their youthful bombast is underpinned by recognition of a simple truth. There is indeed an essential smallness about Evander Holyfield in relation to the title he has held for the past two years, a lack of power and authority that neither his height (6 ft 2 in) nor the manufactured bulk of his upper body can obscure. Holyfield is a genuine warrior, a fighting man to the marrow, but he is a synthetic heavyweight and at first-hand here in the Nevada desert he seems alarmingly vulnerable against a challenger who stands 6 ft 5 in tall, is likely to enter the ring at slightly more than 16½ st and can box and punch well enough to make those advantages tell. Whereas Bowe was born to be big, his opponent is a natural cruiserweight who had bigness thrust upon him by strength coaches and dieticians, and money-men keenly aware that every muscular pound he gained could be worth the equivalent in gold. With the co-operation of a junk-food mountain named James 'Buster' Douglas, who surrendered the world championship while philosophising in a supine posture, the grand strategy of Holyfield's career achieved its objective, and wealth has come in a tidal wave. When he collects on the percentage deal that is expected to give him something like $15 million for Friday's engagement at the Thomas and Mack Center in Las Vegas, the aggregate of his purses will be about $80 million. That figure will put him comfortably ahead of Muhammad Ali and Mike Tyson, though still well behind boxing's most prodigious earner, Sugar Ray Leonard. The gap would narrow considerably, of course, if Holyfield survived Bowe's challenge and went on to a bonanza against the latest vehicle of British dreams, Lennox Lewis.

But it must be said that so far the marketing of his title defences has been far more triumphant than the performances. For mildly vandalising two ancient monuments of the heavyweight division – the former champions George Foreman and Larry Holmes, both of whom were aged 42 when laboriously outpointed – he was paid the staggering total of $40 million. Between those enriching embarrassments, Bert Cooper, a journeyman drafted in at a week's notice as a substitute for a substitute, pounded Holyfield to the brink of a knockout before reverting to type and being stopped in the seventh round. Everything about these three blemished victories has been a reminder that a fighter's validity as a heavyweight can never be established by a reading of the scales. True heavyweights are a separate species. They come in many shapes and sizes and in the past some of the best (Dempsey and Marciano, to mention only two) have been a great deal lighter than Holyfield's recent fighting average of around 15 st. But, inside the ropes, the work of such men had a destructive substance, a violent conviction, that Holyfield has conspicuously failed to produce. For all the tapered and rippling impressiveness of his physique, and the testimony of a professional record that shows 28 straight wins (22 inside the distance), he does not hit with the power of a real out-and-out heavyweight. That belief is certainly reinforced by the memory of how Mike Tyson annihilated a Holmes four years younger than the man who faced Holyfield, and the frightening thought of what Tyson would have done to the bloated, lumbering Foreman. Holyfield's time as champion has been not so much a reign as a regency, one that has been extended by the imprisonment of the natural ruler of the division (Tyson) and the absence of any clamour of young pretenders. Now, however, youth and size, in the shape of Bowe and Lewis, are back to claim their due and most of the omens appear to be in their favour.

Yet the Las Vegas odds-makers have installed the champion as the 6–4 on favourite, with Bowe at 11–10 against. Their assessment points to the issue that is the most intriguing and perhaps the most crucial in this, as in so many other fights – the question of heart. In Holyfield's case, there simply isn't any question. Courage, like his endearing warmth and honesty, is in the inviolable core of his nature. It is the quality of Bowe's resolve that many are inclined to doubt, which might seem remarkable considering how much character he has required just to emerge healthy and uncorrupted from an inner-city environment as desperate as any in America. As the seventh son and 12th child in a family of 13 that had been left fatherless, he had only the unbreakable spirit of his mother, Dorothy, and his own resources to shield him against the crowding dangers of the Brownsville ghetto in Brooklyn. Brownsville has become notorious as the area in which Tyson served an apprenticeship in thuggery but even the ex-champion's immediate locality was less threatening than the nearby block at 250 Lott Avenue, where Bowe's family had an apartment in a building ruthlessly controlled by crack dealers. Men with Uzis, pump-action shotguns and an assortment of pistols were posted as lookouts at glassless windows and sentries on the landings. Life was so cheap that when a man was shot dead on the fifth floor of the building no one was in any hurry to call the police and his body lay where it had fallen for nearly 12 hours.

Three years ago *The New York Daily News* did a story about Bowe's achievement in managing to grow up clean in the midst of such murderous desperadoes. The desperadoes were not amused. A few days after the story was published, one of Dorothy's daughters sent her some flowers. The flowers, as Mike Katz reported in the *News*, were dead on arrival. So was the delivery man. He and they were stuffed into a garbage can and left for Mrs Bowe. Her son got the message and before long he had moved himself and his mother out of Brownsville. He, his wife and three children now live in suburban Fort Washington, Maryland. 'The first thing I noticed about not being in New York was that I didn't hear shots fired every night,' he says. 'I realised I could let my kids walk around and nobody was going to steal them. That's beautiful but I still tell my wife: "Maryland is where we live – Brooklyn is our home."'

The loyalty is notable, in view of what Brooklyn did to them. Bowe's own sister Brenda was knifed to death by crack sellers after she refused to be a buyer. The murder happened three weeks before he won a place in the 1988 US Olympic team. By the time he went into the ring in Seoul he knew one of his brothers was dying of Aids, which made the boxer's fitness problems (recent surgery on his right hand and a barely healed hairline fracture of an ankle) rather trivial. Perhaps it is no overwhelming surprise that neither his heart nor his mind seemed totally committed to the battle when he was stopped by Lennox Lewis in the Olympic final. It is true, nevertheless, that four years on, at the age of 25 and with a growing family, Bowe remains engagingly boyish. With his gentle humour (he fancies himself as an impressionist, specialising in Stevie Wonder, Bill Cosby and Ronald Reagan) and the easy-going attitude that allows his weight between fights to balloon close enough to 20 st to alarm his newly recruited nutritionist, Dick Gregory, he encourages critics to ask if he can ever develop the meanness to inherit Iron Mike Tyson's boxing territory. He has been insisting quietly this past week that he does not have to be as consistently hostile as Tyson to hold the same titles and add a string of gargantuan pay-days to the $7 million he will pick up for his exertions at the Thomas and Mack Center. 'I do think I am a decent guy, and Evander Holyfield is a nice fella, too, but we're in the hurt business here and I'll be mean all right when we get at it on Friday.'

While he is five years younger than Holyfield, the challenger's unbeaten record includes three more fights than the champion has had, with more stoppages, and he refuses to believe he is at a disadvantage in terms of experience. Neither will suffer from a shortage of enlightened advice between rounds, for they will have the competing services of two of the world's finest corner-men. George Benton, who is 59, and Eddie

236

Futch, who has been around a couple of decades longer, first met when Benton was a feared middleweight and Futch brought wisdom to his corner. They later teamed up to help Joe Frazier among others and, since Bowe sparred many rounds with Holyfield in the '80s, this fight will be awash in mutual knowledge.

Benton is happy that Holyfield will be coming in lighter than of late (maybe as low as 14 st 9 lb), having cut down drastically on his sessions with weights to avoid sluggishness in his arms. Explosive speed, the master trainer confirms, will be their key currency, that and assiduously practised defensive manoeuvres meant to let the champion neutralise Bowe's longer reach and fine jab by operating at close quarters without being punished for it. 'We want to be like the Indians with Custer,' Benton told me. 'They would jump on Custer's ass, do their own thing, and then get out and regroup. Then jump on him again.' Holyfield admits that the eyebrow cut inflicted by Holmes, the first of his pro career, undermined his confidence in the gym for a while afterwards, especially when another, smaller one developed on the adjacent eyelid. But he says that is all behind him and he is a warrior again.

The opposition are convinced he is about to be a vanquished warrior. 'Name a heavyweight with a better jab than Bowe has or, regardless of size, more mobility?' demands Futch. 'He can box and punch, work inside as well as outside and he has an excellent uppercut, which is traditionally the best punch a heavyweight can use. Styles make fights and I've known for years Riddick has the style to beat Holyfield.'

I thoroughly agree. But, looking into Evander Holyfield's face, where the hard determination of the eyes contradicts the slightly dandified curve of moustache and beard, there is the feeling that the right style may not be enough. What Riddick Bowe needs can be drawn from the mean streets of his youth. If he can summon it, he should be the new champion of the world.

Bowe the King of Hearts

The Observer, 15 November 1992

Even the bravest of the brave cannot hold reality at bay indefinitely and the truth about Evander Holyfield's physical limitations closed on him like a plundering army in Las Vegas on Friday night. At the end of 12 violently compelling rounds in the hurtful company of the younger, bigger Riddick Bowe, Holyfield had lost a unanimous decision, the undisputed heavyweight championship of the world and the inclination to continue his career as a professional fighter. What remained gloriously intact was the great fortress of his heart, one of the most remarkable boxing has ever known.

Given the memorable intensity of this conflict, and especially of a tenth round that ranked in terms of drama with any ever fought between heavyweights, and an 11th that saw Holyfield survive a knockdown, it seemed insulting that the immediate aftermath should be dominated by talk of another, future fight. However, as soon as Bowe had claimed the three belts that signify the most lucrative dominion in sport, the air in the Thomas and Mack Center was alive with speculation about when and how the new champion will respond to the pressing challenge of Lennox Lewis, who emerged as Britain's most threatening contender this century when he blasted the highly rated Razor Ruddock out of his way two weeks ago.

There were, of course, good reasons why interest in a Bowe–Lewis confrontation was not confined to the British. Bowe, who has won all 32 of his pro fights, last suffered defeat in a ring at the powerful hands of Lewis, who stopped him convincingly four years ago in the Olympic final that climaxed their amateur careers. That humiliation, which burdened the loser with accusations of cowardice he is only now shaking off, still rankles deeply. The man from the Brooklyn ghetto abandoned the quick-witted banter of his victory press conference to abuse Lewis as 'a big ugly bum' and a 'faggot' and told him: 'I got sisters that could whup you.' Lewis may have invited the New Yorker's hostility in the past with taunting references to his Olympic superiority but here he contented himself with being a handsome, smilingly dismissive presence, concentrating his verbal aggression on the growing evidence that Bowe will delay facing him in order to accommodate a high-earning voluntary defence of his titles against some unmenacing opponent such as the vast and decrepit George Foreman, whose name has been linked with a perhaps fanciful multi-million dollar promotion in Communist China.

Such application of commercial priorities would, the World Boxing Council have declared, cause them to strip Bowe of their version of the championship and hand it instantly to Lewis. When Rock Newman – the volatile and loquacious manager of the champion – had recovered his breath after punching a photographer in the turmoil that developed around the winner's corner following the final bell, he sneered at the WBC, suggesting that their initials stood for Will Be Corrupt and condemning their president, José Sulaiman, as a dictator and exploiter he would be happy to ignore. So there was plenty to justify the crackle of anticipation surrounding the promised showdown between Bowe and the unbeaten Lewis.

Nevertheless, nothing that lies ahead should be allowed to detract in the slightest from appreciation of the unquenchable courage and nobility of spirit exhibited by Evander Holyfield as he lost his grip on a kingdom his natural physique never equipped him to rule. His own extraordinary strength of character and a collusive set of circumstances (not least the imprisonment of the era's deadliest genuine heavyweight, Mike Tyson) enabled him to flourish profitably for a time within the fiction that he belonged among the truly big men. There might have been resentment of his prodigious income from defences against relics like the former champions Foreman and Larry Holmes (who were both 42 when he beat them) had it not been for the feeling that Holyfield's honourable nature and the purity of his will entitled him to whatever good fortune he enjoyed, even as his purses piled up towards a current gross estimated at around $80 million.

And, if he generated a flood of warmth with the decency and commitment he showed through the 28 straight victories he had amassed before he entered the ring on Friday, his performance turned it into a tidal wave. Some of us were always sure that all the effort he had put in with weights and diets and relentless sessions in the gym could never compensate for the basic reality that he was born to be no more than a cruiserweight. We were irrevocably persuaded that when he met a young and vigorous challenger who not only could fight but had been destined from the womb to be a heavyweight, Holyfield's invented world would crumble painfully around him.

Riddick Bowe, five years younger at 25, three inches taller at 6 ft 5 in and 30 pounds heavier at 16 st 11 lb, vindicated the theory by inflicting a comprehensive beating. But any concern with being proved right was utterly swamped by emotional admiration for the quality of Holyfield's defiance. Bowe, too, was brave, silencing his many doubters with the unswerving sense of purpose that informed his persistent exploitation of his advantages in height, reach, bulling strength and power of punch. But the images that will stay longest in the memory grew out of Holyfield's refusal to yield, not merely his insistence on remaining upright on teetering legs under bombardments that should have flattened him but the unmistakable signs that in the midst of his worst crises he was positively seeking ways to win the fight.

All of that was exemplified in the astonishing tenth round, the recollection of which will bring a shiver of awe to most of those who witnessed it from among the live audience of more than 17,000. For about two-thirds of its duration Holyfield was a helpless, reeling victim of unbridled assault. He had staggered back to his corner after being badly shaken right at the end of the ninth, and, as he answered the next bell still weak and vulnerable, Bowe settled into his most sustained and controlled attack of the night. Jolting left jabs and plunging overhand rights were mixed with two-handed hooking as he drove his target across the ring and it seemed that the older man could not possibly come through the nightmare.

But if you want to know how the mind of a fighting man of the truest calibre functions in such moments, listen to Holyfield's subsequent report of what he was thinking then: 'He was laying a lot of leather on me. He hurt me and he had me going from pillar to post. Yet I felt, "This is the round I have the chance to knock him out." Even though he had me hurt he was expending a lot of energy. I knew he was going to miss one and I was going to have a chance to catch him. I did catch him and he was hurt but he proved he was a champion by staying in there.'

There is characteristic understatement in Holyfield's description of what he achieved in the last minute of that round. Having punched himself close to exhaustion in pursuit of a stoppage, Bowe found that his habitual tendency to slow towards the finish of every round was desperately compounded. Soon it was his turn to suffer as Holyfield, dredging hostile force from a place that only heroes know, swarmed over him with hooks and uppercuts. The fury and surging fluctuations of those three minutes of action left spectators wondering if they, let alone the fighters, could take any more of this war.

In fact, Holyfield had to weather another brush with calamity early in the 11th. As the champion reached out both arms to put a restraining embrace on his opponent's shoulders, Bowe suddenly ducked under his left elbow and smashed a looping right into the back of his skull. Having lurched sideways on to his right knee, Holyfield stayed down for only about three seconds but he was obviously glad of the respite granted when the referee, Joe Cortez, extended the count to eight. Once again Bowe's attempts to terminate resistance were courageously frustrated and again he found himself tiring before the 30-year-old. But, automatically, that 11th went 10–8 in favour of Bowe on the scorecards of all three judges and a coronation was already just about inevitable. The tiny residue of uncertainty was duly obliterated when Holyfield lost a final round in which both men, at last, revealed the wearing effects of the cruel pace they had sought to maintain.

The loser did not deserve the two cards that gave him just 110 points against 117 for Bowe. Chuck Giampa's 115–112 was fairer, though I would have made the gap one point wider. When all credit is given to the new champion for the systematic effectiveness of his work, particularly the patience with which he applied damaging pressure to the body and declined to be discouraged by the failure of his heavy rights to bring a knockout, it must be said that the decisive factor was, predictably, Holyfield's lack of a true heavyweight's hitting power.

He had a number of impressive rounds (the first, the fifth, the eighth and ninth come to mind) and even in his bad times he could connect with some good clean blows, ranging from the jab to the left hook to the right cross. But none did more than discomfit Bowe, whereas Bowe's punches were brutalising Holyfield. The contrast of their faces afterwards told a story. Holyfield's was sadly misshapen by swellings and cuts that needed stitching. The winner showed limited marks around the right eye, some of them caused by thumbing in the eighth round.

As congratulations poured in on Bowe, and on his peerless 81-year-old trainer Eddie Futch, who has now handled six heavyweight world champions, the most heartfelt tributes were reserved for Evander Holyfield. He is the kind of man who makes you feel it is a privilege to share the same planet.

A Robbery with Violence

The Observer, 11 February 1993

Pernell Whitaker now has bitter proof that professional boxing is the most truly egalitarian of sports, a world in which great champions and obscure journeymen are equally exposed to barefaced robbery. The scorecards that turned the simple reality of Whitaker's clear points victory over Julio Cesar Chavez into the squalid fantasy of a draw may have to be explained in terms of nothing more sinister than the distorted vision and demented logic of two of the three ringside judges. But the desperately wronged fighter is entitled to feel like a victim of larceny on the grand scale.

Through at least eight of the 12 rounds fought at the Alamodome on Friday night, Whitaker exploited lithe movement and swift, precisely targeted punching to such undeniable effect that he had the right to believe he was dismantling a legend. Chavez had been borne into the ring on a tide of success without comparison in the modern era, an uninterrupted sequence of 87 wins over 13½ years that hinted at invincibility. But before the fight had gone halfway the implacable destructiveness that invested most of those performances with a sense of the inevitable had given way to lunging frustration and, though both his body and his spirit remained so defiantly strong that he took the last round, it seemed impossible that any objective witness could fail to acknowledge that he had been soundly beaten.

Even the vast Mexican majority in the crowd of 63,000 that equalled the indoor record for a boxing promotion, a concentration of nationalist fervour in which fair-mindedness was as improbable as good manners in a riot, indicated unmistakably by the rapid dwindling of their din that they knew their hero was lurching to the first defeat of his magnificent career. No people anywhere have a more basic affinity than Mexicans with the harsh imperatives of fist-fighting, or a clearer understanding of what is happening inside the ropes, and all their partisan emotion could not blind the army of Chavez supporters who had streamed across the nearby border to the superiority relentlessly established by Whitaker.

Later, having been rescued from the nightmare of the truth by wildly eccentric scoring, many of them would try to persuade themselves that perhaps the judges had seen something they had missed. Was there, they would ask, validity in Julio's protestations that he deserved reward for persistently advancing on his opponent, forcing the pace of the action, whereas Whitaker deserved to suffer for recurring use of illegal methods, particularly when punching low or frequently ducking unacceptably close to the floor? While the intense battle was being waged, however, the anxious silence that settled over the Hispanic spectators, like the reluctant lowering of the thousands of flags they had brought to wave in celebration, betrayed their inability to delude themselves about what they were watching.

They were struggling to accept the mounting evidence that Chavez, who has held five versions of world titles in three separate weight categories between 9 st 4 lb and 10 st (he is currently the World Boxing Council champion at super-lightweight – 10 st), had gone a division too far by challenging for Whitaker's WBC welterweight (10 st 7 lb) crown. Mutual agreement had fixed Friday's weight limit at 10 st 5 lb but from the early rounds such niceties were rendered irrelevant by the technical excellence of the Virginian, whose own accumulation of titles is as impressive as that of Chavez (his welterweight reign was preceded by the capturing of four world championships in the 9 st 9 lb and 10 st classes).

That Whitaker, at 29, had the depth and range of education as a fighter to represent extreme danger for Chavez was made obvious by the fact that he had fought more than 200 times as an amateur before winning an Olympic gold medal in Los Angeles in 1984 and that the pro career begun immediately afterwards had included only one setback, a loss in Paris to Jose Luis Ramirez which owed much to local prejudice and was soon avenged. Moving up the weights to confront such a seasoned champion left the 31-year-old Mexican phenomenon open to the charge of hubris, and perhaps the only major shock about the ordeal he endured was that it had its origins not in any disadvantage in physical strength but in the gulf between the planned and disciplined effectiveness of Whitaker's boxing and the unconvincing, often ragged response it drew from Chavez.

Bewilderingly, that glaring discrepancy in the quality of the fighters' work failed to intrude on the thinking of the two European judges whose deliberations gave the contest its ludicrously unjust outcome. Franz Marti of Switzerland and Mickey Vann from Yorkshire both contrived to produce a confusion of scoring that added up to 115 points for each man, thus ensuring a draw by majority decision. In less outlandish circumstances, the third judge, Jack Woodruff from Dallas, might have been considered severely ungenerous to Whitaker by putting him ahead by 115–113 (my card had the welterweight champion a winner by eight rounds to four, or 116 points to 112) but his fellow officials obliterated any chance that the Texan would be criticised. The peculiarity of the identical conclusions of Vann and Marti was compounded by the realisation that they disagreed over the scoring of no fewer than six individual rounds.

Vann said subsequently that he had been influenced by the conviction that much of Whitaker's activity was blemished by illegality. It was, of course, a theme echoed in Chavez's interpretation of the fight and there was special significance in the similarity of their opinions concerning the low left hook with which Whitaker hurt his opponent in the sixth round. Chavez, who staggered away from that blow clutching his groin and had to be granted time to recover before hostilities were resumed, condemned the referee, Joe Cortez, for declining to insist on the deduction of a point from Whitaker for the offence. He must have been gratified to learn that Vann had independently decided to punish Whitaker, giving Chavez a 10–9 edge in the sixth, a round that contained sufficient legitimate aggression from Whitaker to satisfy the other two judges that it should be scored 10–9 for the American.

There can be no vehement objection to the deduction of a point for a punch as conspicuously low as that left hook. But it is hard to have sympathy with Chavez's sweeping allegation that he was abused by dirty tactics throughout the 36 minutes, most damagingly by intentional punches below the belt and grabbing that inhibited his use of his own left hooks, especially his favourite slashes to the liver. The truth, as Whitaker suggested at the post-fight press conference, is that there was a two-way traffic in questionable ploys, but one that never threatened to get viciously out of hand. This was an enthralling conflict between champions of the highest calibre and fiercest commitment, men too serious and knowledgeable about their violent trade to regard Corinthian etiquette as a priority on such a night. It has certainly never been high on Chavez's list of concerns and, as frustration welled in him like bile, he displayed all his familiar adroitness at following through on his punches with the forearm or the shoulder and was not averse to landing blows in places as unlikely as the thighs or the buttocks. At least, he was willing to do so on those occasions when he was within reach of Whitaker. Chavez's abiding problem was that such opportunities were painfully, unwontedly sporadic.

Movement was always bound to be the key for Whitaker. As long as he could stay loose and fluid, his evasive speed and gift for presenting an even more awkward target than southpaws usually do – often effecting twisting sideways manoeuvres that deploy a shoulder to close the door on an attacker's most telling assaults – were likely to keep him away from drastic harm and allow him to counter with quick straight punches and selectively applied flurries of hooks. But in the ring elusiveness can evaporate under the heat generated by a Chavez. When he is building the stalking, hounding pressure that is the essence of his method, the apprehensive quarry is liable to find that nothing feels loose but his bowels. Chavez had sought to stir that dread in Whitaker. 'He does not have the one thing you need to have a chance against me,' he said a couple of days ago, holding his right hand out in front of him as if weighing something. 'You need balls, and he does not have them.'

The taunt amounted to an each-way bet. If Whitaker did not yield to fear, he might be provoked into the macho recklessness that was Sugar

Ray Leonard's undoing in his first meeting with Roberto Duran. In the event, Whitaker committed neither blunder. He proved his manhood by fighting his natural fight, parading all those fluent skills previously mentioned so calculatingly that the great Chavez was almost in danger of being outclassed. Once or twice, as the Mexican's groping, ineffectual pursuit was joltingly halted and Whitaker switched to outright aggression, driving in unanswered punches to the head, there was a faint shudder of suspicion that the incredible might occur and the proudest competitor in sport would be left sprawling at a conqueror's feet. That was an unrealistic worry. But – though he had the odd round when he managed to shrink the ring with a semblance of his accustomed authority and delivered a number of thudding punches (a notable example was the fifth, in which Whitaker's face briefly assumed a chastened, slightly wistful expression) – he could never achieve a percussive rhythm. By the time he was labouring through a rough passage in the eleventh, it seemed that his only hope was a small miracle of the kind that transformed apparently unavoidable defeat into a last-second technical knockout of Meldrick Taylor in 1990. His final round was a triumph of will, and it had to be scored for him, but it was well short of a miracle. It took the judges to provide that.

An hour after their baffling verdict had been handed down, amid seething resentment deepened by awareness of how much the preservation of Chavez's record means to the principal promoter of the Alamodome extravaganza, Don King, Whitaker voiced his dissatisfaction with unexpected restraint. 'The fans were always going to be my real judges tonight,' he said. 'I'm glad we had TV putting what happened in front of millions of viewers. The public gets to decide.'

No one was more eager to vote than Terry Norris, the intimidating super-welterweight (11 st) champion of the world who had just effortlessly defended his title by destroying a hapless Joe Gatti in half a round. 'I saw that fight and Pernell Whitaker won it easily,' said Norris in a tone to discourage argument. He is right, but the history of the fight business will show, astonishingly, that in San Antonio on Friday, 10 September 1993, two world championship matches ended in draws. The other involved Azumah Nelson's WBC super-featherweight (9 st 4 lb) title. Nelson was ill-served by being obliged to share the honours with a challenger called Jesse James Leija.

But the most dastardly robbery of the night had nothing to do with Jesse James.

The Terrible Beauty of Chavez

The Observer, 9 May 1993

It is a classic plot-line that runs through the boxing career of Julio Cesar Chavez, the timeless theme of the man whose greatness contains the seeds of his own destruction. By being the best fighter of his generation, and one of the very best of any era, Chavez has exhausted the competition in the weight divisions most natural to him and driven himself towards the dangerous company of heavier men. Each achievement he added to the most astonishing record of invincibility in modern boxing created more risk, increased the chances that the dizzying climb would end in a cruel fall.

There is a remote possibility that as you read these words the unthinkable has already happened and Chavez's flawless sequence of victories has ended with a raging anticlimax in his 87th professional fight. In the early hours of Sunday British time, he was due in the ring at the Thomas and Mack Center in Las Vegas to defend his World Boxing Council super-lightweight title against a solid, experienced pro from Guyana called Terrence Alli in a contest providing sorely needed promotional support for the heavyweight championship action between Lennox Lewis and Tony Tucker.

However, though there is always hazard in making assumptions about the outcome of any fight, after watching Chavez and talking to him over the past week it is hard to avoid writing as if his business with Alli is just another opportunity to demonstrate how exceptional he is. This Sunday is unlikely to be a day of mourning in Mexico, as it certainly would be if the country's most celebrated son tasted failure at last.

The 30-year-old who ducked through the ropes at the Thomas and Mack Center has a strength of body and will, a depth of skill and fierce clarity of intent that encouraged Angelo Dundee, mentor to Muhammad Ali, Sugar Ray Leonard and a clutch of other champions, to say of him: 'The toughest fighter I've ever seen – bar none.' Dundee had the good fortune to acquire that respect without suffering. Such notable performers as Meldrick Taylor, Edwin Rosario, Juan LaPorte and Hector 'Macho' Camacho were permanently diminished by the systematic beatings Chavez inflicted on them, especially the relentless hooking to the body that is the foundation of his technique.

For opponents, Chavez brings a quality of nightmare to the ring, pressing in so remorselessly that he seems to surround them, allowing no escape from the percussive intensity of assaults mounted with a patient, apparently passionless fury. In fact, he told me last week, he does sometimes carry deep anger into a fight, which is not surprising in view of the remarkable inclination of so many of his challengers to fill the days before their violent meetings with taunts and insults. 'Their big mouths

245

do bother me,' he admitted, communicating seriousness as much with the hard stare of eyes so dark that the irises are almost indistinguishable from the pupils as through the words of the excellent female interpreter who is constantly at his disposal here. 'I walk to the ring with anger but my concentration is so strong that nothing can interfere with it. The insults only make me even more motivated.'

In Mexico City two and a half months ago, in front of 136,000 of his countrymen who made up the largest (and probably the most noisily partisan) live audience ever drawn to a prize fight, he taught Greg Haugen, a tough but under-talented American of distinctly red-neck tendencies, the folly of reinforcing his motivation with provocative mockery of Mexico and Mexicans. The five rounds it took to reduce Haugen to a penitent wreck afforded Chavez scope to display barely half of the frightening arsenal of destructive gifts he has perfected since, after only 13 amateur fights, he turned professional at the age of 17 in February 1980.

Against more menacing rivals, the dismantling process is deliberately less abrupt, marked by a cumulative sense of inevitability. Once he has begun to rip the substance out of his man with rhythmic pounding of the torso, the mastery of range that governs his punching enables him to switch smoothly to the vulnerable head, and every time one punch lands several others are almost sure to thud home with equal accuracy. Just when the opponent is trying to regroup in a brief respite from the hooks and uppercuts, a sudden long right cross will jump in a blur on to his jaw and the agony will start again. Chavez, bringing a terrible beauty to the execution of fell purposes, reaches far into the ambivalence many of us feel about boxing.

Born fourth of a family of ten to a railway worker, Rodolfo Chavez, and his wife Isabel, Julio took to boxing because older brothers were involved and because fighting is not an unnatural pursuit in their home town of Culiacan, which is reputed to be the drug capital of Mexico and is rarely short of the gunfire to back the claim. In remaining unbeaten through more than 13 years, he has won five versions of world championships in three separate weight categories – super-featherweight (9 st 4 lb), lightweight (9 st 9 lb) and super-lightweight (10 st) – and went to face Terrence Alli with 74 stoppages included in his 86 straight wins.

He stays so persistently within hitting distance that he occasionally seems to absorb an unhealthy amount of return fire. But his head moves evasively on the wide, rolling shoulders, frequently denying the retaliator a clean shot, and a certain thickening of the nose is the only noticeable impairment of his virile handsomeness. Grounds for fearing that Omar, the second of his three sons, was developing meningitis had been removed by doctors shortly before we talked in his suite at the Mirage Hotel and his high spirits showed in wide smiles and an eagerness to shout out the new phrases of English he can summon.

'Wait a minute . . . Take it easy,' he called playfully as his regal progress to the elevators was interrupted constantly by requests for autographs and handshakes. 'My Gawd,' he said as the lift was filled by an entourage that was tiny compared with the posse of subsidised relatives and friends with whom he insists on surrounding himself in Culiacan. His lack of English is blamed for the failure of his earnings to equate with his peerless talent. But once settled in an armchair, with his slim legs stretched to park his trainers on a coffee table, he suggested that, while he had been paid a lot less than heavyweights with a fraction of his ability, he would have enough to keep him happy when he retires in 1994.

He dismissed, perhaps too readily, the thought that he might find the dramas of his years in boxing irreplaceable. 'Every good thing comes to an end,' he said. 'Everything that is born dies. I am sure my people will not forget me. My record will last for a long time. I have met many goals in boxing. Now I must meet the goals of being a father and a husband. And I want to prove myself as a businessman.'

But first, he acknowledged, he had to deal with Terrence Alli and clear the way for the next major project of his fighting life – his challenge in September for the welterweight (10 st 7 lb) world championship of Pernell Whitaker, a Virginian of dazzling speed and virtuosity. Chavez refuses to believe that by aspiring to domination of a yet higher weight division he may be risking the penalties of hubris.

'Whitaker is actually a smaller man than I am,' he said. 'I will not go up all the way to 147 lb, only to 144 lb, and there will be absolutely no physical advantage for him. I am stronger than he is and I hit harder. He is a very agile fighter with an awkward style but Whitaker cannot play with me as he has with other opponents. I am going to be throwing punches all the time, giving him more pressure than he has ever known. He is one who likes to twist around and make those fancy turns. If he turns away from me the punches will keep coming, even if they hit his back. I'll throw punches everywhere, at his butt if necessary.'

It sounds like a fairly typical evening with Julio Cesar Chavez.

Bruno Should Retire, and Lewis Needs to Improve

The Observer, 26 September 1993

When Welsh rain gave way to Caribbean thunder, Frank Bruno provided far more than his expected share of it and Lennox Lewis had to survive some of the most alarming moments of his boxing life before keeping his version of the world heavyweight title by battering the challenger into a state of piteous helplessness in the middle of the seventh round.

The destructive fury of the World Boxing Council champion's final, overwhelming assault at Cardiff Arms Park obliterated Bruno's resistance, leaving him in the familiar and frightening predicament of remaining upright long after the scattering of his senses had made him an utterly defenceless target. But all the merciless energy Lewis poured into that conclusive attack could not blur the memory of how amateurish and vulnerable he had looked in previous rounds or of how magnificently Bruno had exploited his own restricted talent to its absolute limits. Bruno, who found his third attempt to be world champion ending in circumstances that offered a cruel echo of his losses in the '80s to Tim Witherspoon and Mike Tyson, should not hesitate to retire immediately. His stock as a sentimental favourite of the nation is probably higher than ever after a performance that brimmed with courage and determined honesty of purpose. He is approaching his 32nd birthday financially sound, and he must know now that the biggest prize is simply beyond him.

On paper, it should be onward and upward for Lewis, who recently turned 28 and boasts a professional record of 24 straight victories, only two of which have been on points. But across his seemingly bright future there falls the considerable shadow of Riddick Bowe, the American who is the alternative (some would say true) champion of the heavyweights and with whom Lewis is meant to engage in a showdown within the coming year. Bowe has his troubles, not least the undisciplined eating habits that can send his weight soaring by 50 or 60 pounds when he takes a rest from training, but his enthusiasm for a decisive collision with the man who beat him out of a gold medal at the 1988 Olympics would be substantially increased by the sight of Lewis's struggling form in the early rounds against Bruno. Having developed his own skills impressively since Seoul under the peerless tuition of Eddie Futch, Bowe will be persuaded by this latest contribution from his rival that Lewis has not made nearly as much technical progress towards the kind of repertoire a top pro requires.

The claim by the winner in Cardiff that the main message he had delivered to the many Americans still sceptical about his credentials was that he possessed a potent left hook as well as a big right hand was dubious in the extreme. A wide, crunching left hook to the jaw did indeed constitute the beginning of the end for Bruno. However, critics were more likely to dwell on the raggedness of much of what had come from Lewis before that blow – the muddle of mistimed punches, the lunging and sprawling, the questions about his stamina raised by recurring signs that he had difficulty in sustaining a high work-rate all the way through a round (evidence that recalled similar hints of damaging tiredness in his defence against Tony Tucker last May) and the failure to punch in telling combinations.

Lewis's subsequent declaration that most of the flaws he betrayed in the first phase of the contest were due to the cold the Welsh climate had planted deep in his muscles fell well short of being an acceptable explanation of his inadequacies. The weather obviously bothered him a great deal more than it did the non-combatants in the stadium, who were just glad the rain that had threatened us with a postponement held off and left conditions far milder than those who foolishly organised an open-air promotion in Britain at this time of year had any reason to expect. He showed the depth of his concern over the chill in the air by remaining covered up so late in the preliminaries that it seemed he might decide to fight in his tracksuit, and afterwards swathing himself in a blanket between rounds. Given such precautions, and the warming-up he must have done in his dressing-room, the cold does not stand up as a comprehensive excuse. It certainly did not freeze Bruno. Perhaps part of the truth is that, surprisingly, the tensions of the occasion affected the 5–1 on favourite more than they did the 3–1 outsider.

All the talk of this event as the first all-British heavyweight championship match in history (though perfectly accurate in terms of where the two boxers were born) could not obscure the reality that the serious element of needle had its origins in the fact that both men are black West Indians. Bruno's resentment of comments Lewis is reported to have made about him is so profound and bitter that, even while he was graciously accepting his defeat as 'fair and square', he abruptly started banging a large fist on a press conference table and declaring that no man would ever get away with accusing him of lacking pride in his race. 'I'm a proud, proud, proud hombre,' he said, and managed to make the melodramatic statement moving.

The pride he carried into the ring overrode the nervousness he was bound to be feeling and from the opening bell it was clear that he was resolved to make Lewis, and the many forecasters (including this one) who had been dismissive of his chances, do a lot of word-eating. His ambitions were too genuine, his intentions too bad, to permit any truck with the kind of charging impersonation of valour favoured by fighters who believe, deep down, that their case is hopeless and are content to make a flourish on the way to an early exit. He meant to win and he sought to advance on Lewis with controlled menace. His method was to move in behind a driving jab, often trying to fire in two or three in one sequence, before attempting to land his heavy, clubbing right hand, and now and then loosing the left hook that once proved powerful enough to stun Mike Tyson.

Bruno was not outstandingly successful during most of the first round and, although by the end of it the champion was already boxing with a distressing slovenliness, Lewis's more active start warranted a score of 10–9 in his favour. The second round was, however, thoroughly different. Bruno began to stalk the discomfited Lewis to noticeable effect, and one hefty right hand might have been crucial had it made a solid rather than a glancing contact. The loser was to admit, naturally enough, in post-fight interviews that his major regret was that his heaviest rights had never landed with full-blooded impact on Lewis's head. But Bruno definitely won the second and in the third he gave every indication of producing the fight of his life. Lewis's corner had been obliged in the interval to work on a reddened swelling high on their man's left cheekbone and he looked unmistakably sorry for himself as he staggered away from a thudding right. The champion's legs were briefly unreliable and further left- and right-hand punches took him closer to exhaustion. When he dropped his hands and essayed an unconvincing shuffle it was a feeble effort to conceal how badly hurt he was.

The crowd were roaring Bruno on in the fourth but at the finish of three minutes of ungainly action it was hard to give him the edge and he, too, was now carrying an unsightly contusion close to his left eye. Then Lewis allowed himself to be trapped for more punishment in the fifth (one penalty of which was a cut to his left eyebrow) and here, as when Bruno was at his best in the third, shortage of foot speed and agility prevented the challenger from profiting fully from the opportunities his periods of dominance created. There was already a sense that this was to be a nearly night for Bruno and it was reinforced in the sixth, which belonged so blatantly to Lewis that we had to suspect an irreversible shifting of fortunes. Yet Bruno went on the attack again at the beginning of the seventh, making it difficult to foresee the horrors that were about to engulf him with terrible suddenness. He had pinned the champion in a neutral corner and was seeking to pummel Lewis as he crouched behind the protective covering of forearms and gloves, apparently with no thought of retaliation.

Lewis was to say later that, as he peered out through his gloves, he saw Bruno lower his right to wind up for a special shot. What is certain is that Lewis's exploitation of the opening was devastating. Springing from his crouch, he unleashed the massive left hook and at once Bruno's face told us he was finished. As Lewis mounted a terrifying bombardment with both fists, able to load for maximum effect against an unresisting victim, the referee stepped in to admonish him for steadying the target of Bruno's head with one hand the better to batter it with the other. Mickey Vann might have been more sensible to stop the slaughter there and then, rather than waving Lewis in for a second onslaught that saw Bruno's head brutally abused by a stream of violent punches, most significantly with horrible, raking uppercuts. After such a blood-curdling conclusion, score-cards are not likely to be uppermost in anybody's mind – but I must say that those who had Bruno several points in front surprised me. I agreed precisely with one of the American judges, Jerry Roth, who scored three rounds for each fighter before the seventh.

But that hardly matters. The truth about this fight is that Frank Bruno, perhaps at the cost of excessive suffering, did himself proud while Lennox Lewis tarnished his reputation.

Champions Still Have to Settle Their Score

The Observer, 10 October 1993

The bitterest feud in British boxing remained unresolved last night after
12 rounds of unrelenting, cruelly intense action in the autumn chill of Old
Trafford left Chris Eubank and Nigel Benn to share a draw. Arguments
will rage about the details of the scoring – Britain's veteran judge Harry
Gibbs had it 115–113 for Eubank while one American official sided with
Benn and another made the men absolutely level – but it is impossible to
argue that the outcome did an injustice to either one. And if neither
fighter should feel cheated, the same can be said with vehemence of the
stadium crowd of more than 40,000 and the millions who watched live on
television.

These were two supremely fit and committed fighters performing to
their limits, producing a clamorous echo of the 1990 war between them
that Eubank won with a ninth-round stoppage, and the conclusion should
encourage both of them to dilute their notorious mutual hostility with a
large injection of respect.

It was Eubank who finished the stronger, forcing a weary Benn around
the ring before intermittent clusters of jarring punches, and some of us felt
that he might have edged ahead in that final phase of the contest,
especially since the referee, Larry O'Connell, had deducted a point from
Benn in the sixth round after administering a fourth warning for low
blows. However, the early rounds had been desperately close and so
difficult to score that a conflict of opinion was almost inevitable.

It was significant that one of the most informed neutrals at ringside,
Mickey Duff, had an almost unprecedented sprinkling of even rounds
across his card. 'I'm a pretty opinionated man,' Duff acknowledged super-
fluously. 'But there were so many rounds in which it was just impossible
to separate them.' The truth of that observation is a tribute to the raw
competitiveness Eubank and Benn brought to the ring for a battle that put
at stake Benn's World Boxing Council super-middleweight (12 st) title
and the World Boxing Organisation championship in the same division
held by Eubank. There was no sign of the monocled dandy here as
Eubank was forced to reach deep into his fighting instincts to prevent his
frequently proclaimed dreams of invincibility from being buried under
the swarming pressure Benn sought to maintain.

The WBO champion is naturally the bigger, more powerful man and it
was widely believed that he would enter the ring at least half a stone
heavier than his opponent, who did indeed look lighter and slighter when
they made an entrance to the arena that was totally in keeping with the
showbusiness flamboyance that has surrounded this rematch. But once
Eubank had vaulted the top rope and indulged in his customary ritual of
posing, and his adversary had come down the aisle to the ominous

251

recorded tolling of Big Ben, reality asserted itself as it always does when a genuine fight gets under way.

Even while another champion, Crisanto Espana, holder of the World Boxing Association welterweight crown, was systematically demolishing the challenge of a game contender from Canada, Donovan Boucher, chants of the rival super-middleweights' names had been rolling down from the stands and now that Eubank and Benn were answering the bell the tumult in the old football ground became deafening. There was heat in the ring to justify the excitement beyond and, though Eubank dominated the first round, the sense of a cumulative equality was soon building. The second was fairly even and the third had an element of ambiguity, too, because Eubank was superior early on but was discomfited by Benn's pressure later.

That impression of equality was in danger of being shattered in the fourth round when Benn caught Eubank with a damaging right hand and a following left that sent him teetering backwards across the ring to topple shoulders-first into the ropes near his own corner. Soon Benn was driving in a right cross and for a moment it seemed that Eubank might need not so much his favourite jodhpurs as a getaway horse. But he has considerable physical resilience and once again he showed the spirit to go with it. Benn won that round clearly but, although Eubank's corner forced him to sit on his stool during the interval instead of engaging in his previous posturing routine, the Brighton man was a long way from being subdued.

At the start of the fifth he walked straight across the ring and blasted Benn with an explosive left that put a stagger into the WBC champion's legs. There was more serious punishment for Benn in the fifth and his own spirited responses did not prevent him from losing it. But that setback was a lot less important than what happened in the sixth, when Larry O'Connell lost patience with Benn over low punching and deducted the point that had a decisive influence on the ultimate result.

The furious, seesawing action continued and Benn's success in taking the seventh and eighth rounds (at least on my card) guaranteed that there would never be mu:ᴸ between the fighters if it went to a points verdict. So it proved and in spite of moments when it appeared possible that there would be a premature ending, the struggle carried on into the 12th round. In those three minutes Eubank's dominance was undeniable and when it was over I felt, with Harry Gibbs, that he was slightly ahead. But Carol Castellano scored the fight 114–113 for Benn and her fellow American Chuck Hassett made it 114–114, guaranteeing a draw.

Heavyweight Reading for the Scholar-Pugilist

The Sunday Times, 13 February 1994

Nobody would wish to be sceptical about the bright new dawn of the intellect and spirit that is said to have broken across the grey prison existence of Mike Tyson. If the sentence he is serving for a rape conviction has been transformed by books into something apocalyptic and enriching, he deserves nothing but congratulations and encouragement. But some of us who spent a fair amount of time around Tyson while he was the deadliest heavyweight in boxing may be forgiven our surprise at the sheer scale of the assault on the world's literature with which he is being credited. Recent articles in American magazines and newspapers, pieces based on interviews with the 27-year-old himself or with voluble friends, suggest that since being locked away in the misleadingly named Indiana Youth Center early in 1992 he has become the undisputed champion of autodidacts.

We are told not only that his reading has embraced Tolstoy, Voltaire, Plato, Socrates, Machiavelli, Dumas, Francis Bacon and Hemingway, along with seminal black activist writers such as Frederick Douglass, W.E.B. Dubois, George Jackson and Maya Angelou, but that he has devoured biographies of Mao, Marx, Genghis Khan and Hernando Cortes with the same gusto as he has read histories of organised crime and lives of great gangsters. He still talks of fights and fighters but his conversation is as likely to be about Hannibal, Oliver Cromwell and Alexander the Great as any of the names in the current heavyweight rankings. That list of sources represents a remarkable exercise in dedicated eclecticism for somebody whose early schooling owed as much to the dangerous streets of the Brownsville ghetto in Brooklyn as to any reformatory or orthodox classroom and who, prior to imprisonment, gave little indication of possessing anything beyond the rudiments of literacy.

It is made to appear even more impressive when we discover that within his monumental reading schedule Tyson manages to accommodate sufficient time in the prison gym to keep the great, intimidating slab of his body hard and fit and under 16 st, not to mention the five prayers a day that his conversion to Islam requires, regular study of the Koran, sessions with the visiting tutor who is reported to be teaching him Chinese and specific preparation for an imminent high school equivalency examination. What is happening on the outskirts of Indianapolis is either slightly miraculous or a tad exaggerated. Apparently, Tyson does not want to talk these days about his relationship with Don King, the promoter who was once a pervasive influence in his financial and personal affairs, and maybe the burgeoning association with the Muslims will put permanent distance between them. But in the reports of Tyson's voracity for learning there are unavoidable echoes of King's account of how he used his jail time after a manslaughter conviction sent him to the Marion Correctional Institution in Ohio for four years.

Behind the older man's flourishes of dubious erudition (he was once heard praising the teachings of 'St Thomas Aquinine') a high intelligence and fecund imagination are undoubtedly at work. If he has travelled through intellectual territory as though on a speeding train, glimpsing the names of stations from the window rather than becoming familiar with the terrain, who will be snobbish enough to argue that he gained nothing worthwhile from the journey? Perhaps Tyson's commitment to self-education and spiritual enlargement will prove more profound than King's was (many will say that in the second category it could hardly be less) and even if it is not, the word from Indianapolis should be welcomed.

The only reservation offered here concerns the claims blithely made about the pace and breadth of the scholar-pugilist's enlightenment. To learn as much as his more ardent admirers say he already has, he would surely have to spend as long in the slammer as the Birdman of Alcatraz. In fact, devotion to study should shorten his term. According to Phil Slavens, the assistant superintendent of operations at the Indiana Youth Center, if Tyson passes that high school equivalency exam, three months will be deducted from his six-year sentence, giving him a release date fairly early next year. When he does come out, his recently acquired comprehension of percentages and decimals should help him to handle a revival of his fighting career that is confidently expected to involve sums of money never previously generated by boxing or any other professional sport. One of the authors he most admires should come in handy, too.

Niccolo Machiavelli versus Don King? It looks like a pretty even match.

Moorer Takes the Title but Chaos Reigns

The Sunday Times, 24 April 1994

After a night on which age and the limited talents of Michael Moorer combined to persuade Evander Holyfield that he no longer has a career, only an honourable history, the one certainty about the heavyweight division is that it is dominated more than ever by the squat shadow of America's most famous convict. From his cell at the Indiana Youth Center, Mike Tyson spreads a pervasive influence across the hopes and plans of every leading fighter, manager and promoter in the most lucrative domain in professional sport. A majority points decision at the end of 12 rarely enthralling rounds gave Moorer deserved possession of the WBA and IBF titles but the dethronement of Holyfield merely confirmed that, among the heavyweights, it is confusion that reigns.

The avaricious turmoil is sure to be prolonged by a result that blew asunder a carefully negotiated deal to bring Holyfield – had he won – into a unification match with Britain's holder of the WBC championship, Lennox Lewis. And running like a raw hunger through the attitudes of Moorer, Lewis, the former undisputed champion Riddick Bowe and every other principal in the script is the desire to be armed with a title when Tyson completes his sentence for rape (probably around the middle of next year) and makes possible the richest promotion boxing has ever known. Within an hour of Moorer's victory in an open-air arena behind Ceasars Palace Hotel, Seth Abraham, who controls the fight schedule of Home Box Office, the cable television company whose previous elimin- ation series left Tyson as supreme champion in 1987, was identifying that promised bonanza as the biggest single impediment to his ambitions of unifying the championship for a second time. 'All of these guys think that having a belt when Tyson gets out will be worth $50 million,' Abraham said. 'In the back of their minds, all of them can see that retirement fund sitting there.'

On the evidence their collision provided, had Holyfield and Moorer encountered Tyson at his destructive peak, they would have been given violent encouragement to retire early. The 36 minutes of action said at least as much about the weaknesses of the winner as about his strengths and, if they offered yet another unforgettable demonstration of Holy- field's unsurpassable courage, they also emphasised the need to dissuade him from ever putting it to such a brutal test again. It will be sad and alarming if the beaten champion's addiction to combat makes him vulnerable to the false arguments for continuing in the ring that might be created out of the specifics of his defeat. He could, for example, seek to convince himself that his performance was seriously diminished by the shoulder injury which, after the fight, sent him to the local Valley Hospital with his left arm in a sling. If, as reported, the trouble developed in the second round, it is natural to assume that it did indeed impair his subsequent effectiveness to some degree, but any restriction of movement was less than pronounced and even his chief corner-man, Don Turner, was disinclined to present it as an excuse.

The lack of speed and fluency and sustained cohesion that became increasingly marked in Holyfield's work as round followed round seemed to have more to do with the sediment of profound weariness left in the marrow of his bones by exposure to too many wars. Fears that this might be a night when he would grow old before our eyes were largely fulfilled. By the 12th round, as the battered, balding head lolled painfully under the jolting assault of the right-hand jabs that had reached it with punishing ease through most of the fight, he looked what he is: someone who has crowded an inordinate amount of strain and pain into his 31 years.

Yet, before the realities of his decline closed in on him, he had managed to produce the evening's most explosive attack, a vivid reminder of better times that threatened briefly to swing the conflict his way and hardened the conviction that Moorer bears scant resemblance to the overwhelmingly powerful heavyweight his more enthusiastic publicists have made him out to be. That combination of right-hook, left-hook to the challenger's head near the end of the second round pitched the victim off his feet and even a count of eight might not have been sufficient respite had the bell not sounded soon afterwards.

The knockdown proved less than crucial to the pattern of the battle, but the way it registered on the scorecards of the three ringside judges turned out to be utterly decisive in shaping the ultimate verdict in Moorer's favour. Holyfield had been under bombardment for more than two minutes before he dropped his opponent, so it would have been unforgivably irrational if any judge had followed the American tradition of automatically using a knockdown to justify a 10–8 score for the fighter who landed the telling punch. But there was widespread astonishment when it was found that Jerry Roth, one of the most respected scorers in the world, had given feller and felled 10 points each, to make the second an even round.

Many felt that approach was unduly innovative and resentment among Holyfield's supporters intensified when they realised that Roth's originality (his two colleagues gave the champion a 10–9 edge in the round) had been instrumental in depriving their man of his titles. At the finish, Roth's card showed Moorer winning by just one point, while Chuck Giampa had Moorer ahead by 116 to 112 and Dalby Shirley made the fight a draw at 114–114. Had Roth accepted the knockdown as warranting a 10–9 for Holyfield, two of the three cards would have scored a draw and that would have been the majority decision.

My own marking reflected a close fight but not quite as close as the one Shirley and Roth had seen. Allowing Holyfield a one-point advantage in the second meant that my totals put Moorer in front at the end by 115 to 113. It was certainly impossible to agree with the large body of unofficial scorers who considered Moorer a runaway winner. They were right to acknowledge a poignant deterioration in Holyfield, a stripping away of all the familiar vigour and controlled technique, so that he was left eventually with little more than his unbreakable fighting heart. But their reading grossly exaggerated the 26-year-old Moorer's capacity to exploit his youth and the freshness guaranteed by a career that had already brought him 34 straight victories (with 30 stoppages) without exposing him to notable risk.

From the fourth round onwards, the ageing of Holyfield accelerated and the omens were unmistakable after he was cut near the outside corner of his left eye in the fifth. Although Turner coped satisfactorily with the problem, and the refusal to pay the $25,000 fee demanded by the specialist cuts man Ace Marotta never became a desperate issue, the occasional bleeding and the facial contusions, like the wincing withdrawal from body shots, conveyed the clear sense of a championship changing hands. Even in his best rounds, such as the seventh and the ninth, Holyfield could not summon enough of the old fire to contradict that impression.

But, while bravery made his exit memorable, Moorer's entrance as the first southpaw heavyweight champion was thoroughly unimpressive. For a start, there was an essential smallness about his presence, an absence of physical authority in his 15 st 4 lb which reminded us that, like Holyfield, he has raised himself from a lighter division in pursuit of big earnings. And whereas he is not remotely the pulverising hitter of his bloated legend, his own chin may well be as suspect as critics allege (the blows that put him down were good but no better than 50 or 60 that could not budge the decrepit George Foreman).

Moorer's right jab is an admirable weapon but his failure to press in conclusively behind it miserably echoed pre-fight indications that he was seething with insecurity, more Hamlet than Henry V. At one stage in the middle rounds his tough young trainer, Teddy Atlas, was so angered by the lack of enterprise that he suggested he should do the fighting while Moorer stayed in the corner.

To cope with a fit Riddick Bowe or a determined Lennox Lewis, they might have to fight as a tag-team.

From Miami Vice to Gunning for Lewis

The Sunday Times, 1 May 1994

As he works with the latest contender for the heavyweight championship of the world, Patrick Burns wears faded denim shorts, trainers but no socks, and he has a couple of fish leaping around on the back of his white T-shirt to remind us that we are in Florida.

The Leprechaun Gym is a converted warehouse, a low building with breeze-block walls, and rolling up the garage-style doors at one end has not prevented the temperature of its thick air from climbing uncomfortably above the 85 degrees to be encountered outside. So Burns's dress makes sense in the setting, indeed is almost conventional – except, perhaps, for the .38 Smith & Wesson revolver tucked so far into the waistband of the shorts that it is almost, but not quite, invisible. For Burns, wearing the .38 in the gym is slightly unusual, but only because he generally favours the 9mm Glock semi-automatic pistol that is standard issue for the Miami police department, which he serves as a highly decorated sergeant. Always, while supervising the base-camp training of Phil Jackson, the 29-year-old product of a local ghetto who will challenge

Lennox Lewis for the WBC title in Atlantic City on Friday, he has made a point of having a handgun handy. 'I'm a police officer before I am anything else,' is his simple explanation. 'I never go anywhere without a gun.' If he ever felt a temptation to relax into a less alert identity, to leave his firepower at home with his uniform, it would be discouraged by the surroundings in which he goes about his second job.

The Leprechaun stands opposite the headquarters of the international construction company operated by Patrick Gerrits, who paid for the gym and whose Cork origins explain its name, an unlikely one in the predominantly Puerto Rican district of Wynwood in north-west Miami. First impressions of Wynwood can be treacherously ambiguous for a stranger used to associating urban deprivation and crime in America with images of the grim high-rise housing projects of the South Bronx or Chicago. Here, although many of the single-storey homes look shabby and rundown in the warm sunshine, others have a defiant respectability, with bougainvillea spreading vividly across their security grilles.

Like Overtown, the neighbouring, 90 per cent black enclave that is Jackson's home turf, Wynwood has plenty of honest, hard-working residents. On the streets of both, however, the crack dealers hold more sway than the churchgoers. These are places where the visitor is ill-advised to go strolling, unless he has a taste for sudden poverty and intensive care units. Statistically, Overtown is the tougher of the two. Jackson has seen a lot of friends and acquaintances jailed, or buried before their time, and a bullet left the oldest of his six brothers paralysed from the waist down. A story the fighter tells of one friendship, improbably initiated and abruptly terminated, gives a jolting sense of how melodramatically strange and fragile life in the Overtowns of America can be. It involves a contemporary, Greg Hodge, who once tried to take his money. Subsequent events are run together by Jackson, as if in a single jagged sentence: 'I hit him with a fishing pole, we made friends, two months after that he got killed breaking into somebody's house, that was in Little River, lady caught him coming in the window and offed him.'

When we talked last week, Jackson's confident assertion that his environment had never been likely to drag him all the way down ('I always worked and I don't drink or smoke') was balanced by an admission that the boys in the 'hood can exert a seductive pressure. 'You hang with your friends, you want to be down with the crew, to fit in,' he said. For a while, where he fitted was in schools for troubled children. Then, at 15, he joined in ripping off a money-belt stuffed with cash from a spectator at a football game and drew three months in a youth correctional centre. Later he stopped running too soon after snatching a wallet from a woman, found himself surrounded by a dozen police cars, and was sentenced to 13 months' detention. The company of younger boys facing 60 to 70 years inside helped to adjust his priorities in a hurry, steering him towards a renewed faith in God and an early release for good behaviour.

The aunt who gave him a home after he came out (his mother died when he was two) suggested he should take up boxing and – although, at the age of 20, he was far too old to be starting a ring apprenticeship – he put himself under Burns's remarkable guidance. What Burns has done with Jackson, and with many less-talented youths he has rescued from the threatening pavements of Wynwood and Overtown, is one reason why the abolitionist argument legitimately stirred in Britain when Bradley Stone became boxing's latest tragedy cannot have the same force in the violence-ravaged cities of America. The question of whether boxing should be outlawed may create a genuine dilemma in Britain but here, where millions insist on the right to own assault rifles, where the sound of gunfire is commonplace in the streets, fight gyms have no difficulty presenting themselves as sanctuaries, rather than ante-rooms to neurological wards. And men like Burns are credited with saving, not endangering, lives.

In fact, there cannot be many men quite like Burns. The eldest of seven in a second-generation Irish-American family, he had gone through a successful amateur boxing career, suffered multiple wounds while with the Marines in Vietnam, and begun a determined pursuit of higher education under the GI Bill before he joined the Miami police as a 23-year-old in 1973. He went on to collect further degrees but it was not academic achievement that made him something of a legend in the force. During the fierce riots that erupted in Miami in 1980 (a black man died after being beaten by cops, and the officers involved were found not guilty at their trial) the police threw a cordon around the deadly turmoil in the Liberty City area, which adjoins Wynwood. But many innocents trapped inside the perimeter were being dragged from their cars and battered, stabbed and shot. 'A bunch of us were standing around when a lieutenant came up and told us what was happening in there,' Burns recalled last week. 'I was a rookie sergeant but, with the combat experience I had in Vietnam, I felt I had to do something, so I grabbed five other guys I knew from the streets, fellas who would hold up under fire. We got a police car and a paddy wagon and went in. The paddy wagon was like a spaghetti strainer afterwards and the car was a mess too, windows blown away, lights shot out. Some of the people we reached were already dead but we managed to save quite a few.'

Burns received his department's highest award for heroism, the Medal of Honor. Locals feel the service he has rendered since then to the deprived communities of north-west Miami has been no less distinguished. He now has a stable of five professional fighters, including Jackson, with an incredible aggregate record of 79 wins and only one defeat. But he is equally proud of the unpaid work with unpaid boxers, and not just those who have gained 35 national amateur titles. 'No championship can mean more than the thought that you might be saving kids from the streets,' he said.

The odds are that he will be obliged to concentrate on that kind of satisfaction after Friday night in Atlantic City. Jackson has won 30 of his 31 pro fights and Burns claims he is such a hard and versatile puncher that 14 of his 28 stoppages have been precipitated by his left hand, 14 by his right. But the form remains spectacularly unconvincing, a culling of nonentities. His most celebrated victim was Mike Dixon, who has been stopped by both Lewis and Herbie Hide, and his most recent victory was a points decision over elderly Eddie Gonzales, who failed to go beyond the second round with Hide two and a half years ago.

Even more damning, however, is the nature of the defeat he suffered on the only occasion that he faced an opponent of real standing. Donovan 'Razor' Ruddock is listed as scoring a fourth-round knockout, but Jackson said after the fight: 'He didn't hurt me at all. When he hit me with that hook, I went down on one knee. I felt, "Why get up?" My heart wasn't in it. There was no need to prove anything.' The most charitable explanation is that he was overawed by his first major test. 'I wasn't fully there for the Ruddock fight,' Jackson said last week. 'Everything will be completely different with Lewis. I am ready for him. London will know about it when I step into the ring.' At least the $575,000 purse will help to meet the bills of the nine children for whom he is responsible. He fathered three by a former girlfriend and three by his present partner, Orvia Ellis, and also cares for Ellis's three older children.

Inside the ropes, Jackson has quick hands and the heavy shoulders seem to generate a fair amount of power. At 6 ft 1½ in and a probable weight of around 15 st 12 lb, he will be conceding more than three inches and the better part of a stone to the unbeaten Lewis, but those statistics will be less important than the sense of intimidating scale the WBC champion conveys. Lewis's work can be distressingly amateurish, flawed by an absence of combination punching. But he is athletic and destructively powerful and he did destroy Razor Ruddock.

Phil Jackson may be in for a night of violent *déjà vu*.

Lewis Punches Out His Credentials

The Sunday Times, 8 May 1994

The Americans Lennox Lewis impresses most are those he hits on the head. Scepticism about his claim that he is the true heavyweight champion of the world may persist among the non-combatant masses of the US. But Phil Jackson, whose challenge for Lewis's WBC title came to a crumbling, painful end when a sickening right uppercut was followed by the dazing thud of left and right hooks halfway through the eighth round, is not the first opponent to admit he was battered into being a believer.

Jackson found an eloquent simplicity to define the gulf between the
impression of Lewis that often predominates on the safe side of the ropes
– where many critics are so dismayed by a tendency to let his work
become amateurishly dishevelled that they constantly underestimate his
overall effectiveness – and the intimidating reality of sharing a ring with
him. Less than an hour after boxing's most experienced referee, the
septuagenarian Arthur Mercante, alertly intervened to curtail pointless
suffering at the Atlantic City Convention Center on Friday night, the
bruised loser was musing from behind dark glasses on how the man who
punched him into submission differed from the one he had imagined he
was studying in films of earlier fights. 'It seems easy when you are looking
at it on tape but when you are standing up there facing a giant it gets kinda
complicated,' Jackson said quietly.

The complications were so far beyond the capacities of the 29-year-old
from Miami that none of the three judges' scorecards made him the
winner of any of the seven rounds completed. It was a comprehensive
beating which involved being sent to the floor a total of four times and,
although one knockdown came from punches illegally thrown after the
bell for the end of the fifth and actually cost Lewis a point, even that
deduction was academic, since Jackson had already been legitimately
blasted on to the canvas in the same round.

Having been brutally outclassed by the finish, stripped of everything
but the extreme gameness that proudly obliterated the memory of his
abject surrender to Donovan 'Razor' Ruddock in June of 1992, it was
hardly surprising that he chose at the subsequent press conference to laud
Lewis as the best of contemporary heavyweights. He was not about to
suggest that the instrument of his devastation was inferior to Michael
Moorer, who struggled a fortnight ago to take the WBA and IBF titles
from Evander Holyfield on an evening when Holyfield was just a
diagnosis away from qualifying as a cardiac patient. However, if Jackson's
views on the comparative merits of the two champions were obviously
tainted with self-interest, that does not prevent them from being accurate.
Fortunately for Lewis, the most relevant spectator at ringside indicated
that he held a contrary opinion.

When asked if he had been impressed by Lewis's performance, Moorer
shook his head. Questioned about when a reunification match might take
place, he mentioned next spring, which represented major progress.
Previously he had refused to talk of the fight as anything more than a
distant possibility. And hopes that a rational hierarchy might be
reimposed on the heavyweight division inside a year were further
encouraged when a well-placed source within Home Box Office, the
cable television company intent on unifying the championship, confirmed
that talks with the Moorer camp had produced the skeleton of a deal. The
suggestion is that if HBO and their associated promoter, Dan Duva,
provide the WBA/IBF champion with two defences against unthreatening

opponents drawn from a list submitted by his advisers, he will agree to meet Lewis early in 1995.

In the fight business, such plans are invariably at the mercy of a dozen ambushes. It is reasonable to assume that Lewis will cope successfully with Oliver McCall, in a mandatory defence of his WBC belt, perhaps around late August. But there will be plenty of other hazards to the scheme, starting with Moorer's capricious attitude to his newly won crown. He is a strange figure, even by the standards of his trade, at times mildly intriguing and amusing, at others profoundly boring in his determination to be perverse. He is handsome enough, as someone said the other day, to convey faint hints of a black Brando, is noticeably articulate and has a speaking voice that is strikingly attractive, not least to himself. One troublesome effect of all this may be an inclination to enjoy acting like a heavyweight champion outside the ring a lot more than he fancies fighting like one inside it.

Perhaps he realises that, in spite of his unblemished record and the fact that he has stopped all but a handful of his victims, he lacks the physical authority and the ability to survive thunderous blows which he would need to prosper against really big men such as Lewis and the former undisputed champion, Riddick Bowe. If so, Lewis's best chance of getting him on to the opposite stool would be the growth in Moorer's mind of the conviction that the pride of Britain (as well as Canada and Jamaica) is less menacing than Bowe, who would almost certainly generate more spectacular earnings. There were signs in the Convention Center that such a preference might well have taken root.

They were not contradicted by the reaction to the Lewis victory of Teddy Atlas, the intelligent and tough-natured young trainer whose motivational drive meant the difference between winning and losing for Moorer in the Holyfield fight. 'If there was scepticism about Lewis before tonight, it is still there,' Atlas said. 'That performance has certainly not put a fight with Michael Moorer further away. You can't knock a man who keeps winning but I don't think this sent a dramatic message to America. What if the other guy had done more persistent work? In the period when Lennox hadn't woken up, he got away with it. Jackson wasn't jabbing at all and to me that was a guy frozen by the moment. Late on, Jackson was what I call a game quitter – hanging in there, showing gameness but not trying to win any more. Maybe Lennox was hampered for a while by the mind-set he took into the first round, the idea that he would set the guy up, hypnotise him with the jab, then knock him over with the right hand and go home. But by the end he was putting his punches together well. He knows what to do when he gets you hurt. He's got a good chin and he has a confidence about himself; he believes he is going to win.'

That self-belief, fed as it is by all the evidence that he does indeed possess the priceless gift of rising above the difficulties he creates for himself with erratic, often slovenly technique, and somehow finding a way to win, is surely his greatest asset. It manifested itself as early as his defeat of Bowe in the Olympic final of 1988 in Seoul and has always emerged when needed in a pro career that now shows 25 straight wins, with 21 stoppages. He is the most athletic of heavyweights, with a physical scope and flexibility rarely observed in a man of 6 ft 5 in and 16 st 11 lb, unless it is on a basketball court.

Some of his pronounced deficiencies and a great many of his exceptional strengths were mixed into his handling of Jackson. Almost before the fight was properly under way, a firm right cross dropped the American on his backside and although he was upright and composed as the mandatory eight count was completed, the flash knockdown looked like an omen. But, instead of building on it, Lewis began to paw indecisively with his left hand and to miss with extravagant downward rights. He also permitted the disadvantaged challenger (Jackson appeared shorter than the stated height of 6 ft 1½ in and had weighed in at 15 st 8 lb) to catch him with an occasional winging hook.

Lewis maintained a clear superiority through the first four rounds, but without stamping his class on a journeyman whose 30 wins in 31 previous fights had been at the expense of nonentities. Jackson, though already swelling conspicuously under both eyes, was still aggressive in the fifth and Lewis stumbled embarrassingly off balance after taking a straight left. Then, suddenly, the champion unleashed in a single explosive punch the right-hand power that sets him apart from every other heavyweight. After pitching face-down near the ropes, Jackson seemed unlikely to climb back into the fray. When he did at nine, he was soon subsiding again under the violent bombardment that continued two or three seconds after the bell. Weathering the next two rounds was an ordeal for the American. By the eighth he was a sad wreck, swallowing blood, hollow-eyed and drained of resistance. Lewis, breaking his normal habit by operating in close, set him up with a short right, then smashed in the combination of uppercut and two hooks that finished the job.

As the 28-year-old champion smoothly discussed his triumph afterwards, referring to himself portentously in the third person, it was left to Larry Merchant, the perceptive boxing analyst of HBO, to make a definitive comment on a phenomenon most other Americans find baffling. 'This is the kind of guy who looks awkward and knocks your brains out,' Merchant said. 'All he is is the biggest, strongest heavyweight around, and the one who punches harder than anybody else. If America had an Olympic champion who turned pro and kept doing what Lewis does, you wouldn't hear too many questions about his genuineness.'

It is to be hoped that Moorer will put himself forward as an interrogator. But the likelihood is that the real questioning of Lennox Lewis will be done by Riddick Bowe.

Young, Gifted, but Out of Order

The Sunday Times, 15 May 1994

When one man is battering another, does it really matter if he adds insult to injury? Is it fatuous to complain because the legalised assault is accompanied by belittling gestures and derisive expressions?

If boxing means to go on arguing its case for being regarded as a sport, it had better answer yes to the first question and no to the second. More specifically, it had better take action (through the British Boxing Board of Control) to curtail the childish mockery with which Naseem Hamed, the new bantamweight champion of Europe, has compounded the embarrassment of some of the dozen opponents he has met and outclassed so far in a professional career of exceptional promise. Abolitionists who contend that boxing's ethos is hardly more elevated than that of bear-baiting were given a measure of encouragement in Sheffield on Wednesday night as Hamed, a 20-year-old Yorkshireman of Yemeni stock, inflicted an elaborate repertoire of taunts and ridicule on Vincenzo Belcastro, of Italy, in a regrettable climax to the overwhelming points win that earned the European title.

Taunting an opponent to undermine his self-belief is scarcely an unknown phenomenon in the fight business. It has been associated with a number of the biggest names in the history of the ring, particularly in recent decades. But seeking, as apologists have done, to justify Hamed's outrageousness in midweek by invoking the memory of Ray Leonard and Muhammad Ali is, to say the least, a bit rich. For a start, in the course of long and magnificent careers, neither of those great champions approached the extremes of insulting behaviour Hamed had made commonplace in his performances before he was out of the novice stage. Ali's provocations mainly involved a sometimes nasty mixture of verbal and physical chastisement, a technique that had its ultimate expression in the grinding down of Ernie Terrell, who had insisted on calling him Cassius Clay: 'What's my name?' – SMACK. 'What's my name?' – SMACK. But he, like Leonard, was most likely to do his dismissive routines in highly dangerous company, where they represented a considerable risk but carried the promise of substantial reward.

Thus Ali, confronted by George Foreman in Zaire at a stage when Foreman was still widely perceived as an invincible ogre, turned conversational: 'Hit harder, George. That the best you got? They told me you had body punches but that don't hurt even a little bit. Harder, sucker, swing harder. You the champion and you gettin' nowhere. Now I'm gonna jab you.' And he did.

Leonard was at his most extravagant in his second fight with Roberto Duran and in his meeting with Marvin Hagler. Since Duran was the macho man's macho man and had outwarred him in their first collision,

264

Sugar Ray could perhaps be forgiven the element of scornful clowning he introduced in New Orleans. He was intent on challenging the celebrated *cojones* of Duran and the 'No mas' conclusion vindicated his policy, although it was a horror of humiliation, not fear, that made Duran quit.

By the time he fought Hagler, years of absence from the ring had so eroded Leonard's ability to sustain the beautiful fluency of his prime, had so reduced his capacity for deadly explosions, that he had to transform the occasion into a baroque optical illusion. His flawless nerve enabled him to dazzle two of the three judges with a superbly contrived blend of brief, spirited flurries and extended periods of persuasive play-acting. I thought the decision in his favour was an injustice to Hagler. But there was no denying the wonder of what Leonard had achieved in circumstances that would have buried many other men under a swirl of dread. Certainly it is ludicrous to liken the calculated flourishes of arrogance he used as a weapon against Hagler to the prolonged display of theatrical gloating with which Hamed polluted the 12th round in Sheffield.

Brendan Ingle, Hamed's manager, has said that in the 12th the young man was not himself but Leonard in Las Vegas with Marvelous Marvin. Really? Well, this witness, who was ringside in Vegas and watched on television last Wednesday, failed to spot the resemblance. Hamed should be told that Leonard was too dedicated a professional, too serious in his pursuit of immortality, to concern himself with liberty-taking, which is the distasteful thread running through much of the brilliance that has brought the Yorkshire prodigy, with extraordinary swiftness, to a continental championship.

Hamed has remarkable speed and timing, wonderful reflexes and a flexibility of torso and limbs that permits him to be bewilderingly evasive and to strike with a gloriously unorthodox range of punches. He is a spectacular talent and his effortless mastery of Belcastro, a seasoned (if notably undestructive) pro, was an astonishing feat. But, sadly, the excesses of his grandstanding at the finish – the apparent eagerness to treat his demoralised victim as if he were no better than something you might wipe off your shoe – could not be explained in terms of the rush of blood caused by becoming a champion.

As early as his third paid fight, Hamed was revealing a taste for mocking the afflicted. His opponent on 23 May 1992 was Andrew Bloomer from Pontypridd, a man with a perfect record: 11 fights, 11 points defeats. Hamed violated the symmetry by stopping the Welshman in two rounds. But observers of the demolition recall that in the short time they spent together he subjected Bloomer to a wide variety of insults, pulling faces, turning his back on the hapless opponent, conveying offensive derision by any means that occurred to him.

Such behaviour has already drawn disapproving words into Hamed's ear from John Morris, the secretary of the Board of Control, and Morris was again distinctly unamused by what he saw on his screen last week.

'Nobody wants to risk killing the spirit of a youngster but there is no place for ridiculing opponents,' Morris said. 'I'd want to wait for reports from our representatives at the Sheffield fight before deciding on any action we might take, but it does seem that what I said to him previously went in one ear and out the other. In his own interests, he had better change his ways. The higher he goes in the game the more of a threat that nonsense will be to his own welfare.'

A more immediate danger is that television, swooning over the ratings engendered by all the pouting, posturing and showbiz claptrap inseparable from Chris Eubank's performances, might see Hamed's playground arrogance as a quality to emphasise in the marketplace. To their credit, ITV's Jim Watt and Reg Gutteridge both registered disgust with the treatment of Belcastro.

As a fighter, the Yemeni Yorkshireman might conceivably thrill the world. As a professional gloater, he would be a cosmic bore.

A Sudden Leap to the Top

Sports Illustrated, September 1994

It was a night when the most ominous cackle in boxing carried all the way from a northern suburb of London to a cell block in Indiana and sent a shiver down many a spine on both sides of the Atlantic. *Heh, heh, heh, heh, heh*. The signature crowing of Don King – even more than the gusher of self-congratulation and mangled quotation it punctuated – let the other leading connivers in the world's most manipulable sport know exactly what they can expect now that King is back in economic control of the heavyweight division.

There can be little doubt that restoration of King's sovereignty was the immediate and overwhelming implication of the blasting right-hand punch with which Oliver McCall scattered the senses of Lennox Lewis after barely half a minute of the second round at Wembley Arena last Saturday night. When the previously unbeaten champion (25–0) was driven violently onto his back, he sprawled to his right and then rose so uncertainly at the count of six that his legs fluttered like saplings in a breeze, and he responded to the referee's inquiries about his condition by lurching against the official. The stopping of the fight followed as naturally as the awareness that far more than ownership of a WBC title was about to change. The *coup de grâce* was also a *coup d'état*.

McCall, a 29-year-old from the South Side of Chicago, entered the ring as a 5–1 underdog because of his 24–5 record and the belief that his ambition was incurably blunted by having worked too long as a sparring partner; in a stroke he regained power for King, a patron who had been without a stake in the heavyweight championship since James 'Buster' Douglas knocked out Mike Tyson in Tokyo four and a half years ago. Tyson remains imprisoned in the Indiana Youth Center on a rape conviction. But with his release due around May 1995, he is the key to the greatest bonanza professional sport has ever known – a blitzkrieg exploitation of the growing pay-per-view television market that might gross $100 million in a single night. And, in the fevered, gloating aftermath of McCall's sudden destruction of Lewis, King declared with aggressive certainty that *he* is the key to Tyson. 'There is no more equivocation about who is going to fight Tyson,' he said. 'We now know who is going to fight him. Everybody was jockeying for position, but you don't have to worry any more about where Tyson is going to fight if he is fighting.'

At that moment it was difficult to relate the noisy scene in a corner of the arena restaurant, where McCall, wearing the garish green-and-gold championship belt over his sweat clothes, had difficulty making himself heard above the voices of every booster and bucket-carrier in his huge entourage, to the presumably quieter one in that house of correction in mid-America. When King spoke of Tyson and of his own resolve to be master of ceremonies at the convict's comeback, he briefly abandoned the knockabout huckster's persona he likes to present to the public and reverted to the ghetto hardness that brought him up from the Cleveland numbers rackets to richer fields of plunder. His voice, which seconds before had been trilling and fluting at 300 words a minute through the familiar extravagances of his imagination, slowed and dropped an octave or two as he enunciated plans that must have sounded like a knell in the ears of his rivals for promotional supremacy among the heavyweights. McCall would, King said, be ready to fight Bruce Seldon or Peter McNeeley or Frans Botha, 'any one of them top guys'. Since the principal distinction of those three men is that they are all affiliated with King, the point he was making could not have been plainer: the WBC title will be kept in the family until brother Mike emerges from the slammer. Seldon was stopped in nine rounds by McCall in 1991, and neither Botha nor McNeeley is close to a contender's status. But that last consideration is unlikely to faze King, whose ability to vault his fighters over more qualified heavyweights in the rankings of boxing's three major sanctioning bodies has evoked awe lately even among veteran students of his winning ways with a dollar. There was a time when King had to rely heavily on the complaisance of the WBC, whose president, José Sulaiman, has long been regarded as his lapdog. These days, however, King seems to be given an equally easy ride by the WBA and IBF. All three organisations co-operated fully in the swift elevation of McCall – he was unranked at the end of '92 but No. 1 several months before the Lewis bout – and now have a clutch of King's clients at the forefront of their rankings.

With McCall spared a mandatory defence until next September and with two of McCall's toughest possible unincarcerated opponents, Tony Tucker and Michael Moorer, discussing a fight for Moorer's WBA title in April (provided Moorer, who is also the IBF champion, duly vandalises the historic remains of George Foreman on 5 November), life for King at present is almost a rose without a thorn. Almost, but not quite. He is, in fact, pricked by a rather substantial anxiety over an indictment for insurance fraud involving Lloyd's of London. Those who wish King ill, and they are not thin on the ground, drool over the possibility that he may be going to prison as Tyson is coming out. But, as law enforcement agencies and boxing's power brokers can testify, King is a hard man to lock up or lock out, and those embarrassed and alarmed by last week's coup in England dare not assume that a court will come to their rescue. Apart from the sad figure of Lewis – and the British public, who, dismissing the fact that Lewis fought for Canada as an amateur, had readily acclaimed him their first heavyweight champion of the twentieth century – the most shell-shocked victims of the explosive happenings at Wembley had to be Riddick Bowe and his manager, Rock Newman. It seems only yesterday that Bowe, having beaten Evander Holyfield in November 1992, was the undisputed heavyweight champion of the world. Then, rather than fight Lewis, Bowe dropped the WBC belt in a garbage bin, and Holyfield did much the same to Bowe by winning their rematch a year later. Now both Bowe and Lewis are so far out in the cold that their careers are in danger of succumbing to hypothermia. Their match, which was scheduled for March, has been rendered meaningless. At least Bowe, who has one big-money option on the table, against Moorer, can say he's an American who was once recognised as the true champion, the man who beat the man who beat the man. However, Lewis, in spite of having battered Bowe when they met in the Olympics in 1988, has always been seen as an upstart who gained his crown by decree.

In the midst of all this panicky positioning among the heavyweights there is a tendency to forget how improbable McCall's achievement was, how much credit he deserves for transcending the limitations he revealed during nearly nine years as a professional fighter. Despite McCall's never having been knocked off his feet in his 29 pro fights and having actually put Tyson down during one of about 300 rounds of sparring they shared, there was a widespread suspicion that in serious company McCall would be preoccupied with survival. However, four months ago Emanuel Steward, one of boxing's most respected coaches, moved in alongside McCall's regular trainer, Greg Page, and the response was dramatic. McCall's earlier reputation as an idler and delin-quent was deserved. A father of six, he admits he took up boxing because he was too lazy to get a steady job, and in 1988 he was jailed for 60 days and given five years' probation after trying to supplement his ring earnings with a little burglary. But his behaviour over four months of dedicated training for the Lewis fight is proof of the cleansing power of opportunity. Not only did McCall sweat himself into a state of hard and shining fitness, but under Steward's tutelage he began to throw recognisable hooks, which gave his attack a new dimension. Above all, he developed an almost maniacal commitment to winning. By the time he reached the Wembley ring, weighing 231 pounds against Lewis's 238 (the heaviest Lewis had ever scaled), McCall had worked himself into such a wild-eyed frenzy that it looked as if his head might explode. With the muscles of his clenched jaw sticking out like rivets, he paced around the ring like a man possessed as Page spoke urgently at his ear.

Lewis's appearance made a contrast with McCall's. What his face suggested was not so much calm as a kind of passive detachment, as if not all of his spirit had turned up. Such impressions can, of course, come from the spectator's imagination, but there was nothing imaginary about the problems that arose for Lewis in the first round. Though he won it with a couple of decent jabs, he did nothing to discourage McCall from storming him. Throughout the accumulation of his perfect record, Lewis's use of his impressive physical resources in the ring – his 6 ft 5 in height and 83-inch reach, his athletic strength and exceptional reflexes – had remained stubbornly amateurish. Some admirers pointed out that Muhammad Ali's style made him the eternal, if divine, amateur. But the hopeful comparison did not help Lewis in that extraordinary second round, which began with Steward counselling McCall to relax. Lewis said later that his disaster was precipitated by efforts to load up with his own right, which was reckoned the heaviest punch in the division. All that ringside observers saw was Lewis's tentative attempt to throw two punches, a left and a right whose soft arcs were never completed as McCall stepped inside with a left hook to the jaw. That hook was real enough, but its main function was to give McCall the rhythmic shoulder movement that helped to ensure that the driving right which followed was nothing less than the punch of a lifetime.

There is no doubt that in ending the fight after only one knockdown and 31 seconds of the second round, Lupe Garcia, who was refereeing his twelfth title fight but first in the heavyweight division, was breaking with tradition. Had he been on hand to apply the same standards, Larry Holmes would certainly never have come back from the twilight zone to beat Earnie Shavers or Renaldo Snipes, and a lot of other celebrated recoveries would not have occurred. Yet, remembering Lewis's teetering vulnerability, it is impossible to regret Garcia's intervention.

The loser talked afterwards about a flash knockdown. There was definitely a hint of lightning about it, and of a thunderclap. And, as Don King might say, it split the boxing firmament asunder.

Jones Shuts Toney's Big, Bad Mouth

The Sunday Times, 20 November 1994

James Toney's mouth had been a flame-thrower but once in the ring his threat was snuffed out like a candle by the gale of swift and varied aggression that came from Roy Jones Jr, and their fight for Toney's IBF super-middleweight title, which was hailed in advance as a classic war between equals, could not have been more one-sided without involving the use of a stretcher. At the end of 12 rounds, the beaten champion's contribution to the scorecards hardly went beyond marks for attendance.

Boxing has its own way of proving that speed kills and, at the MGM Grand Hotel on Friday night, Jones's repeated spurts of deadly pace did more than anything else to annihilate his opponent's dreams of being recognised as the best pound-for-pound fighter in the world. No doubt this was the wrong time to measure Toney on a worth-for-weight basis, since it is impossible to escape the suspicion that years of undisciplined eating have turned his struggle to make the 12-stone limit into a damaging ordeal. There were rumours, vehemently denied by his camp, that the process of wasting became so extreme at one point that he was reduced to taking nourishment intravenously. What is certain is that after going to scale at 11 st 13 lb on Thursday afternoon (nobody in authority seems particularly appalled by the scandalous nonsense of allowing men to weigh in more than 24 hours before they fight) he increased his bulk so rapidly that by Friday evening he had added 17 lb. Anybody who believes it is healthy for a trained athlete of 26 to boost his body weight by 10 per cent in a single day takes a strange view of fitness. 'I felt sluggish from the weight loss,' Toney said quietly at the press conference following his defeat. Really?

Yet, when the tale of the scales has been given its due significance, there remains the firm conviction that Toney at his most effective would have been outclassed by the range of athletic skills and the convincing power Jones brought through the ropes. The 25-year-old challenger arrived in the ring wearing a false shirt-front and bow tie. He could have been forgiven if he had gone for the full evening dress appropriate to the concert platform, for what he delivered was a recital, a virtuoso performance in which Toney was largely a helpless instrument. 'I'm goin' to break your ass up,' the glowering champion had told Jones at the weigh-in. On the night, even breaking up Jones's unorthodox rhythm was painfully beyond him. 'That's just mouth – and mouths can say anything,' Jones had responded on Thursday. 'They got birds that can talk.'

Toney tried to do some talking during the fight, but when his gumshield showed like a white slash between his lips it was usually so that he could gulp down extra air to stave off the exhaustion that several times appeared to be closing in on him. 'Losing is not an option' was emblazoned on the jackets worn by his entourage, but within a few minutes of the first bell it looked as if winning might be an impossibility. From the start, Jones's left hook clattered against the right side of Toney's head as if the bones were magnetised. Eddie Futch, the 83-year-old who is rated the wisest strategist in boxing and who was in a losing corner against Toney with Mike McCallum, had said that well executed left hooks could be his undoing, and the entire evening was to be a vindication of his theory. But Futch, watching the action on television, would be surprised by the ease with which Jones landed the right, too.

In fact, with his fluent, unpredictable footwork and the blurring speed of his punches, often thrown from improbable, unnerving angles, Jones was able to torment and punish Toney almost at will. As the heavier man sought to press in, with his shaven head bobbing behind a raised left shoulder, Jones would sometimes extend his own left arm and, provocatively, hold the attacker at the end of his glove, before abruptly switching tactics to explode another accurate bombardment. When Toney did penetrate close enough to unload the body assault he had imagined would be a key to success, Jones tied him up without difficulty and bore down on his shoulders until what was meant to be a menacing crouch degenerated into stooping, groping impotence.

Proof that there was a dangerous violence in Jones's flurries came as early as the second round, when Toney staggered briefly under the cumulative force of a sustained attack, and in the third the crowd roared in premature expectation of a sensational finish when yet another left hook from Jones precipitated a prolonged, dramatic stumble. That punch and the follow-up lunge so unbalanced Toney that he lurched into a sitting position as his scrambling legs carried him towards his own corner. Though a further left and right from Jones apparently missed, Toney went thudding against the ringpost. But he remained clear-headed. The seat of his pants never actually touched the canvas and he was both upright and ready to attempt retaliation long before the referee, Richard Steele, had completed the eight-count with which Steele indicated that he saw the incident as a knockdown.

The final seconds of the round found Toney hustling forward, refusing to be unmanned by the frustration and hurt that awaited him. His sufferings in subsequent rounds were frequently shot through with embarrassment (as when Jones's dismissive pirouettes left Toney reaching for a target that had long gone and, once or twice, peering out miserably into the disbelieving faces of the spectators) but his fighting heart guaranteed that the experience would not become outright humiliation. He was entitled to the gross subjectivity with which he interpreted the fight later, even when he said of the knockdown: 'I wasn't hurt. He pushed me after I ducked.' Warriors are allowed to edit their memories.

Plainly, however, Toney was stretching the truth too far when, having stifled his natural inclinations sufficiently to say he took his hat off to

Jones, the loser added: 'He did a good job of running away, of staying away from my power.' If Jones was running away, who was hitting Toney? Maybe he thinks it was the referee. As it happened, Steele, who has been embroiled in more than his share of controversy in the past, did not have an inspired night and on two occasions he signalled the end of a round ahead of the timekeeper. Toney's supporters, grabbing desperately for any hint of a complaint, argued that in the case of the eighth round Steele had done their man a major disservice. It is true that the fierce exchange which marked the conclusion of those three minutes brought forth the most potent aggression Toney produced at any stage and he could ill afford the misfortune of being interrupted by the referee's mistake. But it is lunacy to suggest that Toney had suddenly taken control or that the few seconds he was denied had the remotest likelihood of being crucial.

He lost the eighth round on all three cards and, indeed, it was difficult for this witness to be confident of giving him any round out of the 12. One judge gave him only the sixth, another awarded him the fourth, ninth and tenth and the third made him winner of the sixth and ninth. Such bursts of generosity were academic. They were submerged in score totals of 119–108, 117–110 and 118–109, which meant that if it had been a horse-race the two contestants would have finished in different parishes.

Toney says he will not be despressed by the first defeat inflicted on him in 47 professional fights, that he will move up to light-heavyweight immediately and resurrect his reputation in the 12 st 7 lb division. He is not consistently endearing (it is hard to warm to a fighter who talks of making an opponent 'my bitch'). But he made an affecting sight as the verdict was announced: a tamed macho man in the midst of a mournful group of females that included his manager, Jackie Kallen, his mother, his fiancée and their baby daughter. However, it is unlikely that his trauma will teach him either humility in the street or restraint at the table.

The problem for Jones, who now has an unblemished sequence of 27 wins to his credit, will be locating lucrative opposition. Any British super-middleweight who fancies the work can be confident that the new champion will accept his call. But it might be a good idea to make sure the BUPA payments are up to date.

272

The Guru at the Glutton's Table

The Sunday Times, 27 November 1994

There is a double sadness about the indiscipline that has long threatened to swamp the talent of Riddick Bowe, for it may sour not only his own prime as a fighter but the late twilight of Eddie Futch's career as one of the greatest trainers boxing has known. Futch, at 83, has no years to waste and it troubles him that the handful he has devoted to Bowe have produced far less solid achievement than he had a right to expect from such outstanding raw material. When the 27-year-old Brooklyn heavy-weight meets the competent but unintimidating Larry Donald in Las Vegas on Saturday night, in his latest attempt to persuade a sceptical public that he has finally put the brake on rampant self-indulgence, his remorse over the damage he has done to himself should be compounded by regret about the way he has misused the unique combination of skill, experience and character Futch brings to his corner.

Bowe cannot fail to appreciate the seriousness of his current predicament as an ostracised, title-less onlooker at the feast of big-money promotions on which lesser men are about to gorge themselves. Nor can he have any doubt that his strongest chance of re-emerging as the best heavyweight now at large (Mike Tyson remains imprisoned and, in terms of how much of his deadliness he will have left when he is released next year, an imponderable) must lie in wholehearted submission to the guidance of the old man who took him all the way to the top in the initial, surging phase of their alliance.

It was after he became undisputed champion of the world by beating Evander Holyfield in November 1992 that the slobbish tendencies which had always been discernible in Bowe's attitude to eating and to the conventional rigours of training developed into a real worry for Futch. For the return with Holyfield, the champion's 6 ft 5 in frame was burdened with 11 lb more than it carried in the first match and, at 17 st 8 lb, the slackness of his body surely reflected a slackness of will in his preparation. Holyfield fought with characteristic determination to reclaim the WBA and IBF titles (Bowe had, symbolically, dumped the WBC belt in a garbage bin, from whence it was happily retrieved by Lennox Lewis). But the narrowness of the victory emphasised the self-destructiveness of the loser.

Bowe is not at all a bad liver in the classic tradition of the most wayward fighters; he is not given to tempestuous sorties around night-clubs and his name has never been linked with orgies of boozing or drug-taking, but he can, apparently, eat for a battalion and, according to Futch, 'is inclined to waste time playing with the expensive toys he has been able to afford'. While he was champion, he outlined plans for a lavish new home that included a kitchen in the master bedroom. A severe shrinking of his purses discouraged him from going ahead with the house-building project but the memory of it does nothing to strengthen belief in his capacity to make a belated switch to asceticism.

However, in New Orleans, where he did the core of his training for the Donald fight and shaped much of it around a regime devised by a specialist conditioner of unquestioned credibility, Mackie Shilstone, he gave every sign of sweating towards his highest level of fitness since the first match with Holyfield. Having arrived in Louisiana on 10 October with a weight of 19 st 6 lb and a back problem, Bowe had embraced Shilstone's scientific methods enthusiastically enough to lose 19 lb and all restrictions on his movement by the time I visited him one week into November. At fractionally over 18 st, he still seemed rather heavy for someone within four weeks of action but Shilstone insists that what he is told by heart-rate telemetry, the monitoring of body fat, and the speed with which Bowe can perform and recover from programmed sequences of intensive exercises is much more important than a simple reading of the scales.

The steady improvement of the ratio of body fat to muscle has been a priority. 'Body fat is something you carry around – muscle is something that carries you around' is a Shilstone mantra. 'Riddick is so committed that I've had to hold him back,' the fitness expert said. 'The weight has been shed in a totally controlled way, with an organised diet and a programme of exercise that builds power and endurance, the ability to expend energy and recharge quickly throughout a fight, so that you keep coming back with the same power you had at the start.'

He would not, he said, be in the least dismayed if Bowe went in against Donald (whose record shows 16 straight wins as a professional) at about 17½ stone, because Bowe would be big but not big and fat. 'We are entering a new age in boxing, that of the true, lean heavyweight,' Shilstone added. 'Riddick is equipped to represent that new breed and if, after preparing as he is now, he were let loose on the likes of George Foreman there would be a danger of something terrible happening, maybe even a death in the ring.'

Some of us find it hard to accept that Bowe needs to be heavier than he was for the most impressive performance of his life, which was probably his defeat of Holyfield. But it must be admitted that he looked good in New Orleans, with the features of his face sharply defined and no significant flab around his waist or, as in the past, gathered in tell-tale clumps at the back of his neck. There can at least be a reasonable hope that he will show against Donald a return to the effectiveness that would restore a sense of quality to the heavyweight division and suggest his career might yet provide a worthy last monument to Futch's exceptional attributes as a mentor of fighting men.

Futch was so alert to the risk of squandering whatever working years remained to him that, when first asked to take charge of Bowe, he demanded that the 1988 Olympic silver medallist undergo a trial period

THE GURU AT THE GLUTTON'S TABLE

of training to show he was capable of rising above the dilettante reputation already attaching itself to him. Since that convincing test, Futch has found it necessary from time to time to deliver reminders that failure to meet his standards would be interpreted as a goodbye. The latest occasion was just a few weeks ago when he arrived in New Orleans to discover that Bowe, having had a viral infection diagnosed by a leading doctor in the city, had tossed the prescribed medication into a wastepaper basket. Futch called a meeting of all the principals in the camp and made it clear that he refused to be associated with such irresponsibility. Nobody was likely to mistake the cold anger of his words for an empty threat. In the past, he has not been averse to walking out on world champions if they took liberties with his authority. Both Marlon Starling and Virgil Hill can testify to that. 'They either shape up or I ship out,' he told me.

It is difficult to imagine a fighter who would not be diminished by the loss of Futch's services. His credentials reach all the way back to the Depression, to the years when he was working 17 hours a day as a hotel waiter and using his three-hour break in the middle of the marathon shift to train for the amateur fights that made him Golden Gloves lightweight champion of Detroit. The training was done in the Brewster Recreation Center, where a remarkably promising light-heavyweight regularly insisted that Futch ignore the 40 lb discrepancy in their weights and give him some fast sparring. Those workouts with Joe Louis, who was soon to become one of the greatest of heavyweight champions, formed an early part of a privileged education in the fight business.

That education had to be absorbed outside rather than inside the ring when Futch – as a married 25-year-old with three daughters – was forced to abandon plans to turn pro after doctors told him he had a heart murmur. The strain of overworking had contributed to the problem but, looking back, he sees himself as lucky to have had a job: 'What made me happy in later years was that those little girls never knew there was a Depression. They went through it without knowing it was there.' They, and the brother who was born later, always knew their father was there. Family bonds are precious to him (he speaks to his sister Agnes every day, regardless of where he is in the world) and his close relationship with his children readily survived his migration from Michigan to California in 1951 and marriage to a second wife. The recent loss of his son to cancer obviously opened a wound that will never heal. 'He's a wonderful man – I'd wish my dad on anybody,' his eldest daughter, Yvonne, said recently.

The simple substance of that tribute is relevant to the qualities he brings to the ring. A fighter who enlists Futch's help gains far more than a vast depth of boxing expertise. He draws on the accumulated lessons and values of a long life, rich in challenges and achievements, very much a life of a literate and sensitive black man in 20th-century America. When he talks of fights and fighters he is spellbinding. He was personally acquainted with legendary figures of four, five and six decades ago, men such as Louis and Ray Robinson and Archie Moore, and learned from all of them. And he is at least as likely to talk enthrallingly of less familiar marvels such as Charley Burley, a welterweight and middleweight he considers the finest all-round fighter he ever saw.

Burley frequently fought heavyweights but the merits that caused him to be studiously denied a title shot in any division during 13 years as a pro are perhaps adequately conveyed by the story of how, in 1944, he was summoned from his work in a foundry in San Diego to be a last-minute substitute opponent at a Hollywood arena. He went home to pick up his kit, rode the bus north for 125 miles, then proceeded to punch Archie Moore about the ring, knocking him down twice in the course of the ten-round beating.

Anybody with the slightest interest in boxing is almost bound to have heard of Futch's own exploits as tutor and corner-man, quiet motivator, inspired strategist and, when required, humane protector of fighters. The imprint of his gifts shows in the records of an array of outstanding performers from Joe Frazier, Ken Norton and Larry Holmes to Michael Spinks and Alexis Arguello, and of a small army of other substantial talents in between. He coached Norton and Frazier in the specific moves that enabled them to beat Muhammad Ali while he was still young and vigorous, succeeded in giving the cumbersome Trevor Berbick the tactics to outscore the precision of Pinklon Thomas, and won the admiration of every civilised watcher by cutting the gloves off Frazier at the end of the 14th round of the brutal epic with Ali in Manila.

Yet Futch can be just as compelling when the conversation moves away from boxing, perhaps to the love of poetry engendered when as a child he walked barefoot to the public library in Detroit and came across a verse that resonated in his mind although he could not comprehend it. It was a quatrain from the Fitzgerald translation of the Rubaiyat of Omar Khayyam and a beautifully illustrated edition of the book accompanies him on every long trip from his Las Vegas home. Also in his briefcase are one or two small anthologies and copies of individual poems by Keats and others, carefully enclosed in transparent folders.

His reading accurately indicates a gentleness of spirit. A sense of habitual calm is communicated by the soft voice in which he speaks his well-constructed sentences and the expression of amiable serenity that is usually on his handsome face. He is indeed a kind, polite, thoroughly delightful man. But underneath all that composure there is a fire that is a long way from being quenched, as several bigger and younger men of provocative disposition have found to their cost over the years. He was 74 when he last applied his left hook to silence a stream of dismissive abuse from a fellow 50 years his junior.

Nothing in his whole repertoire of anecdotes is more affecting than the tales of journeys he made southward from Detroit in the late 1940s, driving his Buick down either side of the Mississippi towards New

Orleans, where black fighters shut out of the lucrative engagements in the north could get decent pay-days. 'There would usually be two fighters with me in the car and I always made sure I had at least half a tank of gas, because I never knew what reception I'd get at a gas station. Once you were out of Ohio and into Kentucky you had to be wary. I took pains to avoid trouble but I had a special box of Kleenex clipped above the sun-visor just in case. It was a narrow box that wouldn't attract attention if the cops searched the car, but under three or four layers of tissue there was a .25 automatic. You had to give yourself some chance if things got really bad.'

Even now, though he moves gingerly on an artificial hip and two artificial knee joints, nimbleness of mind makes Mr Futch a handy man to have around if things get really bad.

The Same Old Brutal Truths

The Sunday Times, 5 March 1995

Every time the violence of the ring leads to a quieter battle on a neurosurgeon's operating table, the aftermath is dominated by two depressingly familiar themes. Almost as inevitable as the period of torturous waiting to see if a young life has been snuffed out, or blighted by the failure of an abused brain to regain all of its vital functions, is the sudden intensifying of the eternal debate about whether public fist-fighting should be tolerated by any society that regards itself as civilised.

The case of Gerald McClellan, the 27-year-old American whose challenge for Nigel Benn's WBC super-middleweight championship last weekend left him at the edge of death in the Royal London Hospital, cannot possibly alter the terms of an argument so long governed by entrenched attitudes of mind. But the specifics of what happened at the London Arena and the tenor of the ensuing controversy strengthen the impression that the justifiers of boxing (among whom my lifelong fascination with fights and fighters must place me) will become increasingly beleaguered, especially if the further calamities that are bound to occur are, like McClellan's, enacted in the glare of international television.

One aspect of this tragedy causes it to be even more significant than similar grim episodes in boxing's past. It developed in spite of some of the most thorough and sophisticated medical safeguards ever associated with a fight in Britain, or anywhere else. Five doctors, including an anaesthetist, were on hand to treat McClellan when he collapsed in his corner after being counted out while resting on one knee in the tenth round, and an ambulance was ready to rush him to a neurological unit that was no more than 15 minutes away and had already been put on standby for such an emergency. Here was a dramatic reminder of something about which the most ardent defenders of boxing should never have been able to delude themselves – that when one man is landing full-blooded punches on another man's head, nothing done during intervals in the action, or when it is over, can remove the risk of severe and perhaps fatal brain damage.

If confronted directly, the majority of those prominent in the pro-boxing lobby will acknowledge these chilling dangers. They accept that the issue is not how hazardous the sport is but whether the hazards are acceptable. But it is in this area that their arguments are too often flawed by pathetically simplistic comparisons. Many of them continue – with a blind persistence that is an offence against common sense and an embarrassment to a number of us who remain uneasily on their side of the debate – to suggest that boxing should be seen in precisely the same light as other high-risk sports such as mountaineering and motor racing.

John Morris, secretary of the British Boxing Board of Control, was playing that old tinny tune again at a press conference last week when he invited everyone to remember how the vast toll of fatalities claimed by the mountains dwarfed the total of deaths in the ring recorded year by year or decade by decade. No one would wish to score points off Mr Morris, who looked like a decent man under dreadful pressure, but how often does it have to be said that motives, not statistics, call pugilism into question? The mountain does not set out to batter the climber, any more than the wall at Imola thrust itself in front of the hurtling Grand Prix car that became a coffin for Ayrton Senna. Boxing can never sidestep the reality that it is the only activity designated a sport in which participants are officially encouraged to knock their competitors unconscious, to inflict what Spanish-speaking fighters have called the little death.

All contact sports are fraught with the possibility of serious injury, but in no other is it so deliberately contrived as it is in boxing. American football leaves more than a few players hideously maimed and most of us know one or two rugby men who betray hints of the condition known as punch-drunkenness. Even in the less violent form of football that is our national game dangers are plentiful. Gary Lineker told me the other day that, while he accepted whatever risks came his way in a competitive match, he studiously avoided heading the ball in training. He felt his brain could do without unnecessary assault. Like many who are more committed to boxing than he is, Lineker shuddered at the thought of how much traumatising force had been applied in the half-hour of sustained ferocity generated by Benn and McClellan as their fortunes seesawed through one of the most brutal fights any of us at ringside had ever witnessed.

It was natural that people who have always been repelled by boxing should consider that occasion, with its relentless, mutually destructive aggression from the principals and the fevered, roaring involvement of the crowd, a vindication of their deepest prejudices, a happening scarcely less abhorrent than a snuff movie. No doubt they would find incomprehensible the reaction of Brendan Ingle, who received £20 for handing up the stool and spittoon in McClellan's corner. Ingle, a respected professional mentor who guided the skilful middleweight Herol Graham during the best years of a distinguished, title-winning career and has been responsible for nurturing the Yemeni Yorkshireman Naseem Hamed to his present status as the outstanding prospect in British boxing, was hardly in need of the menial job or the few pounds that it earned him. But he says he would have paid to be working, however marginally, at 'one of the greatest fights ever seen in a British ring'.

His testimony is, admittedly, as partisan as that of the most rabid abolitionist. Born 54 years ago into a poor Dublin family, one of ten brothers, nine of whom boxed, Ingle has been in thrall to gloved fighting for as long as he can remember and not even the kind of disaster that overtook McClellan can diminish by a fraction his enthusiasm for it. What makes him an important, unignorable witness is his character, which utterly refutes the assumption harboured by some in the anti-boxing faction that the fight business is strictly for low-lifes, exploiters and those drawn to it by bloodlust and a hunger for cheap, vicarious thrills. Ingle is a highly individual personality, whose views on several subjects would strike many as joltingly unorthodox, but the last thing anybody could say about him is that he is amoral. He is a Christian with a serious interest in other religions (he is so impressed by the discipline of the Muslims that he has long been living among that for 15 years now he has gone without food and drink from sunrise to sunset throughout Ramadan) and is renowned for the fatherly devotion he shows to his protégés and for running a gym that serves almost as a social centre in one of the most deprived areas of Sheffield.

'I tell the kids at my gym that boxing at its worst is a dirty, horrible, prostitutin', vindictive game,' he said from Glasgow, where he was preparing to be in Hamed's corner last night. 'But at its best it is the purest sport there is, a place where you will meet some of the finest people you'll ever come across. It is a theatre of life. I've convinced a lot of kids there is an alternative to robbin' and fightin' in the streets, and doin' drugs. I tell them there is no room at the bottom, it's crowded down there, but there's room at the top if they lift themselves up. Anybody who wants me to justify boxing should come to that gym and watch what goes on there. I boxed amateur myself until I was 25 and then professionally after that until I was about 33. As a not very good middleweight, I had 38 pro fights, winning 20-odd, meeting a few good performers along the way (I lost on a cut eye to Chris Finnegan in the last seconds of an eight-rounder). I came back to my work on building sites with plenty of bumps and bruises, and I have had more than 100 stitches in my face, but I've no doubt I was part of a wonderful game. I used to tell my wife to stop worrying about me. I said, "I know the dangers and if I get killed so be it. I like fighting and I can get a few extra quid doing it."'

Abolitionists may say that such a man should be protected from himself. However, as was argued recently by Jim Watt, a former light-weight champion of the world turned television commentator who retains the good looks and sharpness of mind to prove that he came through his numerous wars unscathed, it would run counter to the permissive ways of modern society to tell mature men who wanted to box that they were forbidden to do so. Of course, allowing consenting adults to behave as they wish in private has little relevance to the broader question of whether we should, in our collective role as citizens, sanction the immense, elaborately hyped and hugely lucrative business of professional boxing. Yet it must be recognised that the irreplaceable excitement certain men find in the ring is inseparable from public performance, from the adrenalin flood of proving themselves by combat in clamorous arenas – the opportunity such a context thrusts upon them for the most basic kind of heroism.

Maybe they are cruelly misguided in craving such harsh examination of their natures, but to deny them by law the right to have it is to run the risk of playing God. When the legitimacy of prohibition is discussed, Johnny Owen unfailingly invades my thoughts, along with images of the heartbreaking night at the Olympic Auditorium in Los Angeles in the autumn of 1980 when that alarmingly thin, poignantly appealing bantam-weight from Merthyr Tydfil was fatally injured in a world championship fight with Lupe Pintor of Mexico. Anyone unacquainted with Owen might have suspected, on first seeing the skeletal frailty of his body and the mild, childlike expression on his face, that his very presence in a ring amounted to exploitation. But, in fact, he was an extreme example of someone who desperately wanted to box.

So where does all this leave those of us who get our thrills on the safe side of the ropes? For me, strangely, the genuine shock, sorrow and guilt felt over the sufferings of Gerald McClellan have not removed the desire to watch fights, especially when the world's best are coming off their stools. It is, at times, an appetite as worrying as an addiction. But most addicts pay with their own health. It seems worse when the cost of a high is met by others.

Am I entitled to go on seeking the fix? A lot of voices chorus no, and sometimes I think my own is among them.

Looking for a Fight

The Sunday Times, 26 March 1995

Some ex-convicts do not need a map to know where the loot is buried. When, early yesterday, Mike Tyson ceased to be prisoner 922335 of the Indiana Youth Center and teamed up with Don King, formerly inmate 125734 of a more forbidding correctional institution at Marion, Ohio, the two men had a right to be thinking about longer strings of digits – all with dollar signs attached.

Now that Tyson has been freed after serving three years for rape, the biggest money-making operation in the history of sport can move from the realm of drooling anticipation into the world of boot-in-the-balls reality in which the major deals of professional boxing are made. Since no one ever swung a kick at a competing promoter's crotch with more accuracy or *élan* than King, it was always odds-on that he would be the architect of his brother lag's rehabilitation as a world heavyweight champion and the Godzilla of sporting earners. Of the two most obvious complications that beset the great salesman's plans for mutual enrichment, the fact that Tyson's conversion to Islam has brought his Muslim associates into the heart of the action would appear to be less of an obstacle than the trial awaiting King in May on charges of insurance and other frauds produced by a two-year Federal investigation into his business practices. For all their spiritual seriousness, the American Muslims have never been slow to recognise commercial opportunities and King worked profitably enough with them while they were exerting a crucial influence on the career of Muhammad Ali.

The very language employed by Tyson's closest religious adviser, Muhammad Siddeeq, strikes a note that suggests he would not find corporate America alien territory. 'We're facilitating a prayer situation,' he said of the arrangements for the fighter's release (there was indeed a visit to a mosque before Tyson travelled on to his home in Ohio). When it comes to facilitating co-operation with the Muslims, King can be expected to do whatever it takes. 'If the right move is to be in Mecca next week, you can be sure that's where he'll be,' a seasoned observer of King's methods told me on the eve of Tyson's liberation. But where will he be if that trial in May goes the wrong way? Back as a reluctant guest of the US government? Those of us who have watched King's various feats of courtroom escapology are not easily persuaded that he will go down this time. Apart from the attentions of the FBI, which were focused on him for several years in the early 1980s, he has blithely weathered the intensive probings of Grand Juries and the hostility of the IRS, the US tax authorities whose persistence proved too much even for Al Capone. Indicted by a Federal Grand Jury in Manhattan late in 1984 on 23 counts of income tax evasion, filing fraudulent tax returns and conspiracy, he was exposed to the risk of up to 46 years in jail. But he was acquitted and members of the mainly female jury clustered around him afterwards for autographs.

He has learned a great deal since his days as a leading figure in the numbers rackets of Cleveland, where a manslaughter conviction over the death of a fellow hustler, Samuel Lee Garrett, in a street fight (he had earlier shot and killed another man but that was deemed justifiable homicide) put him in room 10, cellblock 6, at Marion for four years. If his subsequent celebrity as the most flamboyant promoter of modern times has been accompanied by a reputation for ruthlessness, and in particular for gouging extortionate percentages from client fighters, it is also true that he has dined at the White House and won a battery of awards for contributions to ethnic and humanitarian causes. And his successful plea for a pardon from the Governor of Ohio in the Garrett case was backed by Jesse Jackson and the widow of Martin Luther King. Yet that record of emerging from dung-heaps of trouble smelling, at least to himself, of roses, does not discourage the belief among his pursuers that they can make the latest charges stick. They seem to feel that by narrowing the target area of their accusations, taking a sniper's approach rather than relying on the scatter-gun tactics that have failed in the past, they can afflict King with concerns more urgent than the role in Tyson's comeback presaged by his prominent part in the brief, theatrical happenings outside the prison gates yesterday morning. Though they may be exaggerating their prospects of success against such a slippery adversary, their efforts do constitute a worry for all the potential deal-makers whose thoughts have been concentrated for so long on the large red-brick building, surrounded by fence, wire and guard towers, that sits starkly isolated on an Indiana plain. The scale of that worry was firmly conveyed by Larry Merchant, a respected broadcaster and knowledgeable insider with HBO, the cable company who are experienced power-brokers around the heavyweight division, when he said on Friday: 'Amid all the fancy sums that are being identified with Tyson's return to the ring, the talk of using pay-per-view to generate $200 million or $250 million, the problems involved have been oversimplified. Apart from the fundamental question of how much of the original Iron Mike is coming out of jail – you would have to bet he'll win a version of the title, because there are so many of them out there, but the real issue is whether he can be the elemental force he once was – there is the confusion over how and with whom negotiations will be conducted. Where is King going to be when the big show is put on the road? This court case could be a fairly serious matter. It goes without saying that HBO are very interested in Tyson's comeback, but it is difficult to negotiate when you don't know what is going to happen between King and Tyson and between King and the law.'

Perhaps more thought should be given at this time to Desiree Washington, who was an 18-year-old beauty contestant in the Black Expo of 1991 when she was raped by Tyson in an Indianapolis hotel room, but that is not the way of the world, and certainly not the way of the boxing business. Regardless of how distasteful many people find all the avaricious speculation about the truckloads of money soon to be prised from the global public, there is undoubtedly a raw fascination in wondering if Tyson can recreate himself as an invincible ogre of the ring, and the hucksters are forming a rowdy queue. The fact that his aura of invincibility had been stripped away long before he was imprisoned is conveniently forgotten in the clamour. Anybody who can present the feeblest claim to being a heavyweight contender has been thrust forward as a possible opponent. Getting lucratively knocked cold in a warm-up match seems to have become the soaring ambition of every has-been and never-could-be from Tommy Morrison to Peter McNeeley to our own ageing national pet, Frank Bruno. Among other, more exotic candidates for walk-on, or carry-off, parts in the reintroduction of the former champion are the Cuban Jorge Luis Gonzalez and the native American Joe Hipp, one Indian whose vocabulary does not include how, at least as far as beating Tyson is concerned.

If King does remain at liberty and retains editorial rights over the script, he will surely make use of one or two of his protégés who are due to perform in Las Vegas on 8 April. On that night, Bruce Seldon and the invariably boring veteran Tony Tucker will meet for the vacant WBA crown, which guarantees King a second championship to add to the WBC title that came under his control when Oliver McCall blasted out Lennox Lewis in London last September. McCall defends on the same promotion against the dwindling residue of Larry Holmes's once formidable gifts. Holmes is reported to have achieved good physical condition and an impressive honing of his attitude but, unless the wayward champion has drifted so far off course that he is a disgrace to his youth, the 45-year-old should have little chance. Weirdly, it is an even more venerable relic of a bygone age, 46-year-old George Foreman, who made himself a world champion for the second time (after a gap of 20 years) five months ago by taking full advantage of the incompetence and porcelain jaw of Michael Moorer, who represents the most obvious jackpot for Tyson. Foreman has the IBF belt around his expanding waist, but he is a legend masquerading as an athlete, a bloated giant who moves as slowly as the seasons. Awareness of the troubles Tyson at his best often had with conspicuously larger opponents cannot undermine the assumption that if he could reassert just a fraction of his old ferocity he could obliterate the ancient coming from the other corner.

The only two men whose size, scope and destructive capacity might encourage them to be genuinely hopeful about beating Tyson – even if he were to return with most of his consuming aggression and hurtful skills restored – are, of course, Riddick Bowe and Lennox Lewis. But Bowe is handicapped by his ability to out-eat a squad of navvies, and the lumbering passivity that is the corollary of such indiscipline, and Lewis is flawed by an amateurishness which may prove impervious to the recently hired expertise of Emanuel Steward. Their shortcomings emphasise that Tyson is extremely fortunate to find himself coming back into a division blissfully free of the kind of frightening ambushes that awaited Muhammad Ali when he rejoined the fray in 1970 after the three-and-a-half-year exile imposed because of his refusal to be inducted into the American army. There is no Frazier, no Norton, no young Foreman in the wings.

Tyson, at 28, is the same age as Ali was then, but there the comparison ends. When Ali's career was interrupted, he was at the height of his powers, the most miraculous combination of speed and athletic fluency heavyweight boxing has known. On his last appearance before incarceration, in Las Vegas on 28 June 1991, Tyson was so miserably undistinguished in outpointing Razor Ruddock that my own report said it 'made his accelerating decline as undeniable as it is astonishing'. Ali was able to spar during his enforced absence, Tyson was not. Whereas Ali could finesse himself out of the problems produced by his loss of leg speed, Tyson was always the incarnation of controlled fury and if he has lost his inner fire and animal vigour he will be doomed to mediocrity. Also, 'The Greatest' withstood a punch as well as anyone who ever fought in the ring. James 'Buster' Douglas demonstrated that when Tyson was receiving rather than delivering onslaughts he could be battered into submission.

The uncertainties proliferate. Only the earnings are assured. When Don King was pulled in on the Garrett charges, he told the arresting officer his occupation was 'self-employed grocer'. For the moment, he holds sway over the fanciest supermarket in sport. There will be no cut-price offers.

Lewis on Way Back by Mean Streets

The Sunday Times, 7 May 1995

It might be called the Detroit factor, since no city in America better represents the streak of meanness from the streets that Emanuel Steward insists is the key to greatness for Lennox Lewis. Steward, the 50-year-old coach and motivator brought in to rescue Lewis's career from the after-shocks of the devastating loss of his WBC heavyweight title to Oliver McCall last September, is a native of Detroit, and the gym he runs in one of its harshest neighbourhoods is a distillation of urban survival instinct. He believes it is the unforgiving spirit of that place, a basement sweatshop known as the Kronk, that Lewis must carry into the ring against Lionel Butler at the Arco Arena in Sacramento on Saturday night – and must absorb permanently into his psyche if he is to exercise what the trainer sees as his natural right to dominate the heavyweight division.

Bare statistics suggest that Butler has the credentials of a victim, for he has lost ten and drawn one of his 34 fights. But his tenth defeat was back in April 1991, and since then he has accumulated 17 victories inside the distance, eight of them in the first round. Admittedly, the list of those he has stopped is largely as anonymous as a bus queue and when a couple of familiar names do appear (ex-champion Tony Tubbs and James 'Bonecrusher' Smith) they reflect the willingness of totally spent fighters to go on taking meagre purses for impersonating their former selves.

Given the unimpressive provenance of these opponents, and wild, mainly upward fluctuations in his weight that do nothing to dispel strong rumours of a drug problem, Butler might seem to be no more of a threat now than he was when he sparred with Lewis in England four and a half years ago (and left behind an unpaid telephone bill that indicated he had a girlfriend on Mars). Yet Steward is not alone in asserting that the intrinsic aggression of the 27-year-old from Louisiana could be dangerous if not ruthlessly checked in the early rounds.

'All those losses don't mean much on the record of a man who had no real amateur career and had to learn the business in the pros,' Steward said. 'He has suffered, too, by being a bit of a nomad. But he has a hard street mentality and you can be sure that he will come out with very little respect for Lennox Lewis. Like all the guys Lewis is liable to face now, Butler will take confidence from the memory of how Lennox was stopped in the second round by McCall. From the time he battered Riddick Bowe in the 1988 Olympics, Lennox had looked like the unbeatable giant, but then McCall got to him and the giant crumbled.

'It was the first time he had met a really aggressive, street-mentality fighter, a guy with the kind of internal rage that can count for more than superior talent in the ring. The fellas he had been dealing with in racking up 25 straight wins as a pro were essentially passive people. Butler won't be passive and Lennox had better take some ferocity of his own in there if he is to do what he should, which is win inside four rounds, maybe inside one.'

As the tutor and corner-man accorded much of the credit for the warrior hostility McCall produced in London, Steward is being true to the credo of the Kronk when he seeks to stir a controlled, destructive fire in Lewis. 'As a fighter, Lennox has been too analytical, not instinctive enough. He likes to think things out before he does something. That's why he loves chess, but boxing isn't chess. In the ring, he is too inclined to wait for the other guy to do something and then react to it. He should be making opponents react to him, imposing his superiority on them. With somebody like Butler, he should be saying, "I'm a big man and, dammit, I'm going to make you respect me. Bring your little ass in here – you're just something for me to look good with."

'This is the only heavyweight around with the ability to be a super-star, to be great, to put himself into history along with Johnson, Louis, Marciano and Ali. If I didn't believe that, why would I leave McCall when he was a winner to go with a loser? Why would I pass up a chance to work with Mike Tyson when he came out of jail, turning my back on a million dollars that I could have earned in the next few months? My credibility is on the line here. I told Lennox, "If you're interested in being just a good fighter, I'd rather forget it."

'We're talking about a guy who is 6 ft 5 in and is probably the best-built heavyweight I ever saw, with big, long muscles that give him tremendous power while leaving his body flexible and athletic. He has a good chin, strong legs and excellent stamina, and he is an amazingly accurate puncher. Properly prepared, and going out as a confident, kick-ass Lennox Lewis, he whips every heavyweight in sight, and Tyson would be one of the easiest. With his talent and dedication – he practically lives in training camps – it is a disgrace that he has not achieved far more than he has, that he has had so many reluctant, drag-out wins against men he should have annihilated.

'But, of course, Lennox is still a big baby in many ways. He is surrounded by so much love, people happy to devote their lives to him. It helps him that his mother Violet is with us to cook his food and look after him, and Courtney Shand, who has been his friend since they were 12 or 13 years old in Canada and has done such a marvellous job on his conditioning, is always there for him to rely on. But some of those working with Lennox on his boxing have given him an easy ride, ducked the responsibility of making him confront the realities of this very tough and violent business. For me there is an advantage in all this, because the fact that he has never been taught very much means he is not set in too many bad habits.'

Steward found that positive interpretation of his task coming under strain during a midweek sparring session at Big Bear Lake, a resort village 7,000 feet up in the San Bernardino Mountains. Sluggish passivity was only one of several disturbing tendencies Lewis manifested and his mother, a warm, charmingly benign presence at ringside, was alone in thinking he had earned praise. Neither the knowledge that the three partners from the Kronk who provided nine rounds of work have an aggregate of 40 pro wins and just one defeat among them, nor the constant awareness of the punishing, if ultimately rewarding demands of altitude training, tempered Steward's dissatisfaction. The trainer is not content to watch from outside the ropes, preferring to skip about the ring, as close to the boxers as a referee. He told me afterwards he had scored two of the sparring rounds against Lewis, which he had never done before. 'I got on his ass at the end and he promised me I'd see a different Lennox tomorrow,' Steward said. 'I'm sure I will. That was just an off day, a lazy day. But he knows he has to be sharp and focused for Butler, that to re-establish himself he has to do more than beat this man. He has to do a number on Butler.'

Lewis acknowledged the imperative when we talked on a veranda overlooking the wide expanse of Big Bear Lake, with snow-capped peaks in the distance. Behind a thick growth of moustache and beard and the heavy shades he wore as protection against the hurtful light slanting off the water, his face showed a fitness that had been equally discernible on his body in the gym. Frank Maloney, the small, agreeable Londoner who manages the 29-year-old Lewis under the auspices of the boxer's principal financial backer, Panos Eliades, was there and agreed that an outstanding performance was made all the more essential by the WBC's decision to install Tyson immediately as their number one contender. The ruling contradicts a declaration at their convention in Spain last November that Butler–Lewis would be a final eliminator for McCall's title and that Tyson would not be ranked until he had had a fight. If necessary, Eliades will fund a legal battle over the right to the first challenge. But a swift demolition of Butler, who must be vulnerable after allowing the weight on a frame that stands short of 6ft to balloon to 18½ st for his most recent fight in March, would obviously strengthen their case.

'I've benefited from the real coaching Emanuel gives me,' Lewis said. 'When he talks it's reality, not bullshit. Before he came, I wasn't getting that quality of training. If I'm doing bad, I don't want to be told I'm great. He's got me shortening my punches, not winding up so much, and he's correcting my tendency to tilt over to my left and lose balance when I jab. Things feel good.' Manny Steward is convinced prolonged submersion in the educative turbulence of the Kronk will make things feel better still. 'He's a whole different fighter there, fast and mean and full of aggression. Basically he is a proud man who hates losing. That crazy-assed place brings out the real Lennox Lewis.'

Maybe the Arco Arena will be crazy-assed enough.

Don't Get Too Excited, Lennox

The Sunday Times, 21 May 1995

In a heavyweight division that pays various levels of homage to four world champions, a sense of perspective is difficult to establish and harder to maintain. The effect is like that of a hall of mirrors with cracked and dirty glass, a place where reputations are ballooned grotesquely for profit and just claims are attenuated, or conveniently disappear behind the grime.

No one, it goes without saying, is better equipped to manipulate this grubby confusion than Don King, and recently he has been back in full fairground barker's voice to inform Lennox Lewis, and every other fighter who is not on his list of clients, that he means to run the next lucrative phase of the heavyweight show. The calculated rant with which King denigrated Lewis's fifth-round victory over a blubber mountain of bad habits called Lionel Butler in California last weekend must be regarded as more relevant to future developments in the division than all the oily circumlocutions of José Sulaiman, the president of the World Boxing Council.

It was the WBC's championship that was battered out of Lewis's possession by a thunderous right-hand punch from Oliver McCall last September and a chance to recapture the title was supposed to be the reward for winning in Sacramento. Sulaiman says his organisation will not renege on their formal promise to recognise Lewis–Butler as a final eliminator for a match with the survivor of the fight McCall is due to have with Frank Bruno in July, but that declaration became hollow the moment he was pressed about the WBC's decision to install Mike Tyson as their number one contender as soon as the former undisputed champion completed his prison sentence for rape. Yes, said the trickiest president since Nixon, if Tyson chose to insist on the rights implicit in his status in the rankings, 'there could be a legal problem'. The fact that he and his cronies had created the problem with their double standards was something he took in his nimble stride.

As usual, any attempt to identify the realpolitik in Sulaiman's word-spinning was helped by reference to the even more verbose but sharper-edged utterances of King, for whom José has often been accused of being a lapdog. King began by stressing, in his Mr Sincerity mode, that he proposed to avoid any hypotheses involving boxing politics, since his statements on such matters were invariably 'misconstrued', especially when they concerned his friendship with Sulaiman. Then he proceeded to deliver a speech that could not have sounded more political if he had been wearing a campaign rosette.

'This fight was an example of what is going on in boxing, what is wrong with it,' he said. 'You had one man in the ring who couldn't fight because of his physical condition and another man who wouldn't fight. The people are not going to continue supporting the business unless some real excitement is restored to it, and the comeback of Mike Tyson is the one factor capable of doing that. He is deservedly ranked No 1. Lennox Lewis as the No. 1 contender would be a joke. Against Butler, he was out to lunch. He ran all night until Butler became so exhausted that he just sat down and got counted out. The crowd spoke to the issue quite candidly. They booed Lewis, and booed him and booed him.'

The finish, said King, wasn't a knockout at all. And he interpolated an English colloquialism to emphasise that he was merely trying to impart a little friendly enlightenment to his listeners from across the Atlantic: 'The bloke just sat down and couldn't get up. His legs were gone. It was remarkable, considering the terrible shape Butler was in when he got to the ring, that he was able to last five rounds. If you guys are going to make this out to be impressive, you'll have a hard job. You will be running a scam on your reading constituency.

'Faced with an opponent in Butler's condition, Mike Tyson would have destroyed him instantly. There is no one else who brings excitement to this business like Tyson does, who makes the adrenalin flow and gives you heart palpitations and makes the perspiration jump off your head when you just see him walk in the room. Once he starts fighting, he will deal with all of them. There will be no need for mandatory defences or purse offers. It will be a case of step in line, get served, and get on outa there.'

Allowing for the self-serving propaganda inseparable from everything said by a man who expects to earn millions from Tyson's comeback, there was plenty in that measured outburst to command attention. The first point of significance was, of course, the extent to which its aggressive, take-no-prisoners tone confirmed the natural assumption that the Tyson–King axis is resolved to be the decisive force in relation to the WBC title and (provided the ex-convict resumes ring action with most of his fighting powers in vigorous working order) in shaping the overall heavyweight picture. There had, undeniably, been a deterioration in his abilities before he went to jail and it is reasonable to imagine that now he will be still less like the frightener he was half a dozen years ago. But even a respectable impersonation of that old ferocity would make him a trump card in King's devious hands.

A second worthwhile point in the diatribe was the underlining of the need to judge what Lewis achieved in Sacramento in the context of Butler's abysmal lack of fitness. Obviously King's comments on that issue were distorted by excess born of naked prejudice, but those of us with warmer feelings for Lewis have an obligation to keep sight of the reality that he was meeting somebody whose body was shameful testament to a destructively undisciplined way of life. Butler has a record of drug abuse and two interviewers who found themselves uncomfortably close to him in the week preceding the fight told me they were convinced they smelled alcohol on his breath.

Emanuel Steward, Lewis's trainer, said in the aftermath of victory that the total absence of any hint of an orthodox commitment to training on Butler's part had made it difficult to predict how he would behave when he came off the stool at the opening bell. 'You don't know what to expect from a guy like that,' Steward said. 'You don't know if, maybe, he was drinking before the fight.'

What Lewis knew he should not anticipate was anything resembling athletic fluency or stamina. Afterwards, some who were eager to applaud the winner's work dwelt on the threat Butler, a heavy-handed puncher who had won his previous 17 fights inside the distance, presented for a round or two. It is true that he was fleetingly dangerous but only in the way that any large, belligerent man in a bar might be dangerous. He was certainly large enough, but mainly in the wrong places. Though standing a touch short of 6 ft, he weighed over 18 st and – in common with his 19 st 4 lb fellow American Ray Evans, who had crumbled in front of Frank Bruno in Glasgow a few hours earlier – demonstrated that sometimes the bigger they are the quicker they fall.

Confronted by Butler and Evans, officials may have been tempted to throw away the scales and drive them on to a weighbridge. There was justification for King's assertion that Lewis, who was himself 10 lb heavier than for any of his previous fights but had spread the extra weight acceptably over his huge physique, took too long to do the demolition job. However, criticism must be tempered by awareness that the ex-champion had to conquer his own demons before he could concentrate on Butler. The anxieties left by the trauma of the McCall defeat showed briefly but vividly in his face when he was caught by a long, overhand right in the first round, and his subsequent insistence that he had not been troubled by the blow was the kind of denial that would have intrigued a psychiatrist.

Lewis's tendency in those first three minutes to respond to Butler's lunges with hasty, sprawling retreats, during which his feet occasionally became entangled and his arms were employed in frantic grabbing and smothering tactics, was probably the most worrying aspect of the short encounter from his point of view. Against a more organised assault, such dishevelment would have been costly.

But, inevitably, the lumbering Butler was soon running short of both breath and appetite for the fray. As the American degenerated into a spiritless, almost stationary target, Lewis's reluctance to put him out of his misery brought chants of 'Bullshit' from the crowd. More constructive shouts were coming from Steward, who had counselled his man to keep the first two or three rounds undramatic by using reach and movement to imprison Butler in 'a zone' where he could be hit but would not have the opportunity to generate leverage for his own punches. Now that the adversary had become a victim, the trainer felt Lewis was too coy. With his right hand cocked, he was circling Butler like a bomb-disposal officer approaching a suspect dustbin. But, in boxing terms, Butler was empty. 'Let it go, let it go,' Steward urged repeatedly, and Lewis eventually began to release his right.

When he jumped it into Butler's head at the start of the fifth, hurling the recipient backwards for an eight count, hostilities were effectively over. The conclusion, near the end of the round, was precipitated by a decent but unspectacular right cross. It encouraged Butler to subside towards the bottom two ropes like a fat man sinking into a deep armchair, and two more looping, upward rights strengthened his conviction that he had endured enough.

Quite a few observers were persuaded that in the quarter of an hour of action Lewis had revealed substantial improvements attributable to his recently formed alliance with Manny Steward. That reaction seemed to me to owe more to wishful thinking than hard evidence. Once the rapid draining away of Butler's scant reserves of energy gave Lewis the luxury of doing as he liked, he apparently did remember at leisure some of Steward's teaching. The trajectory of his punches was sensibly shortened and he sought to throw them in combinations rather than relying on isolated blasts with the right hand. But in that first round, when Butler still carried the semblance of a threat, such positive developments were undetectable amid alarming signs of a familiar vulnerability.

What matters, however, is that he has coped with the problems of his return to the wars. No doubt he *will* improve under Steward's tutelage. His main worry may be that the WBC will let him continue his education in the wilderness.

Tyson Tests His Drawing Power

The Sunday Times, 13 August 1995

When Peter McNeeley is labelled 'The Irish Hurricane' it is proof that reality, which is never an assertive presence in Las Vegas, has been run right out of town. There is an acid irony in the publicity men's nonsense since McNeeley has been cheaply hired to be blown away.

If the 26-year-old from Boston stays in front of Mike Tyson for more than a minute or two in the ring at the MGM Grand Hotel on Saturday night, he will become an embarrassing blemish on an occasion that is meant to be about as competitive as a ticker-tape parade. What is planned is not a fight but an elaborate festival of rehabilitation, complete with an assembly line of celebrities and the theatrical effects of a rock concert – a spectacular relaunching of a fighting career that once seethed with excitement and money but must now recover from the pulverising impact of a rape conviction and the prison sentence it brought. Already the money is pouring back but if it is to swell into the predicted flood, Tyson must re-enter the public imagination on Saturday as the dramatic destroyer of old.

That is why McNeeley's credentials have been thoroughly vetted to ensure that the essence of his contribution to the party will be brevity. During less than four years as a professional, he has won 36 of 37 fights, with 30 stoppages, and has not allowed any of his last dozen engagements to go beyond the second round. However, when names are attached to those statistics, a truer perspective emerges: Lopez McGee, Wayne Perdue, Quinton Hardy, and so on, a list of characters who could not embody obscurity more convincingly if they were called John Doe. Hurricane? A zephyr would have flattened that lot.

All but seven of McNeeley's fights have taken place in his native Massachusetts, so it is not surprising that first-hand witnesses of his work are hard to find. But the evidence of a few brief film clips is sufficient to confirm that his attacking method has slightly less subtlety than a bayonet charge. 'Controlled fury, technical brawling' is his own description of his approach to the job. Such eagerness to rush into the cannon's mouth may enliven the seconds after the opening bell but, unless Tyson's artillery has been severely rusted by his three years in jail (and more than four out of the ring), the rashness should bring early destruction.

The real test here is not of Tyson's fighting capacities but of his post-prison earning power, particularly through pay-per-view television. That medium is opening up new horizons of plunder for professional boxing. Increasingly condemned as an anachronism too primitive to be tolerated in civilised society, the fight business is nevertheless approaching the millennium with a swaggering demonstration that its commercial vigour is undiminished. It is the dinosaur that adapted, effortlessly modifying its rich traditions of larcenous ingenuity to suit the electronic age.

No one is ready to dismiss out of hand the claims of Don King and his promotional associates that Tyson–McNeeley will break all records for sales of a boxing event on pay-per-view. The best return hitherto was achieved when Evander Holyfield beat George Foreman in Atlantic City in 1991, attracting 1.36 million armchair customers at an average cost of rather more than $35 to produce a gross take of $48.9 million. In talking confidently of pulling in 1.5 million buyers this time, King is reassured by the fact that the number of sets that can be reached by his signal is substantially greater than was the case four years ago.

Apparently reasonable estimates say the pool of potential customers across America, what the jargon of the trade calls 'the universe of addressable systems', may have grown by nearly 50 per cent since 1991, to around 24 million. It is a figure that obviously makes the 1.5 million sales target more attainable and, with the average price of connection for next weekend's show boosted close to $45, a gross of almost $60 million may not be outrageously optimistic. Even if the regional cable operators who do the connecting get the 50 per cent of that booty they regard as their due – rather than the 30 per cent originally proposed by Showtime Event Television, the company responsible for transmission – there should be unanimous satisfaction.

How much Tyson personally will gain from all this is a mystery the shrewdest outsiders are unable to penetrate. The series of deals he and his two managers, John Horne and Rory Holloway, have negotiated with King, Showtime and the MGM Grand is the subject of much speculation but, apart from the fact that the hotel has him contracted for six fights, no solid information has been released. It has been postulated, perhaps wildly, that when signing-up fees and other fancy inducements go into the pot, completion of Saturday's assignment will leave him $35 million ahead of the game. There are certainly immense fortunes to come, especially if the 17,000 spectators who are expected to fill the Grand Garden at the MGM, and the millions around the world who will watch a telecast, live or delayed, are thrilled by what they see.

If the star's wages are secret, the bit-player's are common knowledge. McNeeley is being paid $700,000 for the fight and nothing for training expenses, a deprivation that has obliged him to settle for one sparring partner. In spite of the modesty of his purse, he has been publicising the promotion with gusto, which sometimes makes him sound like a man using a loud hailer to attract a crowd to his own funeral. 'I am going to wrap Mike Tyson in a cocoon of horror,' he declared at a press conference in Los Angeles last week, treating us to a New England accent complicated by a nasal problem which will eventually require surgery. In his seat a few feet away, Tyson smiled broadly, as if contemplating operating procedures of a cruder kind. Asked if he would use McNeeley for an extended workout or go for a quick win, he smiled again at the naïvety of the question. 'I'll do my thing,' he said. 'You know what I do.'

Well, we know what he did at his best, which was deliver punches of frightening power in swift, calculated combinations while moving his head and shoulders in rolling, weaving patterns that made him deceptively elusive to opponents brave enough to counter-attack. But before his imprisonment he showed alarming signs of having lost his fire and his discipline (not only in Tokyo, when James 'Buster' Douglas inflicted the one defeat of his 42-fight career, but in two subsequent meetings with Donovan 'Razor' Ruddock). He became ponderous, almost static, abandoning the sequences of blows he had thrown in a blur for laboured attempts to load up for single, murderous shots. Inevitably, there was a suspicion that the extraordinary precocity which saw him claim a world title as a boy-ogre of 20, and made him undisputed champion nine months later, might carry the penalty of premature burn-out for a rather squat body blatantly abused by his rampaging social life.

As he comes back at the age of 29, he has the good fortune to find a heavyweight division devoid of truly outstanding performers, one bearing no resemblance to the concentration of threatening excellence that greeted Muhammad Ali when he returned following the three-and-a-half-year exile imposed for his refusal to be drafted into the US armed forces. But if Tyson were to exhibit the weaknesses manifest when he was last seen as a fighter, even today's leading heavyweights might be more than he could handle.

Eddie Futch, who turned 84 the other day but is in no danger of losing the title of the wisest man in boxing, has no doubt about the central question Tyson must answer. 'He must prove that the root of his effectiveness is still there, and that means his quickness,' Futch said.

'What made him so effective was the speed with which he delivered his power. He had the quickest delivery of any hard puncher since Joe Louis. There have been harder hitters, Earnie Shavers and Sonny Liston to name two. What set him apart was his speed. We must wait and see if he is still capable of the same lightning-fast delivery.'

Here it must be said that, on the limited evidence of his appearance in shirt and tie at the LA press conference, he looks well enough to make his assertions of physical and mental rejuvenation believable. His face is planed to leanness behind thin lines of moustache and beard and it has a glow of fitness that had deserted it by 1991. Under the clothes, his body gave an impression of hardness and of a bulk in astonishing contrast to the sense of diminution conveyed when he left jail. A carefully devised diet and programme of conditioning are credited with the rapid build-up of muscle. It must be quite a regimen.

Presumably his conversion to Islam has helped to rid his life of its tendency towards destructive chaos. Jay Bright, who was in Tyson's corner for seven fights before the fateful court case in Indiana and has just been appointed principal trainer for the comeback, said on Thursday: 'When Mike started to get his priorities wrong, letting people drag him here and drag him there, we had to track him down to get him to work. Now he is waiting with his bags packed, ready to go to the gym, getting us there early.' Once in the gym, according to Bright, he has been so brutal with a succession of sparring partners that many have fled to nurse their wounds.

The psychological blows Tyson has taken lately seem to have left something deeper than bruising, perhaps incipient paranoia. He talks darkly of forearming himself against betrayal and it is significant that Bright, Horne and Holloway are all friends from happier years in the home of the late Cus D'Amato, his guardian and boxing guru. Bright's lack of experience at his present job, and his habit of invoking the ghost of D'Amato in a manner more appropriate to a medium than a corner-man, raises questions about his ability to be an authoritative mentor. But he should be under no strain on Saturday.

Peter McNeeley's father, Tom, was knocked down ten times when he challenged for Floyd Patterson's world heavyweight title in 1961. The son's execution should be quicker and cleaner.

The Golden Fleece

The Sunday Times, 27 August 1995

If the heavyweight division has always been the Klondike of professional boxing, pay-per-view television has opened up the mother-lode. You might say it offers riches beyond the dreams of avarice, were it not for the fact that the avarice of the men who run the most meretricious enterprise in sport is constantly expanding towards infinity. They are encouraged by the knowledge that followers of the hardest game have invariably been a soft touch. In all the wide realm of suckerdom, there is no gullibility more gluttonous than that of boxing fans, and those who complain about being short-changed over the Mike Tyson–Peter McNeeley fiasco in Las Vegas last weekend sound like someone bemoaning the lack of true love in a whorehouse. Did such people actually imagine that the expenditure of $1,500 on a ringside seat, or up to $50 for a cable connection with happenings at the MGM Grand Hotel, would entitle them to see a fight? If they did they should lie down quietly on a couch and await the arrival of men in white coats.

It is more plausible that many of them paid up in the hope of witnessing a ritual slaughter and felt cheated when McNeeley was taken into protective custody by his manager halfway through the first round. Others presumably decided that, given the morbid momentousness lent to the occasion by Tyson's return to the ring after three years in an Indiana prison, they wanted to be part of history. That group had their wish, for the 89-second farce did represent a kind of watershed in the annals of boxing's electronic junk-trade. This was a looting exercise distinguished not only by its scale but by the matter-of-factness of its execution. Don King, as promoter, made a few perfunctory noises in justification of McNeeley's involvement but in general he and the Tyson camp behaved as if it were perfectly natural that the former world champion – who currently holds no title and whose previous public performance had been a sluggishly unimpressive victory more than four years ago over Donovan 'Razor' Ruddock, a Canadian who has since spent much of his ring-time on the horizontal – should earn $25–30 million for loosening up against an opponent with a record so contrived that it suggested he had a mortician as matchmaker. And the sobering truth is that these perpetrators of the financial coup had every right to regard the public as sheep for the fleecing, and to be confident that the rapidly developing pay-per-view market would bring unprecedented efficiency to the shearing process.

Perhaps the only significance of that brief, depressing episode in Las Vegas was as a demonstration of how TV has relieved King and his ilk of even the obligation to work at conning their customers. Out there in tellyland, there is a multitude whose criteria have been drained of all rigour by a ceaseless bombardment with the cheapest of showbiz values. How else could we explain the extraordinary audience of 13.1 million drawn to ITV when Chris Eubank, a fighter who learned early that posturing was more profitable than punching, laboured to a points win against Graciano Rocchigiani in Berlin in February 1994? Those viewers were able to watch that banal exhibition without adding to their licence fee and it is obvious that only a minority of them switched on because of a genuine interest in boxing. Most were attracted to Eubank as a 'turn', a figure who might have fitted as readily into ITV's light entertainment schedule as into their sports programming. Anyone asked to pay heavily for the privilege of access to a specific transmission will clearly be more choosy. But Tyson–McNeeley dramatically confirmed earlier indications that in the case of boxing it is not necessary to have the promise of anything resembling competitive action to generate lavish revenue from pay-per-view. Here, too, the showbiz factor is increasingly relevant and non-fights can be successfully peddled as 'events'.

The technique has never been as extravagantly applied as it was with this dubious collision in the desert. Overselling blatant mismatches is, of course, an ancient tradition in the fight business, especially at heavyweight. W.C. Fields should be the patron saint of promoters, who operate on the principle that giving suckers an even break leads them into bad habits, like keeping their money in their pockets. But in the past most of the major plundering was done by exploiting a world title, with unthreatening contenders being unearthed and promptly reburied for the benefit of the champion's (or his handlers') bank balance. That was the pattern with Joe Louis's bum-of-the-month campaign, and several subsequent champions, notably Floyd Patterson, favoured the same routine. However, one important distinction to be made between then and now is that the ploy had at least a whiff of validity when the man concerned could claim undisputed supremacy in the heavyweight division. Another is that the sums being looted were scarcely within a telephone number of Tyson's purse, even if we allow for the changes in the worth of money across the decades.

Tyson's present lack of a title must, admittedly, be seen as a technicality, considering the shortcomings of the assorted scufflers who are in possession of the principal belts or about to fight for them. Nevertheless, screwing at least $25 million out of his first comeback engagement against a carefully selected victim was an outrageous triumph of hucksterism that bodes ill for the prospects of seeing him excitingly tested in the near future. When John Horne, who manages Tyson in partnership with Rory Holloway, says that they will not be pressured into deviating from their calculated agenda, we can assume that their immediate strategy will concentrate on maximising returns while minimising risks. They could implement such a policy and still be challenging for a championship in, perhaps, Tyson's third fight, so miserable is the standard of competition they will encounter. Meanwhile, they should be happy to find themselves armed with compelling evidence that, in an age when the box shapes boxing, there are fortunes to be had from so-called contests that are as far removed from the realities of conflict as the choreographed absurdities of professional wrestling.

It was difficult in Vegas to hold at bay a feeling of having been plunged into the fantasy world of the grapplers. McNeeley seemed to have borrowed extensively from them and one must hope that his tongue was as firmly in the cheek as theirs usually are. One of the reliable badges of identification among those muscled rhetoricians is a hoarseness brought on by their habit of expending more energy on shouting about what they will do than on actually doing it. McNeeley put his voice similarly at hazard and much of what he bellowed, such as his vow that he would 'wrap Tyson in a cocoon of horror', was straight out of their fevered scripts. To his credit, he did at least mount a charge when the opening bell sounded. Plainly, he had less chance of success than the Light Brigade and it was no stunning shock when he landed on his backside within a few seconds. Observers who saw Tyson as being worryingly disconcerted by the Bostonian's initial attempt to live up to his improbable nickname, 'The Irish Hurricane', were searching for form pointers where none existed. Good fighters far less rusty than Tyson would have been temporarily inconvenienced by such a headlong rush, and his decision to batter rather than finesse his way out of the neutral corner in which he had been pinned was not merely sensible but unavoidable. When he had risen after the first, comparatively unhurtful knockdown, McNeeley headed away from Tyson with the briskness of a jogger who was ready for his orange juice. But the pursuer caught up with his prey on the other side of the ring and began winging punches to the head. Tyson's attack climaxed with two undevastating left hooks and a far more telling right uppercut. The unbalancing effect of that blow was compounded when Tyson followed up by swinging his right arm behind his opponent's head and spinning him towards the ropes, where he fell in a heap. Once upright again, McNeeley stumbled sideways against the ropes but looked sufficiently in control to justify the conviction of the referee, Mills Lane, that he was able to continue. It was then that Vinny Vecchione, McNeeley's manager, deprived the referee of any discretion in the matter by jumping into the ring and forcing Lane to disqualify his man. Generous interpretations have recognised an admirable compassion in Vecchione's conduct. But where was that compassion when he signed for the match? Did he think Tyson *wasn't* going to hit McNeeley on the head? My own opinion is that his intervention fully warranted the inquiry ordered by the Nevada State Athletic Commission and the withholding of his substantial percentage of McNeeley's purse pending its findings. No one would wish to fault a corner-man for being protective but, remembering the money Vecchione was due to collect, it is hard to avoid thinking that his conscience made sure it wasn't roused too early.

If the architects of the great comeback adhere to preliminary plans for having Buster Mathis Junior as the next opponent, that assignment, too, is likely to be both undemanding for Tyson and unenlightening for students of his progress. Mathis has some boxing skills but he hits so lightly that if he battered on your door you wouldn't be sure to hear him. Tyson would not have to rediscover much of his old ferocity to make that evening a short one. At 29, his body looks as formidable as it ever did. Against McNeeley, he weighed 15 st 10 lb and every ounce was impressive. Superficially, his attitude is equally intimidating, conveying the sense that the paranoid resentments apparently festering in his mind can be channelled outwards into destructive hostility. But such signs could be misleading. Unless his conversion to Islam gives him lasting discipline, he may have trouble sustaining a fierce edge through more than a handful of fights and the slackness that was eroding his gifts before incarceration may return. For the present, he remains an enigma, which does nothing to hurt his marketability.

So who can ask him the kind of serious questions that will tell us whether or not his ogreish streak survives? Surely not Bruce Seldon, the WBA champion, who encapsulates everything that is unconvincing about heavyweight boxing today. Definitely not George Foreman, America's favourite war memorial. And could anyone fancy the winner of Saturday's Wembley fight in which Tyson's former sparring partner, Oliver McCall, defends his WBC title against Frank Bruno? Evander Holyfield, Lennox Lewis and Riddick Bowe have better qualifications. But Holyfield, though his iron resolve must be respected, has never been a true heavyweight and he is battle-worn. Lewis's size and power are too often neutralised by amateurishness. Bowe has the equipment to beat Tyson but the tools he most likes using are his knife and fork. He tends to eat himself out of condition. Mike Tyson could hardly have invented a more vulnerable bunch of rivals.

Bruno the World Champ

The Sunday Times, 3 September 1995

Even Bobby Charlton has never produced a happier sound at Wembley Stadium than the roar that swept across the ground for Frank Bruno last night as he buried the frustrations of a lifetime with a points victory which, at long last, made him a heavyweight champion of the world.

As Oliver McCall, the defending WBC champion from Chicago, barged and punched the reeling, grappling Bruno around the ring in the

12th and final round, fears grew that the 33-year-old Londoner's fourth challenge for the big prize would end in much the same mixture of suffering and failure as the previous three. But a combination of his own courage and McCall's ineptitude kept him upright on his unsteady legs until the last bell sounded – and left the judges with no alternative but to recognise the superiority he had established in earlier rounds.

The Australian official, Malcolm Bulner, made Bruno the winner by 115 points to 113 and the other two judges, Newton Campos from Brazil and Ray Solis from Mexico, were rather more emphatic in scoring the fight identically at 117–111 for the British challenger. My own card showed the margin of victory somewhere between those two assessments, but certainly there could not be a sliver of doubt about Bruno's right to talk happily of realising his dream.

As a blizzard of confetti burst above the ring and the winner's corner-men went into rehearsal for a party that is sure to be a marathon, it seemed churlish to be over-analytical about the quality of the contest that had delivered the triumph. But the simple truth is that Bruno's fortunes changed because of the dramatic difference in the quality of company he was keeping in this title fight compared with those he lost to Tim Witherspoon in 1986, Mike Tyson in 1989 and Lennox Lewis in 1993. McCall was exposed here as nothing more than a sparring partner who got lucky.

His huge surge of luck came on the night last September when he transcended everything he had done before by throwing one murderous right-hand punch that blasted Lennox Lewis away from his WBC crown. That was along the road at Wembley Arena, but in the Stadium last night he gave barely a glimpse of the menace he had borne in on Lewis. It is true that McCall totally dominated the last two rounds, but his supremacy in those six minutes owed as much to the notorious deficiencies of his opponent's stamina as to his own raising of momentum. Throughout that period the deep current of emotional support that ran through the crowd of about 30,000 was contaminated by nervous suspicions that victory would be battered from the national hero's grasp at the last gasp.

There was nothing surprising about the early lead Bruno had established with competent use of his long, jolting left jab, an occasional sharp left hook off that jab and clubbing right crosses. Against better men than McCall he has been able to set such a pattern for a number of rounds, but always there has been the justified dread of an abrupt decline in the middle of the fight and a wilting into helplessness as a better stayer from the other corner applied pressure.

But in this instance no real pressure was generated by McCall until it was far too late. He had a substantial bruise under his left eye, and in spite of his attempts to affect a dismissive smile when hurt, he looked increasingly troubled and short of ideas through fully three-quarters of the fight. Bruno, at 6 ft 3 in, is appreciably taller than the American, and at nearly 17 st 10 lb almost a stone heavier, and he was the dominating physical presence in that period. His familiar shortcomings, an intrinsic lack of spontaneity and fluency, were blatant enough, but McCall's slow-pulsed and ponderous responses made such defects unimportant. The champion was close to being an insult to his status, and only intermittently – notably in the fourth round, which he won clearly – did he emerge from brawling mediocrity to jab decently with his left hand and follow with some fairly methodical hooking. He brought blood from Bruno's mouth in that round and it continued to brighten the challenger's lips for the rest of the contest, but it was a false beacon of hope for McCall.

The two principal impressions as the untidy conflict wore on, often with less grace than might be found in a wrestling bout, was that its quality was dire, but that any credit due had to go to Bruno. He did manage some remarkably lively, almost witty contributions, such as a right uppercut in the tenth which was so trickily surprising that it almost looked playful. Less entertaining were his ill-advised efforts to operate as a southpaw. What such peculiarities revealed more than anything else was the waning of his energy and he had to be grateful that he had an extremely healthy lead by the time the 11th round began. Soon he was unable to offer even a jab to discourage McCall as the champion, belatedly galvanised by his corner's exhortations and the clear opportunities in front of him, came boring in. However, the only effect of McCall's overdue aggression was to create a dramatic finish and add to the satisfaction of by far the greatest night in the 13½ years and 44 fights of Frank Bruno's career.

Almost immediately, almost inevitably, there was talk of putting the big man in with Mike Tyson, his fifth-round conqueror of six years ago. They tell us it will be in London a year from now. They say many things in boxing. What they can no longer say is that Frank Bruno is not a champion.

Hard Road to Hopesville

The Sunday Times, 1 October 1995

There was never any great temptation to associate the Main Street Gym in downtown Tulsa with leotards and aerobics classes, least of all on the day last week when a rat the size of a small dog loped across the concrete floor for the full width of the back wall before making a leisurely exit at a far corner of the big, shabby warehouse of a room.

If the four-legged visitor hoped to cause a stir, he should have waited until somebody other than Tommy Morrison was the main tenant of the gym. In his 26 years, Morrison has seen too much of the rough side of life to be disconcerted by a passing rodent. He merely paused to make an

Oklahoma country boy's joke about the dimensions of the creature ('It's either a rat or a possum') and continued with our conversation. Morrison is due to meet Lennox Lewis in Atlantic City on Saturday in what might be seen as a fight for the heavyweight championship of Hopesville. They were scheduled to collide nearly two years ago for huge purses and the WBC title then held by Lewis. But Morrison's credibility was blown away in a first-round loss to Michael Bentt (soon to disappear from the picture because of the health problems that emerged after he was badly beaten by Herbie Hide) and Lewis's fortunes plummeted, too, as a result of one big right hand from Oliver McCall.

Frank Bruno has since taken the WBC belt from McCall and informed whispers suggest that Mike Tyson, the economic sun of the heavyweight division, may choose to warm Bruno with a title challenge while leaving the apparently superior Lewis out in the cold. If, as must be expected, Tyson dispossessed Bruno, Don King's cosy relationship with José Sulaiman, the WBC president, would presumably ensure Tyson the standard year of voluntary engagements before he had to face a mandatory defence. All the earlier promises of championship involvement Sulaiman made to Lewis might then prove unenforceable. It is a predicament that reminds the former Olympic gold medallist of how much was lost when his failure to shed his amateur ways permitted the severely limited McCall to land a punch he may never reproduce.

As Morrison wistfully acknowledged in Tulsa, he has a double dose of such regrets. Whereas Lewis's career figures show one defeat in 28 fights, his include two setbacks so brutal that they outweigh the 46 wins and one draw which make up the rest of his record. He had been a professional for less than three years but had 29 victories to his credit when an attempt to capture the WBO title from Ray Mercer in October 1991, produced an extraordinary torrent of mayhem. 'I beat the hell out of him for four rounds but when I found he was still standing I didn't know what to do,' Morrison told me. 'I was a one-dimensional fighter, used to seeing people go down from my heavy shots. I didn't know how to relax and take a breather and when he caught me on the ropes in the fifth I was gone. The referee should have stopped it earlier than he did. I took a bunch of punches I shouldn't have. After that, a lot of guys would have been gun-shy, but I never was.'

He felt he had learned from the savage experience as a successful comeback climaxed in the winning of the WBO crown from George Foreman. Having signed to fight Lewis for $7.5 million, he sought to sharpen up by defending against Bentt. His headlong assault from the bell looked certain to abbreviate the action but, in a moment of uncharacteristic inspiration, Bentt came off the ropes to throw a perfect right that put Morrison down. 'I got up and went right back at him without having my legs under me,' the loser recalled in the Main Street Gym. He went down twice more, forcing the referee to stop the fight.

Suddenly several men who had been eager to identify with his earning power as the latest White Hope, notably Bill Cayton, who combined with the late Jim Jacobs to plan the young Tyson's climb to the heavyweight championship, were heading for the horizon – and Morrison, not for the first time, was heading for the bars and nightclubs of Kansas City, Missouri, committing himself to a monumental binge that might have become a slide to permanent oblivion but for the intervention of Tom Virgets.

Virgets, who is in his early forties, is probably the most highly educated trainer in the fight business, with a doctorate in exercise physiology to reinforce the lessons absorbed while being raised in a New Orleans boxing family. Since he left his previous career as boxing coach and athletics director at military establishments and universities to begin working full time with Morrison in 1990, Virgets has considered it politic to spend the bulk of every year under the same roof as the wayward fighter, settling for brief sojourns at home in Carrollton, Georgia, with his wife and three children. He and Morrison have no contract but the bond between them has been put at risk only when the younger man has gone on the rampage with a large cast of hangers-on Virgets describes as 'an entourage of assholes'.

Morrison says his breeding (his mother, Flossie, is a full-blooded American Indian and his father is of Irish stock, with a distant link to John Wayne) has given him a dual penchant for fighting and drinking. With a strong, slightly forbidding face and an impressive array of muscles spread over a 6 ft 2 in physique which weighs a few pounds more than 16 st when honed to fitness, he is also, according to Virgets, 'the world's greatest bimbo-magnet' and has seldom shown any sign of regretting it.

'There has never been a problem with Tommy while in training,' Virgets said. 'The trouble has been that the day after a fight Tommy would start partying and for maybe six weeks – after the Bentt fiasco it was more like four or five months – there wouldn't be a day when he wasn't going at it, when he would be in bed before sun-up. Then, when I finally persuaded him to come back to work, he would be carrying a load of guilt. He's the most guilt-prone person I know. And it would turn him sour in the gym. He would be there physically but not in spirit, more or less saying: "All right, I'm here, now you train me."

'Tommy desperately wants to be a good guy but he has yet to find out who he really is. When he is not working he doesn't know what to do with himself and, since he can't stand being alone, he is vulnerable to the assholes. That's why I try to minimise the idle time between fights. He has stopped charging around as he once did, but he still drinks too much and he can't handle alcohol. Going back recently to his family's religion – they are Seventh Day Adventists – is a stabilising influence, but he is still battling a lot of demons.'

That is hardly surprising. Morrison's life story resembles a particularly lurid country and western lyric, with elements of a Raymond Carver short story thrown in. He was born in Gravette, Arkansas, and when his parents' divorce caused his mother to move him and his brother and sister across the border into Oklahoma it wasn't much of a journey, in terms of miles or social conditions. There have been fighters on his father's side for five generations and the grandfather had gone 30 fights unbeaten and was lined up to meet Homicide Henry Armstrong when, perhaps wisely, he made an abrupt switch to preaching. 'He is 83 years old but in fantastic shape,' Morrison reported fondly. 'He jumps up and down on a miniature trampoline every day and keeps saying he could still take me.'

For as long as the Morrisons have been boxers, his mother's clan have been turning out nurses. Flossie is obviously not a squeamish nurse. When Tommy was about ten years old, she took a needle and some thread and used an old Indian technique to fashion a crude tattoo of a pair of boxing gloves on his upper left arm. It reflected an active interest in the ring, one he reckons brought him 242 bouts as a juvenile amateur (and just 20 losses) between the ages of seven and 13. By the time another volunteer artist superimposed the head of a cougar on the boxing gloves, so that today there are conspicuous remnants of the laces between the big cat's eyes, Morrison had lived through a year of amazing experiences away from home.

'When I was 13, I moved out on my own and I got a job in construction over in the western part of the state, in the Oklahoma panhandle near the Texas line. One day the Toughman circuit rolled into town, setting up rough-and-ready fights for money. The minimum age was supposed to be 21 but I had a fake driver's licence I got through my sister's boyfriend, and the organisers didn't care so long as their butt was covered. It was fraud, but we did the same thing to get away with under-age drinking. Me and three or four of my friends would go into a bar and we would all be the same person. We'd have different pictures on the licences but they'd all be issued in the same name.

'I got $300 for winning that first Toughman tournament as a 13-year-old. It involved fighting three times. Between then and when I graduated from high school (a year later than I should have done because of my time on the road) I'd had 60 Toughman contests and lost just one. It was rugged but I could handle most of those guys comfortably, even the ones that weren't half drunk. There was no biting or kicking but you could get away with elbowing, lacing and head-butting, and I was pretty good at that stuff if it was needed. Mainly I outboxed them and even as a kid I had power, especially with the natural left hook that has always been my best weapon. I had always done plenty of fighting back home in Jay, Oklahoma, which has only 2,300 people but wasn't too quiet. I was never a bully but if somebody wanted to fight it didn't take a lot to get me interested. My older brother Tim and I had a reputation but I think it was a good one. When we walked into a bar-room everybody's attitude kind of calmed down a little bit.'

Tranquillity was not a noticeable theme of Morrison's time at school, where sport alone held his attention. Finding his baseball ambitions thwarted by a coach who objected to his wildness, he laid hands on some gasoline and went off to the school stadium to scorch a rude message on the grass. 'But the wind picked up and the whole sonofabitch caught fire and the stadium burned down,' he said. 'They knew I did it but they couldn't prove it.'

'That's why I've never ordered him out of the gym,' Virgets said, adding more seriously that Morrison had talked of going back and building a new baseball stadium in Jay, which is close to the home he now shares with his girlfriend, Dawn. It was the morning after the day of the rat and the fighter was preparing for a session in a different, more sedate gym, followed by a flight to Kansas City for an appointment with a chiropractor. Since his youth he has had an alarming susceptibility to injuries. As an outstanding high-school football player, he had four leg operations, including the total reconstruction of one knee, yet remained sufficiently effective to be offered a college scholarship.

He was in the midst of considering it when, urged on by his mother, he entered the Kansas City Golden Gloves tournament. That was the start of an outrageously compressed career as a senior amateur. Within three months, he swept all the way to the final trials for the 1988 Olympics, fatefully losing to Ray Mercer, who was to collect the gold medal in Seoul. After that run, turning professional was almost inevitable and at the age of 19 he stepped on to a plane for the first time, flew to New York and made his paid debut in Madison Square Garden. Soon peroxide was altering the dirty fair colouring of his hair and a brown-eyed golden boy was on his way. There was genuine ability for his pitchmen to promote, above all the exceptional speed of his hands and the blasting authority of that left hook. But his new trade was soon taking its toll of his bones and sinews and he was showing a persistent aptitude for damaging his image. He has had several fractures of both hands, had his jaw broken, required an operation to relieve pressure on his calf muscles and, since the sixth-round stoppage of Donovan 'Razor' Ruddock, has had further surgery to cure a problem in his right shoulder.

Along the way, he has fathered two sons, six-year-old Trey and five-year-old Mackenzie, by different mothers, taken a major role in *Rocky V* and set a few long-distance carousing records. He is aware that his limousine tours of the entertainment centres exposed him to predators. 'For a while there, if I farted in an elevator somebody was ready to sue me. But I've come through pretty much unscathed.' That is true, although a pushing incident in an Iowa restaurant cost him $40,000 in an out-of-court settlement.

Virgets estimates that Morrison is 'maybe $800,000 to the good and should have a couple of million after Lewis'. Can he qualify for a Tyson jackpot? 'It depends on whether he stays low and fights from his crouch.

According to the level of his hips, he goes from being an exceptional fighter to being less than mediocre. With low hips, he murders people to the body and is positioned to deliver the killing head punches. High, he doesn't amount to much. My biggest dread is the part of the fight around the fifth round, when Tommy remembers Mercer and looks for fatigue. He has never fought a good fifth round in his life.' Morrison, who appeared fit enough but often technically uncertain in training, doubts Lewis's resolution. A line of moustache and beard, and single dangling earring, give the country boy a piratical aspect these days, but he did not bother to look bloodthirsty when he said: 'I question Lewis's balls. I don't think he is mentally a tough person.'

What no one can deny is that Lewis is a very large person, and his physical scope, especially the length of arm that grants him the octopus option, may neutralise Morrison's early threat. Lewis is a clear favourite to win in the ring. If the fight were moved to the Irish pub along the boardwalk, the odds would have to be adjusted.

'I'm Ready to Rumble'

The Sunday Times, 10 December 1995

Talking with Mike Tyson, listening to that light, slightly lisping voice convey a sense of confidence bordering on serenity, makes it impossible to believe that his next opponent can be anything but the merest punctuation mark in the story of the most lucrative comeback in the history of boxing. Buster Mathis Jr is unbeaten after 22 fights, but he is a heavyweight with a silhouette disturbingly similar to that of Humpty Dumpty. Come Saturday night at the Spectrum in Philadelphia, he will have much the same prospects of avoiding a fall.

He may not break apart, but he has every chance of sagging to the floor like a sack of marshmallows. How long that process takes will depend on the quality of his own spirit and the sharpness of Tyson's timing. But the limitations of Mathis's physique, and the technical shortcomings exposed by the abuses he suffered during an appalling session of sparring on Thursday, suggest he will be lucky to survive more than a round or two. Mathis represents the softest of soft targets and if Tyson lingers over the easy task of demolition he will provide unexpected encouragement for Frank Bruno, who is due to defend the WBC title against the former undisputed champion on 16 March. Big Frank should not hold his breath waiting for such a licence to be optimistic.

While Mathis has been showing a pathetic vulnerability to his sparmates, Tyson has been brutal with the hired help in his training camp. Reports that he has forced as many as 15 sparring partners to slink off in search of more congenial employment may contain as much hyperbole as is standard in the fight business. There is, however, no need for his PR team to elaborate on the impression made by his appearance. The taut lines of his face, accentuated by a neat moustache and small beard, combine with the trim condition of his body to make acceptable the claims of a current weight around 15 st 10 lb, which is exactly what he scaled for the 89-second destruction of the egregious Peter McNeeley last August in the one-ring engagement he has faced since completing three years for rape. And there was nothing stage-managed about the flurry of precisely executed violence that hurled Nate Tubbs to the canvas and curtailed a rare open-day in Tyson's training at a gym in north Philadelphia (home turf of the Hollywood slugger Rocky) last week.

In four impressive rounds with the 6 ft 7 in, 20 st 5 lb Tyrone Evans, Tyson had given no indication of protecting the right hand which caused the Mathis fight to be postponed from 4 November to next weekend, and fears that he might be inhibited by that thumb fracture disappeared altogether as he started to pummel Tubbs, a 6 ft 2 in, 18-stoner from Cincinnati. It was, in fact, a couple of rights, one to the body and another to the temple, that first severely distressed Tubbs. Then, after permitting the bigger man a brief respite, Tyson unloaded a swift left-right-left combination of hooks to the head that blasted his victim sideways to the floor and into a state of confusion which took half a minute to clear.

Having given that public demonstration of his aggressive well-being, and coped with a concentrated onslaught of media attention afterwards, he instantly reverted to the reclusive ways that have been the norm since he left prison. But there have been signs here in Pennsylvania that his inaccessibility is less armour-plated than it was even a few weeks back. Some say this is because the necessity to sell this fight is more pressing than was the case with the first phase of the second coming against McNeeley (the Fox network television company are understood to be putting up only half of the $10 million they were going to pay for the original 4 November date with Mathis). Other close observers conclude less cynically that, as Tyson slowly adjusts to the complex consequences of his release, he is gradually thawing towards a more relaxed attitude.

There was certainly not a trace of tension or awkwardness in his manner when, on Friday evening, he responded to requests for a private conversation by making a telephone call to my hotel room. The unmistakable voice answered questions with an agreeableness and gentle courtesy which, in conjunction with the televised images of the dumping of Tubbs, created a faintly eerie effect. When he uses the term 'Sir', as he did frequently, there is a tendency for the *listener* to touch the forelock.

'I am happy with the way things are going,' he said. 'Right now, at this stage of my life, I have no hang-ups. I'm not concerned with what people think about me. I am content to live my life for me and my children. People underestimate the strain, the pressures of coming back from where

I have been to where I am now. Prison was a dismal experience and the horrific ordeal didn't end the moment I was freed. I had to deal with so many things, a different mentality, a different value-system. But I am pretty loose now. I am smiling more than I ever did. I'm in good shape and I am having fun.'

The very relaxation he celebrates at 29 is seen by many as a powerful argument against believing that he can ever again be the forest fire of aggression he was nearly a decade ago as he began the devastating surge which made him, at 20, the youngest ever holder of a heavyweight championship and rapidly carried him on to total supremacy in the division. He was, such critics justifiably emphasise, declining noticeably long before he was jailed. Given all the disparate influences that have been at work on him since, from the eroding effects of four years of idleness to the spiritual impact of conversion to Islam, can he possibly rediscover the single-minded zeal for fighting he once had?

'This is a job I take very seriously,' was his direct, if less than comprehensive response. 'Being the best out there is still extremely important to me. The money obviously matters a lot but ego and pride are vital elements, too. I always had a hunger to win and it is still there, intact. I can feel my powers coming back. The speed is back, the hooks, the combinations. In due time we will discover, in the ring, whether I am as good as I was, or better.'

That phrase, 'in due time', recurred in his conversation and it had a special resonance when he talked of Riddick Bowe and Bowe's insistence that, in spite of holding nothing more meaningful than the WBO crown, he is the world's No. 1 heavyweight. Both men are from Brownsville, a Brooklyn district that is one of the bleakest ghettoes in America, and there is an almost fraternal respect mixed with the hard implications when Tyson refers to the rival who may bring him the ultimate jackpot of his career.

'A lot of people say they are going to do great things and then when the day of judgement comes they don't fare too well,' he said mildly. 'But Riddick is a good fighter. He has earned his reputation. I have been away and he has been performing, so you can't say I am the best. He has put in his dues. But there will be a day of judgement. In due time, we'll know who is the man.'

Officially, Bowe has only one blemish on his record (a loss to Evander Holyfield sandwiched between two victories over the brave veteran) but there should have been another in August 1994 when he battered Mathis while Mathis was in a kneeling position during the fourth round of their meeting in Atlantic City. Expediency rather than justice produced a ruling of no-contest. However, regardless of the blatant unfairness of that decision, the occasion supplied scant evidence that Mathis can hope to trouble Tyson and there seemed no point in wasting questions on the negligible problems presented by the imminent assignment. Mathis is only a fraction taller than the 5 ft 11½ in optimistically claimed by Tyson. Though the outsider has a substantial advantage in reach, he clearly lacks the superiority in physical scope that enabled really big opponents of reasonable talent to worry Tyson even in his prime.

Bruno does have such troublesome dimensions, but it was the long list of the Londoner's deficiencies that dominated Tyson's thinking when he was asked about the March rematch with a man he stopped in five rounds in 1989. 'No one has to tell me how Frank Bruno will fight,' he said. 'I know how he will fight. I know his strengths and his weaknesses. If somebody wants to make something of the fact that he landed a decent left hook early in our first fight, that's fine. He caught me off guard and the punch was solid enough. But I took it like it was nothing. What I know about Bruno tells me that if I do my work properly I will come out of this championship fight very successfully.'

Naturally, he does not harbour the slightest dread that Saturday will damage career figures which stand at 42 wins and one defeat, with 36 stoppages to his credit. It was another Buster, James Douglas, who violently inflicted the one loss, in Japan nearly six years ago. But surely that spectre will not haunt the Spectrum. A more convincing omen appeared at the Joe Frazier Gym while 25-year-old Mathis was suffering on Thursday. Watching the lanky figure of the retired Michael Spinks engaged in a training routine he insisted had no significance other than as a means of keeping fit, we were reminded of how Spinks, a magnificent light-heavyweight over many years, was annihilated by Tyson in half a round.

The great Frazier himself was on hand to reminisce admiringly about Mathis's late father, who earned a living as a heavyweight in a more distinguished era. 'That Buster could fight,' said Frazier, blinking in the hard sunlight that slanted in from rough streets. 'He could go all right.' Against Tyson, the younger one can be expected to go all wrong, and early. In seeking to explain the miseries of his sparring, Mathis and his handlers stressed that he was exhausted by a complicated transfer from New York which landed him in Philadelphia in the early hours of Thursday. If he had flown economy from Mars, it would scarcely have been an excuse for such a shambles.

No reaction to what we had witnessed was more measured or more damning than that of George Benton, a famous local who has made the transition from outstanding fighter to venerated trainer. 'It will be a miracle if this kid can stay in there with Tyson,' Benton said. 'He doesn't have anything that can stave off Tyson. He is much the same height, his jab isn't much and he doesn't have muscular strength. The kid looks soft and he obviously doesn't hit very hard. His record shows only six wins inside the distance. How can he resist Tyson? Tyson comes at you with a lot of hands, hooking at you, hooking at you. I'd say Buster's chances are slim and none.'

And, as Don King jokes with tiresome regularity, Slim is out of town.

Glory Returns to the Garden

The Sunday Times, 17 December 1995

No doubt all the greatness they have seen has made them a querulous and judgemental crew, but the ghosts of Madison Square Garden could only applaud on Friday night as Oscar De La Hoya reintroduced major boxing to the incomparable arena with a master-class in graceful destruction.

A 22-year-old fighter's six-minute demolition of an opponent half a foot shorter, and infinitely less talented, is hardly the stuff of legend. Yet the calculated precision and seemingly effortless power that forced the referee to rescue Jesse James Leija at the end of the second round of what was scheduled to be a 12-round defence of De La Hoya's WBO light-weight (9 st 9 lb) title strengthened the impression that the slender, handsome stylist from a barrio in East Los Angeles is equipped to make his an enduring name in the history of fist-fighting.

Many of the 16,000 who crowded into the Garden may have been drawn by an undertow of nostalgia, a feeling that the promoter's trum-petings about a 'Return to the Mecca' carried more than a hint of truth. But it was belief in De La Hoya as something exceptional, an exciting reincarnation of the classic abilities and towering performances which a string of unforgettable champions brought to the place in earlier, more glorious eras, that gave validity to the occasion. He came to New York with all the baggage of hype and aggressive marketing considered essential to the shaping of a big career in an age when the capacity to have impact on television is the most vital ingredient of success in boxing. However, his deeds in the ring had engendered faith that the sales pitch was not too seriously divorced from reality, that beyond the exploitation of his looks, and of the priceless appeal of being a Hispanic American who speaks eloquently in English, there was a phenomenal talent. That faith was dramatically reinforced on Friday by a demonstration of concentrated excellence that left him with a professional record of 20 straight wins (18 stoppages) and, more importantly, persuaded a demanding audience that the effectiveness of his outstanding technique is compounded by a natural gift of timing which enables punches not instantly recognisable as decisive to apply stupefying force.

Jesse James Leija has always been more of an artisan than an artist, more noted for sustained, determined scuffling than surges of deadliness. But the 29-year-old is far from negligible. If the statistics he took to the Garden showed that only 14 of his 30 victories had come inside the distance, they also included a win and a draw against the formidable veteran Azumah Nelson, who recently recaptured the WBC super-featherweight championship at the age of 37 by beating Gabriel Ruelas, the man who inflicted the one defeat Leija had suffered before Friday. Hopes that Leija would pose substantial problems were diminished by the knowledge that his notable achievements have been at super-featherweight (9 st 4 lb) – he briefly held the WBC title – and the fact that he stands just 5 ft 5 in, compared with De La Hoya's 5 ft 11 in.

When they came off their stools, they definitely looked like men from different weight categories and, though De La Hoya spent the first round probing to assess the substance of his opposition, his long, slim arms reached Leija's head often enough in rapidly delivered clusters. The challenger is from San Antonio, site of the Alamo, and he may have experienced a little retrospective empathy as he waited to be overwhelmed by another Mexican assault. 'He hits hard,' Leija said as he slumped disconsolately into his corner at the end of the first, and it was impossible to miss the pained resignation in that stark acknowledgement.

Those of us outside the ropes had seen ample justification for a sense of doom. There is a terrible predatory alertness about De La Hoya even when he is apparently concerned with defence. At such times he holds his arms out in front of his body as if preparing to ward off rushes, but he is constantly measuring the critical distances between himself and his opponent, judging precisely the movements of his feet and torso and hands that will minimise the risk of being hit and maximise the opportunities of doing damage. That process is, of course, nothing more or less than the essence of boxing but it is seldom engaged in with such cerebral control. And another quality that sets De La Hoya apart from all but the very best practitioners of his trade is the nerveless certainty with which he pours into openings once he has identified them.

It is then that he proves how blessedly freakish his timing is. A few boxers who do not resemble him in any other way come to mind because they, too, were able to throw punches which did not seem especially dramatic until they detonated on the victim's head with devastating results. Teofilo Stevenson, the Cuban amateur heavyweight who won gold medals at three consecutive Olympics, had the gift and so did an American WBC featherweight champion, Danny 'Little Red' Lopez. They were magicians of violence and De La Hoya suggests he is of their mysterious fraternity.

One obvious component of his power is the advantage that comes from being a natural left-hander who boxes in an orthodox stance, leading with the more powerful arm and thus putting the most hurtful weapon closer to its target. 'I write, play golf, do everything left-handed,' he confirmed happily at the press conference after his triumph, offering the dazzling smile that has been known to make young girls swoon and cause women of riper years to flirt hopefully in restaurants and hotel lobbies. His face, with the strong, stubbled jaw and high cheekbones and wide-set, steady eyes under the short, dark hair, had been all seriousness as he set about dismantling Leija in the second round. 'Although my training in California had been interrupted by flu, and my running was restricted in New York because it was so cold when I came here, I felt strong in the fight,' he reported later. 'The power was there but my timing was less than 100 per cent. I was a bit sluggish.' That was unlikely to be Leija's view as he found his efforts to burrow in on the taller man's midriff punished with counters to the head.

De La Hoya said the first knockdown in that conclusive second round came while he was seeking to catch Leija with high left and right hooks. By switching abruptly to the body, he had brought Leija's hands down and then banged him to the head with sufficient authority to necessitate an eight-count. Once upright again, the Texan was a sad figure and he was pursued with deliberate, unhurried ferocity. Pinning his opponent in a neutral corner, De La Hoya disconcerted him with an accurate flurry and then stepped back to await the lunging attempt at retaliation he knew would come. Having let Leija swing and miss, without taking himself far out of range, De La Hoya stepped in with a briskly brutal straight right and perfect left hook that dropped the challenger in a dazed heap in a neutral corner. He rose to hear the bell arrive while the referee was still counting but his unsteady return to his corner was followed immediately by the sensible announcement that his agonies were over.

Subsequent testimony from the two principals left no doubt that De La Hoya will be moving up through the weight divisions and supported his conviction that he will cope successfully. He says he means to rise in. stages all the way up to middleweight (11 st 6 lb), so he was bound to be encouraged by Leija's rueful assertion that he already hits like someone in that class. 'I knew he was strong but I didn't know he had so much power,' said Leija. 'I've been sparring with welterweights but he punches like a middleweight. He was just stronger and bigger and better than I was. I fought a great fighter and I did my best. A man cannot do more.'

It is difficult to put a limit on what De La Hoya might do on the climb that began with the winning of an Olympic gold medal in Barcelona. He believes he has realised perhaps only 50 per cent of his potential and, if that is an unconvincing estimate, there is probably enough scope for development to make future rivals tremble, particularly as he has sensed the true nature of his punching prowess. 'The main thing I have learned,' he told me when we talked several days before the fight, 'is that I don't have to load up to produce power. If I throw the punches in combinations, with the proper rhythm, the power comes automatically. Rhythm and timing count as much as they do in golf, which is a game I love so much that it was almost becoming a dangerous distraction from my boxing. When I started playing golf I would try to kill the ball and it would go, like, ten feet. If I take an easy, rhythmic swing it will fly 250 yards. And now my handicap is down to ten.'

De La Hoya is still claiming he will curtail his time in boxing so that he can widen his life to accommodate leisure pursuits and a college education, insisting that he intends to retire rich at 25 or 26. We must hope he keeps his word, but in the fight business there is no correlation between brilliance and wisdom. Of course, such issues are far along the road. Now he must ready himself for another fight on 9 February and then, early in May, he is due to meet the legendary Julio Cesar Chavez. He expects the Mexicans of the Los Angeles barrios to root for Chavez, because they like their heroes to be born south of the border. De La Hoya looked at his long, rather fine hands as he talked of the imminent war. He has a right to assume that youth and the magic of those hands will see him through.

Iron Mike Has Plenty in the Fire

The Sunday Times, 24 December 1995

The script called for a couple of hollow men who could be beaten like drums to announce that the circus was back in town. Peter McNeeley and Buster Mathis Jr duly proved themselves empty of threat but, during the short time he spent in their company, Mike Tyson struggled to find his old percussive rhythm. Instead of a big bang, or at least a reverberating boom-boom, the first two fights of his comeback have produced the squelching sound of feeble resistance being clumsily crushed.

McNeeley's impersonation of a dervish with a death-wish had lasted only 89 seconds when it was terminated by the illegal intervention of a manager who found he had less nerve at ringside than he had shown when signing the contract. So complaints about the lack of control and accuracy in Tyson's response to the headlong rushes of the Boston-Irish novice fell somewhere between the hyper-critical and the meaningless. But when the wildly ill-timed hooks in evidence then were repeated in embarrassing volume through most of the eight and a half minutes required to subdue Mathis, there was clearly a case for wondering if the former undisputed heavyweight champion's three years in jail for rape, and four years' absence from boxing, have left him much further from a state of battle readiness than he is willing to acknowledge. However, before such speculation can be translated by the Frank Bruno fan club into a torrent of optimistic assumptions concerning the WBC champion's chances of repelling Tyson's challenge for his title in Las Vegas on 16 March, it behoves us to recognise a few simple facts about the uninspired skirmish in Philadelphia.

That is a process which naturally involves disposing of several fictions, starting with the extraordinary notion that the winner was quite happy to prolong the untidy action because he wanted 'a few rounds under his belt'. Unbelievably, such a view emerged from the discussion conducted by the three British fighting men who made up the studio panel of experts for Sky Television's live broadcast of the fight. A non-combatant must hesitate before questioning the opinions of worthies with as many ring-hours to their credit as Gary Mason, Duke McKenzie and Neville Brown. But nonsense is nonsense, whatever its source, and the idea that Tyson was content to 'carry' Mathis for the sake of the exercise does not bear a moment's scrutiny. In fact, many of the victor's troubles, such as they were, originated in his compulsion to seek his opponent's instant destruction with practically every punch he threw.

Tyson's trainer, Jay Bright – whose contribution continues to suggest that his ability to discipline and channel the fighter's ego is sadly limited – told reporters ten days ago that his employer's strategy was to go out and 'vaporise' the opposition. That was certainly how it looked from the first bell as Tyson loosed hooks of such unbridled violence that their exaggerated arcs brought almost as much danger to those of us in the ringside seats as they did to the flabby but elusive object of their venom. It is difficult to understand how Mason, McKenzie and Brown could watch so many blatant, if badly aimed, attempts at annihilation and imagine that the perpetrator was content to let Mathis hang around.

Perhaps their judgement was affected by the dull, unchanging expression on Tyson's face. It was a look which persuaded some that he was bored, devoid of aggressive fire. They seem to be missing the point about the role in which he had cast himself for the engagement at the Spectrum. He had plainly decided to be the cold, stony-faced destroyer, safe in the knowledge that Mathis was utterly incapable of being more than a temporary irritant. As missile after missile whistled harmlessly around Mathis's frantically bobbing head, it apparently became all the more essential to the effect Tyson was determined to create that his features should retain their expression of patient, relaxed implacability. He was totally free of hazard and entitled to assume that the end could not be long delayed, so why not conceal the frustration he must have felt over his failure to connect promptly with the heavy stuff?

Proof that Tyson was anxious to minimise the bad impression made by his inability to blast Mathis into submission earlier than the final minute of the third round was delivered at the subsequent press conference. There he fantasised at length about having set a trap for Mathis, 'lullabying' him into a false sense of priorities by releasing a stream of careless left hooks before taking him out with right-hand punches. Maybe he was just enjoying a joke at his listeners' expense. Anybody who believed that drivel about the set-up would lose an IQ competition with a plant.

If Tyson's reading of the fight was fanciful, that presented by the loser was faintly ludicrous. By the time he sat down behind the microphones, Mathis appeared to have convinced himself that his performance had been tinged with glory. He is a likeable 25-year-old and if a dollop of delusion helps him to preserve his self-respect, he is welcome to it. But when he started to argue blithely that what he had achieved inside the ropes merited another lucrative assignment against Tyson, he invited the suspicion that the decisive knockdown had done him more damage than we realised. He recently acquired qualifications as a realtor and he might be well advised to plan his future in terms of the property world rather than the fight business, where he will always suffer from the major disadvantages of an incorrigibly unathletic physique and an equally incurable shortage of hitting power.

Burdened with such handicaps, Mathis could hardly be blamed for fighting in a style which made it obvious that avoidance of swift humiliation was the absolute limit of his ambition. He was the one who wanted a few rounds under his belt. He dared not hope for more. Not for a millisecond did he or any other sane person in the Spectrum entertain the possibility that he could win, and it is that reality which should restrain those who are eager to condemn Tyson's work as a revelation of extreme vulnerability.

There is not the slightest doubt that the ex-champion performed unimpressively, that his timing was miserably flawed and his reaction to openings sluggish. But many of his problems came from the combined effect of his lack of respect for Mathis and Mathis's vast respect for him. Tyson's contempt for the negligible armament of the fat man from the other corner made him disdain the basic obligation to build attacks behind his jab. Only once, briefly at the beginning of the second round, did he thrust out a series of effective left leads, and the promise of reward immediately discernible failed to encourage further reliance on such orthodoxy. Instead of developing his assaults with bursts of combination punches, he tried to blow Mathis away with prodigious single shots which, when they hit nothing but air, threatened to wrench the thrower's muscular arms from their sockets.

Much has been made of the speed and skill of Mathis's head movements, and the extent to which they contributed to Tyson's inaccuracy. They were admirable enough, but the outsider's most telling tactic consisted of crowding in on his opponent to envelop him in grappling arms and heaving flesh. Tyson was more likely to be disconcerted by a slap from pendulous breasts than hurt by occasional flurries of feather-duster hooks. The constant proximity of Mathis drastically restricted the heavy puncher's own effectiveness until he began moving abruptly to his left to make space and angles for delivery of the right hand.

When the end came suddenly late in the third round it was from a modified version of that manoeuvre. There has been a tendency to describe the blow that killed Mathis's resistance as a right uppercut but, though it was travelling vertically upwards when it landed cruelly on his mouth, it could not be regarded as a true uppercut, since it was thrown at least 18 inches wide of Tyson's body. A following right hit Mathis on the temple and by the time a third, rather slack punch with the same hand caught him on a shoulder, he was already lurching away from the firing line and into the final count.

Once all the detailed elements of the Philadelphia story have been examined, it can be seen that they provide less encouragement for Bruno than the big man claims. Bruno's long limbs and open style will offer Tyson far more opportunities to apply his leverage than he was permitted by Mathis's smothering approach. Of course, the Londoner has a genuine, jolting left jab and clubbing destruction in his right arm. He is, however, notoriously without fluency or an instinct for improvisation. But will he need such refinements if the 29-year-old Tyson, who has shown his speed and power are back but awaits the return of his timing, turns out to be as rusty as his worst moments in the Spectrum indicated?

Intriguing questions abound. No matter how much of an enigma the reincarnated Tyson remains, I will find it impossible to tip against him in March. But he is heading for the first real test of his comeback. He and his backers know this, and the one certainty is that Bruno will be subjected to as much pre-fight pressure as the Tyson camp can generate. That means plenty.

Have-a-go Hero on Hiding to Nothing

The Sunday Times, 10 March 1996

To most Americans, the very idea of a British fighter as heavyweight champion of the world is a cultural contradiction. They react to the sight of Frank Bruno wearing the garish championship belt of the World Boxing Council as they might to an Amazonian Indian with ice-skating medals. It is an aberration they are sure will be corrected at the MGM Grand Hotel in Las Vegas on Saturday night, when Bruno tries to defend his title against the man America regards as the once and future king of the heavyweights, Mike Tyson. In the casinos along the Vegas Strip Tyson's current odds are 10–1 on. Such certainty is unlikely to be dented by mention of the fact that bare-knuckle mayhem in eighteenth-century England gave birth to the modern era of organised prize-fighting, or by pointing out that this same WBC title was held barely 18 months ago by another boxer who is officially (if not altogether convincingly) a Brit, Lennox Lewis. The American public's scepticism about our heavyweights is almost impervious to recent developments, having been hardened throughout nearly 100 years by a parade of big men from the other side of the Atlantic who entered US rings with little prospect of doing anything more than occupying a substantial area of floorspace.

Coverage of Bruno–Tyson in the British media over the coming week will suggest that it is an apocalyptic event, Armageddon with gloves, but the healthy ticket sales for the 16,700-seat arena at the MGM Grand are based on the expectation of an execution. Bruno is viewed here as a tiresome bit of clutter Tyson must sweep away before moving on to the serious business of reunifying a championship fragmented by the mercenary eagerness of separate governing bodies to install their own champions. Implicit in such dismissiveness is the rather glib assumption that the prominence of British fighters in the heavyweight division these days owes everything to that fragmentation. Bruno can scarcely deny that he has benefited from the process, since his first three efforts to become a world champion all ended in brutal defeat, and political manoeuvring played a big part in giving him the opportunity to succeed at the fourth attempt by outpointing Oliver McCall in London last September.

Lewis, by contrast, lacks the right connections, and the one blemish on his record has been used to freeze him out of contention. The size, power and athleticism of Lewis – who survived early anxiety to win a crushing victory over Bruno before losing the WBC belt to a freakishly explosive punch from the normally pedestrian McCall – would make him less of an outsider than Bruno if he were facing Tyson next weekend. Like Bruno, Lewis is of West Indian blood and happy to call himself British. But perhaps the knowledge that he won his Olympic gold medal in 1988 while boxing as a Canadian will always afford him some protection from the special disdain Americans reserve for Limey heavyweights.

Bruno is being subjected to the full traditional bombardment. The 6,000 supporters reported to be setting out hopefully from Britain can be glad they did not arrive in time to read what the country's most celebrated sports columnist, Jim Murray, had to say in *The Los Angeles Times* last Thursday. Having credited the WBC champion with a good punch, Murray added: 'He also has a chin of such pure Waterford crystal, it gives rise to the adage that people who live in glass jaws shouldn't throw punches. The biggest danger in fighting Bruno is, you might get hit by flying glass . . . he has been on more canvases than Rembrandt. Maybe he just likes the view from down there.' As it happens, Bruno's most frightening characteristic is his capacity to remain upright long after he is thoroughly beaten and his senses have been scattered, a habit which testifies to gallant instincts but leaves him vulnerable to the kind of sustained punishment that could have tragic repercussions. It would be better for him if, when badly hurt, he subsided to the canvas as readily as Murray suggests he does.

What the veteran columnist's flip generalisations represent is, obviously, the American insistence on identifying Britain as the classic breeding ground of horizontal heavyweights. There can be no doubt that history provides justification for the prejudice. Between the point late in the nineteenth century when gloved fighting became internationally acceptable and Lewis's arrival on the scene, the only titleholder we could claim was Bob Fitzsimmons. He was born in Cornwall but emigrated as a boy, and it was in the Antipodes and America that he honed the skills which enabled him to knock out James J. Corbett at Carson City, Nevada, in 1897. Through nine decades afterwards, it was difficult to decide whether our contenders for the championship should be classified as valiant tragedians or bad vaudeville acts forever auditioning for a part far beyond their abilities. One favourite with the Americans was Phil Scott, who reigned as British champion between 1926 and 1931. They dubbed him Phaintin' Phil, in tribute to a succession of groin-clutching collapses that brought him no fewer than six wins on disqualifications. But Scott paid the price for having so often cried wolf. In a final eliminator for the world title, Jack Sharkey actually did punch him low but went unpunished and won.

Of course, we sent out plenty of heavyweights who performed more admirably than Scott. Tommy Farr, born tough in the mining valleys of south Wales, went the full 15 rounds against the young and seemingly irresistible Joe Louis in 1937, and Henry Cooper's renowned left hook inflicted as much pain and embarrassment on Muhammad Ali as any one blow ever did. But Farr and Cooper finished those fights comprehensively beaten, and the myths that have grown up around their limited successes serve only to confirm that the British fascination with heavyweight boxing is a phenomenon utterly divorced from the achievements of our men in the ring. Maybe it is not too fanciful to associate it with folk memories of that distant time when England's bare-knuckle heroes could imagine themselves the best punchers around. Whatever its source, there is always a rich reservoir of national warmth waiting to be tapped by anybody with the slightest pretensions to being a heavyweight contender. Cooper, who remains a darling of the public 30 years after his heyday, is living proof of that. Apparently, it matters little that Our 'Enery lost 14 of his 55 contests or that he, in common with every notable British heavyweight of the period, was demolished by the only European in the past 50 years to hold the undisputed championship of the world, Ingemar Johansson, a fearsome hitter who emerged, improbably, from Sweden.

Cooper's enduring popularity is inseparable from two assets he shares with Bruno; he has an engaging persona and he is a Londoner. Nobody should ever underestimate the advantages for a fighter of having a metropolitan constituency. British fans are unfailingly emotional, rarely objective about their ring representatives – when Don Cockell was brutalised by Rocky Marciano 40 years ago, the greatest of boxing writers, A.J. Liebling, described Cockell as 'a fat man whose gift for public suffering has enlisted the sympathy of a sentimental people' – and the cockneys are the most sentimental of all. They have been mainly responsible for causing Bruno to be treated less like a sportsman than a cherished character in a long-running soap, for enabling him to supplement his considerable earnings in the ring (he admits to being paid

317

£4 million for this assignment) with self-lampooning frolics on the pantomime stage.

It is, of course, easy to discern a totally different kind of sentimentality in the American attitude to the heavyweight championship. Theirs is a harsh, mean-streets version and it helps them to persuade themselves that Tyson, the rapist recently freed from jail, should be given a chance to rehabilitate himself inside the ropes. They are almost mawkishly macho about what they regard as their inalienable right to have the hardest man on the planet. 'When John L. Sullivan said, "I can lick any man in the house," a nation shuddered,' Jim Murray wrote on Thursday. 'When Jack Dempsey fell, small boys wept.'

Bruno is much the likelier to fall on Saturday, but at least he knows he has the cosier place to land.

Time for Bruno to Cry Enough

The Sunday Times, 24 March 1996

As world heavyweight champion, Frank Bruno was regarded by many as a squatter in somebody else's mansion. When Mike Tyson, a man with genuine title deeds to his name, set about repossessing the property, it could be no surprise that Bruno was evicted with only the most perfunctory gestures of protest. Since he managed to grab £4 million on the way out, big Frank's return to the hard pavements of reality was a lot more tolerable than it might have been. As a former holder of the WBC title, he has a secure place in the history of boxing now, and a pile of money in the bank, so it would be reasonable to assume that a quiet, dignified withdrawal into retirement would suit him fine.

Instead there is talk of continuing his career. The British public, who have for so long shown a miraculous willingness to submerge the many proofs of his inadequacy as a fighter in the warm flood of their affection for him, may well be asked to pay for a long goodbye. As justification of the proposed ploy, we are told that it would be unutterably sad if such a national favourite did not go out as a winner. It is a theme calculated to work on the purse strings as much as the heart strings. The truth is that Bruno is already a bigger winner than anyone with his limitations was entitled to dream he could be. He has gained lasting celebrity and serious riches on the strength of a record created by some of the most selective matchmaking even the heavyweight division has ever seen. Three times he was painstakingly built up to the status of championship contender; and each time, when he was found wanting on the big night, his promoters simply raided a few more graves to find opponents who would permit the reconstruction of his reputation. Through it all the man himself performed honestly, training to the highest standards of fitness and striving to improve technique flawed by his lack of athletic fluency and the spontaneity and swiftness with which a natural fighter conceives and executes his moves.

Because he brought so much that was admirable to the dance, no one could complain when Bruno at last found the right partner in Oliver McCall. By outpointing a slothful and unambitious McCall to claim a world title at his fourth attempt, Bruno hit a financial jackpot, but only at the cost of being hit by Tyson in a fight that laid bare the unbridgeable gap between the Londoner's standards and those of true heavyweight champions. The full, yawning extent of that gulf seemed to have a terrible impact on Bruno's mind as he headed for the ring in Las Vegas. In the weeks before he confronted Tyson, his frequently declared confidence came across as sincere. Probably it was. A man whose nerve is unaffected by the sound of distant battles may find it breaking when the guns are thunderously close. Walking taut-faced and dry-mouthed from the dressing-room to that illuminated square of canvas amid a bedlam of exhortations, crossing himself repeatedly, like a cardinal on speed, Bruno gave the impression that the enormity of what he was undertaking was suddenly being borne in on him.

Once the bell rang, he settled almost instantly for the fate of victim. From the moment Tyson drove in to land his first heavy right-hand punch, Bruno was no more competitive than a sheep in an abattoir. Even the restricted arsenal that he has at his command was left largely unused. Instead of pumping out his jab, he employed his long left arm in forlorn, pawing attempts to keep his pursuer at bay. There had, obviously, been plans to catch Tyson with right uppercuts as he came in but that is a demanding tactic, requiring calm and precision, and Bruno was far too preoccupied with survival to achieve more than two or three clumsy, half-hearted efforts at implementing it. When real uppercuts arrived they were delivered with brutal effect by Tyson. Two of them, thrown on a pure vertical line, ripped into Bruno's sagging head in the middle of the battering assault that finished the one-sided exercise early in the third round. Sheer quickness was the tool that made Tyson the absolute master from beginning to end in both abbreviated fights between these men. All of the three other fighters who beat Bruno – James 'Bonecrusher' Smith, Tim Witherspoon and Lennox Lewis – were at least inconvenienced to the point of finding themselves behind in the early stages but Tyson's hand-speed mercilessly exploited the bigger man's ponderousness. After such a comprehensive demonstration of his shortcomings, such a cruel reminder that he was a journeyman who rose profitably above his station, Bruno should admit that enough is enough. None of us will begrudge him a penny of the fortune he has amassed. But to look for more would be outrageous.

Non-contests will, it must be assumed, continue to be the basic currency of Tyson's comeback during the next phase of his campaign to reunify the heavyweight championship. Bruce Seldon, the WBA champion who is likeliest choice as the immediate target, hits so lightly that if he punched the doorbell you wouldn't be certain to hear it. Taking the IBF crown from Frans Botha (or Axel Schulz if Schulz succeeds in his legal action to invalidate his loss to Botha) would surely be a formality for Tyson. He was undisputed ruler of the division in his early twenties and should be restored to that position soon after his 30th birthday, which falls on 30 June. But is there, on the horizon, any prospect of a fight real enough to show how his destructive powers now compare with those of his previous peak? George Foreman, at 47, would offer about as much resistance to Tyson as a condemned building does to the wrecking ball. And it is legitimate to dismiss Evander Holyfield and Michael Moorer. That leaves Riddick Bowe and Lewis but even they have major question marks against their names. Bowe is an attractive, easy-going personality and an excellent fighter, blessed with skill, variety and a punch. He does, however, have the self-discipline of a slob and can never be relied upon to get full value for his talents. Lewis, on available evidence, would have the best chance of troubling Tyson, which is why he can expect to be frozen out for at least another year. Against him, too, Tyson would go in as a clear betting favourite.

Annihilating someone as tailor-made for him as Bruno could hardly prove that Iron Mike was all the way back to his best. But there was a fire in his work, and sufficient volume, accuracy and ferocity about his punching, to send a shudder through anybody who has to come off the other stool.

Lewis Ready to Expel Demons

The Sunday Times, 2 February 1997

It is time for Lennox Lewis to stop being the perennial promising boy and become the delivery man. He will be 32 in September and all the talk about the late maturation of heavyweights cannot quell anxieties over recent indications that his career is stalling and could be in danger of slipping into reverse.

On Friday night at the Las Vegas Hilton he will be given precisely the opportunity he needs to reassure himself and his admirers, not only a chance to avenge the one defeat on his record but an invitation to demonstrate, at Oliver McCall's expense, that he has the will and the professionalism to do justice to his superlative physical gifts. As a technical achievement, beating McCall would scarcely amount to a triumph (Frank Bruno managed as much). But to do a convincing job on an opponent who separated him from the WBC heavyweight title with one thunderous right-hand punch at Wembley in September 1994, Lewis will have to overcome whatever personal demons were created by that trauma. It is in dealing with them that he can make a statement about his future.

This is a fight fraught with so many imponderables concerning the mental state of the contestants that there might be a case of having psychiatrists instead of corner-men. In fact, McCall has gone fairly close to that kind of arrangement during his preparation in Nashville, Tennessee. He must be one of the few boxers in history to have combined intensive training for a championship fight (the vacant WBC crown is at stake) with a full-scale programme of rehabilitative treatment for drug and alcohol abuse. With a doctor and support team constantly on call, he has been seeing almost as much of his counsellors as of his trainer, George Benton, who is a street-hardened Philadelphian and unlikely to be fazed by the peculiarity of his working conditions.

McCall is a Don King fighter and, with characteristic readiness to turn any circumstance to their advantage, the King camp have been suggesting that the discipline imposed by the medical supervision is making their man fitter than he has ever been. The patient-pugilist himself conjures up an entirely new vision of fight training when he acknowledges that failure to go into rehab before his meeting with Bruno largely explains the miserable performance that cost him his title.

On that night in London he looked as if he had overdosed on sedatives. He was unrecognisable as the primed adrenalin-pump who entered the ring against Lewis with the muscles of his clenched jaw sticking out like rivets. However much benefit he is gaining from his current regimen, it is hard to believe that McCall will ever again rise to the level of destructive intensity he reached on that night. Perhaps even then it would have dissipated after a few rounds and become incidental had Lewis's amateurish carelessness not exposed his head to that devastating right barely three and a half minutes into the action.

Sharpened by special tuition from Emanuel Steward, the challenger produced a *coup de grâce* that was also a *coup d'état*, since it restored control of the heavyweight division to the merciless Mr King. Much has changed since that dramatic occasion. Evander Holyfield's exposure of Mike Tyson's limitations has pushed King off centre-stage once again (deepening his hunger for an upset by McCall on Friday) and Steward is firmly established as Lewis's mentor. But how have Lewis and McCall changed and have they done so sufficiently to make a reprise of that shock of two and a half years ago unthinkable? Yes, say the odds-makers of Las Vegas. They have installed Lewis as an almost unbackable favourite – you have to bet 530 dollars to win a hundred – and offer the American at nearly 4–1. Steward, predictably, agrees with the assessment. 'Now the positions are virtually reversed,' the trainer told me last week. 'The people working with Oliver have allowed him to forget most of what I taught him. Whereas I respected Lennox when I was in the other corner, they are filling Oliver's head with the belief that this man lacks the mental toughness to hold up in a brawl. They are saying he will be terrified when he remembers what happened last time and will quit or fold as soon as Oliver gets to him.

'Meanwhile, I've cured Lennox of that nonsense about the right hand being the answer to everything. I'm working on making him a complete fighter, improving his jab and his body movement, getting him to throw left hooks and, above all, to concentrate on maintaining his balance at all times, avoiding those awful habits of crossing his feet and sprawling.

'We are preparing for three different styles McCall could apply in this fight, all of them designed to get him in close, which is his obvious hope of doing damage against a giant like Lennox. One method would be to come in swinging haymakers, brawling from the start. Or he could cover up and try to walk in without getting hurt. He could also bob and weave, slipping punches, moving his body from side to side, staying low, attempting to penetrate that way. Whatever he does, we'll be ready. I feel whichever shape the fight takes, Lennox wins. McCall has never been stopped but he could be in this one. Oliver won't be the same man I sent out and Lennox won't be the fella we beat that night.'

All of this has a rational, if slightly facile, ring. And it was supported by the evidence of extreme wellbeing Lewis presented last week in Arizona, both while relaxing in his quarters at a luxurious resort hotel in the shadow of the double hump of Camelback Mountain and during work sessions in the contrastingly stark setting of a gym in an impoverished Mexican district of Phoenix. His 6 ft 5 in frame is reported to weigh well over 17 stone but his torso is tubular, not flabby, and his face under the new haircut has the clean lines of gradually developed fitness. When he sparred ten rounds on Tuesday against Al Williams, an aspiring heavyweight from Virginia with a record of 16 wins, one loss and one draw, he moved and punched effectively, advertising his stamina by finishing the last round with a swift and accurate combination that made his battered helper grateful for the liberating bell.

But Lewis is notoriously misleading in the gym. Apparently he looked tremendous in training for his most recent fight, with Ray Mercer in May. Yet, once the real activity began, he reverted to his old laborious ways and was glad to emerge with a narrow and controversial verdict whose major consolation was the proof it provided that he has the stomach for a roughhouse. There must be a suspicion that, as far as his amateurish tendencies are concerned, he is a recidivist, doomed to be a repeat offender when the heat is on. Lewis's physical scope (McCall is not small but he will be dwarfed) and his career statistics – he has 29 wins and one defeat with 24 stoppages in his favour against comparable figures for McCall of 28–6–20

– are enough to underpin the bookmakers' faith. It is, however, what is happening in his mind that is most relevant and most mysterious.

'Regardless of what I say or Lennox says, you can never tell what will occur inside a man's head,' said Steward. 'Who knows what memories will come flooding back when he sees McCall rise off the other stool? The first minute or two could be dangerous. There is not just the risk of a bad reaction if big punches are thrown at Lennox but the possibility that he will be hesitant about letting his own stuff fly because last time he was hit while in the process of throwing a punch.'

Lewis insisted he was not haunted by the experience: 'I would expect Mike Tyson to have demons after the Holyfield fight. He knows he was stopped by a man who was far better on the night. Meeting Tyson for the second time, Bruno had demons in him. But why should I? Look at the way the McCall fight ended, with me on my feet. I wasn't beaten up. McCall comes across as a scared fighter, throwing punches with his eyes closed. Basically I beat myself. I'm longing to get in there and prove this man doesn't have anything over me.'

Mentally, Lewis should be in better shape than McCall, who fell foul of the law three times in 1996 because of episodes involving marijuana, cocaine and booze. Some cynics wonder if he can be relied upon to turn up and their doubts are not lessened by grumblings from the King organisation about the problems with payment of their fighter's $3 million share of the purse and a dispute over training expenses.

The chances are that McCall will show, making a raucous entrance and a tamer, loser's exit. Lewis should be enough of a delivery man to send him to obscurity.

The Sick Face of Boxing

The Sunday Times, 9 February 1997

Even heavyweight boxing, where the freakish is commonplace, may never have produced anything more eerily outlandish than the mental unravelling of Oliver McCall that caused him to behave as if he needed a psychiatrist as much as the referee's intervention which stopped his WBC championship fight with Lennox Lewis after 55 seconds of the fifth round.

McCall, who combined his training for Friday night's fight with intensive treatment for the severe drug abuse that has landed him several times in the hands of the police, had made the ending inevitable by abandoning any semblance of competitiveness and choosing to spend the fourth round walking in eccentric patterns around the ring with a look of demented preoccupation on his face. The experienced referee, Mills Lane, tried during those three minutes to talk him out of his often tearful trance, to persuade him to throw punches, and when the round was over the official again attempted to reason with McCall in his corner. Initially the responses were contradictory but when he declared, 'I gotta fight, I gotta fight,' the bell was sounded to begin the fifth.

Immediately, however, he reverted to bizarre passivity and, as Lewis loaded up to deliver his powerful right hand, principally in sweeping uppercuts, McCall remained remote and apparently indifferent to the threat of execution. Once, under assault, he permitted a weird, fleeting smile to cross his features but mainly he gave the impression that he just wanted to be out of there and free to concentrate on whatever strange thoughts were seething in his mind.

When Lane granted his wish, the first announcement from the ring said the referee was 'calling a halt because Oliver refuses to defend himself' and that the result was a technical knockout. But soon came indications that he was to be punished as a non-trier, that the Nevada Athletic Commission were setting up an inquiry and making urgent moves to put a freeze on the Letter of Credit that had lodged McCall's $3 million purse with a bank in New Jersey. Suggestions that the payment might already have reached the man who has been the guiding influence in the fighter's erratic career, the egregious Don King, brought swift assurances that the Nevada Attorney General's office would be taking an interest.

By then poor McCall – who had become a figure of heart-wrenching pathos, weeping frequently, as the shabby denouement unfolded – had disappeared from sight. It was reported that the 31-year-old Chicagoan had left the Las Vegas Hilton (whose management may regret staging such an unedifying drama in their Convention Center) in a red limousine. Neither he nor the drug counsellors who had accompanied him to Vegas from his training camp in Tennessee could be tracked down as Friday slid into Saturday.

It was left to George Benton, McCall's trainer, whose long involvement with boxing has exposed him to most of the squalid problems that abound in the business, to speak about the relevance of drugs to the miseries we had seen: 'Oliver is a good guy but he's a little weak. Maybe in a way it's a good thing this happened here. It shows people what drugs can do. This wasn't a movie. This was real life.'

Lewis's trainer, Emanuel Steward, was sympathetic. Steward trained McCall for the fight in September 1994 in which he became the only opponent ever to beat Lewis by felling the bigger man with a brutal right in the second round, and the corner-man's role in the avenging of that defeat might have encouraged triumphalism. But the circumstances were too sad for that. 'Oliver is one of the sweetest persons I ever dealt with,' said Steward. 'He needs personal attention.'

For Lewis, the night was tainted with anti-climax. In not only beating

McCall but becoming the first man to prevent him from going the distance, he should have cause for celebration. But his win was not the story. He had to content himself with reflecting that he had worked effectively for as long as the action amounted to a legitimate contest, showing form that should certainly be too much for his next challenger, Henry Akinwande.

Perhaps the failure to land the devastating punches that could have toppled the American during his vulnerable, walkabout phase justifies criticism. Claims that Lewis was inhibited by compassion are implausible but McCall's peculiarities obviously made it difficult to sustain a destructive rhythm. 'At first when he was walking around, I thought he was trying to trick me into something and I didn't want to make the kind of slip that let him catch me in our first fight,' the winner acknowledged afterwards. 'Then Manny told me to step up the pace. McCall never managed to get through my jab. Later I was getting to him with my uppercut and that shook him. He doesn't have the skill to contend with me. He just gave up. I would have liked to knock him out cold but I decided to stay composed.'

In spite of weighing just a pound under 18 stone, Lewis had the movement and variety of punches (left jabs interspersed with right crosses and left hooks) to take the first round easily. McCall had made the expected storming entrance to the ring, wet-eyed with emotion, though less convincingly intense than he was in London two and a half years ago. Memories of that blasting upset stirred him to attack with spirit in the second round and Lewis showed signs of the old amateurish dishevelment. But it was still hard to agree with the British judge, Larry O'Connell, who scored the round for McCall.

Throughout the third, Lewis reached McCall with heavy shots and the recipient's inclination to throw his arms wide as if welcoming the blows hinted at his mental disintegration. In the minute between the third and fourth, McCall refused to make himself available for advice in his corner, perambulating aimlessly while Benton fumed. The rest was lunacy – and sadness.

Awed by Ali, the One True King

The Sunday Times, 25 May 1997

A couple of hours spent sitting in the dark of a West End cinema made it difficult last week to be excited by the small dramas of contemporary sport. The FA Cup final had been won and lost, Eric Cantona was leaving Old Trafford, great golfers were in action at Wentworth and the pulse of the cricket season was quickening at Headingley and The Oval. But

Muhammad Ali was back among us and even in the second-hand images on a screen his presence was so vibrant and compelling that all the other sports performers who might have been claiming the attention shrank and receded into shadow.

When We Were Kings, the Oscar-winning documentary about the 1974 fight in Zaire in which Ali recaptured the heavyweight championship of the world against George Foreman, is a marvellous demonstration of modern film's capacity to grant us a glimpse of immortality, to defy time and its erosions at least to the extent of preserving scenes and episodes with sufficient vividness and immediacy to create the illusion that they are being relived again and again. The grained and jerky footage from the early days of the movie camera cannot have that effect. It is fascinating but leaves the impression of dispatches from the realm of the dead. With colour and sound (talk was as inseparable from Ali in his prime as heat is from fire) and the intimacy of advanced lenses, we are given something close to a flesh-and-blood experience.

That is certainly how it was for me in that auditorium off the Haymarket. The years peeled away and I was back by the languid sweep of the Zaire River, covering the most extraordinary event encountered in more than three decades of writing about sport. What was rekindled was not simply the excitement and unique exoticism of the occasion or the sense of wonder at the physical beauty and spellbinding imagination of Ali and the aura of miraculous possibility that always surrounded him. There was also a renewed realisation of his strange ability to spread not merely pleasure but joy just by being around, to light up lives wherever he went.

Everybody knows that his constant assaults on the self-belief of opponents could spill over into taunting too hurtful to be dismissed as harmless mischief. However, as someone who had the privilege of reporting most of his career at close quarters, I find it impossible to associate him with vicious motives. The core of his nature never seemed anything but lovingly generous and when his conduct suggested otherwise the explanation was probably to be found in the conflict between his natural humane warmth and the fierce combative pride that made him the fighter he was. He loved people but he loved to fight, too – hungered for the violent dangers of the ring, and was stimulated by the crises they produced, to a degree I have not discerned in anybody else. And, since putting himself on the line was such a drug for him, and the thought of losing so monstrous, it was his instinct to attack from the moment a match was mooted.

During preparations for the first of his momentous battles with Joe Frazier, which came within five months of Ali's return to competitive action after the three-and-a-half-year exile imposed because of his refusal to be drafted into the United States Army, the verbal bombardment had a darker, crueller tone as Frazier was accused of being an Uncle Tom. The jibe (which contributed substantially to the incurable bitterness felt by Frazier) was as ridiculous as it was wounding. But Ali, who knew the effects of his prolonged absence from the wars made defeat a probability, was reaching for any weapon available. Once he had lost, it was the other side of him that showed during an hour and a half I spent in his hotel suite. 'He's a nice man with a family,' he said of Frazier, 'just another brother workin' to make a living.'

Again in Zaire it was, astonishingly, possible to have private time with Ali a few hours after the historic fight, which was staged shortly before dawn to suit American television. The key to coverage of his activities was to put minimum reliance on press conferences, at which his self-perpetuating stage act could be hilariously entertaining but rarely yielded anything fresh or seriously informative, and instead devote as long as needed to the laying of polite ambushes designed to catch him at those points of the day where his restless energy had outstripped the stamina of his hangers-on. It was an approach vitally aided by the flexibility of Sunday newspaper work and at N'Sele, a government complex 40 miles outside Kinshasa, it led to perhaps the most magical experience of this reporter's professional life.

The fight, in which Ali exploited the flawless diamond of his nerve in letting a previously irresistible ogre punch himself to the edge of exhaustion before sensationally knocking out 'big bad George Foreman, the baddest man alive', in the eighth round, was epic. But lunchtime in the winner's villa was equally unforgettable. With myself, a fellow journalist, his bodyguard and two female cooks (one of whom was his father's sister, Coretta Clay) as the only listeners, Ali rambled for more than two hours through a generally subdued monologue that left out little of what he felt about his triumph and its implications. 'I kicked a lot of asses – not only George's . . . I done fucked up a lot of minds,' was his accurate, if uncharacteristically crude, assessment.

Clear memories of that session in the villa provide a rich counterpoint to the enthralling documentary just released, and act as a corrective to some of the dubious testimony delivered by the heavyweight wordsmiths, Normal Mailer and George Plimpton.

One of several peculiarities is the implied acceptance that the so-called rope-a-dope ploy was the result of pre-fight planning by Ali, whereas it was blatantly a brilliant improvisation in response to the crowding, ring-reducing pressure exerted by Foreman from the first bell. 'Truth is I could have killed myself dancin' against him,' Ali told me. 'I was a bit winded after doin' it in the first round, so I said to myself, "Let me go to the ropes while I'm fresh, while I can handle him there without gettin' hurt. Let him burn himself out. Let him blast his ass off and pray he keeps throwin'."'

Foreman, with plenty of help from the man out of the opposite corner, blasted himself into a psychological trauma from which he took years to recover. But recover he did and now it is Ali who is a figure of sad

327

infirmity. *When We Were Kings* is no more inclined to address directly the horrors visited on Ali by Parkinson's Syndrome brought on by punches to the head than it is to deal adequately with the central role of today's fallen tyrant, ex-President Mobutu, in the financing of the Rumble in the Jungle.

Perhaps a case can be made for the first of those omissions. The film, as its title declares, is a celebration of another time, a time when Muhammad Ali was more effortlessly regal than any other sportsman who ever lived.

Judgement Night Looms for Tyson

The Sunday Times, 22 June 1997

Anybody who unloads adamant opinions about the outcome of the rematch between Mike Tyson and Evander Holyfield should be avoided as a menace to sanity and solvency. Among sensible judges of fights and fighters, the event scheduled for Saturday in Las Vegas evokes not an urge to bet but an admission of bafflement. This fight is awash with psychological imponderables, with questions that beget further questions, and to be confident of the result is to imply that human nature is as easily read as a road map.

Those who blithely seek to oversimplify Tyson's attempt to reverse the beating he took from Holyfield last November, and recapture the WBA heavyweight championship, are missing its true significance. It is the total absence of certainty – the prospect of physical and mental struggle capable of fluctuating dramatically round by round, minute by minute – that sets this occasion apart from the contrived, one-sided banality of most heavyweight confrontations.

For once, the grotesque sums of money involved are related to public fascination with a genuine contest. By earning a guaranteed $35 million for his engagement at the MGM Grand Garden, Holyfield will become the highest earner from a single performance in the history of entertainment. Tyson's wages will be upwards of $20 million. The arena's capacity of more than 16,300 seats (at prices up to $1,500) was entirely sold out for the original date of 3 May. When a cut above Tyson's left eye caused a postponement, only about 50 customers asked for a refund. Their tickets were sold instantly and 3,000 more are expected to pay $70 a head to watch on television screens in the hotel. Across the United States, pay-per-view subscriptions will cost $49.95 and, when all revenue sources are included, the gross from the promotion is likely to break the fight-business record by exceeding $100 million.

In the midst of such a blizzard of banknotes, it is strange to hear the protagonists insist that money is not their principal motivation. It is strange but not unbelievable. Every fighter puts his own sense of himself on the line and that pressure is at its rawest when the heavyweight title is at stake. But, even in that context, what is about to happen is exceptional. Saturday's action may well represent the ultimate measurement of the achievements of two remarkable fighters.

Holyfield always felt that his entire career, his validity as a champion, would be defined by a collision with Tyson. That was why he craved the meeting so intensely long after his two previous tenancies of the championship (one as the undisputed ruler of the division) had made him seriously rich and secured his place in the annals of the ring. He believed the widespread inclination to categorise him as a blown-up light-heavyweight, lacking the congenital destructive power and physical authority of the natural big man, could best be refuted by humbling a contemporary the world regarded as the stuff of nightmares.

Tyson, having plundered fortunes after his release from prison by disposing of a series of intimidated victims, was in no hurry to revert to real conflict and his acceptance of Holyfield as a challenger was plainly based on the belief that boxing's proudest warrior was in swift and terminal decline. The idea was to knock off a formidable name no longer attached to a formidable man. Such a view had seemed justified when Holyfield was stopped in the eighth round by a blubbery Riddick Bowe and followed that with a miserably unconvincing stoppage of the negligible Bobby Czyz. Double-digit odds were quoted against the outsider for weeks and, although his price shortened to around 7–1 on the night, only a tiny minority of eccentric reasoners gave him a hope.

But Holyfield has the kind of faith in himself that can work miracles. He has religious convictions so deep that he has been starting his recent training sessions in a seedy district of downtown Houston, Texas, by linking hands with his gym crew for prayers. He therefore tends to give the Almighty credit for the thrilling defiance of probability that has punctuated his professional life, but the fact that he habitually reported to the gym at 6 a.m. is one of many indications that he is willing to offer God plenty of help. His will is as resolute as any ever employed in the ring and there was never a danger that Tyson would be able to bully him into a feeling of inferiority.

Holyfield was emphasising last week that he has been boxing 26 years (he will be 35 in October) and has never stopped learning or demanding improvement of himself, and it is true that the sharp, accurate punching and economical work at close quarters that are his main assets have never been more effective than they were in November. Encouraged by the unfamiliar experience of exerting a more dominating physical presence than his opponent – he was at least three inches taller at 6 ft 2 in and just half a stone lighter at 15 st 5 lb – he readily withstood Tyson's sporadic flourishes of the old ogreish ways, especially a burst of frightening aggression in the fifth round, and by the tenth the champion was such a battered, reeling wreck that it was easy to feel sorry for him.

The referee's intervention in the next round did not come a second too soon. Long before that stage, Tyson had appeared to shrink before our eyes and by the finish the truth his ferocity had always obscured was blatant: he is a distinctly small, short-armed heavyweight.

Surely then, the most obvious logic suggests, Holyfield can repeat the dismantling process. It is here that the questions begin to engulf analysis in a confusing torrent. Can Holyfield, at 34, lift himself yet again to apparently impossible heights of concentration and commitment? Has the first fight implanted ineradicable doubts in Tyson's mind or will that rough passage, and the suspicion that complacency contributed to it, stimulate him to rediscover his former capacity for blasting opposition aside? He knows that now it is the validity of *his* career that is at stake.

Recent betting made him 2–5 favourite but is Tyson, wealthy and newly married and preparing for the birth of his fourth child, single-minded about re-entering the war zone two days before his 31st birthday? Will it all come down to Holyfield's more conspicuous ability to absorb a brutal punch and keep thinking positively enough through the ensuing dishevelment?

Further relevant uncertainties come crowding in but the most important of all may be that first one. Is it probable that Holyfield can carry through the ropes at the weekend the inspired zealotry that enabled him to inflict horrors similar to those Tyson had suffered at the hands of James 'Buster' Douglas in the only other defeat of his 47-fight career? Putting two great fights together has hitherto been beyond Holyfield. His record shows 33 wins and just three losses, two to Bowe and one, at a time when he was diagnosed as having a heart condition, to the unimpressive Michael Moorer. His heart is sound now but the signs are that his supreme performances call for such intensity that they tend to be followed by a let-down.

Perhaps his obsession with Tyson will overwhelm that trend. But I am not convinced change is likely in a 34-year-old. Accepting that bewildering criteria do not remove the obligation to predict, I will go to the ringside in Las Vegas nervously identifying with the forecast that Mike Tyson will blast his way back to power.

The Most Marketable Psychotic

The Sunday Times, 6 July 1997

It was always savagery that Mike Tyson was selling and nobody should imagine that a flirtation with cannibalism has reduced his market value. When the Nevada State Athletic Commission meets this week to consider sentencing Tyson for biting off part of Evander Holyfield's right ear and bloodily gnawing on the other, the basic issues of crime and punishment will have a rival for the commission's attention. The inquiry will be in Las Vegas, the most money-driven city even America can boast, and commerce of the sleaziest kind will be in there pleading its case.

There may be oily talk about compassion and opportunities for redemption and the cleansing power of contrition. But running through it all will be the infinitely persuasive voice of the dollar. Tyson is the most marketable psychotic in the world and it is his capacity to generate ticket sales and subscriptions to pay-per-view television, and to draw high-rollers to the desert casinos – not any honest concern with improving his chances of climbing out of the behavioural squalor into which he has sunk – that galvanises the majority of those arguing against the lifetime ban from boxing invited by his excesses.

Perhaps permanent banishment, though warranted, could be seen as having a vindictive finality. But anything less than removal from competition for three or four years will be a shamefully inadequate response to the carnivorous wildness that caused him to be disqualified at the end of surely the weirdest third round in the history of the heavyweight championship. One popular prediction has the commission revoking Tyson's licence and then acceding to a request for its reissue after only a year or so. Now 31, the former undisputed champion would not necessarily find that more than a petty inconvenience, in the same category as the maximum financial penalty he faces: a deduction of 10 per cent from the purse of $30 million he is due for last weekend's depravity.

Should the Nevada authorities (who have earned a reputation for putting expediency before ethics) opt for such leniency, whatever battered and soiled claims to integrity professional boxing can still muster will shrink to meaninglessness. Last Tuesday the same commission fined Oliver McCall $250,000 and suspended him for a year as punishment for his bizarre refusal to defend himself against Lennox Lewis during their WBC heavyweight title fight in February. McCall apparently suffered some form of nervous breakdown in the ring, and is undergoing psychiatric treatment, so it could be said that he was punished for being a sick pacifist. Tyson, too, has obvious mental problems but the malevolence he exhibited during and after the Holyfield fight demands measures far harsher than those applied to McCall.

Tyson attracts a few sympathisers as he flounders in the dark turbulence of his mind. But when Emanuel Steward, Lennox Lewis's trainer, suggests that he is 'really a nice person' who has been destructively influenced by the immorality of stronger personalities around him, his defence of the convicted rapist is hopelessly unconvincing. No doubt Tyson's deprived and abused upbringing in the ghetto of Brownsville, Brooklyn, imposed handicaps that only a giant spirit could have survived, but the unavoidable truth is that the man who has emerged from that background, and subsequent exposure to the brutal pressures of the fight business, is anything but nice. Nothing seems to impinge healthily on the resentful core of his nature – not wealth or fame; not prison and all the liberating access to literature it is reported (implausibly) to have brought him; not conversion to Islam or fatherhood or his recent second marriage.

It is, admittedly, difficult to conceive of a more alarming concentration of malign influences than is to be found surrounding Tyson. From the numbers racketeer-turned-promoter Don King to the surly and sinister managers John Horne and Rory Holloway, to the hardcase trainer Richie Giachetti, they are an unedifying bunch. The low-life values prevalent in the camp were neatly encapsulated when Horne sneered at Holyfield for acting 'like a bitch' because of what the non-combatant characterised as a couple of little nips on the ear. Horne spat out the words as dismissively as his employer had spat out a sliver of Holyfield's flesh.

Nevertheless, attempts to excuse Tyson on the basis of the company he keeps are ludicrous. Those people are there because he wants them, because the street meanness and hostility that crackle around them echo his own sour aggression towards the world. There is good reason to believe the biting of Holyfield was premeditated. (Holyfield acknowledges clamping his teeth on an opponent's shoulder as a 17-year-old amateur but says it was an adolescent aberration.) In Las Vegas, Tyson was leaving his corner for the third round without his mouthpiece until the referee sent him back for it. However, I do not subscribe to the view that, after losing two rounds in which Holyfield indicated he was ready to re-establish the dominance that gave him an extraordinary upset victory in their first fight last November, Tyson's objective was to escape protracted humiliation by getting himself disqualified.

My opinion is that he was genuinely infuriated by the butting assaults of Holyfield's head, which had opened a serious cut beneath his right eyebrow, and had resolved to take the battle far beyond the restraints of boxing's rules and down into the kill-or-be-killed depths of ghetto warfare. Here I must say, without seeking to offer any vestige of justification for Tyson's conduct, that if the butting he endured in both fights was an accident it was one that Holyfield helped to happen. Though at least three inches taller than his opponent, the WBA champion persistently contrived to duck underneath Tyson's face and bring his hairless skull rolling upwards in a movement almost certain to do damage. It looked to me like a calculated tactic.

Had Tyson been intent on disqualification, he could have achieved that result more simply by retaliatory use of the head. He wanted to fight all right, but on his own Brownsville terms. Back in that ghetto last week, Julien Grant, who is executive director of the Amboy Neighborhood Center and knew Tyson well during his three years there, said: 'I think the link between what happened in the ring and the environment he grew up in is that at some point you don't let anyone push you any more. And you retaliate without regard for consequences. I'll do anything to let you know you can't do this to me.'

It is only by reference to that mentality that we can explain Tyson's determination to chew lumps out of Holyfield at a stage of the fight when he appeared capable of wrenching the initiative from the champion. He had scored significantly in the third round, and Holyfield was conspicuously disconcerted, but Tyson had left his stool with illegal intentions, so he went ahead and implemented them. Such behaviour suggests, first, that his psychosis is deep and, second, that the ring is the worst place imaginable for him to seek a cure. In there the beast that lurks in all of us is supposed to be kept at bay by a flimsy cage of conventions. You could put Tyson's respect for conventions in your eye and not blink.

Boxing has so much trouble justifying itself at the best of times that its governing bodies should recognise the impossibility of justifying a Mike Tyson. But we must fear that, in Nevada, greed will find a way.

When Cash Outstrips Credibility

The Sunday Times, 20 July 1997

Opponents of boxing must have a strong sense of redundancy these days. Who needs abolitionists when the fight business, at least in the flagship heavyweight division, insists on lurching from the revolting to the pitiful by way of the ridiculous?

We have come to accept that the least likely occurrence when leading heavyweights go through the ropes is that a straightforward fight will break out. There is a case for replacing ring-stools with psychiatrists' couches. Fist-fighting may be such a primitive anachronism at the close of the twentieth century that outbursts of weird behaviour are to be expected. But the sheer volume of outlandish happenings has made regulars at ringside feel like voyeurs in a madhouse.

Mike Tyson's gobbling of Evander Holyfield's ears may have been the most grotesque episode but several of his contemporaries have done their best to be unforgettably awful. Andrew Golota was twice disqualified after aiming so many punches below Riddick Bowe's waist that watchers began to wonder if the Pole was suffering from a peculiarity of vision that caused him to see his adversary upside down. Oliver McCall had a nervous breakdown in the ring against Lennox Lewis and then, last weekend in Lake Tahoe, Lewis was again haplessly embroiled in a sad farce as Henry Akinwande decided that instead of fighting he would attempt to set a world record for marathon hugging.

Suggestions that all of this besmirches the reputation of boxing are, of course, risible. The mayhem trade has never had a good name to lose. It has always had to weather public cynicism and has often had the street-wit to capitalise on its less salubrious aspects by using them to titillate potential customers. Violence with a whiff of skulduggery is marketable and fight followers are not likely to become worked up over occasional flouting of the rules of combat. But, in terms of both offensiveness and tedium, new depths have been plumbed lately. Even boxing's notoriously undiscriminating patrons cannot be relied upon to remain satisfied with the diet of swill they are being served.

What plagues the men who control the crazily bloated finances of the business is the simple fear that the tolerance and gullibility of the paying fans may prove, against all previous evidence, to have limits. Selling worthless fights is second nature to promoters but selling non-fights may be beyond their rich talent for the con. When disqualifications come by the handful the dumbest devotee might start to wonder if there isn't something better he could do with his money than spending it on fight tickets and extravagant subscriptions to pay-per-view television. Setting fire to banknotes would be more fun than occupying an expensive seat to witness the ravening criminality of Tyson or the exhibition of terrified pacifism given by Akinwande eight days ago.

There is undeniably something historic about the recent spate of horrifying anti-climaxes among the heavyweights and it is difficult to resist the suspicion that it is somehow associated with the obscene tide of money coursing through boxing at the moment. Most of us who have had close exposure to the pressure and pain endured by fighters incline to the view that they cannot be overpaid. There is, however, no doubt that the mass of cash currently available has distorted perspectives to the point where the greed-ridden Disneyland of heavyweight boxing must be running the risk of imploding. It is all very well to argue that it is a financial enterprise that just happens to be chronicled on the sports pages, but when it loses touch entirely with some version of sporting standards, however diluted, its claims on public enthusiasm collapse. And that loss of touch becomes more blatant every day.

Heavyweights of moderate ability can earn such monstrous sums of money that an accountancy ethos has overwhelmed the pride in performance and old-fashioned pursuit of glory that once ran in harness with the legitimate desire to pile up profit. Hungry fighters are virtually non-existent (unless the expression is archly applied to Tyson) and the knowledge that even abject failure can be outrageously rewarding asserts itself in many minds when crisis looms in the ring.

The pure, unbreakable commitment of a Holyfield, for whom money means much but pride means more, would have been a precious rarity in any age but in this era it makes him seem like a freak survivor of an extinct species. On the basis of size and strength, and possession of the technical gifts to exploit those advantages, Bowe should have achieved far more

334

than Holyfield as a heavyweight. But the bigger man's intrinsic softness was encouraged by the ease with which he contrived a sybaritic life for himself, and his self-indulgent drift towards overfed obscurity looks irrevocable.

It can be contended that the flaws of temperament revealed steadily by Bowe, and with dramatic suddenness by Akinwande, are too deep-rooted to have been influenced by the values that prevailed in earlier, more rigorous, phases of professional boxing's development. There is certainly no eagerness in this quarter to berate the engaging giant for the disintegration of his nerve against Lewis. Presumably the experience will haunt him for the rest of his days and that thought should stir sympathy in all of us. But there is something profoundly wrong with a so-called sport that allows so many inadequates to reach its highest, most lucrative levels before they are embarrassingly exposed.

Maybe the whole mess should be seen as the pugilists' revenge. Have the fighters resolved to give the audience brain damage?